Principles of Accounting.com

Financial Accounting

2020 Edition

Larry M. Walther
Utah State University

principlesofaccounting.com

Principles of Accounting.com

Financial Accounting

2020 Edition

ISBN-13: 9781729456286

Table of Contents

Chapter Five: Special Issues for Merchants

Chapter Six: Cash and Highly-Liquid Investments

Chapter Seven: Accounts Receivable

Chapter Eight: Inventory

Chapter Nine: Long-Term Investments

Chapter Ten: Property, Plant, & Equipment

Chapter Eleven: Advanced PP&E Issues/Natural Resources/Intangibles

Chapter Twelve: Current Liabilities and Employer Obligations

Chapter Thirteen: Long-Term Obligations

Chapter Fourteen: Corporate Equity Accounting

Chapter Fifteen: Financial Reporting and Concepts

Chapter Sixteen: Financial Analysis and the Statement of Cash Flows

Chapter 1:
Welcome to the World of Accounting

Goals:

The nature of financial and managerial accounting information.
The accounting profession and accounting careers.
The accounting equation: Assets = Liabilities + Owners' Equity.
How transactions impact the accounting equation.
The four core financial statements.

principlesofaccounting.com

Accounting Information

You likely have a general concept of accounting. Information about the transactions and events of a business is captured and summarized into reports that are used by persons interested in the entity. But, you likely do not realize the complexity of accomplishing this task. It involves a talented blending of technical knowledge and measurement artistry that can only be fully appreciated via extensive study of the subject.

You may also know what a surgeon does, but you can certainly appreciate that considerable knowledge and skill is needed to successfully treat a patient. If you were studying to be a surgeon, you would likely begin with a basic human anatomy class.

In this chapter, you will begin your study of accounting by looking at the overall structure of accounting and the basic anatomy of reporting. Be advised that a true understanding of accounting does not come easily. It only comes with determination and hard work. If you persevere, you will be surprised at how much you discover about accounting. This knowledge is very valuable to achieve business success.

Let's begin with a more formal definition of accounting: **Accounting** is a set of concepts and techniques that   *DEFINITIONS*
are used to measure and report financial information about an economic unit. The economic unit is generally
considered to be a separate enterprise. The information is reported to a variety of different types of interested
parties. These include business managers, owners, creditors, governmental units, financial analysts, and even
employees. In one way or another, these users of accounting information tend to be concerned about their
own interests in the entity.

Business managers need accounting information to make sound leadership decisions. Owners and investors
hope for profits that may eventually lead to distributions from the business (e.g., "dividends"). Creditors are
always concerned about the entity's ability to repay its obligations. Governmental units need information
to tax and regulate. Analysts use accounting data to form opinions on which they base investment recom-
mendations. Employees want to work for successful companies to further their individual careers, and they
often have bonuses or options tied to enterprise performance. Accounting information about specific entities
helps satisfy the needs of all of these interested parties.

The diversity of interested parties leads to a logical division in the discipline of accounting. **Financial accounting** is concerned with external reporting to parties outside the firm. In contrast, **managerial accounting** is primarily concerned with providing information for internal management. One may have trouble seeing the distinction; after all, aren't financial facts being reported? The following paragraphs provide a closer look at the distinctions.

FINANCIAL ACCOUNTING

Consider that financial accounting is targeted toward a broad base of external users, none of whom control the actual preparation of reports or have access to underlying details. Their ability to understand and have confidence in reports is directly dependent upon standardization of the principles and practices that are used to prepare the reports. Without such standardization, reports of different companies could be hard to understand and even harder to compare.

Standardization derives from certain well-organized processes and organizations. In the United States, a private sector group called the **Financial Accounting Standards Board** (FASB) is primarily responsible for developing the rules that form the foundation of financial reporting. The FASB's global counterpart is the **International Accounting Standards Board** (IASB). The IASB and FASB are working toward convergence,

such that there may eventually be a single harmonious set of international financial reporting standards (IFRS). This effort to establish consistency in global financial reporting is driven by the increase in global trade and finance. Just as standardization is needed to enable comparisons between individual companies operating within a single economy, so, too, is standardization needed to facilitate global business evaluations.

Financial reports prepared under the generally accepted accounting principles (GAAP) promulgated by such standard-setting bodies are intended to be general purpose in orientation. This means they are not prepared especially for owners, or creditors, or any other particular user group. Instead, they are intended to be equally useful for all user groups. As such, attempts are made to keep them free from bias (neutral). Standard-setting bodies are guided by concepts that are aimed at production of relevant and representationally faithful reports that are useful in investment and credit decisions.

MANAGERIAL ACCOUNTING

Managerial accounting information is intended to serve the specific, and varied, needs of management. Business managers are charged with business planning, controlling, and decision making. As such, they may desire specialized reports, budgets, product costing data, and other details that are generally not reported on an external basis. Further, management may dictate the parameters under which such information is to be accumulated and presented. For instance, GAAP may require that certain product development costs be deducted in computing income; on the other hand, management may see these costs as a long-term investment and stipulate that internal decision making be based upon income numbers that exclude such costs. This is their prerogative. Hopefully, internal reporting is being done logically and rationally, but it need not follow any particular set of mandatory guidelines.

A QUALITY SYSTEM

Both financial accounting and managerial accounting depend upon a strong information system to reliably capture and summarize business transaction data. Information technology has radically reshaped this mundane part of the practice of accounting over the past 50 years. The era of the "green eye-shaded" accountant has been relegated to the annals of history. Now, accounting is more of a dynamic, decision-making discipline, rather than a bookkeeping task.

INHERENT LIMITATIONS

Accounting data are not absolute or concrete. Considerable amounts of judgment and estimation are necessary to develop the specific accounting measurements that are reported during a particular month, quarter, or year. For example, how much profit is actually earned when a car is sold with a 3-year warranty? It will be three years before the final costs of the warranty agreement are all known. One approach would be to wait three years before reporting on the profit or loss for this transaction. However, by the time the information could be reported with certainty, it would be so stale as to lose its usefulness. Thus, in order to timely present information, reasonable estimations are routinely embraced in the normal preparation of periodic financial reports.

In addition, accounting has not advanced to a state of being able to value a business. As such, many transactions and events are reported based on the **historical cost principle** (in contrast to fair value). For example, land is typically recorded and carried in the accounting records at the price at which it was purchased. The historical cost principle is based on the concept that it is best to report certain financial statement elements at amounts that are tied to objective and verifiable past transactions.

The alternative is to value (and periodically revalue) accounts based upon subjective assessments of current worth. Such adjustments are problematic and the subject of much debate. Nevertheless, the current trend in global standard-setting is toward an increased acceptance of the circumstances under which fair value accounting is deemed acceptable for selected financial statement elements.

The ongoing debate about fair value versus historical cost is often cast in the context of a tradeoff between the "relevance" of fair value information and the "reliability" of historical cost information. This debate is apt to continue, and the related accounting standards will likely be in an evolutionary state for many years to come. Nevertheless, it is reasonable to expect that the accountant of the future will be increasingly skilled in valuation issues.

The Accounting Profession and Careers

To decide to be an accountant is no more descriptive than deciding to be a doctor as there are a variety of specialty areas. Many accountants engage in the practice of **public accounting**, which involves providing audit, tax, and consulting services to the general public. To engage in the practice of public accounting usually requires one to be licensed. In the United States, individual states issue a license called a CPA **(Certified Public Accountant)**. Other countries offer similar designations such as the "Chartered Accountant." **Auditing** involves the examination of transactions and systems that underlie an organization's financial reports, with the ultimate goal of providing an independent report on the appropriateness of financial statements. Tax services relate to providing help in the preparation and filing of tax returns and the rendering of advice on the tax consequences of alternative actions. Consulting services can vary dramatically, and include such diverse activities as information systems engineering to evaluating production methods.

Many accountants are privately employed by small and large businesses (i.e., "industry accounting") and not-for-profit agencies (some hospitals and universities, as well as most charitable groups and churches). They may work in areas of product costing and pricing, budgeting, and the examination of investment alternatives, or they may serve as **internal auditors**, who look at controls and procedures in use by their employer. Objectives of these reviews are to safeguard company resources and assess the reliability and accuracy of accounting information and accounting systems. They may also serve as in-house tax accountants, financial managers, or countless other occupations.

Many accountants also work in the governmental sector, whether it be local, state, or national levels. Accountants are employed at the Internal Revenue Service, General Accounting Office, Securities and Exchange Commission, and even the Federal Bureau of Investigation, among other agencies.

ETHICS

Because investors and creditors place great reliance on financial statements in making their investment and credit decisions, it is imperative that the financial reporting process be truthful and dependable. Accountants are expected to behave in an entirely ethical manner. To help insure integrity in the reporting process, the profession has adopted a code of ethics to which its licensed members must adhere. In addition, checks and balances via the audit process, government oversight, and the ever vigilant "plaintiff's attorney" all serve a vital role in providing additional safeguards against the errant accountant. Those who are preparing to enter the accounting profession should do so with the intention of behaving with honor and integrity. Others will likely rely upon accountants in some aspect of their personal or professional lives. They have every right to expect those accountants to behave in a completely trustworthy and ethical fashion. After all, they will be entrusting them with financial resources and confidential information.

The Accounting Equation

The basic features of the accounting model in use today trace roots back over 500 years. Luca Pacioli, a Renaissance-era monk, developed a method for tracking the success or failure of trading ventures. The foundation of that system continues to serve the modern business world well, and is the entrenched cornerstone of even the most elaborate computerized systems. The nucleus of that system is the notion that a business entity can be described as a collection of assets and the corresponding claims against those assets. The claims can be divided into the claims of creditors and owners (i.e., liabilities and owners' equity). This gives rise to the fundamental **accounting equation**:

$$\textbf{Assets = Liabilities + Owners' Equity}$$

ASSETS

Assets are the economic resources of the entity, and include such items as cash, accounts receivable (amounts owed to a firm by its customers), inventories, land, buildings, equipment, and even intangible assets like patents and other legal rights. Assets entail probable future economic benefits to the owner.

LIABILITIES

Liabilities are amounts owed to others relating to loans, extensions of credit, and other obligations arising in the course of business. Implicit to the notion of a liability is the idea of an "existing" obligation to pay or perform some duty.

OWNERS' EQUITY

Owners' equity is the owner's stake in the business. It is sometimes called net assets, because it is equivalent to assets minus liabilities for a particular business. Who are the "owners?" The answer to this question depends on the legal form of the entity; examples of entity types include sole proprietorships, partnerships, and corporations. A **sole proprietorship** is a business owned by one person, and its equity would typically consist of a single owner's capital account. Conversely, a **partnership** is a business owned by more than one person, with its equity consisting of a separate capital account for each partner. Finally, a **corporation** is a very common entity form, with its ownership interest being represented by divisible units of ownership called shares of stock. Corporate shares are easily transferable, with the current holder(s) of the stock being the owners. The total owners' equity (i.e., "stockholders' equity") of a corporation usually consists of several amounts, generally corresponding to the **owner investments** in the capital stock (by shareholders) and additional amounts generated through earnings that have not been paid out to shareholders as dividends (**dividends** are distributions to shareholders as a return on their investment). Earnings give rise to increases in **retained earnings**, while dividends (and losses) cause decreases.

BALANCE SHEET

The accounting equation is the backbone of the accounting and reporting system. It is central to understanding a key financial statement known as the **balance sheet** (sometimes called the statement of financial position). The following illustration for Edelweiss Corporation shows a variety of assets that are reported at a total of $895,000. Creditors are owed $175,000, leaving $720,000 of stockholders' equity. The stockholders' equity section is divided into the $120,000 that was originally invested in Edelweiss Corporation by stockholders (i.e., capital stock), and the other $600,000 that was earned (and retained) by successful business performance over the life of the company.

Does the stockholders' equity total mean the business is worth $720,000? No! Why not? Because many assets are not reported at current value. For example, although the land cost $125,000, Edelweiss Corporation's balance sheet does not report its current worth. Similarly, the business may have unrecorded resources, such as a trade secret or a brand name that allows it to earn extraordinary profits. Alternatively, Edelweiss may be facing business risks or pending litigation that could limit its value. Consideration should be given to these important non-financial statement valuation issues if contemplating purchasing an investment in Edelweiss stock. This observation tells us that accounting statements are important in investment and credit decisions, but they are not the sole source of information for making investment and credit decisions.

EDELWEISS CORPORATION
Balance Sheet
December 31, 20X3

Assets		Liabilities	
Cash	$ 25,000	Accounts payable	$ 50,000
Accounts receivable	50,000	Loans payable	125,000
Inventories	35,000	Total liabilities	$175,000
Land	125,000	**Stockholders' equity**	
Buildings	400,000	Capital stock	$120,000
Equipment	250,000	Retained earnings	600,000
Other assets	10,000	Total stockholders' equity	720,000
Total assets	$895,000	Total liabilities and equity	$895,000

Assets ($895,000) = Liabilities ($175,000) + Stockholders' equity ($720,000)

How Transactions Impact the Accounting Equation

The preceding balance sheet for Edelweiss represented the financial condition at the noted date. But, each new transaction brings about a change in financial condition. Business activity will impact various asset, liability, and/or equity accounts without disturbing the equality of the accounting equation. How does this happen? To reveal the answer to this question, look at four specific cases for Edelweiss. See how each impacts the balance sheet without upsetting the basic equality.

CASE A: COLLECT AN ACCOUNT RECEIVABLE

If Edelweiss Corporation collected $10,000 from a customer on an existing account receivable (i.e., not a new sale, just the collection of an amount that is due from some previous transaction), then the balance sheet would be revised to show that cash (an asset) increased from $25,000 to $35,000, and accounts receivable (an asset) decreased from $50,000 to $40,000. As a result total assets did not change, and liabilities and equity accounts were unaffected, as shown in the illustration on the following page.

CASE B: BUY EQUIPMENT VIA LOAN

If Edelweiss Corporation purchased $30,000 of equipment, agreeing to pay for it later (i.e. taking out a loan), then the balance sheet would be further revised. The Case B illustration on the next page shows that equipment (an asset) increased from $250,000 to $280,000, and loans payable (a liability) increased from $125,000 to $155,000. As a result, both total assets and total liabilities increased by $30,000.

CASE C: PROVIDE SERVICES ON ACCOUNT

What would happen if Edelweiss Corporation did some work for a customer in exchange for the customer's promise to pay $5,000? This requires further explanation; try to follow this logic closely! Retained earnings is the income of the business that has not been distributed to the owners of the business. When Edelweiss Corporation provided a service to a customer, it can be said that it generated revenue of $5,000. **Revenue** is the enhancement resulting from providing goods or services to customers. Revenue will contribute to income, and income is added to retained earnings. Examine the resulting balance sheet for Case C and notice that accounts receivable and retained earnings went up by $5,000 each, indicating that the business has more assets and more retained earnings. Note that assets still equal liabilities plus equity.

CASE D: PAY EXPENSES

Expenses are the outflows and obligations that arise from producing goods and services. Imagine that Edelweiss paid $3,000 for **expenses**. This transaction reduces cash and income (i.e., retained earnings), as shown in the Case D illustration.

CASE A:
COLLECT AN
ACCOUNT
RECEIVABLE

EDELWEISS CORPORATION
Balance Sheet
December 31, 20X3
(before indicated transaction)

Assets		
Cash		$ 25,000
Accounts receivable		50,000
Inventories		35,000
Land		125,000
Building		400,000
Equipment		250,000
Other assets		10,000
Total assets		$895,000
Liabilities		
Accounts payable	$ 50,000	
Loans payable	125,000	
Total liabilities		$175,000
Stockholders' equity		
Capital stock	$120,000	
Retained earnings	600,000	
Total stockholders' equity		720,000
Total liabilities and equity		$895,000

+$10,000
−$10,000

EDELWEISS CORPORATION
Balance Sheet
December 31, 20X3
(after indicated transaction)

Assets		
Cash		$ 35,000
Accounts receivable		40,000
Inventories		35,000
Land		125,000
Building		400,000
Equipment		250,000
Other assets		10,000
Total assets		$895,000
Liabilities		
Accounts payable	$ 50,000	
Loans payable	125,000	
Total liabilities		$175,000
Stockholders' equity		
Capital stock	$120,000	
Retained earnings	600,000	
Total stockholders' equity		720,000
Total liabilities and equity		$895,000

CASE B:
BUY
EQUIPMENT
VIA LOAN

EDELWEISS CORPORATION
Balance Sheet
December 31, 20X3
(before indicated transaction)

Assets		
Cash		$ 35,000
Accounts receivable		40,000
Inventories		35,000
Land		125,000
Building		400,000
Equipment		250,000
Other assets		10,000
Total assets		$895,000
Liabilities		
Accounts payable	$ 50,000	
Loans payable	125,000	
Total liabilities		$175,000
Stockholders' equity		
Capital stock	$120,000	
Retained earnings	600,000	
Total stockholders' equity		720,000
Total liabilities and equity		$895,000

+$30,000

+$30,000

EDELWEISS CORPORATION
Balance Sheet
December 31, 20X3
(after indicated transaction)

Assets		
Cash		$ 35,000
Accounts receivable		40,000
Inventories		35,000
Land		125,000
Building		400,000
Equipment		280,000
Other assets		10,000
Total assets		$925,000
Liabilities		
Accounts payable	$ 50,000	
Loans payable	155,000	
Total liabilities		$205,000
Stockholders' equity		
Capital stock	$120,000	
Retained earnings	600,000	
Total stockholders' equity		720,000
Total liabilities and equity		$925,000

EDELWEISS CORPORATION
Balance Sheet
December 31, 20X3
(before indicated transaction)

Assets

Cash	$ 35,000
Accounts receivable	40,000
Inventories	35,000
Land	125,000
Building	400,000
Equipment	280,000
Other assets	10,000
Total assets	$925,000

Liabilities

Accounts payable	$ 50,000	
Loans payable	155,000	
Total liabilities		$205,000

Stockholders' equity

Capital stock	$120,000	
Retained earnings	600,000	
Total stockholders' equity		720,000
Total liabilities and equity		$925,000

+$5,000 (Accounts receivable)
+$5,000 (Retained earnings)

EDELWEISS CORPORATION
Balance Sheet
December 31, 20X3
(after indicated transaction)

Assets

Cash	$ 35,000
Accounts receivable	45,000
Inventories	35,000
Land	125,000
Building	400,000
Equipment	280,000
Other assets	10,000
Total assets	$930,000

Liabilities

Accounts payable	$ 50,000	
Loans payable	155,000	
Total liabilities		$205,000

Stockholders' equity

Capital stock	$120,000	
Retained earnings	605,000	
Total stockholders' equity		725,000
Total liabilities and equity		$930,000

*CASE C:
PROVIDE
SERVICES ON
ACCOUNT*

EDELWEISS CORPORATION
Balance Sheet
December 31, 20X3
(before indicated transaction)

Assets

Cash	$ 35,000
Accounts receivable	45,000
Inventories	35,000
Land	125,000
Building	400,000
Equipment	280,000
Other assets	10,000
Total assets	$930,000

Liabilities

Accounts payable	$ 50,000	
Loans payable	155,000	
Total liabilities		$205,000

Stockholders' equity

Capital stock	$120,000	
Retained earnings	605,000	
Total stockholders' equity		725,000
Total liabilities and equity		$930,000

-$3,000 (Cash)
-$3,000 (Retained earnings)

EDELWEISS CORPORATION
Balance Sheet
December 31, 20X3
(after indicated transaction)

Assets

Cash	$ 32,000
Accounts receivable	45,000
Inventories	35,000
Land	125,000
Building	400,000
Equipment	280,000
Other assets	10,000
Total assets	$927,000

Liabilities

Accounts payable	$ 50,000	
Loans payable	155,000	
Total liabilities		$205,000

Stockholders' equity

Capital stock	$120,000	
Retained earnings	602,000	
Total stockholders' equity		722,000
Total liabilities and equity		$927,000

*CASE D:
PAY
EXPENSES*

IN GENERAL   In the life of any business entity, there are countless transactions. Each can be described by its impact on assets, liabilities, and equity. Note that no properly recorded transaction will upset the balance of the accounting equation.

TERMS   In day-to-day conversation, some terms are used casually and without precision. Words may incorrectly be regarded as synonymous. Such is the case for the words "income" and "revenue." Each term, however, has a very precise meaning. Revenues are enhancements resulting from providing goods and services to customers. Conversely, expenses can generally be regarded as the costs of doing business. This gives rise to another accounting equation:

$$\textbf{Revenues - Expenses = Income}$$

Revenue is the "top line" amount corresponding to the total benefits generated from all business activity. Income is the "bottom line" amount that results after deducting expenses from revenue. In some countries, revenue is also referred to as "turnover." As you will see, revenue is summarized first in the company's income statement.

The Four Core Financial Statements

Your future will be marked by opportunities to invest money in the capital stock of a corporation. Another option that will present itself is to lend money to a company, either directly, or by buying that company's debt instruments known as "bonds." Stocks and bonds are two of the most prevalent financial instruments of the modern global economy. The financial press and television devote seemingly endless coverage to headline events pertaining to large public corporations. Public companies are those with securities that are readily available for purchase/sale through organized stock markets. Many more companies are private, meaning their stock and debt is in the hands of a narrow group of investors and banks.

In contemplating an investment in a public or private entity, there is certain information that will logically be needed to guide the decision process. What types of information is desired? What should be known about the companies in which an investment is being considered? If preparing a list of questions for the company's management, what subjects would be included? Whether this challenge is posed to a sophisticated investor or to a new business student, the listing almost always includes the same basic components.

What are the corporate assets? Where does the company operate? What are the key products? How much income is being generated? Does the company pay dividends? What is the corporate policy on ethics and environmental responsibility? Many such topics are noted within the illustrated "thought cloud." Some of these topics are financial in nature (noted in blue). Other topics are of more general interest and cannot be communicated in strict mathematical terms (noted in red).

FINANCIAL STATEMENTS   Financial accounting seeks to directly report information for the topics noted in blue. Additional supplemental disclosures frequently provide insight about subjects such as those noted in red. And, additional information is available by reviewing corporate websites (many have separate sections devoted to their investors), filings with securities regulators, financial journals and magazines, and other similar sources. Most companies will have annual meetings for shareholders and host webcasts every three months (quarterly). These events are very valuable in allowing investors and creditors to make informed decisions about the company, as well as providing a forum for direct questioning of management.

Some investors might even call a company and seek "special insight" about emerging trends and developments. Be aware, however, that the company will likely not be able to respond in a meaningful way. Securities laws include very strict rules and penalties that are meant to limit selective or unique disclosures to any one investor or group. It is amusing, but rarely helpful, to review "message boards" where people anonymously post their opinions about a company. Company specific reports are often prepared by financial statement analysts. These reports may contain valuable and thought-provoking insights but are not always objective.

Financial accounting information is conveyed through a standardized set of reports. The balance sheet has already been introduced. The other **financial statements** are the income statement, statement of retained earnings, and statement of cash flows. There are many rules that govern the form and content of each financial statement. At the same time, those rules are not so rigid as to preclude variations in the exact structure or layout. For instance, the earlier illustration for Edelweiss was first presented as a "horizontal" layout of the balance sheet. The subsequent Edelweiss examples were representative of "vertical" balance sheet arrangements. Each approach is equally acceptable.

INCOME STATEMENT

A summary of an entity's results of operation for a specified period of time is revealed in the **income statement**, as it provides information about revenues generated and expenses incurred. The difference between the revenues and expenses is identified as the **net income** or **net loss**.

The income statement can be prepared using a single-step or a multiple-step approach, and might be further modified to include a number of special disclosures relating to unique items. These topics will be amplified in several subsequent chapters. For now, take careful note that the following income statement illustration relates to activities of a specified time period (e.g., year, quarter, month), as is clearly noted in its title.

QUARTZ CORPORATION Income Statement For the Year Ending December 31, 20X9		
Revenues		
Services to customers	$750,000	
Interest revenue	15,000	
Total revenues		$765,000
Expenses		
Salaries	$235,000	
Rent	115,000	
Other operating expenses	300,000	
Total expenses		650,000
Net income		$115,000

STATEMENT OF RETAINED EARNINGS

Previous illustrations showed how retained earnings increases and decreases in response to events that impact income. A company's overall net income will cause retained earnings to increase, and a net loss will result in a decrease. Retained earnings is also reduced by shareholder dividends.

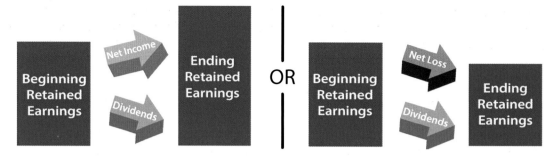

The **statement of retained earnings** provides a concise reporting of these changes in retained earnings from one period to the next. In essence, the statement is nothing more than a reconciliation or "bird's-eye view" of the bridge between the retained earnings amounts appearing on two successive balance sheets.

QUARTZ CORPORATION Statement of Retained Earnings For the Year Ending December 31, 20X9	
Retained earnings - January 1, 20X9	$400,000
Plus: Net income	115,000
	$515,000
Less: Dividends	35,000
Retained earnings - December 31, 20X9	$480,000

Many companies provide a statement of stockholders' equity in lieu of the statement of retained earnings. The statement of stockholders' equity portrays not only the changes in retained earnings, but also changes in other equity accounts. An expanded statement of stockholders' equity is presented in a future chapter.

BALANCE SHEET

The balance sheet focuses on the accounting equation by revealing the economic resources owned by an entity and the claims against those resources (liabilities and owners' equity). The balance sheet is prepared as of a specific date, whereas the income statement and statement of retained earnings cover a period of time. Accordingly, it is sometimes said that the balance sheet portrays financial position (or condition) while other statements reflect results of operations. Quartz's balance sheet is as follows:

QUARTZ CORPORATION Balance Sheet December 31, 20X9				
Assets		**Liabilities**		
Cash	$192,000	Salaries payable	$ 34,000	
Accounts receivable	128,000	Accounts payable	166,000	
Inventories	120,000	Total liabilities		$200,000
Land	300,000	**Stockholders' equity**		
Building	100,000	Capital stock	$220,000	
Equipment	50,000	Retained earnings	480,000	
Other assets	10,000	Total stockholders' equity		700,000
Total assets	$900,000	Total liabilities and equity		$900,000

The statement of cash flows details the enterprise's cash flows. This operating statement reveals how cash is generated and expended during a specific period of time. It consists of three unique sections that isolate the cash inflows and outflows attributable to (a) operating activities, (b) investing activities, and (c) financing activities.

QUARTZ CORPORATION Statement of Cash Flows For the Year Ending December 31, 20X9		
Operating activities		
Cash received from customers	$ 720,000	
Cash received for interest	15,000	
Cash paid for salaries	(240,000)	
Cash paid for rent	(115,000)	
Cash paid for other items	(300,000)	
Cash provided by operating activities		$ 80,000
Investing activities		
Purchase of land		(250,000)
Financing activities		
Payment of dividends		(35,000)
Decrease in cash		$(205,000)
Cash, January 1		397,000
Cash, December 31		$ 192,000

Notice that the cash provided by operations is not the same as net income found in the income statement. This result occurs because some items generate income and cash flows in different periods. For instance, remember how Edelweiss (from the earlier illustration) generated income from a service provided on account? That transaction increased income without a similar effect on cash. These differences tend to even out over time. Other cash flow items may never impact operations. For instance, dividends paid are an important financing cash outflow for a corporation, but they are not an expense. They are a distribution of income. The proceeds of a loan would be an example of a nonoperating cash inflow. It would be shown as a financing activity cash flow item.

The statement of cash flows requires a fairly complete knowledge of basic accounting. Do not be concerned by a lack of complete comprehension at this juncture. Comprehension develops as studies progress, and a future chapter is devoted to the statement of cash flows.

Finally, it is important to note that the income statement, statement of retained earnings, and balance sheet articulate. This means they "mesh together" in a self-balancing fashion. The income for the period ties into the statement of retained earnings, and the ending retained earnings ties into the balance sheet. This final tie-in causes the balance sheet to balance. These relationships are illustrated in the summary diagram on the following page.

It may almost seem magical that the final tie-in of retained earnings will exactly cause the balance sheet to balance. This is reflective of the brilliance of Pacioli's model, and is indicative of why it has survived for centuries.

QUARTZ CORPORATION
Income Statement
For the Year Ending December 31, 20X9

Revenues

Services to customers	$750,000	
Interest revenue	15,000	
Total revenues		$765,000

Expenses

Salaries	$235,000	
Rent	115,000	
Other operating expenses	300,000	
Total expenses		650,000
Net income		$115,000

QUARTZ CORPORATION
Statement of Retained Earnings
For the Year Ending December 31, 20X9

Retained earnings - January 1, 20X9	$400,000
Plus: Net income	115,000
	$515,000
Less: Dividends	35,000
Retained earnings - December 31, 20X9	$480,000

QUARTZ CORPORATION
Balance Sheet
December 31, 20X9

Assets

Cash		$192,000
Accounts receivable		128,000
Inventories		120,000
Land		300,000
Building		100,000
Equipment		50,000
Other assets		10,000
Total assets		$900,000

Liabilities

Salaries payable	$ 34,000	
Accounts payable	166,000	
Total liabilities		$200,000

Stockholders' equity

Capital stock	$220,000	
Retained earnings	480,000	
Total stockholders' equity		700,000
Total liabilities and equity		$900,000

Chapter 1 Quiz

Goals Achievement

Q1-1. Which of the following branches of accounting is concerned primarily with external reporting or communicating the results of economic activities to parties outside the firm?

managerial accounting or financial accounting

Q1-2. The economic resources owned by a company that are expected to benefit future periods are:

assets or liabilities

Q1-3. Withdrawals of assets by the stockholders ("dividends") causes retained earnings to:

increase or decrease

Q1-4. Payment of accounts payable with cash causes retained earnings to:

change or remain the same

Q1-5. Which financial statement most closely corresponds to the accounting equation?

balance sheet or statement of cash flows

Fill in the Blanks

Q1-6. _____ accounting involves reporting results of operating activity to administrators within an organization.

Q1-7. The private sector agency that currently oversees external financial reporting is the

_____.

Q1-8. The shortened form of the accounting equation is _____ equals

_____ plus _____.

Q1-9. The historical cost principle holds that accounting valuations be tied to

_____ and _____ past transactions.

Q1-10. The four primary financial statements are the _____,

_____, _____, and _____.

Q1-11. _____ appears in both the income statement and the statement of retained earnings.

Q1-12. The accounting profession can be divided into three major categories; specifically, the practice of public accounting, private accounting, and governmental accounting. A somewhat unique and important service of public accountants is:

a. Financial accounting.

b. Managerial accounting.

c. Auditing.

d. Cost accounting.

Q1-13. Which of the following equations properly represents a derivation of the fundamental accounting equation?

a. Assets + liabilities = owner's equity.

b. Assets = owner's equity.

c. Cash = assets.

d. Assets - liabilities = owner's equity.

Q1-14. Wilson Company owns land that cost $100,000. If a "quick sale" of the land was necessary to generate cash, the company feels it would receive only $80,000. The company continues to report the asset on the balance sheet at $100,000. Which of the following concepts justifies this?

a. The historical-cost principle.

b. The value is tied to objective and verifiable past transactions.

c. Neither of the above.

d. Both "a" and "b".

Q1-15. Retained earnings will change over time because of several factors. Which of the following factors would explain an increase in retained earnings?

a. Net loss.

b. Net income.

c. Dividends.

d. Investments by stockholders.

Q1-16. Gerald had beginning total stockholders' equity of $160,000. During the year, total assets increased by $240,000 and total liabilities increased by $120,000. Gerald's net income was $180,000. No additional investments were made; however, dividends did occur during the year. How much were the dividends?

a. $20,000.

b. $60,000.

c. $140,000.

d. $220,000.

Chapter 1 Problems

Basic Problems

Definitions, concepts, and awareness of accounting	B-01.01

Professor Pacioli was recently asked the following five questions by his aspiring accounting students. Prepare a summary of the professor's reply to each question.

(a) Professor, I'm not sure why, but your name sounds familiar . . .why is that?

(b) Professor, I have no interest in being a bookkeeper. Why should I study accounting?

(c) Professor, I am not sure I understand why there is a distinction between financial and managerial accounting. If you are accounting for one business, how can there possibly be two separate approaches?

(d) Professor, haven't computers and modern information systems made accountants obsolete?

(e) Professor, I am interested in becoming a CPA. Do I need to apply to the FASB?

Classification of items as assets, liabilities, revenues, or expenses	B-01.02

Determine whether each of the following items is a(n):

Asset   Liability   Revenue   Expense   Owners' equity   Other

(a) Cash

(b) Dividend to shareholders

(c) Land

(d) Accounts payable

(e) Capital stock

(f) Notes payable

(g) Accounts receivable

(h) Salaries

(i) Rent paid

(j) Cost of utilities used

(k) Customer order not yet filled

(l) The value of completed services provided to customers

(m) Obligation to pay for utilities consumed

SPREADSHEET TOOL:

Using drop down lists

Impact of transactions on fundamental accounting equation	B-01.03

Indicate the impact (increase/decrease/no change) for each of the following transactions on total assets, liabilities, and owners' equity.

(a) Paid the current month's rent.

(b) Provided services to customers for cash.

(c) Provided services to customers on account.

(d) Recorded receipt of an electric bill to be paid next month.

(e) Paid an electric bill received in a prior month.

(f) Purchased land for cash.

(g) Purchased equipment in exchange for a note payable (loan).

(h) Collected a previously recorded account receivable.

(i) Purchased a building by paying 20% in cash and agreeing to pay the remainder over future years.

(j) Declared and paid a dividend to shareholders.

B-01.04   *Basic identification of revenues, expenses, assets, liabilities*

Goudar Bloodcare is a blood donation center where eligible donors give a pint of blood about once every other month. Assess each of the following to decide if Goudar should record the item as an asset, a liability, a revenue, or expense.

(a) The monthly fee paid to maintain Goudar's website.

(b) Needles, bags, plastic bandages, etc. that *were used* to collect blood.

(c) Needles, bags, plastic bandages, etc. that will be used *in the future* to collect blood.

(d) Amounts received from hospitals to pay for the blood products.

(e) A loan that is owed to a bank.

(f) The building and equipment that serves as the home office for Goudar.

(g) Amounts owed to a printing company that prepared T-shirts given away at a recent blood drive campaign.

(h) The salaries of employees of Goudar.

B-01.05   *To develop an understanding of the nature of changes in equity*

Magee Corporation provided the following summary balance sheet information:

	Dec. 31, 20X1	Dec. 31, 20X2
Total assets	$1,500,000	$2,300,000
Total liabilities	700,000	1,400,000

Compute net income for the year ending December 31, 20X2, under each of the following independent scenarios:

(a) Magee paid no dividends, and no additional capital was raised via share issuances.

(b) Magee paid $100,000 in dividends, and no additional capital was raised via share issuances.

(c) Magee paid no dividends, but raised $250,000 via issuances of additional shares of stock.

(d) Magee paid $100,000 in dividends, and raised $250,000 via issuances of additional shares of stock.

CUE Corporation was formed at the beginning of 20X2, and presents the following incomplete financial statements for three years. CUE has requested your help in completing the missing values for each year. Begin by solving the unknowns in the 20X2 year, and work forward to subsquent years. Remember that 20X2 is the first year of business, so Cue begins with a zero balance in 20X2 beginning retained earnings.

Income Statements for the Years Ending December 31, 20XX

	20X4		20X3		20X2	
Revenues						
Services to customers	$200,000		?		$100,000	
Expenses						
Wages	?		$117,000		?	
Interest	3,000	?	3,000	?	5,000	?
Net income		?		$ 40,000		?

Statements of Retained Earnings for the Years Ending December 31, 20XX

	20X4	20X3	20X2
Beginning retained earnings	?	?	$ -
Plus: Net income	?	40,000	?
	?	?	$ 25,000
Less: Dividends	30,000	?	?
Ending retained earnings	$ 60,000	?	?

Balance Sheets as of December 31, 20XX

	20X4		20X3		20X2	
Assets						
Cash	?		?		$ 50,000	
Accounts receivable	65,000		50,000		?	
Land	180,000		180,000		180,000	
Total assets	?		$289,000		?	
Liabilities						
Interest payable	?		$ 1,000		$ 2,000	
Loan payable	10,000		?		?	
Total liabilities		$11,000		$31,000		?
Stockholders' equity						
Capital stock	?		?		$228,000	
Retained earnings	?		30,000		?	
Total stockholders' equity		?		?		238,000
Total liabilities and equity		$299,000		?		$300,000

B-01.07   *Broad ideas about the role of accounting and its concepts*

Think very broadly about accounting, its societal role, and its underlying premises; then, provide a general answer to each of the following.

(a)   What is the role of accounting in society?

(b)   Is accounting complete? Does it provide all of the information that investors and creditors need for rational decision making?

(c)   Consider an intrinsic principle of accounting, such as the historical cost principle. Are the underlying principles and assumptions of accounting immutable truths, or is there some degree of arbitrariness that is apt to evolve over time?

B-01.08   *Differentiating between "right" and "wrong" accounting*

As you study accounting, you will become increasingly familiar with a variety of generally accepted accounting principles. Already, you are beginning to appreciate some of the fundamental principles, rules, and procedures. Evaluate the following ten comments, and state whether you agree or disagree:

(a)   The fundamental accounting equation precludes a situation where liabilities exceed assets.

(b)   A complete set of financial statements would include a cash flow statement.

(c)   The balance sheet can be prepared in a vertical or horizontal format.

(d)   The period of time covered by each financial statement is identical.

(e)   Many assets are reported at their historical cost.

(f)   Revenue should not be recognized before it is collected.

(g)   The term income is synonymous with the term revenue.

(h)   Dividends are reported as an expense on the income statement.

(i)   Retained earnings will equal cash on hand.

(j)   Issuing stock does not increase a company's revenue or income.

B-01.09   *Interpreting financial statement outcomes to assess profit/loss*

SPREADSHEET TOOL:

Cell comments/ narratives

Review the following facts for four separate companies. Identify the two companies that lost money during the year, explaining how you reached your conclusion for each.

COMPANY A   Ending retained earnings was less than beginning retained earnings, and dividends were twice as much as income during the year.

COMPANY B   Ending retained earnings was more than beginning retained earnings, but the company issued stock in an amount greater than the increase in retained earnings; no dividends were declared or paid.

COMPANY C   No stock was issued and no dividends were declared or paid; total liabilities increased more than total assets.

COMPANY D   Expenses exceeded revenues, but the company issued additional shares of stock in an amount that exceeded the difference between revenues and expenses.

Involved Problems

Accounting, GAAP, careers, and ethics	I-01.01

Provide a carefully constructed narrative reply to each of the following requirements. You may consider using internet resources beyond your textbook to gather supporting information.

(a)   Define accounting, and define generally accepted accounting principles (GAAP).

(b)   Identify several different career paths that one might consider as an accounting professional.

(c)   What is ethical behavior, and why is it very important to the accounting profession? What challenges might arise that cause an otherwise "good person" to engage in unethical behavior?

Accounting equation and entity types	I-01.02

Financial statements are typically prepared for a specific entity, or circumscribed area of accountability. There are a variety of legal forms of entities.

(a)   What is the fundamental accounting equation, and how does the legal form of entity impact the basic equation?

(b)   What three entity forms were broadly identified in the textbook? How does the entity form influence the reporting of assets, liabilities, and equity?

(c)   Conduct internet research into other forms of entities (LLP, LLC, etc.). Why are there so many different types of entities, and does this newly discovered information change your answer to parts (a) or (b).

Preparing and formatting basic financial statements from selected data	I-01.03

Prepare Bisceglia's income statement, statement of retained earnings, and balance sheet for the year ending December 31, 20X5. The following information is all that is available. Be sure to prepare proper headings and dates on each financial statement.

Capital stock	$41,000	Rent expense	$10,000
Wage expense	37,000	Accounts payable	4,000
Revenue	90,000	Equipment	80,000
Cash	9,000	Dividends	5,000
Utilities expense	6,000	Accounts receivable	19,000
Beginning retained earnings	11,000	Notes payable	20,000

I-01.04 *Moderately complex assessment to determine income for four years*

Sketchy Company provided the following very limited set of data. Use this information to determine net income for the years ending December 31, 20X1, 20X2, 20X3, and 20X4. The company was formed at the beginning of January, 20X1 by issuing $100,000 of capital stock. No additional shares were issued during the 4-year period. The company's 20X4 dividends were equal to 50% of the 20X4 net income.

Revenues, 20X2	$ 90,000
Dividends, 20X3	15,000
Total equity, December 31, 20X3	210,000
Total liabilities, December 31, 20X3	220,000
Retained earnings, December 31, 20X1	41,000
Expenses, 20X2	44,000
Retained earnings, December 31, 20X2	80,000
Dividends, 20X1	10,000
Total assets, December 31, 20X4	500,000
Increase in liabilities, 20X4	50,000

I-01.05 *Analysis of impact of transactions on complete financial statements*

Bingo Corporation is a newly formed company. Below are the first 10 transactions that Bingo encountered. Prepare an income statement, statement of retained earnings, and balance sheet immediately following each of these consecutive transactions.

(1)   Issued capital stock for $50,000 cash.

(2)   Purchased building for $120,000, making a $20,000 down payment and signing a promissory note payable for the balance.

(3)   Paid wages expense of $5,000.

(4)   Provided services to customers for $15,000 cash.

(5)   Paid utilities expense of $2,000.

(6)   Reduced note payable with an $8,000 cash payment (ignore interest costs).

(7)   Provided services to customers on account, $10,000.

(8)   Incurred wages expense of $3,000, to be paid in the future.

(9)   Collected $4,000 on an outstanding account receivable.

(10) Declared and paid dividend of $6,000.

Computing income and extended analysis based on partial data   *I-01.06*

Winterbotham Corporation provided the following listing of financial statement elements and their respective balances. The periodic amounts relate to the year ending December 31, 20X5, and the point-in-time amounts reflect balances as of December 31, 20X5, unless otherwise implied. Unfortunately, the company has been unable to locate its listing of assets; but, all other information is complete, although in disarray.

				SPREADSHEET TOOL:
Capital stock	$250,000	Utilities expense	11,000	
Wage expense	40,000	Accounts payable	12,500	
Revenue	80,000	Dividends	2,500	*Cell*
Rent expense	22,000	Notes payable	50,000	*references*
Beginning retained earnings	89,000			

(a)   Determine Winterbotham's net income for the year ending December 31, 20X5.

(b)   How much are total assets of the company, as of December 31, 20X5?

(c)   If you were told that assets included an accounts receivable of $5,000 for services provided during 20X5, and that such transactions had been excluded in calculating the given "revenue" amount, how would this influence your answer to part (a) above?

Team-based identification of errors and corrections   *I-01.07*

Efendi Company hired an accounting intern, Pat Morgan, to prepare its income statement, statement of retained earnings, and balance sheet. Pat was reluctant to undertake this task due to a lack of adequate training, but, agreed to if someone would examine the work in detail and provide useful suggestions for improvement. Pat's work follows:

PAT MORGAN'S Income Statement December 31, 20X5		
Net income		
Services to customers		$125,000
Expenses		
Dividends	$13,500	
Rent	11,000	24,500
Revenues		$100,500

PAT MORGAN'S Statement of Retained Earnings For the Year Ending December 31, 20X1	
Beginning retained earnings	$ 45,000
Plus: Net income	100,500
	$145,500
Less: Capital stock	200,000
Ending retained earnings	$ (54,500)

PAT MORGAN'S
Equation Sheet
December 31, 20X1

Assets

Cash	$ 92,700
Accounts receivable	37,400
Equipment	239,000
Total assets	$369,100

Liabilities

Accounts payable	$ 7,500	
Wages expense	64,000	
Total expenses		$ 71,500

Stockholders' equity

Notes payable	$80,100	
Retained earnings	(54,500)	
Total stockholders' equity		25,600
Total liabilities and equity		$ 97,100

(a) Find specific errors in Pat's work. Prepare written review notes sufficient to allow Pat to understand the errors and make necessary corrections. To get started, you may assume Pat did manage to get the listing of total assets correct.

(b) Provide your notes to a fellow classmate (just call your classmate Pat for purposes of this exercise), and have him or her prepare corrected reports, based solely on your notes -- right or wrong! Remember that achieving professional success not only depends on technical proficiency but also your ability to communicate and mentor others.

(c) Prepare corrected financial statements and compare them to the set provided by your classmate in requirement (b).

I-01.08   *Preparing financial statements and cash calculations based on a narrative*

Skousen Exploration Corporation was formed on January 1, 20X3. The company was formed by Cliff and Chris Skousen with the goal of conducting geophysical support services related to natural gas drilling operations in the Uinta Basin region of eastern Utah. The company's initial capitalization consisted of shareholder investments of $1,000,000 and an additional bank loan of $750,000.

During the first year of operation, the company purchased land, buildings, and equipment in the amount of $200,000, $500,000, and $300,000, respectively. (Hint: In subsequent chapters you will be introduced to the concepts of depreciation relating to certain of these assets; for now you may ignore this issue).

During 20X3, the company signed contracts to deliver consulting services with a total value of $2,500,000. By year's end, $1,600,000 of services had been provided and billed under these agreements. The remaining $900,000 of work will not be performed until 20X4. All amounts billed had been collected during 20X3, with the exception of December's billings in the amount of $125,000. The Skousen's are quite confident that the December billing will be collected in the normal course of business in early 20X4.

Expenses paid during 20X3 included rent ($140,000), wages ($780,000), interest ($75,000), and taxes ($215,000). In addition, the company had incurred rent ($10,000), wages ($30,000), and interest ($6,000) related to 20X3 activity that was not yet paid as of the end of 20X3.

Skousen Exploration declared and paid dividends to shareholders in the amount of $75,000 during 20X3. Skousen also repaid $50,000 of the original bank loan.

(a)   Prepare an income statement for Skousen Exploration Corporation for the year ending December 31, 20X3.

(b)   Prepare a statement of retained earnings for Skousen Exploration Corporation for the year ending December 31, 20X3.

(c)   Prepare calculations showing that cash is $890,000 as of December 31, 20X3.

(d)   Prepare a balance sheet for Skousen Exploration Corporation as of December 31, 20X3.

Basic cash flow analysis and statement of cash flows	*I-01.09*

Harish Company was formed on January 1, 20X1. The company's accountant prepared the following income statement, statement of retained earnings, and balance sheet at the conclusion of the first full year of operations. Mr. Harish desires for the company to declare and pay a dividend equivalent to the company's net income for the year.

HARISH COMPANY
Income Statement
For the Year Ending December 31, 20X1

Revenues		
Services to customers		$70,000
Expenses		
Wages	$30,000	
Rent	12,000	42,000
Net income		$28,000

HARISH COMPANY
Statement of Retained Earnings
For the Year Ending December 31, 20X1

Beginning retained earnings	$ -
Plus: Net income	28,000
	$28,000
Less: Dividends	-
Ending retained earnings	$28,000

HARISH COMPANY Balance Sheet December 31, 20X1		
Assets		
Cash		$ 4,000
Accounts receivable		15,000
Equipment		50,000
Total assets		$69,000
Liabilities		
Rent payable	$ 1,000	
Notes payable	30,000	
Total liabilities		$31,000
Stockholders' equity		
Capital stock	$10,000	
Retained earnings	28,000	
Total stockholders' equity		38,000
Total liabilities and equity		$69,000

(a) Is the company currently able to declare and pay the dividend? Why or why not?

(b) Explain why net income can differ from cash provided by operations.

(c) In addition to operating activities, what other "categories" of business activity can generate or expend cash? Provide examples for each category.

(d) Prepare a statement of cash flows for Harish Company for the year ending December 31, 20X1.

I-01.10　　　　　　　　　　　　　　　*Accessing and examining financial statements of a public company*

There are many corporations, and most of them have a relatively small group of shareholders. These are considered to be privately held entities, and it is difficult to obtain much financial information about them. There are also many large "public" companies, and their shares of stock are readily traded on organized stock market exchanges. In the USA, such companies must regularly file financial reports and other documents with the Securities and Exchange Commission (SEC). You can go to the SEC website (www.sec.gov) and access filings for public companies.

(a) Go to the SEC website, and probe until you find the section that includes filings. You might find it helpful to work through the related tutorial on the site.

(b) Find the filings from the SEC website for one of your "favorite" public companies.

(c) The annual report that must be filed with the SEC is known as a "10K." Locate the 10K for your target company, and find the balance sheet and income statement (note that the statement of retained earnings illustrated in the textbook is likely replaced by a more comprehensive statement of stockholders' equity). What are the revenues, income, assets and liabilities of your target company?

Chapter 2:
Information Processing

Goals:

Accounts, debits and credits.
The journal.
The general ledger.
The trial balance.
Computerized processing systems.
T-Accounts.

principlesofaccounting.com

The previous chapter showed how transactions caused financial statement amounts to change. "Before" and "after" examples were used to develop the illustrations. Imagine if a real business tried to keep up with its affairs this way! Perhaps a giant marker board could be set up in the accounting department. As transactions occurred, they would be communicated to the department and the marker board would be updated. Chaos would quickly rule. Even if the business could manage to figure out what its financial statements were supposed to contain, it probably could not systematically describe the transactions that produced those results. Obviously, a system is needed.

It is imperative that a business develop a reliable accounting system to capture and summarize its voluminous transaction data. The system must be sufficient to fuel the preparation of the financial statements, and be capable of maintaining retrievable documentation for each and every transaction. In other words, some transaction logging process must be in place.

In general terms, an accounting system is a system where transactions and events are reliably processed and summarized into useful financial statements and reports. Whether this system is manual or automated, the heart of the system will contain the basic processing tools: accounts, debits and credits, journals, and the general ledger. This chapter will provide insight into these tools and the general structure of a typical accounting system.

ACCOUNTS

The records that are kept for the individual asset, liability, equity, revenue, expense, and dividend components are known as **accounts**. In other words, a business would maintain an account for cash, another account for inventory, and so forth for every other financial statement element. All accounts, collectively, are said to comprise a firm's general ledger. In a manual processing system, imagine the general ledger as nothing more than a notebook, with a separate page for every account. Thus, one could thumb through the notebook to see the "ins" and "outs" of every account, as well as existing balances. The following example reveals that the Cash account has a balance of $63,000 as of January 12. By examining the account, one can see the various transactions that caused increases and decreases to the $50,000 beginning-of-month cash balance.

Cash				
Date	Description	Increase	Decrease	Balance
Jan. 1, 20X3	Balance forward			$ 50,000
Jan. 2, 20X3	Collected receivable	$ 10,000		60,000
Jan. 3, 20X3	Cash sale	5,000		65,000
Jan. 5, 20X3	Paid rent		$ 7,000	58,000
Jan. 7, 20X3	Paid salary		3,000	55,000
Jan. 8, 20X3	Cash sale	4,000		59,000
Jan. 8, 20X3	Paid bills		2,000	57,000
Jan. 10, 20X3	Paid tax		1,000	56,000
Jan. 12, 20X3	Collected receivable	7,000		63,000

In many respects, this Cash account resembles the "register" one might keep for a wallet-style checkbook. A balance sheet on January 12 would include cash for the indicated amount (and, so forth for each of the other accounts comprising the entire financial statements). Notice that column headings for this illustrative Cash account included "increase" and "decrease" labels. In actuality, these labels would instead be "debit" and "credit." The reason for this distinction will become apparent in the following discussion.

DEBITS AND CREDITS

References to debits and credits are quite common. A business may indicate it is "crediting" an account. "Debit" cards may be used to buy goods. **Debits** and **credits** (abbreviated "dr" and "cr") are unique accounting tools to describe the change in a particular account that is necessitated by a transaction. In other words, instead of saying that cash is "increased" or "decreased," it is said that cash is "debited" or "credited." This method is again traced to Pacioli, the Franciscan monk who is given credit for the development of our enduring accounting model. Why add this complexity -- why not just use plus and minus like in the previous chapter? There is an ingenious answer to this question that will soon be discovered!

Understanding the answer to this question begins by taking note of two very important observations:

(1) every transaction can be described in debit/credit form

and

(2) for every transaction, debits = credits

THE FALLACY OF A "+/-" SYSTEM

The second observation above would not be true for an increase/decrease system. For example, if services are provided to customers for cash, both cash and revenues would increase (a "+/+" outcome). On the other hand, paying an account payable causes a decrease in cash and a decrease in accounts payable (a "-/-" outcome). Finally, some transactions are a mixture of increase/decrease effects; using cash to buy land causes cash to decrease and land to increase (a "-/+" outcome). In the previous chapter, the "+/-" nomenclature was used for the various illustrations. Take time to review the comprehensive illustration that was provided in Chapter 1, and notice that various combinations of pluses and minuses were needed.

As one can tell by reviewing the illustration, the "+/-" system lacks internal consistency. Therefore, it is easy to get something wrong and be completely unaware that something has gone amiss. On the other hand, the debit/credit system has internal consistency. If one attempts to describe the effects of a transaction in debit/credit form, it will be readily apparent that something is wrong when debits do not equal credits. Even modern computerized systems will challenge or preclude any attempt to enter an "unbalanced" transaction that does not satisfy the condition of debits = credits.

The debit/credit rules are built upon an inherently logical structure. Nevertheless, many students will initially find them confusing, and somewhat frustrating. This is a bit similar to learning a new language. As such, memorization usually precedes comprehension. Take time now to memorize the "debit/credit" rules that are reflected in the following diagrams. Going forward, one needs to have instant recall of these rules, and memorization will allow the study of accounting to continue on a much smoother pathway. Full comprehension will follow in short order.

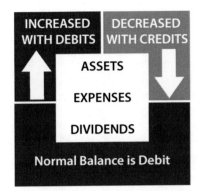

*ASSETS/
EXPENSES/
DIVIDENDS*

As shown at left, asset, expense and dividend accounts each follow the same set of debit/credit rules. Debits increase these accounts and credits decrease these accounts. These accounts normally carry a debit balance. To aid recall, rely on this mnemonic: D-E-A-D = Dividends, Expenses, and Assets are increased with Debits.

Liability, revenue, and equity accounts each follow rules that are the opposite of those just described. Credits increase liabilities, revenues, and equity, while debits result in decreases. These accounts normally carry a credit balance. To aid recall, rely on this mnemonic: R-E-L-I-C = Revenues, Equity and Liabilities are Increased with Credits.

*LIABILITIES/
REVENUES/
EQUITY*

*TRANSACTION
ANALYSIS*

It is now apparent that transactions and events can be expressed in "debit/credit" terminology. In essence, accountants have their own unique shorthand to portray the financial statement consequence for every recordable event. This means that as transactions occur, it is necessary to perform an analysis to determine (a) what accounts are impacted and (b) how they are impacted (increased or decreased). Then, debits and credits are applied to the accounts, utilizing the rules set forth in the preceding paragraphs.

*SOURCE
DOCUMENTS*

Usually, a recordable transaction will be evidenced by a **source document**. A disbursement will be supported by the issuance of a check. A sale might be supported by an invoice issued to a customer. A time report may support payroll costs. A tax statement may document the amount paid for taxes. A cash register tape may show cash sales. A bank deposit slip may show collections of customer receivables. Suffice it to say, there are many potential source documents, and this is just a small sample. Source documents usually serve as the trigger for initiating the recording of a transaction. The source documents are analyzed to determine the nature of a transaction and what accounts are impacted. Source documents should be retained (perhaps in electronic form) as an important part of the records supporting the various debits and credits that are entered into the accounting records. To illustrate, assume that Jill Aoki is an architect. Concurrent with delivering completed blueprints to one of her clients, she also prepared and presented an invoice for $2,500. The invoice is the source document evidencing the completed work for which payment is now due. Therefore, Accounts Receivable is to be increased (debited) and Revenues must be increased (credited). When her client pays, the resulting bank deposit receipt will provide evidence for an entry to debit Cash (increased) and credit Accounts Receivable (decreased).

A properly designed accounting system will have controls to make sure that all transactions are fully captured. It would not do for transactions to slip through the cracks and go unrecorded. There are many such safeguards that can be put in place, including use of prenumbered documents and regular reconciliations. For example, an individual might maintain a checkbook for recording cash disbursements. A monthly reconciliation should be performed to make sure that the checkbook accounting system has correctly reflected all disbursements. A business must engage in similar activities to make sure that all transactions and events are recorded correctly. Good controls are essential to business success. Much of the work performed by a professional accountant relates to the design, implementation, and evaluation of properly functioning control systems.

AN ACCOUNT'S BALANCE

The balance of a specific account can be determined by considering its beginning (of period) balance, and then netting or offsetting all of the additional debits and credits to that account during the period. Earlier, an illustration for a Cash account was presented. That illustration was developed before the introduction of debits and credits. However, accounts are maintained by using the debit/credit system. The Cash account is repeated below, except that the increase/decrease columns have been replaced with the more traditional debit/credit column headings. A typical Cash account would look similar to this illustration:

Cash				
Date	**Description**	**Debit**	**Credit**	**Balance**
Jan. 1, 20X3	Balance forward			$ 50,000
Jan. 2, 20X3	Collected receivable	$ 10,000		60,000
Jan. 3, 20X3	Cash sale	5,000		65,000
Jan. 5, 20X3	Paid rent		$ 7,000	58,000
Jan. 7, 20X3	Paid salary		3,000	55,000
Jan. 8, 20X3	Cash sale	4,000		59,000
Jan. 8, 20X3	Paid bills		2,000	57,000
Jan. 10, 20X3	Paid tax		1,000	56,000
Jan. 12, 20X3	Collected receivable	7,000		63,000

Bear in mind that each of the debits and credits to Cash shown in the preceding illustration will have some offsetting effect on another account. For instance, the $10,000 debit on January 2 would be offset by a $10,000 credit to Accounts Receivable. The process by which this occurs will become clear in the following sections of this chapter.

A COMMON MISUNDER-STANDING ABOUT CREDITS

Many people wrongly assume that credits always reduce an account balance. However, a quick review of the debit/credit rules reveals that this is not true. Where does this notion come from? Probably because of the common phrase "we will credit your account." This wording is often used when one returns goods purchased on credit. Carefully consider that the account (with the store) is *on the store's books* as an asset account (specifically, an account receivable). Thus, the store is reducing its accounts receivable asset account (with a credit) when it agrees to credit the account. On the customer's books one would <u>debit</u> (decrease) a payable account (liability).

On the other hand, some may assume that a credit always increases an account. This incorrect notion may originate with common banking terminology. Assume that Matthew made a deposit to his account at Monalo Bank. Monalo's balance sheet would include an obligation ("liability") to Matthew for the amount of money on deposit. This liability would be credited each time Matthew adds to his account. Thus, Matthew is told that his account is being "credited" when he makes a deposit.

What is already known about a journal (not an accounting journal, just any journal)? It's just a log book, right? A place where one can record a history of transactions and events, usually in date (chronological) order. Likewise, an accounting **journal** is just a log book that contains a chronological listing of a company's transactions and events. The accounting journal serves to document business activity as it occurs. However, rather than including a detailed narrative description of a company's transactions and events, the journal lists the items by a form of shorthand notation. Specifically, the notation indicates the accounts involved, and whether each is debited or credited.

The general journal is sometimes called the book of original entry. This means that source documents are reviewed and interpreted as to the accounts involved. Then, they are documented in the journal via their debit/credit format. As such the general journal becomes a log book of the recordable transactions and events. The journal is not sufficient, by itself, to prepare financial statements. That objective is fulfilled by subsequent steps. But, maintaining the journal is the point of beginning toward that end objective.

The following illustration draws upon the facts for the Xao Corporation. Specifically it shows the **journalizing** process for Xao's transactions. Review it carefully, specifically noting that it is in chronological order with each transaction of the business being reduced to the short-hand description of its debit/credit effects. For instance, the first transaction increases both cash and equity. Cash, an asset account, is increased via a debit. Capital Stock, an equity account, is increased via a credit. The next transaction increases Advertising Expense "with a debit" and decreases Cash "with a credit."

JOURNAL EXAMPLE

Note that each transaction is followed by a brief narrative description; this is a good practice to provide further documentation. For each transaction, it is customary to list "debits" first (flush left), then the credits (indented right). Finally, notice that a transaction may involve more than two accounts (as in the January 28 transaction); the corresponding journal entry for these complex transactions is called a "compound" entry.

In reviewing the general journal for Xao, note that it is only two pages long. An actual journal for a business might consume hundreds or thousands of pages to document its many transactions. As a result, some businesses may maintain the journal in electronic form only.

GENERAL JOURNAL		Page 1	
Date	**Accounts**	**Debits**	**Credits**
01-01-X3	Cash	25,000	
	Capital Stock		25,000
	Issued stock to shareholders for cash		
01-04-X3	Advertising Expense	2,000	
	Cash		2,000
	Paid for initial advertising programs		
01-08-X3	Cash	4,000	
	Service Revenue		4,000
	Provided services to customers for cash		
01-15-X3	Utilities Expense	1,000	
	Accounts Payable		1,000
	Received bill for utility cost incurred		

GENERAL JOURNAL			Page 2
Date	Accounts	Debits	Credits
01-17-X3	Accounts Receivable	8,000	
	Service Revenue		8,000
	Provided services to customers on account		
01-18-X3	Accounts Payable	500	
	Cash		500
	Paid half of the utility bill received on Jan. 15		
01-25-X3	Cash	4,800	
	Accounts Receivable		4,800
	Received 60% of the amount due on the receivable that was established on Jan. 17		
01-28-X3	Land	15,000	
	Cash		5,000
	Notes Payable		10,000
	Purchased land by giving $5,000 cash, and promising to pay the remainder in 90 days		

SPECIAL JOURNALS

The illustrated journal was referred to as a "general" journal. Most businesses will maintain a general journal. All transactions can be recorded in the general journal. However, a business may sometimes find it beneficial to employ optional "special journals." Special journals are deployed for highly repetitive transactions.

For example, a business may have huge volumes of redundant transactions that involve cash receipts. Thus, the company might have a special cash receipts journal. Any transaction entailing a cash receipt would be recorded therein. Indeed, the summary total of all transactions in this journal could correspond to the debits to the Cash account, further simplifying the accounting process. Other special journals might be used for cash payments, sales, purchases, payroll, and so forth.

The special journals do not replace the general journal. Instead, they just strip out recurring type transactions and place them in their own separate journal. The transaction descriptions associated with each transaction found in the general journal are not normally needed in a special journal, given that each transaction is redundant in nature. Without special journals, a general journal can become quite voluminous.

PAGE NUMBERING

Second, notice that the illustrated journal consisted of two pages (labeled Page 1 and Page 2). Although the journal is chronological, it is helpful to have the page number indexing for transaction cross-referencing and working backward from financial statement amounts to individual transactions. The benefits of this type of indexing will become apparent in the general ledger exhibits within the following section of the chapter. As an alternative, some companies will assign a unique index number to each transaction, further facilitating the ability to trace transactions throughout the entire accounting system.

RECAP

The general journal does nothing to tell a company about the balance in each specific account. For instance, how much cash does Xao Corporation have at the end of January? One could go through the journal and net the debits and credits to Cash ($25,000 - $2,000 + $4,000 - $500 + $4,800 - $5,000 = $26,300). But, this is tedious and highly susceptible to error. It would become virtually impossible if the journal were hundreds of pages long. A better way is needed. This is where the general ledger comes into play.

The General Ledger

As illustrated, the general journal is, in essence, a notebook that contains page after page of detailed accounting transactions. In contrast, the **general ledger** is, in essence, another notebook that contains a page for each and every account in use by a company. As examples, the ledger accounts for Xao would include the Cash and Accounts Receivable pages illustrated below:

Cash

Date	Description	Debit	Credit	Balance
Jan. 1, 20X3	Balance forward			$ -
Jan. 1, 20X3	Journal page 1	$ 25,000		25,000
Jan. 4, 20X3	Journal page 1		$ 2,000	23,000
Jan. 8, 20X3	Journal page 1	4,000		27,000
Jan. 18, 20X3	Journal page 2		500	26,500
Jan. 25, 20X3	Journal page 2	4,800		31,300
Jan. 28, 20X3	Journal page 2		5,000	26,300

Accounts Receivable

Date	Description	Debit	Credit	Balance
Jan. 1, 20X3	Balance forward			$ -
Jan. 17, 20X3	Journal page 2	$ 8,000		8,000
Jan. 25, 20X3	Journal page 2		$ 4,800	3,200

Xao's transactions utilized all of the following accounts:

Cash	Accounts Payable	Service Revenue
Accounts Receivable	Notes Payable	Advertising Expense
Land	Capital Stock	Utilities Expense

Therefore, Xao's general ledger will include a separate page for each of these nine accounts.

POSTING

Next, consider how the details of each specific account can be determined through a process known as **posting**. To "post" means to copy the entries listed in the journal into their respective ledger accounts. In other words, the debits and credits in the journal will be accumulated ("transferred"/"sorted") into the appropriate debit and credit columns of each ledger page. The following illustration shows the posting process. Arrows are drawn for the first journal entry posting. A similar process would occur for each of the other transactions to produce the resulting ledger pages.

In reviewing the ledger accounts on the following page, notice that the "description" column includes a cross-reference back to the journal page in which the transaction was initially recorded. This reduces the amount of detailed information that must be recorded in the ledger, and provides an audit trail back to the original transaction in the journal. The check marks (✓) in the journal indicate that a particular transaction has been posted to the ledger. Without these marks (in a manual system), it would be very easy to fail to post a transaction, or even post the same transaction twice.

GENERAL JOURNAL			Page 1
Date	**Accounts**	**Debits**	**Credits**
01-01-X3	Cash ✓	25,000	
	Capital Stock ✓		25,000
	Issued stock to shareholders for cash		
01-04-X3	Advertising Expense ✓	2,000	
	Cash ✓		2,000
	Paid for initial advertising programs		
01-08-X3	Cash ✓	4,000	
	Service Revenue ✓		4,000
	Provided services to customers for cash		
01-15-X3	Utility Expense ✓	1,000	
	Accounts Payable ✓		1,000
	Received bill for utility costs		

GENERAL JOURNAL			Page 2
Date	**Accounts**	**Debits**	**Credits**
01-17-X3	Accounts Receivable ✓	8,000	
	Service Revenue ✓		8,000
	Provided services to customers on account		
01-18-X3	Accounts Payable ✓	500	
	Cash ✓		500
	Paid half of the utility bill received on Jan. 15		
01-25-X3	Cash ✓	4,800	
	Accounts Receivable ✓		4,800
	Received 60% on the amount due on the receivable that was established on Jan. 17		
01-28-X3	Land ✓	15,000	
	Cash ✓		5,000
	Notes Payable ✓		10,000
	Purchased land by giving $5,000 cash, and promising to pay remainder in 90 days		

Cash

Date	Description	Debit	Credit	Balance
Jan. 1, 20X3	Balance forward			$ -
Jan. 1, 20X3	Journal page 1	$25,000		25,000
Jan. 4, 20X3	Journal page 1		$ 2,000	23,000
Jan. 8, 20X3	Journal page 1	4,000		27,000
Jan. 18, 20X3	Journal page 2		500	26,500
Jan. 25, 20X3	Journal page 2	4,800		31,300
Jan. 28, 20X3	Journal page 2		5,000	26,300

Accounts Receivable

Date	Description	Debit	Credit	Balance
Jan. 1, 20X3	Balance forward			$ -
Jan. 17, 20X3	Journal page 2	$ 8,000		8,000
Jan. 25, 20X3	Journal page 2		$ 4,800	3,200

Land

Date	Description	Debit	Credit	Balance
Jan. 1, 20X3	Balance forward			$ -
Jan. 28, 20X3	Journal page 2	$15,000		15,000

Accounts Payable

Date	Description	Debit	Credit	Balance
Jan. 1, 20X3	Balance forward			$ -
Jan. 15, 20X3	Journal page 1		$ 1,000	1,000
Jan. 18, 20X3	Journal page 2	$ 500		500

Notes Payable

Date	Description	Debit	Credit	Balance
Jan. 1, 20X3	Balance forward			$ -
Jan. 28, 20X3	Journal page 2		$ 10,000	10,000

Capital Stock

Date	Description	Debit	Credit	Balance
Jan. 1, 20X3	Balance forward			$ -
Jan. 1, 20X3	Journal page 1		$ 25,000	25,000

Service Revenue

Date	Description	Debit	Credit	Balance
Jan. 1, 20X3	Balance forward			$ -
Jan. 8, 20X3	Journal page 1		$ 4,000	4,000
Jan. 17, 20X3	Journal page 2		8,000	12,000

Advertising Expense

Date	Description	Debit	Credit	Balance
Jan. 1, 20X3	Balance forward			$ -
Jan. 4, 20X3	Journal page 1	$ 2,000		2,000

Utilities Expense

Date	Description	Debit	Credit	Balance
Jan. 1, 20X3	Balance forward			$ -
Jan. 15, 20X3	Journal page 1	$ 1,000		1,000

Thus far the following accounting "steps" should have been grasped:

TO REVIEW

- STEP 1: Each transaction is analyzed to determine the accounts involved

- STEP 2: A journal entry is entered into the general journal for each transaction

- STEP 3: Periodically, the journal entries are posted to the appropriate general ledger pages

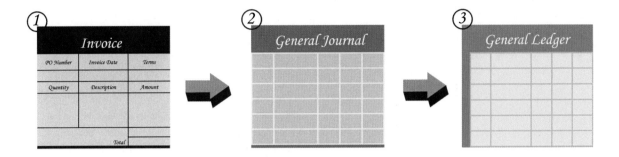

The Trial Balance

After all transactions have been posted from the journal to the ledger, it is a good practice to prepare a **trial balance**. A trial balance is simply a listing of the ledger accounts along with their respective debit or credit balances. The trial balance is not a formal financial statement, but rather a self-check to determine that debits equal credits. Following is the trial balance prepared for Xao Corporation.

XAO CORPORATION
Trial Balance
January 31, 20X3

	Debits	Credits
Cash	$26,300	
Accounts receivable	3,200	
Land	15,000	
Accounts payable		$ 500
Notes payable		10,000
Capital stock		25,000
Service revenues		12,000
Advertising expense	2,000	
Utilities expense	1,000	
	$47,500	$47,500

Since each transaction was journalized in a way that insured that debits equaled credits, one would expect that this equality would be maintained throughout the ledger and trial balance. If the trial balance fails to balance, an error has occurred and must be located. It is much better to be careful as one proceeds, rather than having to go back and locate an error after the fact. Be aware that a "balanced" trial balance is no guarantee of correctness. For example, failing to record a transaction, recording the same transaction twice, or posting an amount to the wrong account would produce a balanced (but incorrect) trial balance.

DEBITS EQUAL CREDITS

FINANCIAL STATEMENTS FROM THE TRIAL BALANCE

The next chapter reveals additional adjustments that may be needed to prepare a truly correct and up-to-date set of financial statements. But, for now, a tentative set of financial statements could be prepared based on the trial balance. The basic process is to transfer amounts from the general ledger to the trial balance, then into the financial statements:

In reviewing the following financial statements for Xao, notice that *italics* are used to draw attention to the items taken directly from the previously shown trial balance. The other line items and amounts simply relate to totals and derived amounts within the statements.

XAO CORPORATION
Income Statement
For the Year Ending January 31, 20X3

Revenues		
Services to customers		*$12,000*
Expenses		
Advertising	*$2,000*	
Utilities	*1,000*	3,000
Net income		$ 9,000

XAO CORPORATION
Statement of Retained Earnings
For the Year Ending January 31, 20X3

Retained Earnings - January 1, 20X3	$ -	
Plus: Net Income	9,000	
	$9,000	
Less: Dividends	*-*	
Retained Earnings - January 31, 20X3	$9,000	

XAO CORPORATION
Balance Sheet
January 31, 20X3

Assets		
Cash		*$26,300*
Accounts receivable		*3,200*
Land		*15,000*
Total assets		$44,500
Liabilities		
Accounts payable	*$ 500*	
Notes payable	*10,000*	
Total liabilities		$10,500
Stockholders' equity		
Capital stock	*$25,000*	
Retained earnings	9,000	
Total stockholders' equity		34,000
Total liabilities and equity		$44,500

CHART OF ACCOUNTS

A listing of all accounts in use by a particular company is called the **chart of accounts**. Individual accounts are often given a specific reference number. The numbering scheme helps keep up with the accounts in use and the classification of accounts. For example, all assets may begin with "1" (e.g., 101 for Cash, 102 for Accounts Receivable, etc.), liabilities with "2," and so forth. The assignment of a numerical value to each account assists in data management, in much the same way as zip codes help move mail more efficiently. Many computerized systems allow rapid entry of accounts by reference number rather than by entering a full account description. A simple chart of accounts for Xao Corporation might appear as follows:

No. 101: Cash

No. 102: Accounts Receivable

No. 103: Land

No. 201: Accounts Payable

No. 202: Notes Payable

No. 301: Capital Stock

No. 401: Service Revenue

No. 501: Advertising Expense

No. 502: Utilities Expense

Another benefit is that each account can be further subdivided into subsets. For instance, if Accounts Receivable bears the account number 102, one would expect to find that individual customers might be numbered as 102.001, 102.002, 102.003, etc. This facilitates the maintenance of "subsidiary" account records which are the subject of the next section of this chapter.

Some general ledger accounts are made of many sub-components. For instance, a company may have total accounts receivable of $19,000, consisting of amounts due from Compton, Fisher, and Moore. The accounting system must be sufficient to reveal the total receivables, as well as amounts due from each customer. Therefore, sub-accounts are used. In addition to the regular general ledger account, separate auxiliary receivable accounts would be maintained for each customer, as shown in the following detailed illustration:

CONTROL AND SUBSIDIARY ACCOUNTS

ACCOUNTS RECEIVABLE: Control Ledger

Accounts Receivable				#102
Date	Description	Debit	Credit	Balance
Jan. 1	Balance forward			$ 30,000
Jan. 11	Journal page 1/Compton	$ 6,000		36,000
Jan. 12	Journal page 1/Fisher		$ 11,000	25,000
Jan. 24	Journal page 2/Sunderman		8,000	17,000
Jan. 30	Journal page 2/Moore	2,000		19,000

ACCOUNTS RECEIVABLE: Subsidiary Ledgers

Compton				#102.001
Date	Description	Debit	Credit	Balance
Jan. 1	Balance forward			$ -
Jan. 11	Journal page 1	$6,000		6,000

Fisher				#102.002
Date	Description	Debit	Credit	Balance
Jan. 1	Balance forward			$15,000
Jan. 12	Journal page 1		$11,000	4,000

Sunderman				#102.003
Date	Description	Debit	Credit	Balance
Jan. 1	Balance forward			$ 8,000
Jan. 24	Journal page 2		$ 8,000	-

Moore				#102.004
Date	Description	Debit	Credit	Balance
Jan. 1	Balance forward			$ 7,000
Jan. 30	Journal page 2	$2,000		9,000

The total receivables are the sum of all the individual receivable amounts. Thus, the Accounts Receivable general ledger account total is said to be the **control account** or control ledger, as it represents the total of all individual **subsidiary account** balances. It is simply imperative that a company be able to reconcile subsidiary accounts to the broader control account that is found in the general ledger. Here, computers can be particularly helpful in maintaining the detailed and aggregated data in perfect harmony.

Computerized Processing Systems

Notice that much of the material in this chapter involves mundane processing. Once the initial journal entry is prepared, the data are merely being manipulated to produce the ledger, trial balance, and financial statements. It is no wonder that the first business applications that were computerized years ago related to transaction processing. In short, the only "analytics" relate to the initial transaction recordation. All of the subsequent steps are merely mechanical, and are aptly suited to computers.

Many companies produce accounting software. These packages range from the simple to the complex. Some basic software products for a small business may be purchased for under $100. In large organizations, millions may be spent hiring consultants to install large enterprise-wide packages. Some software companies offer cloud-based accounting systems, with the customers utilizing the internet to enter data and produce their reports.

HOW DO THEY WORK? As one might expect, the look, feel, and function of software-based packages varies significantly. Following is a very typical data entry screen. It should look quite familiar. After the data are input, the subsequent processing (posting, etc.) is totally automated.

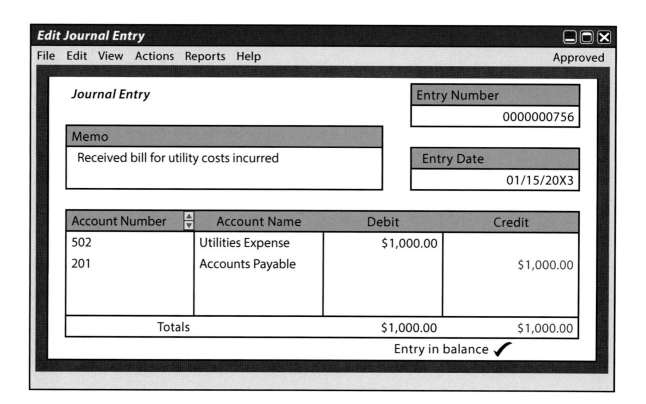

Each company's product must be studied to understand its unique attributes. Accounting software packages generally:

- Attempt to simplify and automate data entry (e.g., a point-of-sale terminal may actually become a data entry device into the accounting system).

- Divide the accounting process into modules related to functional areas such as sales/collection, purchasing/payment, and others.

- Attempt to be "user-friendly" by providing data entry blanks that are easily understood in relation to the underlying transactions.

- Attempt to minimize key-strokes by using "pick lists," automatic call-up functions, and auto-complete type technology.

- Are built on database logic, allowing transaction data to be sorted and processed based on any query structure (e.g., produce an income statement for July).

- Provide up-to-date data that may be accessed by key business decision makers.

- Are capable of producing numerous specialized reports.

Despite each product's own look and feel, the persons primarily responsible for the maintenance and operation of the accounting function must still understand accounting basics such as those introduced in this chapter: accounts, debits and credits, journal entries, etc. Without that intrinsic knowledge, the data input decisions will quickly go astray, and the output of the computerized accounting system will become hopelessly trashed. Accounting knowledge is essential in the successful implementation and use of most any computerized system and the reports it produces.

T-Accounts

A useful tool for demonstrating certain transactions and events is the **T-account**. Importantly, one would not use T-accounts for actually maintaining the accounts of a business. Instead, they are just a quick and simple way to figure out how a small number of transactions and events will impact a company. T-accounts would quickly become unwieldy in an enlarged business setting. In essence, T-accounts are just a "scratch pad" for account analysis. They are useful communication devices to discuss, illustrate, and think about the impact of transactions. The physical shape of a T-account is a "T," and debits are on the left and credits on the right. The "balance" is the amount by which debits exceed credits (or vice versa).

Below is the T-account for Cash for the transactions and events of Xao Corporation. Carefully compare this T-account to the actual running balance ledger account which is also shown (notice that the debits in black total to $33,800, the credits in red total to $7,500, and the excess of debits over credits is $26,300 -- which is the resulting account balance shown in blue).

Cash

25,000	2,000
4,000	500
4,800	5,000
33,800	7,500
26,300	

Cash

Date	Description	Debit	Credit	Balance
Jan. 1, 20X3	Balance forward			$ -
Jan. 1, 20X3	Journal page 1	$ 25,000		25,000
Jan. 4, 20X3	Journal page 1		$ 2,000	23,000
Jan. 8, 20X3	Journal page 1	4,000		27,000
Jan. 18, 20X3	Journal page 2		500	26,500
Jan. 25, 20X3	Journal page 2	4,800		31,300
Jan. 28, 20X3	Journal page 2		5,000	26,300

Chapter 2 Quiz

Goals Achievement

Q2-1.   Assets and expenses may be increased with a:

debit   or   credit

Q2-2.   All accounts are increased with credits and decreased with debits.

correct   or   incorrect

Q2-3.   The transactions in the journal and the accounts in the ledger are linked together by a transfer process called:

posting   or   audit trail

Q2-4.   A trial balance is compiled from the account balance information contained in the ledger.

correct   or   incorrect

Q2-5.   Which form of account is more popular in practice?

T-account form   or   running balance form

Fill in the Blanks

Q2-6.   The general ledger is comprised of numerous individual asset, liability, equity, revenue, and

expense _____.

Q2-7.   The normal balance of an expense account is a _____ balance.

Q2-8.   The normal balances of accounts correspond to the fundamental _____.

Q2-9.   In any transaction, total debits must _____.

Q2-10.   A _____ is a listing of the general ledger accounts along with the dollar

balances contained therein.

Q2-11.   The individual accounts in a general ledger are frequently assigned a number according to

the _____.

Q2-12. Of the following account types, which would be increased by a debit?

a. Liabilities and expenses.

c. Assets and expenses.

b. Assets and equity.

d. Equity and revenues.

Q2-13. The following comments all relate to the recording process. Which of these statements is correct?

a. The general ledger is a chronological record of transactions.

c. The trial balance provides the primary source document for recording transactions into the general journal.

b. The general ledger is posted from transactions recorded in the general journal.

d. Transposition is the transfer of information from the general journal to the general ledger.

Q2-14. The proper journal entry to record $1,000 of Dividends paid by Myer's Corporation is:

a. Dividends   1,000
       Cash   1,000

c. Dividends Expense   1,000
       Cash   1,000

b. Accounts Payable   1,000
       Cash   1,000

d. Dividends Expense   1,000
       Service Revenue   1,000

Q2-15. The trial balance:

a. Is a formal financial statement.

c. Provides a listing of every account in the chart of accounts.

b. Is used to prove that there are no errors in the journal or ledger.

d. Provides a listing of the balance of each account in active use.

Q2-16. The basic sequence in the accounting process can best be described as:

a. Transaction, journal entry, source document, ledger account, trial balance.

c. Transaction, source document, journal entry, trial balance, ledger account.

b. Source document, transaction, ledger account, journal entry, trial balance.

d. Transaction, source document, journal entry, ledger account, trial balance.

Chapter 2 Problems

Basic Problems

B-02.01 *Understanding the basic "tools" of accounting*

Perhaps you have watched the game show known as "Jeopardy." Contestants must prepare a question that is answered by a given prompt. It is your turn to play "Jeopardy" and your category is "tools of accounting."

For instance, if your prompt was "book of original entry," you would reply:

"What is the general journal?"

And remember, the prompts get harder as you go. Don't forget to answer in the form of a question!

(a) Debits must equal these

(b) Used to increase expense accounts

(c) The process of transferring data from journal to ledger

(d) Not a financial statement, showing balance

(e) The offspring of a control account

(f) A "scratch pad" for accountants

B-02.02 *Debit/Credit rules and normal balances*

Review the following list of accounts. Indicate the debit/credit rules for the account as well as the account's normal balance. The first one is done as an example.

		Increased with a:	Decreased with a:	Normal Balance:
(a)	Cash	Debit	Credit	Debit
(b)	Capital Stock			
(c)	Accounts Payable			
(d)	Revenues			
(e)	Rent Expense			

continued...

	Increased with a:	Decreased with a:	Normal Balance:
(f) Equipment			
(g) Dividends			
(h) Utilities Expense			
(i) Accounts Receivable			
(j) Loan Payable			

Basic journal entries	B-02.03

Mo Lambert formed a corporation to provide concrete construction work. His jobs typically involve building parking lots, drives, and foundations. Mo provided the following information about transactions occurring during the first month of operation. Evaluate the transactions and prepare journal entries for this activity.

Jan. 2, 20X5	Mo Lambert invested $10,000 cash in the capital stock of the newly formed corporation.
Jan. 4, 20X5	Purchased equipment on account for $7,500.
Jan. 12, 20X5	Received $15,000 from customers for services rendered.
Jan. 15, 20X5	Received a bill for construction supplies used in the amount of $2,000.
Jan. 18, 20X5	Provided $3,200 of services on account.
Jan. 20, 20X5	Paid employees $2,300 for wages earned.
Jan. 22, 20X5	Collected 60% of the amount due for the work provided on January 18.
Jan. 23, 20X5	Paid 40% of the amount due on the equipment purchased on January 4.
Jan. 25, 20X5	Purchased (and immediately used) construction supplies for cash in the amount of $600.
Jan. 31, 20X5	The company paid Mo Lambert a $1,500 dividend.

Determining the nature of transactions by examination of entries	B-02.04

Yorkston Corporation was formed in 1961. The company came into existence concurrent with the beginning of construction of super highways throughout the country. It seems the company's founders had innovated a unique process of applying high-gloss luminescent paint to street signs, and these were in high demand for the new high-speed roadways.

The company has gone on to develop a full line of highway safety products. Yorkston is now in the process of building a company museum. Someone has dug up the first page from the company's original general journal. This page will be on display in the museum. When you examine this page, you will note that the bookkeeper simply recorded the debits and credits, but included no descriptions.

Your job is to review the journal page and write a description for each transaction. These descriptions will be included on an explanatory diagram included in the display case. The diagram should also include some information that would allow a museum visitor to know what the document is and how it was used.

GENERAL JOURNAL				Page 1
Date	Accounts		Debits	Credits
January 2, 1961	Cash	✓	25,000	
	Capital Stock	✓		25,000
January 3, 1961	Paint	✓	500	
	Accounts Payable	✓		500
January 5, 1961	Ladders and Tools	✓	1,200	
	Cash	✓		1,200
January 7, 1961	Accounts Payable	✓	200	
	Cash	✓		200
January 8, 1961	Accounts Receivable	✓	1,500	
	Revenues	✓		1,500
January 9, 1961	Wage Expense	✓	400	
	Cash	✓		400
January 11, 1961	Cash	✓	400	
	Accounts Receivable	✓		400

B-02.05　　　　　　　　　　　　　　　　　　　　　　　　*Posting entries to the ledger*

Bikash Mishra recently formed a financial services and consulting firm in Nepal. He was very busy during the first month and has not yet had an opportunity to install his computerized accounting package. But, he did understand the need to keep track of all transactions as they occurred. Following is a manual journal that he maintained for transactions occurring during January. All amounts are in the Nepalese rupee (NPR).

SPREADSHEET TOOL:

Using formulas

Bikash has requested that you prepare a ledger of the company's accounts, and post these transactions to determine the balance of each account. He needs this data in order to begin the process of transitioning to his new computerized accounting system.

GENERAL JOURNAL		Debits	Credits
			Page 1
Date	Accounts	Debits	Credits
02-Jan-X5	Cash	1,000,000	
	Capital Stock		1,000,000
	Bikash invested cash in exchange for stock		
			continued...

Date	Accounts	Debits	Credits
04-Jan-X5	Equipment	200,000	
	Loan Payable		200,000
	Purchased equipment with proceeds of loan		
06-Jan-X5	Accounts Receivable	300,000	
	Revenues		300,000
	Provided services to customers on account		
07-Jan-X5	Supplies Expense	10,000	
	Accounts Payable		10,000
	Purchased (on account) and used supplies		
11-Jan-X5	Accounts Payable	10,000	
	Cash		10,000
	Paid for purchase of Jan. 7		
15-Jan-X5	Wage Expense	100,000	
	Cash		100,000
	Paid employee		

GENERAL JOURNAL			Page 2
Date	**Accounts**	**Debits**	**Credits**
17-Jan-X5	Cash	150,000	
	Accounts Receivable		150,000
	Collected partial payment on receivables		
18-Jan-X5	Cash	180,000	
	Revenues		180,000
	Provided services to customers for cash		
20-Jan-X5	Supplies Expense	20,000	
	Accounts Payable		20,000
	Purchased (on account) and used supplies		
31-Jan-X5	Wage Expense	100,000	
	Cash		100,000
	Paid employee		
31-Jan-X5	Loan Payable	200,000	
	Interest Expense	2,000	
	Cash		202,000
	Paid off the loan with interest		

SPREADSHEET TOOL:

Goal Seek function

The CEO of newly formed Targus Company printed a copy of the company's general ledger prior to a recent plane flight. She settled into seat 7A next to where you were sitting. Once airborne, she removed the printed "GL" from her brief case and began examining the report. Unfortunately, she realized that her printer had run out of ink on the very last page. She is frustrated because she is not able to determine the company's exact profitability to date, and is on her way to a shareholder meeting where she is to issue a report on the company's progress. She happened to note that you were studying an accounting book, and asked if you might help her.

Prepare a trial balance from the general ledger, determine the missing amount for salaries expense, and determine the company's profit for its first month.

Cash

Date	Description	Debit	Credit	Balance
Jan. 2, 20X8	Balance forward			$ -
Jan. 3, 20X8	Journal page 1	$ 250,000		250,000
Jan. 10, 20X8	Journal page 1		$ 75,000	175,000
Jan. 14, 20X8	Journal page 1		15,000	160,000
Jan. 18, 20X8	Journal page 2	40,000		200,000
Jan. 21, 20X8	Journal page 2		4,000	196,000
Jan. 26, 20X8	Journal page 2		3,000	193,000
Jan. 31, 20X8	Journal page 2	26,000		219,000

Accounts Receivable

Date	Description	Debit	Credit	Balance
Jan. 2, 20X8	Balance forward			$ -
Jan. 6, 20X8	Journal page 1	$ 55,000		55,000
Jan. 18, 20X8	Journal page 2		$ 40,000	15,000

Land

Date	Description	Debit	Credit	Balance
Jan. 2, 20X8	Balance forward			$ -
Jan. 10, 20X8	Journal page 1	$ 75,000		75,000

continued...

Salaries Payable

Date	Description	Debit	Credit	Balance
Jan. 2, 20X8	Balance forward			$ -
Jan. 31, 20X8	Journal page 2		$ 18,000	18,000

Capital Stock

Date	Description	Debit	Credit	Balance
Jan. 2, 20X8	Balance forward			$ -
Jan. 3, 20X8	Journal page 1		$ 250,000	250,000

Revenues

Date	Description	Debit	Credit	Balance
Jan. 2, 20X8				$ -
Jan. 6, 20X8	Journal page 1		$ 55,000	55,000
Jan. 31, 20X8	Journal page 2		26,000	81,000

Supplies Expense

Date	Description	Debit	Credit	Balance
Jan. 2, 20X8				$ -
Jan. 26, 20X8	Journal page 2	$ 3,000		3,000

Utilities Expense

Date	Description	Debit	Credit	Balance
Jan. 2, 20X8				$ -
Jan. 21, 20X8	Journal page 2	$ 4,000		4,000

Salaries Expense

Date	Description	Debit	Credit	Balance
Jan. 2, 20X8				$ -
Jan. 14, 20X8	Journal page 1	$ 15,000		
Jan. 31, 20X8	Journal page 2			

Professor Drebin's Executive MBA students were recently discussing the benefits of a chart of accounts. Following is a transcript of the discussion. Most of the comments were correct, but two students were off base. Assume the role of Professor Drebin, and identify and adjust the incorrect statements.

Susie	I am a sales manager, but I occasionally need to review our company's general journal. It frustrates me because the accounts are often listed only by a number. What's up with that?
Professor	What you are likely seeing are references to the chart of accounts. Chart of accounts are quite typical. Why would a company use a chart of accounts?
Miguel	I am an IT manager, and I can tell you that computer programming is much simpler when numeric values are used in lieu of text descriptions. This aids the construction of underlying computer programs that are able to match and sort.
Roberta	Miguel may be right, but I work in our cash department and I have to monitor receivables, payables, and cash. A key benefit for me is that I can determine the total of all receivables by doing a query of our 1002 accounts. If I want data by customer, I can refine the query to look for sub accounts like 1002.003, etc. And, the same thing is true for cash and payables. For example, our cash account is 1001, but we have unique sub accounts for each bank account (1001.001, 1001.002, etc.). So, I think one key benefit is to have a unique master account that can easily be broken down into many sub components.
Fletcher	This is all interesting to me. I guess you don't even need textual names for accounts if you use a numeric system.
Randy	I had no idea about this. All I know is that I am in charge of managing our delivery trucks, and I track individual trucks for scheduled maintenance based on an asset ID tag number. Each truck has a unique long number, but it just occurred to me that it always begins with the digits 10005. I wonder if that "10005" might tie back to the company's chart of accounts as well.
Jana	Randy, I doubt it. We have trucks, and I know for a fact that they are numbered 1500 in our chart of accounts. I am pretty sure that all companies must use the same chart of accounts. Otherwise, comparing data from different companies would be chaos.
Louis	Jana makes an interesting point. But, I don't think everyone uses the same chart of accounts. Although, I must add that I recently read about a project called XBRL that purports to develop some uniform data management schemes that will aid data comparison and exchange. And, it involves a lot more than just the chart of accounts.
Arman	I am a divisional manager, and I regularly review our unit's ledger accounts and compare them to balances of other divisions. It is very helpful to be able to identify all assets, expenses, and so forth by uniform account numbering. This uniformity greatly aids data mining and evaluation. For example, our travel costs all start with a 503 digit, but 503.01 further identifies air travel, 503.02 relates to lodging, and so forth. This scheme enables me to look at overall data, as well as its components. It sure helps me control costs and compare results to other divisions. Without a numeric system of account numbering, I would surely be lost.

| T accounts -- an analytical tool | B-02.08 |

The following narratives describe transactions impacting cash, accounts receivable, accounts payable, revenues, and selected expense accounts. Use T-accounts to analyze this activity and determine the ending balances for accounts receivable and accounts payable. At the beginning of the period, accounts receivable totaled $54,300, while accounts payable totaled $31,275. The company started the period with $85,000 in cash.

Transaction #1   Services were provided to customers for cash in the amount of $15,230.

Transaction #2   Supplies were purchased and used. This purchase occurred on account, in the amount of $2,400.

Transaction #3   Collections of outstanding receivables occurred in the amount of $19,410.

Transaction #4   Utilities costs in the amount of $763 were incurred and paid in cash.

Transaction #5   Payments on outstanding accounts payable were made for $23,900.

Transaction #6   Services were provided to customers on account in the amount of $48,654.

| Understanding subsidiary ledger concepts | B-02.09 |

Narmadha Narayan distributes electronic parts. Most transactions with customers are immediately paid with cash or check. But, Narayan has five major customers that have established accounts. These approved customers routinely buy on credit. The terms of the credit agreement provide that payment must occur within 30 days, and each customer has a maximum credit limit of $10,000.

Following is information for May regarding each of the credit customers:

Customer #1   Beginning balance, $1,403. Purchases on account on May 5, $7,237.
               Payment on account on May 17, $1,403.

Customer #2   Beginning balance, $5,275. Purchase on account on May 15, $2,275.
               Payment on account on May 26, $4,275.

Customer #3   Beginning balance, $0. Purchase on account on May 9, $9,550.

Customer #4   Beginning balance, $7,557. Purchase on account on May 7, $2,100.
               Purchase on account on May 22, $9,444. Payment on account on May 11, $7,557.

Customer #5   Beginning balance, $2,990. Payment on account on May 18, $2,990.

(a) Prepare a subsidiary accounts receivable ledger account for each of Narayan's customers.

(b) Prepare the general ledger Accounts Receivable "control" account. Be sure the total in this account reconciles to the sum of the individual balances in the subsidiary ledgers.

(c) What is the purpose of a subsidiary ledger? What other control accounts might be supported by subsidiary ledgers?

(d) Review Narayan's subsidiary ledgers and identify which customer should be put on credit watch for being delinquent, and which customer has exceeded their credit limit.

Involved Problems

Tom Pryor formed a management consulting firm specializing in cost management systems. Below are the transactions that occurred during the initial month of operation.

June 2	Tom Pryor invested $25,000 cash in the capital stock of the newly formed corporation.
June 3	Hired an administrative assistant, to be paid $3,000 per month. Leased office space at the rate of $1,000 per month. Signed a contract with Pomero to deliver consulting services valued at $7,500.
June 8	Purchased (and immediately used) office supplies on account for $750.
June 9	Received $2,500 from Pomero for work performed to date.
June 15	Paid $1,200 for travel costs associated with consultation work.
June 16	Provided services on account to Arpy for $3,000.
June 17	Paid $1,500 to administrative assistant for salary.
June 23	Billed Farris for $4,000 consulting engagement performed.
June 25	The company paid Tom Pryor a $1,000 dividend.
June 26	Collected 50% of the amount due for the billing on June 23.
June 27	Purchased computer furniture for $4,000, paying $1,000 down.
June 27	Paid $750 on the open account relating to the June 8 purchase.
June 28	Completed the Pomero job and billed the remaining amount.
June 30	Paid $1,500 to administrative assistant for salary.
June 30	Paid rent for June, $1,000.

Pryor consulting uses the following accounts:

Cash
Accounts Receivable
Equipment
Accounts Payable
Capital Stock
Revenues
Salary Expense
Rent Expense
Travel Expense
Supplies Expense
Dividends

(a)   Journalize the listed transactions.

(b)   Post the transactions to the appropriate general ledger accounts.

(c)   Prepare a trial balance as of June 30.

Paul Morris is a doctor of veterinary medicine specializing in horses. At the beginning of March, he incorporated his practice, and has completed his first month in business. He has come to you seeking help setting up his "books." The following is a transcript of your conversation with Dr. Morris.

Dr. Morris	"I specialize in embryo transplants for horses that will be used in cutting horse competitions. I started the month by investing $30,000 of my own money in the stock of the business."
You	"By stock, do you mean livestock animals or capital stock?"
Dr. Morris	"I mean the capital stock of the business -- I don't actually own any animals. I work with clients' animals only."
You	"Ok, is that all the money you had to start out the business? Were there any other investors?"
Dr. Morris	"I am the only owner, but the business did borrow $50,000 to buy some land on which I plan to build a barn next year. Is that what you mean by other investors?"
You	"Not exactly. The loan will need to be listed as a liability of the business. Have you paid off any of the loan yet?"
Dr. Morris	"Not yet. The loan is not due for several years. But, I did pay $400 interest on the loan for the month."
You	"I see. So, you plan to build a barn next year on the land. I guess that is where you will be working with animals in the future. But, where are you caring for animals currently?"
Dr. Morris	"I rent stalls from Tri-County arena. That costs me $1,500 per month. Which reminds me, I need to pay them for the first month. I forgot to send them their check!"
You	"Besides the interest, what other bills have you paid so far?"
Dr. Morris	"I knew you would ask that, so I kept a list. I paid for salaries of $2,000, for supplies used of $3,300, and utilities of $700. That's it so far."
You	"Do you have any other bills that have not been paid yet?"
Dr. Morris	"Nope, just the rent, but we already talked about."
You	"Good. Let's talk about your revenues. Do you have a list of what customers paid you this month?"
Dr. Morris	"No, just a total of all my bank deposits. They come to a total of $26,315 -- excluding the cash deposits for my original investment and the $50,000 loan."
You	"I see, and this $26,315 all relates to services provided to customers? Have you done any work for which you have not been paid?"

Dr. Morris   "Yes, my wife keeps up with the outstanding balances due from customers. She told me that we are still owed $9,500."

You   "Well, Dr. Morris, I think that gives me enough information to get started. I will prepare a set of financial statements for your first month of business, and we will see where you stand. Then, I think the first order of business for next month will be to get you set up with a computerized accounting system. You really will need an organized accounting system going forward, and that is best handled with a basic computer program. There are many from which to choose."

Dr. Morris   "Great, that is what I was hoping you would say. I cannot tell you how much I appreciate your help on this."

(a)   Prepare summary journal entries that reflect the first month of business.

(b)   Use T-accounts to capture the impact of the transactions on the accounts.

(c)   Prepare a trial balance as of the end of March.

(d)   Prepare an income statement and statement of retained earnings for the month of March. Prepare the resulting balance sheet as of the end of the month.

I-02.03   *Team-based approach to learn about information processing*

Form a team with six other classmates. Each team member will assume an "organizational" function, as defined below. Each member should discharge their duties according to instructions from the project manager.

Project Manager   Your job is to keep this project on task. You will need to coordinate communication between team members. Further, you should identify a time schedule for completion of each task, and make sure the project stays on schedule. Your CEO is authorized to "fire" a team member that is not performing and find a replacement if necessary. If you experience a problem, you will need to discuss this with the CEO and identify an appropriate solution. Remember, it is not your job to do a specific task; your job is to organize labor so the task is successfully completed.

CEO   As chief executive officer, you must prepare a list of ten transactions for the first month of operation for your business. These transactions can be modeled after those found in earlier problems and the textbook illustrations. The 'transactions' should be unique, and include consideration of raising capital to start the business and operate for the first month. You can decide what business you are in, but assume it is a service business rather than one that manufacturers or resells products.

CIO   As chief information officer, you must design the information system that will be used by your company. You will need to meet with the accounting team members (bookkeeping, controller, and the CFO) and decide what method will be utilized to help them complete their tasks. You might develop a manual "paper only" system, but you are encouraged to use the computer to innovate an electronic method of processing. Worksheet templates from earlier problems may provide a good point of beginning. Or, if you are proficient with database software or an accounting program, you might consider implementing one of those alternatives. The final design is up to you.

Bookkeeping
You have an important role to fill. You must "record" the transactions described by the CEO. This recording should describe the accounts that are impacted and serve as a chronological record of the business activity. The CIO should provide the "template" that you are to use for this task.

Controller
You are to post the bookkeeper's records into a ledger of accounts and prepare a balanced trial balance for the business.

CFO
As chief financial officer, you must convert the trial balance into financial statements. Unlike in real life, if the business lost money or ran out of cash, you can go back and tell the CEO to redo a transaction or two! Your business needs to be profitable for purposes of this exercise.

Audit
The auditor should review everyone's work and make sure that the final report of the CFO is accurate. In addition to crunching numbers, a good auditor will test the systems and make sure they function correctly. Be sure to examine any software developed by the CIO. Finally, prepare an abbreviated report about the results of your audit -- just a few sentences giving an opinion about the results of your audit.

Comprehensive processing exercise (with beginning balances)   *I-02.04*

Morgan Corporation opened the year 20X6, with the following trial balance information:

MORGAN CORPORATION Trial Balance January 1, 20X6		
	Debits	**Credits**
Cash	$ 25,000	
Accounts receivable	75,000	
Land	150,000	
Accounts payable		$ 60,000
Loan payable		30,000
Capital stock		50,000
Retained earnings		110,000
Dividends		
Revenues		
Salaries expense		
Rent expense		
Supplies expense		
Interest expense		
	$250,000	$250,000

January's transactions are listed below:

Jan. 2	Collected $10,000 on an open account receivable.
Jan. 3	Purchased additional tract of land for $20,000 cash.
Jan. 5	Provided services on account to a customer for $15,000.
Jan. 7	Borrowed $12,000 on a term loan payable.
Jan. 11	Paid salaries of $3,000.
Jan. 12	Provided services to customers for cash, $11,000.
Jan. 15	Purchased (and used) office supplies on account, $2,000.
Jan. 17	The company paid shareholders a $2,500 dividend.
Jan. 20	Paid rent of $1,700.
Jan. 23	Paid salaries of $4,000.
Jan. 24	Paid $16,000 on the open accounts payable.
Jan. 29	Collected $50,000 on accounts receivable.
Jan. 31	Repaid loans of $22,000.
Jan. 31	Paid interest on loans of $600.

(a) Create the general ledger accounts, and enter the initial balances at the start of the month of January. This requirement is already completed on the worksheets.

(b) Prepare journal entries for January's transactions.

(c) Post January's transactions to the appropriate general ledger accounts.

(d) Prepare a trial balance as of January 31.

(e) Prepare an income statement and statement of retained earnings for January, and a balance sheet as of the end of January.

I-02.05   *Determining missing values from a limited information set*

Moncrief Corporation is a small business operating in a state where a tax on income is contrary to the state's constitution. In an effort to raise revenue, the state has imposed a tax on business receipts for services provided to customers (total revenues, whether collected during the period or not). The tax is equal to 1% of revenues in excess of $300,000.

Moncrief prepared its state tax return by adding up the total deposits to the company's bank account during the year. Total deposits were $1,240,000, and the company paid taxes of $9,400 (($1,240,000 - $300,000) X 1%).

Assume you are an auditor for the state, and Moncrief has been randomly selected for a routine review. You immediately find that the company does not maintain a typical journal/ledger system, and is fundamentally clueless about proper accounting procedures.

You have discovered the following limited information as part of your examination:

Fact 1   Total deposits included $150,000 that resulted from issuing shares to stockholders.

Fact 2   The total deposits included $25,000 of interest income on investments.

Fact 3   The total deposits included $900 that was the result of a bank error. The bank subsequently discovered the error, and removed the funds from Moncrief's account.

Fact 4   Moncrief provides some services for cash, and portions of that money are never deposited to a bank. The company maintains a cash receipts book, and you have determined that $24,700 was collected from customers but never deposited.

Fact 5   Bank deposits during the period included a $1,200 refund check from a vendor relating to an overpayment for supplies.

Fact 6   The company deposits included $14,000 that was the result of a refund of an overpayment of federal income taxes.

Fact 7   During the year, Moncrief collected a customer deposit toward a future contract. This $10,000 advance was deposited and subsequently refunded when both parties mutually agreed to cancel the contract.

Fact 8   Moncrief has many customers for which services are provided on account. As of the beginning of the year, the balance due from customers was $130,000. By the end of the year, accounts receivable had grown to $390,000. Moncrief has never experienced a problem with non-payment, and all customers pay their accounts in full within 90 days of a transaction.

(a)   Prepare an analysis to determine the correct amount of revenue for purposes of computing the tax.

(b)   Prepare journal entries for the "revenue" cycle, as well as the other cash items described.

(c)   Prepare a general ledger account supporting the revenue calculation.

Evaluation of errors and corrections	I-02.06

The following trial balance for Williams Corporation does not balance. You have conducted an extensive review to help Laura Williams find the nature of the problem. Below the trial balance is information about six errors you have discovered. Use this additional information to prepare a corrected trial balance.

WILLIAMS CORPORATION Trial Balance December 31, 20X1		
	Debits	Credits
Cash	$123,432	
Accounts receivable	76,409	
Land		$ 688,004
Accounts payable		32,611
Loan payable		76,400
Capital stock		340,000
Retained earnings		456,332
Revenues		879,998
Wages expense		575,988
Rent expense	112,654	
Interest expense	4,654	
Dividends	9,000	
	$326,149	$3,049,333

Error # 1 All accounts have normal balances, but two amounts are in wrong columns!

Error # 2 Services provided on account for $1,500 was debited to Accounts Payable and credited to Revenues.

Error # 3 Supplies Expense of $104,300 was completely omitted from the trial balance.

Error # 4 The amount recorded for Revenues was transposed. It should have been $789,998.

Error # 5 A $5,000 shareholder investment was debited to Cash and credited to Dividends.

Error # 6 An interest payment of $1,000 was debited to Loan Payable for $100 and credited to Cash for $1,000.

I-02.07   *Computerized processing*

SPREADSHEET TOOL:

Vertical/ Horizontal Lookup Formula

There are numerous commercial accounting software packages, and they greatly simplify the drudgery of basic accounting tasks. Each software package has its unique features and strengths. Even a very basic spreadsheet can be developed to handle much of the day-to-day bookkeeping. This problem illustrates the benefits of an electronic system. You only need to select the transaction number and the account numbers you wish to debit or credit (in the shaded portions of the *journal worksheet*). Then, enter the dollar value for the debit. The rest will be automatic.

Your assignment is to enter the following seven transactions in Lei Han Corporation's electronic *journal worksheet*, and print the resulting financial statements from the *financials worksheet* (the worksheet can be downloaded from the website). You can view the T-accounts worksheet and trial balance worksheet if you wish, but no action is required on those pages.

Transaction	Date	Description	Amount
701001	Jan. 3, 20X7	Issued capital stock for cash	$25,000
701002	Jan. 5, 20X7	Purchased land for note payable	30,000
701003	Jan. 6, 20X7	Provided services on account	10,000
701004	Jan. 9, 20X7	Provided services for cash	5,000
701005	Jan. 10, 20X7	Collected cash on account	4,000
701006	Jan. 15, 20X7	Paid salaries with cash	7,000
701007	Jan. 16, 20X7	Recorded utilities expense incurred on account	2,000

Lei Han Corporation uses the following chart of accounts.

10001	Cash
10002	Accounts Receivable
10003	Land
20001	Accounts Payable
20002	Loan Payable
30001	Capital Stock
30002	Retained Earnings
40001	Revenues
40002	Interest Income
50001	Salaries Expense
50002	Utilities Expense
50003	Rent Expense
50004	Miscellaneous Expense
60001	Dividends

Using T-accounts to evaluate business activity   *I-02.08*

Problem I-01.05 provided the following data for Bingo Corporation. In that problem, financial statements were prepared after each transaction. This problem requires you to use T-accounts to capture the transactions and produce a final set of financial statements.

(1)   Issued capital stock for $50,000 cash.

(2)   Purchased building for $120,000, making a $20,000 down payment and signing a promissory note payable for the balance.

(3) Paid wages expense of $5,000.

(4) Provided services to customers for $15,000 cash.

(5) Paid utilities expense of $2,000.

(6) Reduced note payable with an $8,000 cash payment (ignore interest costs).

(7) Provided services to customers on account, $10,000.

(8) Incurred wages expense of $3,000, to be paid in the future.

(9) Collected $4,000 on an outstanding account receivable.

(10) Declared and paid dividend of $6,000.

(a) Prepare T-accounts for the above transactions.

(b) Prepare the resulting trial balance.

(c) Prepare the income statement, statement of retained earnings, and balance sheet that results from these 10 transactions.

(d) Comment on the value of an information processing system. Would T-accounts provide a sufficient data processing system?

Chapter 3:
Income Measurement

Goals:

"Measurement triggering" transactions and events.
The periodicity assumption and its accounting implications.
Basic elements of revenue recognition.
Basic elements of expense recognition.
The adjusting process and related entries.
Accrual versus cash-basis accounting.

principlesofaccounting.com

"Measurement Triggering" Transactions and Events

GENERAL CONCEPTS

Economists refer to income as a measure of "better-offness." Thus, economic income represents an increase in command over goods and services. Such notions of income capture operating successes, as well as good fortune from holding assets that may increase in value. In contrast, accounting income tends to focus on the effects of transactions and events that are evidenced by exchange transactions. For example, land is recorded at its purchase price.

In recent years, however, accounting rules around the globe have increasingly reflected greater acceptance of fair value measurements for selected financial statement elements. Whether and when accounting should measure changes in value has long been a source of debate. This debate is ongoing, and rules that establish measurement principles will continually evolve.

Generalizing: (a) accounting measurements tend to be based on historical cost determined by reference to an exchange transaction with another party (e.g., a purchase) and (b) income is "revenues" minus "expenses" as determined by reference to those transactions. More specifically:

Revenues   Inflows and enhancements from delivery of goods and services that constitute central ongoing operations

Expenses   Outflows and obligations arising from the production of goods and services that constitute central ongoing operations

Gains/Losses   Like revenues/expenses, but from peripheral transactions or events

Thus, it may be more precisely said that income is equal to Revenues + Gains - Expenses - Losses. Be aware that in some countries revenues is an all-inclusive term, including both revenues and gains.

NON-EXCHANGE EVENTS

Although accounting income will typically focus on recording transactions and events that are exchange based, some items must be recorded even though there is not an identifiable exchange between the company and some external party. What types of nonexchange events logically should be recorded to prepare correct financial statements? How about the loss of an uninsured building from fire or storm? Clearly, the asset is gone, so it logically should be removed from the accounting records. This would be recorded as an immediate loss. Even more challenging may be to consider the journal entry: debit a loss (losses are increased with debits since they are like expenses), and credit the asset account (the asset is gone and is reduced with a credit).

The Periodicity Assumption

Business activity is fluid. Revenue and expense generating activities are in constant motion. Just because it is time to turn a page on a calendar does not mean that all business activity ceases. But, for purposes of measuring performance, it is necessary to draw a line in the sand of time. A **periodicity assumption** is made that business activity can be divided into measurement intervals, such as months, quarters, and years.

ACCOUNTING Accounting must divide the continuous business process, and produce periodic reports. An annual reporting
IMPLICATIONS period may follow the calendar year by running from January 1 through December 31. Annual periods are usually further divided into quarterly periods containing activity for three months.

In the alternative, a **fiscal year** may be adopted, running from any point of beginning to one year later. Fiscal years often attempt to follow **natural business year** cycles, such as in the retail business where a fiscal year may end on January 31 (allowing all of the holiday rush, and corresponding returns, to cycle through). Note in the following illustration that the "20X8 Fiscal Year" is so named because it ends in 20X8:

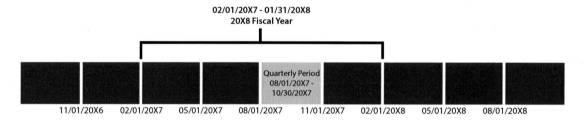

Also consider that internal reports may be prepared on even more frequent monthly intervals. As a general rule, the more narrowly defined a reporting period, the more challenging it becomes to capture and measure business activity. This results because continuous business activity must be divided and apportioned among periods; the more periods, the more likely that ongoing transactions must be allocated to more than one reporting period. Once a measurement period is adopted, the accountant's task is to apply the various rules and procedures of generally accepted accounting principles (GAAP) to assign revenues and expenses to the reporting period. This process is called **accrual-basis** accounting. Accrue means to come about as a natural growth or increase. Thus, accrual-basis accounting is reflective of measuring revenues as earned and expenses as incurred.

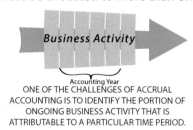

ONE OF THE CHALLENGES OF ACCRUAL ACCOUNTING IS TO IDENTIFY THE PORTION OF ONGOING BUSINESS ACTIVITY THAT IS ATTRIBUTABLE TO A PARTICULAR TIME PERIOD.

Correctly assigning revenues and expenses to time periods is pivotal in the determination of income. It goes without saying that reported income is of great concern to investors and creditors, and its proper determination is crucial. Measurement issues can become complex. For example, if a software company sells a product for $25,000 (in year 20X1), and agrees to provide updates at no cost to the customer for 20X2 and

20X3, then how much revenue is "earned" in 20X1, 20X2, and 20X3? Such questions make accounting far more challenging than most realize. Suffice it to say that one would need more information about the software company to answer their specific question. But, there are basic rules about revenue and expense recognition that should be understood, and they will be introduced in following sections.

Before moving away from the periodicity assumption, and its accounting implications, there is one important factor to note. If accounting did not require periodic measurement, and instead, took the view that one could report only at the end of a process, measurement would be easy. For example, if the software company were to report income for the three-year period 20X1 through 20X3, then revenue of $25,000 would be easy to measure. It is the periodicity assumption that muddies the water. Why not just wait? Two reasons: first, one might wait a long time for activities to close and become measurable with certainty, and second, investors cannot wait long periods of time before learning how a business is doing. Timeliness of data is critical to its relevance for decision making. Therefore, procedures and assumptions are needed to produce timely data, and that is why the periodicity assumption is put in play.

Basic Elements of Revenue Recognition

To recognize an item is to record it into the accounting records. **Revenue recognition** normally occurs at the time services are rendered or when goods are sold and delivered. The conditions for revenue recognition are (a) an exchange transaction, and (b) the earnings process being complete.

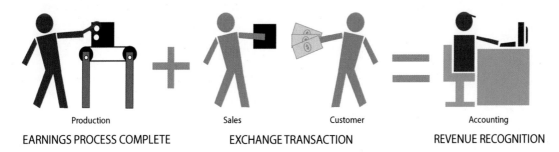

Production	Sales	Customer	Accounting
EARNINGS PROCESS COMPLETE	EXCHANGE TRANSACTION		REVENUE RECOGNITION

For a manufactured product, should revenue be recognized when the item rolls off of the assembly line? The answer is no! Although production may be complete, the product has not been sold in an exchange transaction. Both conditions must be met. In the alternative, if a customer ordered a product that was to be produced, would revenue be recognized at the time of the order? Again, the answer is no! For revenue to be recognized, the product must be manufactured and delivered.

Modern business transactions frequently involve complex terms, bundled items (e.g., a cell phone with a service contract), intangibles (e.g., a software user license), order routing (e.g., an online retailer may route an order to the manufacturer for direct shipment), achievement of milestones (e.g., payment contingent on reaching research and development results), and so forth. Many past accounting failures involved misapplication of revenue recognition concepts. As a result the profession has moved to provide further guidance that should be instructive on how to account for more complex contracts. Stepwise, the approach is as follows:

> **Step 1:** Identify the contract(s) with a customer.
> **Step 2:** Identify the performance obligations in the contract.
> **Step 3:** Determine the transaction price.
> **Step 4:** Allocate the transaction price to the performance obligations in the contract.
> **Step 5:** Recognize revenue when (or as) the entity satisfies a performance obligation.

As one may well imagine, a great deal of judgment is needed to apply this general framework to case specific situations. Expect to consider this topic in advanced accounting courses and beyond.

Basic Elements of Expense Recognition

Expense recognition will typically follow one of three approaches, depending on the nature of the cost:

* Associating cause and effect: Many costs are linked to the revenue they help produce. For example, a sales commission owed to an employee is based on the amount of a sale. Therefore, commission expense should be recorded in the same accounting period as the sale. Likewise, the cost of inventory delivered to a customer should be expensed when the sale is recognized. This is what is meant by associating cause and effect, and is also referred to as the **matching principle**.

* Systematic and rational allocation: In the absence of a clear link between a cost and revenue item, other expense recognition schemes must be employed. Some costs benefit many periods. Stated differently, these costs expire over time. For example, a truck may last many years; determining how much cost is attributable to a particular year is difficult. In such cases, accountants may use a systematic and rational allocation scheme to spread a portion of the total cost to each period of use (in the case of a truck, through a process known as depreciation).

* Immediate recognition: Last, some costs cannot be linked to any production of revenue, and do not benefit future periods either. These costs are recognized immediately. An example would be severance pay to a fired employee, which would be expensed when the employee is terminated.

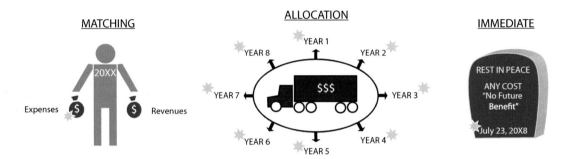

PAYMENT VS. It is important to note that receiving or making payments are not criteria for initial revenue or expense
RECOGNITION recognition. Revenues are recognized at the point of sale, whether that sale is for cash or a receivable. Expenses are based on one of the approaches just described, no matter when payment occurs. Recall the earlier definitions of revenue and expense, noting that they contemplate something more than simply reflecting cash receipts and payments. Much business activity is conducted on credit, and severe misrepresentations of income could result if the focus was simply on cash flow.

The Adjusting Process and Related Entries

In the previous chapter, tentative financial statements were prepared directly from a trial balance. However, a caution was issued about adjustments that may be needed to prepare a truly correct and up-to-date set of financial statements. This occurs because of multi-period items (revenue and expense items that relate to more than one accounting period) and accrued items (revenue and expense items that have been earned or incurred in a given period, but not yet entered into the accounting records). In other words, the ongoing business activity brings about changes in account balances that have not been captured by a journal entry. Time brings about change, and an **adjusting process** is needed to cause the accounts to appropriately reflect those changes. These adjustments typically occur at the end of each accounting period, and are akin to temporarily cutting off the flow through the business pipeline to take a measurement of what is in the pipeline. This is consistent with the revenue and expense recognition rules.

There is simply no way to catalog every potential adjustment that a business may need to make. What is required is a firm understanding of a particular business's operations, along with a good handle on accounting measurement principles. The following discussion describes typical adjustments. Strive to develop a conceptual understanding of these examples. Critical thinking skills will then allow extension of these basic principles to most any situation. The specific examples relate to:

MULTI-PERIOD ITEMS
PREPAID EXPENSES:
Prepaid Insurance
Prepaid Rent
Supplies
DEPRECIATION
UNEARNED REVENUE

ACCRUED ITEMS
UNRECORDED EXPENSES:
Accrued Salaries
Accrued Interest
Accrued Rent
UNRECORDED REVENUES:
Accrued Revenue

PREPAID EXPENSES

It is common to pay for goods and services in advance. Insurance is typically purchased by prepaying for an annual or semi-annual policy. Or, rent on a building may be paid ahead of its intended use (e.g., most landlords require monthly rent to be paid at the beginning of each month). Another example of **prepaid expense** relates to supplies that are purchased and stored in advance of actually needing them. At the time of purchase, such prepaid amounts represent future economic benefits that are acquired in exchange for cash payments. As such, the initial expenditure gives rise to an asset. As time passes, the asset is diminished. This means that adjustments are needed to reduce the asset account and transfer the consumption of the asset's cost to an appropriate expense account.

As a general representation of this process, assume that one prepays $300 on June 1 to receive three months of lawn mowing service. As shown in the following illustration, this transaction initially gives rise to a $300 asset on the June 1 balance sheet. As each month passes, $100 is removed from the balance sheet account and transferred to expense (think: an asset is reduced and expense is increased, giving rise to lower income and equity).

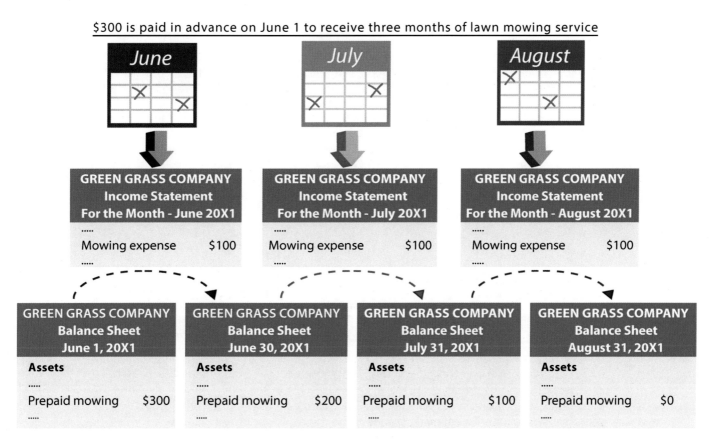

Examine the journal entries for this illustration, and take note of the impact on the balance sheet account for Prepaid Mowing (as shown by the T-accounts below):

06-01	Prepaid Mowing	300	
	Cash		300
	To record prepayment of mowing service		
06-30	Mowing Expense	100	
	Prepaid Mowing		100
	To record mowing service for June		
07-31	Mowing Expense	100	
	Prepaid Mowing		100
	To record mowing service for July		
08-31	Mowing Expense	100	
	Prepaid Mowing		100
	To record mowing service for August		

Prepaid Mowing			Prepaid Mowing			Prepaid Mowing			Prepaid Mowing	
300		**6/30** →	300	100	**7/31** →	300	100	**8/31** →	300	100
							100			100
										100

ILLUSTRATION OF PREPAID INSURANCE Insurance policies are usually purchased in advance. Cash is paid up front to cover a future period of protection. Assume a three-year insurance policy was purchased on January 1, 20X1, for $9,000. By December 31, 20X1, $3,000 of insurance coverage would have expired (one of three years, or 1/3 of $9,000). The following entries would be needed to record the transaction on January 1 and the adjustment on December 31:

01-01-X1	Prepaid Insurance	9,000	
	Cash		9,000
	Prepaid a three-year insurance policy		
12-31-X1	Insurance Expense	3,000	
	Prepaid Insurance		3,000
	To adjust prepaid insurance to reflect portion expired ($9,000/3=$3,000)		

As a result of the above entry and adjusting entry, the income statement for 20X1 would report insurance expense of $3,000, and the balance sheet at the end of 20X1 would report prepaid insurance of $6,000 ($9,000 debit less $3,000 credit). The remaining $6,000 amount would be transferred to expense over the next two years by preparing similar adjusting entries at the end of 20X2 and 20X3.

Assume a two-month lease is entered and rent paid in advance on March 1, 20X1, for $3,000. By March 31, 20X1, half of the rental period has lapsed, and financial statements are to be prepared. The following entries would be needed to record the transaction on March 1, and adjust rent expense and prepaid rent on March 31: *ILLUSTRATION OF PREPAID RENT*

03-01-X1	Prepaid Rent	3,000	
	Cash		3,000
	Prepaid a two-month lease		
03-31-X1	Rent Expense	1,500	
	Prepaid Rent		1,500
	To adjust prepaid rent for portion lapsed ($3000/2 months=$1,500)		

In the illustration for insurance, the adjustment was applied at the end of December, but the rent adjustment occurred at the end of March. What's the difference? What was not stated in the first illustration was an assumption that financial statements were only being prepared at the end of the year, in which case the adjustments were only needed at that time. In the second illustration, it was explicitly stated that financial statements were to be prepared at the end of March, and that necessitated an end of March adjustment. *HOW OFTEN ARE ADJUSTMENTS NEEDED?*

There is a moral to this: adjustments should be made every time financial statements are prepared, and the goal of the adjustments is to correctly assign the appropriate amount of expense to the time period in question (leaving the remainder in a balance sheet account to carry over to the next time period(s)). Every situation will be somewhat unique, and careful analysis and thoughtful consideration must be used to determine the correct amount of adjustment.

The initial purchase of supplies is recorded by debiting Supplies and crediting Cash. Supplies Expense should subsequently be debited and Supplies credited for the amount used. This results in expense on the income statement being equal to the amount of supplies used, while the remaining balance of supplies on hand is reported as an asset. The following illustrates the purchase of $900 of supplies. Subsequently, $700 of this amount is used, leaving $200 of supplies on hand in the Supplies account: *ILLUSTRATION OF SUPPLIES*

12-08-X1	Supplies	900	
	Cash		900
	To record purchase of supplies		
12-31-X1	Supplies Expense	700	
	Supplies		700
	Adjusting entry to reflect supplies used		

One might find it necessary to "back in" to the calculation of supplies used. Assume $200 of supplies in a storage room are physically counted at the end of the period. Since the account has a $900 balance from the December 8 entry, one "backs in" to the $700 adjustment on December 31. In other words, since $900 of supplies were purchased, but only $200 were left over, then $700 must have been used.

The following year is slightly more challenging. If an additional $1,000 of supplies is purchased during 20X2, and the ending balance at December 31, 20X2, is $300, then these entries would be needed:

XX-XX-X2	Supplies		1,000	
	Cash			1,000
	Purchased supplies for $1,000			
12-31-X2	Supplies Expense		900	
	Supplies			900
	Adjusting entry to reflect supplies used			

The $1,000 amount is clear enough, but what about the $900 of expense? One must take into account that 20X2 started with a $200 beginning balance (last year's "leftovers"), purchases were an additional $1,000 (giving the total available for the period at $1,200), and the year ended with $300 of supplies on hand. Thus, $900 was used up during the period:

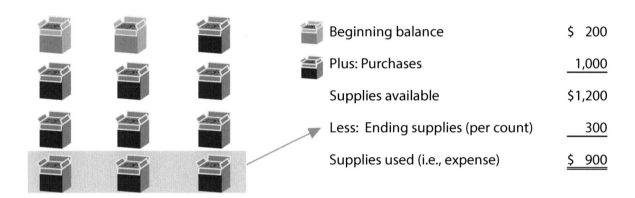

Beginning balance	$ 200
Plus: Purchases	1,000
Supplies available	$1,200
Less: Ending supplies (per count)	300
Supplies used (i.e., expense)	$ 900

DEPRECIATION Long-lived assets like buildings and equipment will provide productive benefits to a number of periods. Thus, a portion of their cost is allocated to each period. This process is called **depreciation**. A subsequent chapter will cover depreciation in great detail. However, one simple approach is called the straight-line method, where an equal amount of asset cost is assigned to each year of service life.

By way of example, if a $150,000 truck with a 3-year life was purchased on January 1 of Year 1, depreciation expense would be $50,000 per year ($150,000/3 = $50,000). This expense would be reported on each year's income statement. The annual entry involves a debit to Depreciation Expense and a credit to Accumulated Depreciation (rather than crediting the asset account directly):

12-31-XX	Depreciation Expense		50,000	
	Accumulated Depreciation			50,000
	To record annual depreciation expense			

Accumulated depreciation is a unique account. It is reported on the balance sheet as a **contra asset**. A contra account is an account that is subtracted from a related account. As a result, contra accounts have opposite debit/credit rules. In other words, accumulated depreciation is increased with a credit, because the associated asset normally has a debit balance. The following statements show how accumulated depreciation and depreciation expense would appear for each year:

As one can see on each year's balance sheet, the asset continues to be reported at its $150,000 cost. However, it is also reduced each year by the ever-growing accumulated depreciation. The asset cost minus accumulated depreciation is known as the **book value** (or "net book value") of the asset. For example, at December 31, 20X2, the net book value of the truck is $50,000, consisting of $150,000 cost less $100,000 of accumulated depreciation. By the end of the asset's life, its cost has been fully depreciated and its net book value has been reduced to zero. Customarily the asset could then be removed from the accounts, presuming it is then fully used up and retired.

Often, a business will collect monies in advance of providing goods or services. For example, a magazine publisher may sell a multi-year subscription and collect the full payment at or near the beginning of the subscription period. Such payments received in advance are initially recorded as a debit to Cash and a credit to Unearned Revenue. **Unearned revenue** is reported as a liability, reflecting the company's obligation to deliver product in the future. Remember, revenue cannot be recognized in the income statement until the earnings process is complete.

As goods and services are delivered (e.g., the magazines are delivered), the Unearned Revenue is reduced (debited) and Revenue is increased (credited). The balance sheet at the end of an accounting period would include the remaining unearned revenue for those goods and services not yet delivered. This amount reflects the entity's obligation for future performance. Equally important, the reported revenue only reflects goods and services actually delivered. Following are illustrative entries for the accounting for unearned revenues:

UNEARNED REVENUES

04-01-X1	Cash		1,200	
	Unearned Revenue			1,200
	Sold a one-year software license			
12-31-X1	Unearned Revenue		900	
	Revenue			900
	To adjust unearned revenue to reflect earned portion ($100 per month for 9 months)			

ACCRUALS

Another type of adjusting journal entry pertains to the accrual of unrecorded expenses and revenues. **Accruals** are expenses and revenues that gradually accumulate throughout an accounting period. **Accrued expenses** relate to such things as salaries, interest, rent, utilities, and so forth. **Accrued revenues** might relate to such events as client services that are based on hours worked.

ACCRUED SALARIES

Few, if any, businesses have daily payroll. Typically, businesses will pay employees once or twice per month. Suppose a business has employees that collectively earn $1,000 per day. The last payday occurred on December 26, as shown in the 20X8 calendar that follows. Employees worked three days the following week, but would not be paid for this time until January 9, 20X9. As of the end of the accounting period, the company owes employees $3,000 (pertaining to December 29, 30, and 31). As a result, the adjusting entry to record the accrued payroll would appear as follows:

12-31-X8	Salaries Expense		3,000	
	Salaries Payable			3,000
	To record accrued salaries			

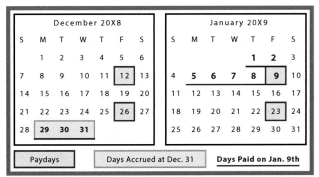

| Paydays | Days Accrued at Dec. 31 | Days Paid on Jan. 9th |

Before moving on to the next topic, consider the entry that will be needed on the next payday (January 9, 20X9). Suppose the total payroll on that date is $10,000 ($3,000 relating to the prior year (20X8) and another $7,000 for an additional seven work days in 20X9).

The journal entry on the actual payday needs to reflect that the $10,000 is partially for expense and partially to extinguish a previously established liability:

01-09-X9	Salaries Expense		7,000	
	Salaries Payable		3,000	
	Cash			10,000
	To record payment of payroll relating to two separate accounting periods			

ACCRUED INTEREST

Most loans include charges for interest. The amount of interest therefore depends on the amount of the borrowing ("principal"), the interest rate ("rate"), and the length of the borrowing period ("time"). The total amount of interest on a loan is calculated as Principal X Rate X Time.

For example, if $100,000 is borrowed at 6% per year for 18 months, the total interest will amount to $9,000 ($100,000 X 6% X 1.5 years). However, even if the interest is not payable until the end of the loan, it is still logical and appropriate to accrue the interest as time passes. This is necessary to assign the correct interest cost to each accounting period. Assume that an 18-month loan was taken out on July 1, 20X1, and was due on December 31, 20X2. The accounting for the loan on the various dates (assume a December year end, with an appropriate year-end adjusting entry for the accrued interest) would be as follows:

07-01-X1	Cash	100,000	
	Loan Payable		100,000
	To record the borrowing of $100,000 at 6% per annum; principal and interest due on 12-13-X2		
12-31-X1	Interest Expense	3,000	
	Interest Payable		3,000
	To record accrued interest for 6 months ($100,000 X 6% X 6/12)		
12-31-X2	Interest Expense	6,000	
	Interest Payable	3,000	
	Loan Payable	100,000	
	Cash		109,000
	To record repayment of loan and interest (note that $3,000 of the total interest was previously accrued in 20X1)		

ACCRUED RENT

Accrued rent is the opposite of prepaid rent discussed earlier. Recall that prepaid rent related to rent that was paid in advance. In contrast, accrued rent relates to rent that has not yet been paid, even though utilization of the asset has already occurred.

For example, assume that office space is leased, and the terms of the agreement stipulate that rent will be paid within 10 days after the end of each month at the rate of $400 per month. During December of 20X1, Cabul Company occupied the lease space, and the appropriate adjusting entry for December follows:

12-31-X1	Rent Expense	400	
	Rent Payable		400
	To record accrued rent		

When the rent is paid on January 10, 20X2, this entry would be needed:

01-10-X2	Rent Payable	400	
	Cash		400
	To record payment of accrued rent		

ACCRUED REVENUE

Many businesses provide services to clients with an understanding that they will be periodically billed for the hours (or other units) of service provided. For example, an accounting firm may track hours worked on various projects for their clients. These hours are likely accumulated and billed each month, with the periodic billing occurring in the month following the month in which the service is provided. As a result, money has been earned during a month, even though it won't be billed until the following month. Accrual accounting concepts dictate that such revenues be recorded when earned. The following entry would be needed at the end of December to accrue revenue for services rendered to date (even though the physical billing of the client may not occur until January):

12-31-X2	Accounts Receivable	500	
	Revenue		500
	Year-end adjusting entry to reflect "earned" revenues for services provided in December		

RECAP OF ADJUSTING

The preceding discussion of adjustments has been presented in great detail because it is imperative to grasp the underlying income measurement principles. Perhaps the single most important element of accounting judgment is to develop an appreciation for the correct measurement of revenues and expenses. These processes can be fairly straightforward, as in the preceding illustrations. At other times, the measurements can grow very complex. A business process rarely starts and stops at the beginning and end of a month, quarter or year – yet the accounting process necessarily divides that flowing business process into measurement periods.

ADJUSTED TRIAL BALANCE

Keep in mind that the trial balance introduced in the previous chapter was prepared before considering adjusting entries. Subsequent to the adjustment process, another trial balance can be prepared. This **adjusted trial balance** demonstrates the equality of debits and credits after recording adjusting entries. Therefore, correct financial statements can be prepared directly from the adjusted trial balance. The next chapter provides a detailed look at the adjusted trial balance.

ALTERNATE PROCEDURE

The mechanics of accounting for *prepaid expenses and unearned revenues* can be carried out in several ways. At left below is a "balance sheet approach" for Prepaid Insurance. The expenditure was initially recorded into a prepaid account on the balance sheet. The alternative approach is the "income statement approach," wherein the Expense account is debited at the time of purchase. The appropriate end-of-period adjusting entry establishes the Prepaid Expense account with a debit for the amount relating to future periods. The offsetting credit reduces the expense to an amount equal to the amount consumed during the period. Note that Insurance Expense and Prepaid Insurance accounts have identical balances at December 31 under either approach.

BALANCE SHEET APPROACH		
Jan. 1	Prepaid Insurance	9,000	
	Cash		9,000
	Prepaid a three-year policy		
Dec. 31	Insurance Expense	3,000	
	Prepaid Insurance		3,000
	To adjust prepaid insurance to reflect expired portion ($9,000/3 = $3,000)		

Insurance Expense: (3,000)

Prepaid Insurance: 9,000 | 3,000 — (6,000)

INCOME STATEMENT APPROACH		
Jan. 1	Insurance Expense	9,000	
	Cash		9,000
	Prepaid a three-year policy		
Dec. 31	Prepaid Insurance	6,000	
	Insurance Expense		6,000
	To adjust prepaid insurance to reflect unexpired portion ($9,000 X 2/3 = $6,000)		

Insurance Expense: 9,000 | 6,000 — (3,000)

Prepaid Insurance: (6,000)

Accounting for unearned revenue can also follow a balance sheet or income statement approach. The balance sheet approach for unearned revenue is presented at left below. At right is the income statement approach, wherein the initial receipt is recorded entirely to a Revenue account. Subsequent end-of-period adjusting entries reduce Revenue by the amount not yet earned and increase Unearned Revenue. Again, both approaches produce the same financial statement results.

BALANCE SHEET APPROACH		
Apr. 1	Cash	1,200	
	Unearned Revenue		1,200
	Sold annual software license		
Dec. 31	Unearned Revenue	900	
	Revenue		900
	To adjust unearned revenue to reflect earned portion ($100 per month for 9 months)		

Revenue		Unearned Revenue	
(900)		900	1,200
			(300)

INCOME STATEMENT APPROACH		
Apr. 1	Cash	1,200	
	Revenue		1,200
	Sold annual software license		
Dec. 31	Revenue	300	
	Unearned Revenue		300
	To adjust revenue to reflect unearned portion ($100 per month for 3 months)		

Revenue		Unearned Revenue	
300	1,200		(300)
	(900)		

The income statement approach does have an advantage if the entire prepaid item or unearned revenue is fully consumed or earned by the end of an accounting period. No adjusting entry would be needed because the expense or revenue was fully recorded at the date of the original transaction.

Accrual Versus Cash-Basis Accounting

Generally accepted accounting principles require that a business use the accrual basis. Under this method, revenues and expenses are recognized as earned or incurred, utilizing the various principles introduced throughout this chapter. An alternative method in use by some small businesses is the **cash basis**. The cash basis is not compliant with GAAP, but a small business that does not have a broad base of shareholders or creditors does not necessarily need to comply with GAAP. The cash basis is much simpler, but its financial statement results can be very misleading in the short run. Under this easy approach, revenue is recorded when cash is received (no matter when it is earned), and expenses are recognized when paid (no matter when incurred).

MODIFIED APPROACHES

The cash and accrual techniques may be merged together to form a **modified cash-basis** system. The modified cash-basis results in revenue and expense recognition as cash is received and disbursed, with the exception of large cash outflows for long-lived assets (which are recorded as assets and depreciated over time). However, to repeat, proper income measurement and strict compliance with GAAP dictates use of the accrual basis; virtually all large companies use the accrual basis.

EXAMPLE

Look at an example for Ortiz Company. Ortiz provides web design services to a number of clients and has been using the cash basis of accounting. The following spreadsheet is used by Ortiz to keep up with the business's cash receipts and payments. This type of spreadsheet is very common for a small business. The "checkbook" is in green, noting the date, party, check number, check amount, deposit amount, and resulting cash balance. The deposits are spread to the revenue column (shaded in orange) and the checks are spread to the appropriate expense columns (shaded in yellow). Note that total cash on hand increased by $15,732.70 (from $7,911.12 to $23,643.82) during the month.

Spreadsheet ☐◻☒

	F16		*fx*	=F15-D16+E16							
	A	B	C	D	E	F	G	H	I	J	K
1	DATE	PARTY	REF #	CHECK	DEPOSIT	Balance	Revenue	Payroll	Rent	Server	Admin
2											
3	04-01-X5		Balance			$ 7,911.12					
4	04-03-X5	Aldridge	1097	$ 700.00		7,211.12		$ 700.00			
5	04-04-X5	Rama	1098	555.13		6,655.99					$ 555.13
6	04-07-X5	Kane	Deposit		$ 9,000.00	15,655.99	$ 9,000.00				
7	04-12-X5	Lipe	1099	1,207.89		14,448.10					1,207.89
8	04-15-X5	Zhou	1100	1,416.22		13,031.88				$1,416.22	
9	04-17-X5	Lobo	Deposit		3,545.23	16,577.11	3,545.23				
10	04-19-X5	Forgione	1101	1043.99		15,533.12					1043.99
11	04-20-X5	Vermeer	Deposit		11,788.45	27,321.57	11,788.45				
12	04-23-X5	Aldridge	1102	700.00		26,621.57		700.00			
13	04-24-X5	Entwistle	Deposit		1,500.00	28,121.57	1,500.00				
14	04-26-X5	Fletham	1103	300.00		27,821.57			$ 300.00		
15	04-29-X5	Mbagwu	1104	498.99		27,322.58				498.99	
16	04-30-X5	Jenkins	1105	3,678.76		23,643.82		3,678.76			
17				$10,100.98	$25,833.68		$25,833.68	$5,078.76	$ 300.00	$1,915.21	$2,807.01
18											

CASH-BASIS INCOME STATEMENT The information from this spreadsheet was used to prepare the following cash-basis income statement. The increase in cash that is evident in the spreadsheet is mirrored as the cash-basis income:

ORTIZ CORPORATION
Cash-Basis Income Statement
For the Month Ending April 30, 20X5

Revenues		
Services to customers		$25,833.68
Expenses		
Payroll	$5,078.76	
Rent	300.00	
Server	1,915.21	
Administrative	2,807.01	
Total expenses		10,100.98
Cash Basis Income		$15,732.70

Internal Use Only: Cash Basis -- Not prepared under generally accepted accounting principles!

Ortiz has been approached by Mega Impressions, a much larger web-hosting and design firm. Mega has offered to buy Ortiz's business for a price equal to "100 times" the business's monthly net income, as determined under generally accepted accounting principles. An accounting firm has been retained to prepare Ortiz's April income statement under the accrual basis. The following additional information is gathered in the process of preparing the GAAP-based income statement:

Revenues:

- The $9,000 deposit on April 7 was an advance payment for work to be performed equally during April, May, and June.

- The $11,788.45 deposit on April 20 was collection of an account for which the work was performed during January and February.

- During April, services valued at $2,000 were performed and billed, but not yet collected.

Expenses:

- Payroll -- Of the $700 payment on April 3, $650 related to the prior month. An additional $350 is accrued by the end of April, but not paid.

- Rent -- The amount paid corresponded to the amount used.

- Server -- Of the $1,416.22 payment on April 15, $500 related to prior month's usage.

- Administrative -- An additional $600 is accrued by the end of April, but not paid.

The accounting firm prepared the following accrual-basis income statement and calculations in support of amounts found in the statement. Although Ortiz was initially very interested in Mega's offer, he was very disappointed with the resulting accrual-basis net income and decided to reject the deal. This illustration highlights the important differences between cash- and accrual-basis accounting.

Cash-basis statements are significantly influenced by the timing of receipts and payments, and can produce periodic statements that are not reflective of the actual economic activity of the business for the specific period in question. The accrual basis does a much better job of portraying the results of operations during each time period. This is why it is very important to grasp the revenue and expense recognition concepts discussed in this chapter, along with the related adjusting entries that may be needed at the end of each accounting period.

ORTIZ CORPORATION Income Statement For the Month Ending April 30, 20X5		
Revenues		
a. Services to customers		$10,045.23
Expenses		
b. Payroll	$4,778.76	
Rent	300.00	
c. Server	1,415.21	
d. Administrative	3,407.01	
Total expenses		9,900.98
Net income		$ 144.25

SUPPORTING
CALCULATIONS

Cash basis	$ 25,833.68
Less: Advance payment	(9,000.00)
Plus: Portion of advance payment earned	3,000.00
Less: Collection of prior receivable	(11,788.45)
Plus: Unbilled services	2,000.00
Accrual-basis revenues	$ 10,045.23 a.
Cash basis	$ 5,078.76
Less: Payment for prior month	(650.00)
Plus: Accrued payroll at end of month	350.00
Accrual-basis payroll expenses	$ 4,778.76 b.
Cash basis	$ 1,915.21
Less: Payment for prior month	(500.00)
Accrual-basis server expenses	$ 1,415.21 c.
Cash basis	$ 2,807.01
Plus: Accrued administrative expenses	600.00
Accrual-basis administrative expenses	$ 3,407.01 d.

Chapter 3 Quiz

Goals Achievement

Q3-1. Which concept holds that an organization's life can be divided into discrete accounting periods (months, quarters, years)?

transactions approach   or   periodicity assumption

Q3-2. Business expenses should be recognized in the same period as the revenues they helped to produce. This concept is known as the:

matching principle   or   cash basis of accounting

Q3-3. An appropriate journal entry to record accrued interest would involve a debit to Interest Expense and a credit to:

Interest Payable   or   Unearned Interest

Q3-4. Prepaid expenses would initially be recorded in an expense account under which adjusting entry approach?

balance sheet approach   or   income statement approach

Q3-5. Which method of accounting is theoretically preferred and used by virtually all large companies?

accrual basis   or   cash basis

Fill in the Blanks

Q3-6. The _____ is paramount to income measurement, and holds that an organization's life can be divided into discrete measurement intervals.

Q3-7. Accrual basis revenue is generally recognized at the time services are _____ or when goods are _____ and _____ to a customer.

Q3-8. _____ are goods and services purchased for future consumption and paid for in advance.

Q3-9. _____ revenue represents future revenue that has been collected but not yet earned, whereas _____ revenues have been earned but not yet received.

Q3-10. Financial statements may be prepared directly from the _____.

Q3-11. The method wherein prepaid expenses are initially recorded into the expense account is called the _____ approach.

Multiple Choice

Q3-12. For purposes of measuring business income, the life of a business is:

a. divided into specific points in time.

b. divided into irregular cycles.

c. divided into discrete accounting periods.

d. considered to be a continuous cycle.

Q3-13. Blankenship Company pays its employees every Friday for work rendered that week. The payroll is typically $10,000 per week. Which of the following journal entries would Blankenship ordinarily record on the Friday payday?

a. Salary Expense 10,000
    Salary Payable 10,000

b. Salary Expense 10,000
    Cash 10,000

c. Salary Payable 10,000
    Cash 10,000

d. Salary Payable 10,000
    Salary Expense 10,000

Q3-14. Blankenship Company pays its employees every Friday for work rendered that week. The payroll is typically $10,000 per week. Blankenship's year-end occurred on Wednesday, at which time a correct adjusting entry was recorded. On the following Friday, which of the following payroll journal entries should be recorded?

a. Salary Expense 10,000
    Cash 10,000

b. Salary Expense 4,000
    Salary Payable 6,000
    Cash 10,000

c. Salary Expense 6,000
    Salary Payable 4,000
    Cash 10,000

d. Salary Payable 10,000
    Cash 10,000

Q3-15. At the end of the current accounting period, Johnson Company failed to record utilities consumed during the period. Johnson will be billed for the utilities during the next accounting period. As a result, current period assets, liabilities, equity, and income, respectively, are:

a. Overstated, overstated, correct, correct

b. Correct, understated, overstated, overstated

c. Overstated, understated, overstated, overstated

d. Overstated, understated, correct, correct

Q3-16. Under the the income statement approach to adjusting entries, the receipt of $5,000 of unearned revenue would be recorded by debiting Cash. What account should be credited?

a. Cash

b. Revenue

c. Unearned Revenue

d. Prepaid Revenue

Chapter 3 Problems

Basic Problems

This chapter introduces important concepts in income measurement. Accountants oftentimes discuss these concepts using accounting "jargon" or "terminology." Effective business communication requires that all parties attach the same meaning to the words that are used to express concepts. Match the accounting terms in the list on the left to the accounting concept described in the list on the right.

(1) Depreciation

(2) Calendar Year

(3) Revenue Recognition

(4) Cash Basis

(5) Prepaids

(6) Unearned Revenue

(7) Balance Sheet Approach

(8) Adjusting Entry

(9) Accruals

(10) Periodicity Assumption

(a) The basic conditions require that an exchange has occurred and the earnings process is complete.

(b) An asset reflecting advance payment for something that will be consumed over the future.

(c) An entry usually prepared coincident with the end of accounting period to update the accounting for prepaids, accruals, and other allocations.

(d) An annual reporting period that runs from January 1 through December 31.

(e) Monies collected from customers for services that have not yet been provided.

(f) An approach that results in the initial recording of prepaids to an asset account and unearned revenues to a liability account.

(g) The notion that continuous business process can be divided into time intervals such as years, quarters, or months for reporting purposes.

(h) A systematic and rational allocation scheme to spread a portion of the total cost of a productive asset to each period of use.

(i) Expenses and revenues that gradually accumulate with the passage of time.

(j) A simplified non-GAAP based method to record revenues as received and expenses as paid.

Accounting "failures" occur when reported results are not presented in accordance with generally accepted accounting principles. These failures can produce significant financial losses to investors and creditors. Oftentimes, an accounting failure results from an incorrect application of revenue recognition concepts.

Revgression Corporation included each of the following described transactions in revenue during 20X5. Three of these transactions were appropriate, and three were not. Determine which are "ok" and which are "not ok."

(1)   Goods were sold and shipped in late 20X5, but the product still requires substantial installation and setup services. The price and terms of sale stipulate that seller must satisfactorily complete all installation and setup at the buyer's location.

(2)   Goods were produced according to a customer purchase order but had not yet been shipped by the end of 20X5.

(3)   Goods were delivered to customers during early 20X5, but the customers had ordered and paid for the goods during 20X4.

(4)   Customers purchased goods and services during late 20X5, but credit terms permitted them to delay payment until early 20X6. Full payment is expected eventually.

(5)   Advance payment from a customer in a foreign country was received in 20X5 for services to be provided in 20X6.

(6)   Goods were purchased and paid for by customers during 20X5, but customers may return defective goods for warranty work or a refund. The expected warranty/refund claims are subject to reasonable estimation and not anticipated to be significant.

B-03.03   *Expense recognition principles*

The recognition of an expense usually occurs based on one of the following three intrinsic principles:

(a)   Associating cause and effect

(b)   Systematic and rational allocation

(c)   Immediate recognition

Evaluate the following items and determine the intrinsic principle that establishes the basis by which it is to be recorded as an expense.

(1)   The cost of a building used in the business.

(2)   The cost of merchandise sold to customers.

(3)   Rental costs under a three-year lease agreement.

(4)   The cost of a rebate offered on goods sold to customers.

(5)   An uninsured storm loss.

(6)   Commissions paid to a sales person.

(7) Cost of land seized as the result of a change in government in a foreign venue.

(8) The cost of paper used by a publishing company.

(9) The cost of an unfavorable verdict in a civil lawsuit.

| *Prepaid expenses* | *B-03.04* |

Following are three separate transactions that pertain to prepaid items. Evaluate each item and prepare the journal entries that would be needed for the initial recording and subsequent end-of-20X3 adjusting entry. Assume the company uses the balance sheet approach, and the initial recording is to an asset account. The company has a calendar year-end and does not make any adjusting entries prior to December 31.

SPREADSHEET TOOL:

Date functions

(1) The company purchased an 18-month insurance policy for $18,000 on June 1, 20X3.

(2) The company started 20X3 with $20,000 in supplies (this was previously recorded, and you do not need to make an entry for the beginning balance), purchased $30,000 in supplies during the year, and found only $13,000 in supplies on hand at the end of 20X3.

(3) The company paid $2,500 to rent a truck. The rental period began on December 16, 20X3, and ends on February 14, 20X4.

| *Depreciation* | *B-03.05* |

Mohamed Bakar Alidini recently formed a business in the Republic of Yemen to process liquefied natural gas for export to other countries. Natural gas can be converted to a liquid by cooling it to -163 degrees Celsius. It then assumes a highly compressed state and can be transported by specially designed cryogenic vessels. Mohamed's business invested 80,000,000 (Yemeni Rials/YER) in a cooling/containment chamber with a 4-year life. The chamber will have no remaining value at the end of the 4-year period.

(a) Prepare journal entries to record annual depreciation for each of the four years, assuming Alidini uses the straight-line method.

(b) Show how the annual depreciation will appear in each year's income statement.

(c) Show how the asset, and related accumulated depreciation, will appear in each year's balance sheet.

| *Unearned revenue* | *B-03.06* |

Stargate Publishing issues the *Weekly Window*. The company's primary sources of revenue are sales of subscriptions to customers and sales of advertising in the *Weekly Window*. Stargate owns its building and has excess office space that it leases to others.

The following transactions involved the receipt of advance payments. Prepare the indicated journal entries for each set of transactions.

(1)   On September 1, 20X5, the company received a $24,000 payment from an advertising client for a 6-month advertising campaign. The campaign was to run from November, 20X5 through the end of April, 20X6. Prepare the journal entry on September 1 and the December 31 end-of-year adjusting entry.

(2)   The company began 20X5 with $120,000 in unearned revenue relating to sales of subscriptions for future issues. During 20X5, additional subscriptions were sold for $1,230,000. Magazines delivered during 20X5 under outstanding subscriptions totaled $1,020,000. Prepare a summary journal entry to reflect the sales of subscriptions and the end-of-year adjusting entry to reflect magazines delivered.

(3)   The company received a $3,000 rental payment on December 16, 20X5 for the period running from mid-December to Mid-January. Prepare the December 16 journal entry as well as the December 31 end-of-year adjusting entry.

B-03.07   *Accrued expenses and accrued revenues*

Creative Hearing Technologies of London recently introduced a Bluetooth-enabled hearing aid that allows hearing-disabled users to not only hear better, but also interface with their cell phones and digital music players.

The company reports the following four transactions and events related to December of 20X7 and is seeking your help to prepare the end-of-year adjusting entries needed at December 31.

(1)   On December 1, the company borrowed £10,000,000 at an 8% per annum interest rate. The loan, and all accrued interest, is due in 3 months.

(2)   Early in December, the company licensed its new technology to Apple Bites Computer, Inc., for use in Apple's existing product lines. The agreement provides for a royalty payment from Apple to Creative based on Apple's sales of products using the licensed technology. As of December 31, £45,000 is due under the agreement for actual sales made by Apple to date.

(3)   Creative pays many employees on an hourly basis. As of December 31 there are 5,320 unpaid labor hours already worked at an average hourly rate of £17.

(4)   The company estimates that utilities used during December, for which bills will be received in January, amount to £20,000.

B-03.08   *Various adjustments from trial balance and other information*

Anthony Asher's administrative assistant maintains a very simple computerized general ledger system. This system includes intuitive routines for recording receipts, payments, and sales on account. However, the system is not sufficiently robust to automate end-of-period adjustments. Following is the trial balance for the month ending January 31, 20X8. This trial balance has <u>not</u> been adjusted for the various items that are described on the following page. Review the trial balance and narratives, and prepare the necessary adjusting entries.

ASHER CORPORATION
Trial Balance
January 31, 20X8

	Debits	Credits
Cash	$ 37,500	
Accounts receivable	12,410	
Prepaid insurance	2,400	
Supplies	7,113	
Equipment	35,000	
Accumulated depreciation		$ 10,000
Accounts payable		7,569
Unearned revenue		8,500
Loan payable		15,000
Capital stock		24,000
Retained earnings, Jan. 1		15,457
Revenues		43,995
Salary expense	12,098	
Rent expense	13,000	
Office expense	2,500	
Dividends	2,500	
	$124,521	$124,521

Asher Corporation's equipment had an original life of 140 months, and the straight-line depreciation method is used. As of January 1, the equipment was 40 months old. The equipment will be worthless at the end of its useful life.

As of the end of the month, Asher Corporation has provided services to customers for which the earnings process is complete. Formal billings are normally sent out on the first day of each month for the prior month's work. January's unbilled work is $25,000.

Utilities used during January, for which bills will soon be forthcoming from providers, are estimated at $1,500.

A review of supplies on hand at the end of the month revealed items costing $3,500.

The $2,400 balance in prepaid insurance was for a 6-month policy running from January 1 to June 30.

The unearned revenue was collected in December of 20X7. Sixty percent of that amount was actually earned in January with the remainder to be earned in February.

The loan accrues interest at 1% per month. No interest was paid in January.

T-account analysis and adjusting entries

Professor Wayne Campbell recently lectured on adjusting entries. As he did so, he prepared T-accounts on a marker board to illustrate the key points he was making.

As he was erasing his illustrations from the board, Candice Greenhaw arrived late to class. She was only able to copy the following portions of the T-account illustrations from the board.

You are to help Candice recreate the lecture by completing the missing portions of each T-account. Then, prepare the adjusting entries for December 31, 20X1.

Example 1:

Unearned Revenues			
12/31/X1	18,000	25,000	12/1/X1
		23,900	12/15/X1
	18,000		
		30,900	

Revenues			
		178,976	Various
			12/31/X1

Example 2:

Prepaid Insurance		
Beg. Bal.	15,000	
12/10/X1	5,000	
	20,000	
	13,000	

Insurance Expense	
12/31/X1	

Example 3:

Salaries Expense		
Various	21,500	
12/15/X1	2,500	
12/31/X1		
	27,000	

Salaries Payable	
	12/31/X1

Example 4:

Depreciation Expense		
Various	23,900	
12/31/X1		
	25,200	

Accumulated Depreciation		
	89,000	Beg. Bal.
		12/31/X1

Example 5:

Supplies				Supplies Expense	
Beg. Bal.	0		12/31/X1		
12/9/X1	3,400				
	3,400				
	1,600				

Cash to accrual conversion **B-03.10**

Evaluate the following items, and determine the correct amount to report on the income statement for each using the accrual basis of accounting for the referenced period of time.

Revenues   A Company had beginning accounts receivable of $8,000. The company reported cash basis revenues of $100,000. The ending accounts receivable amounted to $18,000.

Supplies   B Company purchased $25,000 of supplies. Supplies on hand decreased by $5,000 during the period.

Rent   C Company started the year with no prepaid rent, and ended the year with $1,000 in prepaid rent. Rent expense on a cash basis was $13,000.

Equipment   At the beginning of the year, D Company purchased and expensed an item of equipment for $20,000. The equipment has a 4-year life and will be worthless after four years.

Wages   There were no wages payable at the beginning of the year. E Company paid $145,000 in wages during the year and owed an additional $12,000 at year's end.

Involved Problems

Income measurement terms and concepts **I-03.01**

This chapter introduces many important terms and concepts. Certain of these terms and concepts are noted in the following listing. Find quotes/descriptions that explain/contrast each of the matched pairs below. It is ok to "copy" and "paste" text from the website to your solution to expedite the preparation of your answer.

SPREADSHEET TOOL:

Copy and Paste Data

Accounting Income vs. Economic Income

Revenues vs. Gains

Expenses vs. Losses

Fiscal Year vs. Calendar Year

Revenue Recognition vs. Expense Recognition

Accruals vs. Prepaids

Balance Sheet Approach vs. Income Statement Approach

Cash Basis vs. Accrual Basis

Although the basic principles for revenue recognition are straightforward, complex business transactions often give rise to difficulties in reaching an appropriate accounting conclusion. More than half (and perhaps as high as 80%) of all accounting failures are attributable to misapplication of accounting rules relating to revenue recognition.

The accounting profession has developed detailed guidance on revenue recognition. Review the website of the Financial Accounting Standards Board (FASB.org), and determine the status of various projects on revenue recognition. Be prepared to have a general discussion with classmates about current issues and developments in standard setting that pertain to this topic.

Divide your class into ten teams. Each team should obtain the annual reports of three different companies. These reports are usually readily available on the corporate websites, and will ordinarily include a footnote to financial statements that details the summary of significant accounting policies. Within that footnote is apt to be a discussion of general policies relative to revenue recognition. Compare and contrast the revenue recognition policies and issues for the three companies, and select the one that seems to involve the most interesting measurement issues.

In class, have each team discuss their most interesting find, and then have the class "rank" the issues from most complex to least complex. Use this as a basis for discussing a general frame of reference for revenue recognition.

Identification of items in need of adjustment is not automatic. It requires careful monitoring of the business environment and can entail assessment of information found on various source documents within the business organization.

This problem introduces typical "business papers" that document transactions of the W. Brian Voss Company. You are to examine the provided information, and determine what related adjusting entry is needed for each item on December 31, 20X1.

(a) Following is a deposit ticket. This item is usually prepared to accompany money that is taken to a bank for deposit to the company's bank account. The W. Brian Voss Company provides security services, and the following deposit was from a customer that fully prepaid a 6-month contract commencing on the date of the deposit. The proceeds were initially entered into Voss's Unearned Revenue account.

W. Brian Voss Company	Cash and coins	
6th Avenue	Checks:	
Austin, TX	D. Dutter	$750.00
Account #　　4567654		
Date　　November 1, 20X1		
Austin Capital Bank	TOTAL	$750.00

(b) The W. Brian Voss Company wrote these checks to purchase supplies during 20X1. Voss began the year with $1,297 of supplies on hand. At year's end only $560 of supplies remained. Each of these transactions was initially recorded in the Supplies account, and no adjusting entries were made during the year.

W. Brian Voss Company 6th Avenue Austin, TX	Check #	11034
	Date:	January 5, 20X1
Pay to the order of: Everything Office Supply Company		$1,175.⁰⁰

**************ONE-THOUSAND, ONE-HUNDRED SEVENTY-FIVE AND NO/100 DOLLARS*************

Austin Capital Bank

MEMO   office supplies   W. Brian Voss

W. Brian Voss Company 6th Avenue Austin, TX	Check #	11164
	Date:	June 6, 20X1
Pay to the order of: Ink Jet Now Company		$90.⁰⁰

***********************************NINETY AND NO/100 DOLLARS***********************************

Austin Capital Bank

MEMO   office supplies   W. Brian Voss

W. Brian Voss Company 6th Avenue Austin, TX	Check #	11202
	Date:	November 5, 20X1
Pay to the order of: Everything Office Supply Company		$940.⁰⁰

*************************NINE-HUNDRED, FORTY AND NO/100 DOLLARS*************************

Austin Capital Bank

MEMO   office supplies   W. Brian Voss

continued...

(c)   The W. Brian Voss Company purchased a new computer. The company estimates that the computer will last four years and have no salvage value at the end of the four-year period. Following is the invoice that was received at the time the computer was purchased.

DEAL COMPUTER COMPANY
1825 Pecan
Pflugerville, TX

Bill To: W. Brian Voss Company   Invoice #34848
           6th Avenue
           Austin, TX

P.O. NUMBER	INVOICE DATE	F.O.B. POINT	TERMS
593CCG	July 1, 20X1	Austin	30 days

QTY.	PART #	DESCRIPTION	UNIT PRICE	TOTAL
1	PC4456	MegaPlex Computer w/FlexPlex Monitor	$2,424	$2,424

THANK YOU FOR YOUR BUSINESS!	TOTAL	$2,424

(d)   The W. Brian Voss Company received the following electric utility bill. It has not been recorded into the accounts.

AUSTIN POWER AND LIGHT
711 Capitol Avenue
Austin, TX

ELECTRIC UTILITIES

Your payment is due by January 15

W. Brian Voss Company
6th Avenue
Austin, TX

Amount Due	$374.00
Account #	0707BB6AVATX

Electric utility service for December, 20X1 - meter #5340757

Meter Read:

Prior month	334346	
End of current month	338086	
Current months usage	3740	KWH
Rate	X 0.1	
	374	

(e) W. Brian Voss leases office space from Trammell Raven Property Management Company. The leasing market was very soft at the time the lease agreement was made, and the lease includes terms that are very favorable to Voss. Below is the lease agreement. No entry has been recorded for this lease.

LEASE AGREEMENT

This agreement is entered into by and between TRAMMELL RAVEN PROPERTY MANAGEMENT COMPANY (lessor) and W. Brian Voss Company, (lessee). Lessee agrees to lease from lessor the office space described as 6th Avenue, Austin, Texas.

The term of the lease shall be for 4 years commencing on January 1, 20X1 and continuing until December 31, 20X4. The annual rental rate is $20,000. Lessee is hereby granted the option to renew and extend the lease for one additional successive four-year period at the then prevailing market rate of rent.

Rent is payable in arrears, annually, on the 1st day of each year following the year of use. The first payment is due January 1, 20X2 (for the preceding year), and continues in similar fashion thereafter for the duration of the lease, including periods of renewal and extension.

Lessor is responsible for all taxes, insurance, and property maintenance. Lessee is responsible for all electric utilities. Lessee agrees to use reasonable care in protecting and preserving the quality of the property covered by this lease.

Date: January 1, 20X1

Trammel Raven	*W. Brian Voss*
for TRPMC	for W. Brian Voss Company

Comprehensive fact set and adjustments   I-03.04

Plicta Motors is an automobile service center offering a full range of repair services for high performance cars. The following information is pertinent to adjusting entries that are needed for Plicta as of March 31, 20X5. Plicta has a fiscal year ending on March 31 and only records adjusting entries at year end.

Plicta has a large investment in repair equipment and maintains detailed asset records. These records show that depreciation for fiscal "X5" is $123,400.

As of March 31, 20X5 accrued interest on loans owed by Plicta is $21,678.

Auto dealerships outsource work to Plicta. This work is done on account and billed monthly. As of March 31, 20X5 $54,800 of unbilled services have been provided.

Plicta maintains a general business liability insurance policy. The prepaid annual premium is $6,000. The policy was purchased on October 1, 20X4. Another policy is a 6-month property and casualty policy obtained on December 1, 20X4 at a cost of $3,000. Both policies were initially recorded as prepaid insurance.

The company prepared a detailed count of shop supplies at March 31, 20X4 with $37,904 on hand at that date. Management believed this level was greater than necessary and undertook a strategy to reduce these levels over the next year. During the fiscal year 20X5, Plicta purchased an additional $125,000 of supplies and debited the Supplies account. By March 31, 20X5, the effort to reduce inventory was successful as the count revealed an ending balance of only $13,600.

During the fiscal year, Plicta began offering a service contract to retail customers entitling them regular tire rotations, car washing, and other routine maintenance items. Customers prepay for this service agreement, and Plicta records the proceeds in the Unearned Revenue account. The service plan is a flat fee of $219, and Plicta sold the plan to 456 customers. At March 31, 20X5, it is estimated that 25% of the necessary work has been provided under these agreements.

Plicta's primary advertising is on billboards. Lamzar Outdoor Advertising sold Plicta a plan for multiple sign locations around the city. Because Plicta agreed to prepay the full price of $26,000, Lamzar agreed to leave the signs up for 13 months. Plicta paid on June 1, 20X4 and recorded the full amount as a prepaid. However, the advertising campaign was not begun until July 1, 20X4. It will conclude on July 31, 20X5.

Plicta leases shop space. Monthly rent is due and payable on the first day of each month. Plicta paid the March rent on March 1, and expects to pay the April rent on April 1.

Prepare adjusting entries (hint: when necessary) for Plicta, as of March 31, 20X5.

I-03.05   *Evaluation of adjustment errors and corrections*

Fenco Corporation's stock price recently collapsed on news that its chief financial officer resigned. It seems the company had deliberately failed to follow generally accepted principles in an attempt to support a 30% income growth rate. The company announced that it would be restating the 20X7 results. Information about Fenco's financial condition and stock price follow:

	Reported Annual Net Income	Reported Assets	Reported Liabilities	Reported Stockholders' Equity	Stock Price Per Share
Dec. 31, 20X4	$ 2,500,000	$ 7,600,000	$3,800,000	$ 3,800,000	$20.20
Dec. 31, 20X5	3,275,000	9,804,000	2,729,000	7,075,000	35.00
Dec. 31, 20X6	4,323,000	13,627,560	2,229,560	11,398,000	60.75
Dec. 31, 20X7	5,576,670	18,942,308	1,967,638	16,974,670	98.90
Jan. 31, 20X8	n/a	n/a	n/a	n/a	11.50

The following information is necessary to correct 20X7's data.

As of December 31, 20X7, Fenco's CFO withheld adjusting entries for accruals relating to wages, utilities, and similar items. The total of such items amounted to $855,000.

During the year, Fenco presold certain services to its clients. All such sales were booked as revenues even though $625,000 had not been "earned" as of the end of 20X7.

Fenco purchased $3,000,000 of equipment on July 1, 20X7. These assets had a 5-year life and no salvage value. Fenco neglected to depreciate these assets during 20X7.

Fenco began 20X7 with $50,000 in a Prepaid Rent account. The rent related to 20X7, but no adjusting entry was recorded in this account during 20X7.

Fenco offered customer rebates for services delivered in 20X7. As of the end of 20X7, Fenco owes $135,000 in rebates. The rebates will not be processed before February, 20X8. The CFO indicated that no entry was necessary before actual payment.

(a) Determine the correct amounts to report for 20X7 (net income, and assets, liabilities, and equity).

(b) Is the collapse in stock price justified, and what pressures might a CFO face to participate in a scheme to manipulate income?

(c) How can business persons prepare themselves to avoid succumbing to pressures to "fudge" on accounting numbers?

Balance sheet versus income statement approaches to adjustments	*I-03.06*

Examine each of the following fact scenarios, then prepare initial and end-of-year adjusting entries (when needed) assuming (a) use of a "balance sheet" approach versus (b) use of an "income statement" approach. You may assume a calendar year end for each scenario. Use T-accounts to show how the same financial statement results occur under either approach. The worksheet on the website includes an illustrative solution for the first scenario.

Scenario 1   A $1,500, one-year insurance policy was purchased on June 1, 20X1.

Scenario 2   Unearned revenue of $20,000 was collected on August 1, 20X1, and 40% of this amount was earned by the end of the year.

Scenario 3   On December 1, 20X1, $3,000 was prepaid for space in a trade-show booth. The trade show is in February of 20X2.

Scenario 4   A $1,000 customer deposit for future services was received on April 1, 20X1. On June 20, 20X1 the customer canceled the agreement and received a full refund.

Roger Wilde is a CPA. He has numerous clients, one of which is Wedding World (WW). WW is a full service bridal consulting firm and is interested in buying Wedding Wonders Photography Studio (WWPS). WWPS uses the cash basis of accounting. Roger has been retained to help WW acquire WWPS, and you are a staff accountant working for Roger. Begin by evaluating the following facts for June.

Revenues	WWPS provides a complete wedding-day package for $2,950. The package requires a $1,000 down payment at the time the contract is signed, a $1,200 payment on the date of the wedding, and a final $750 payment 30 days after the wedding. The company uses a mobile digital processing lab and is able to deliver a complete wedding portfolio at the close of the reception on the wedding day itself!
	Seventy-five weddings were photographed during June. All of these events were booked in earlier months. During June, an additional 92 weddings were booked for future months. Final payments were received during June for 47 weddings performed in May. None of the June weddings resulted in receipt of the final payment before July 1, but full payment is expected.
Expenses	During June $70,000 was actually paid for wages. Accrued wages at the beginning of the month totaled $12,000. At the end of the month, $23,000 was owed to employees.
	At the close of June, the WWPS bought new photography equipment for $13,000. Entering June, WWPS owned equipment with a total cost of $700,000. This equipment has an average life of 50 months.
	Supplies on hand at the beginning of the month totaled $123,500 and $76,000 was expended for supplies during the month. Supplies on hand were $81,200 at the end of the month.

(a) Prepare a cash basis income statement for June. Preliminarily, WW is willing to pay a price equal to 75 X June's monthly income.

(b) On further review of the facts relating to WWPS, Roger suggested that a fair offer should be based on accrual basis income. Calculate accrual basis income.

(c) What is the proposed purchase price? What is the value of utilizing a CPA to assist in the business decision process?

(d) As a general rule, could a CPA like Roger give an unqualified audit opinion on the cash basis financial statements? Why or why not?

(e) Why might some businesses that are not required to follow GAAP use the cash basis?

(f) What is the modified cash basis of accounting?

Chapter 4:
The Reporting Cycle

Goals:

Preparation of financial statements.

The accounting cycle and closing process.

The nature of "optional" reversing entries.

Classified balance sheets.

The importance of business liquidity and the concept of an operating cycle.

principlesofaccounting.com

The previous chapter presented adjustments that might be needed at the end of each accounting period. These adjustments were necessary to bring a company's books and records current in anticipation of calculating and reporting income and financial position. This chapter begins by illustrating how such adjustments would be used to actually prepare financial statements.

Assume that England Tours Company began operation early in 20X3. In the process of preparing its financial statements for the year ending December 31, 20X3, England determined that various adjusting entries were needed. These adjusting journal entries are shown on the following page. The numbers are all "assumed." But, if it is unclear as to why any one of these entries might be needed, definitely review the detailed discussion in the previous chapter. The illustration shows:

- England's trial balance before the adjusting entries
- the adjusting journal entries
- the posting of the adjusting journal entries to the general ledger
- the adjusted trial balance

If England attempts to prepare its financial statements based only on the unadjusted trial balance, the reported information would be incomplete and incorrect.

Most of the time, a company will prepare its trial balance, analyze the trial balance for potential adjustments, and develop a list of necessary adjusting entries. Knowing what to adjust is not necessarily intuitive. It usually requires hands-on review by someone who is very knowledgeable about the business. As a practical matter, a company should not allow everyone to have access to the accounting system for purposes of entering year-end adjustments; too many errors and rogue entries will appear. Instead, a company will usually have a defined process where proposed entries are documented on a form (sometimes called a journal voucher). These forms are submitted to a chief accountant/controller for review and approval. The approved journal vouchers then serve as supporting documents to authorize data entry into the accounting system.

THE ADJUSTING PROCESS

ENGLAND TOURS COMPANY
Trial Balance
December 31, 20X3

	Debits	Credits
Cash	$15,500	
Accounts receivable	4,500	
Equipment	45,000	
Accounts payable		$ 4,000
Unearned revenue		3,000
Notes payable		20,000
Capital stock		30,000
Revenue		31,000
Salaries expense	15,000	
Advertising expense	5,000	
Fuel expense	2,000	
Dividends	1,000	
	$88,000	$88,000

 Record Adjusting Entries in Journal

12-31-X3	Depreciation Expense		5,000	
	Accumulated Depreciation			5,000
	To record annual depreciation expense			
12-31-X3	Salaries Expense		2,000	
	Salaries Payable			2,000
	To record accrued salaries due to employees			
12-31-X3	Interest Expense		1,200	
	Interest Payable			1,200
	To record accrued interest on note payable			
12-31-X3	Unearned Revenue		1,800	
	Revenue			1,800
	To record earned portion of advance sales			

 Post Entries to the Ledger

Cash

Date	Description	Debit	Credit	Balance
Dec. 31, 20X3	Balance			$15,500

Accounts Receivable

Date	Description	Debit	Credit	Balance
Dec. 31, 20X3	Balance			$4,500

Equipment

Date	Description	Debit	Credit	Balance
Dec. 31, 20X3	Balance			$45,000

Accumulated Depreciation

Date	Description	Debit	Credit	Balance
Dec. 31, 20X3	Adjusting entry		$5,000	$5,000

Accounts Payable

Date	Description	Debit	Credit	Balance
Dec. 31, 20X3	Balance			$ 4,000

Unearned Revenue

Date	Description	Debit	Credit	Balance
Dec. 31, 20X3	Balance			$3,000
Dec. 31, 20X3	Adjusting entry	$1,800		$1,200

Salaries Payable

Date	Description	Debit	Credit	Balance
Dec. 31, 20X3	Adjusting entry		$2,000	$ 2,000

Notes Payable

Date	Description	Debit	Credit	Balance
Dec. 31, 20X3	Balance			$20,000

Revenue

Date	Description	Debit	Credit	Balance
Dec. 31, 20X3	Balance			$31,000
Dec. 31, 20X3	Adjusting entry		$1,800	$32,800

Advertising Expense

Date	Description	Debit	Credit	Balance
Dec. 31, 20X3	Balance			$ 5,000

Depreciation Expense

Date	Description	Debit	Credit	Balance
Dec. 31, 20X3	Adjusting entry	$5,000		$ 5,000

Dividends

Date	Description	Debit	Credit	Balance
Dec. 31, 20X3	Balance	$1,000		$ 1,000

Interest Payable

Date	Description	Debit	Credit	Balance
Dec. 31, 20X3	Adjusting entry		$1,200	$ 1,200

Capital Stock

Date	Description	Debit	Credit	Balance
Dec. 31, 20X3	Balance			$30,000

Salaries Expense

Date	Description	Debit	Credit	Balance
Dec. 31, 20X3	Balance			$15,000
Dec. 31, 20X3	Adjusting entry	$2,000		$17,000

Fuel Expense

Date	Description	Debit	Credit	Balance
Dec. 31, 20X3	Balance			$ 2,000

Interest Expense

Date	Description	Debit	Credit	Balance
Dec. 31, 20X3	Adjusting entry	$1,200		$ 1,200

 Prepare Adjusted Trial Balance from Ledger

ENGLAND TOURS COMPANY
Adjusted Trial Balance
December 31, 20X3

	Debits	Credits
Cash	$15,500	
Accounts receivable	4,500	
Equipment	45,000	
Accumulated depreciation		$ 5,000
Accounts payable		4,000
Unearned revenue		1,200
Salaries payable		2,000
Interest payable		1,200
Notes payable		20,000
Capital stock		30,000
Revenue		32,800
Salaries expense	17,000	
Advertising expense	5,000	
Fuel expense	2,000	
Depreciation expense	5,000	
Interest expense	1,200	
Dividends	1,000	
	$96,200	$96,200

FINANCIAL STATEMENTS

The adjusted trial balance is ordinarily sufficient to facilitate preparation of financial statements. Take time to trace the amounts from England's adjusted trial balance to the following statements.

ENGLAND TOURS COMPANY
Income Statement
For the Year Ending December 31, 20X3

Revenues

Tour services		$32,800

Expenses

Salaries	$17,000	
Advertising	5,000	
Fuel	2,000	
Depreciation	5,000	
Interest	1,200	30,200
Net income		$ 2,600

ENGLAND TOURS COMPANY
Statement of Retained Earnings
For the Year Ending December 31, 20X3

Beginning retained earnings	$	-
Plus: Net income		2,600
		$2,600
Less: Dividends		1,000
Ending retained earnings		$1,600

ENGLAND TOURS COMPANY
Balance Sheet
December 31, 20X3

Assets

Cash		$15,500
Accounts receivable		4,500
Equipment	$45,000	
Less: Accum. depreciation	(5,000)	40,000
Total assets		$60,000

Liabilities

Accounts payable	$ 4, 000	
Salaries payable	2,000	
Interest payable	1,200	
Notes payable	20,000	
Unearned revenue	1,200	
Total liabilities		$28,400

Stockholders' equity

Capital stock	$30,000	
Retained earnings	1,600	
Total stockholders' equity		31,600
Total liabilities and equity		$60,000

ACCOUNTING SOFTWARE

The financial statement preparation process is mostly mechanical, and easily automated. Once the adjusting entries have been prepared and entered, every accounting software package will race through the steps of processing the data to produce the financial statements. As such, one might be inclined to discount the need to understand how to move amounts from an adjusted trial balance into a set of financial statements. In some respects that is true, just as it is true that one does not need to know how to add and subtract if they own a calculator. Of course, there is value in understanding addition and subtraction even with a calculator. In the same light, please consider that understanding the flow of transactions into financial statements is essential.

WORKSHEET APPROACH

Occasionally, one may desire to prepare financial statements that take into account necessary adjustments, but without actually updating journals and ledgers. Why? A manager may desire monthly financial reports even though the business may not formally prepare and book adjusting entries every month. A worksheet approach can be used for this purpose. Or, an auditor may use a worksheet to prepare financial statements that take into account recommended adjustments, before proposing that the actual journal/ledger be updated.

The following illustrates a typical worksheet. The data and adjustments correspond to information previously presented for England. The first set of columns is the unadjusted trial balance. The next set of columns reveal the end-of-period adjustments. The information in the first two sets of columns is combined to generate the adjusted trial balance columns. The last three pairs of columns are the appropriate financial statement extensions of amounts from the adjusted trial balance columns.

For example, Cash is an asset account with a debit balance, and is "appropriately" extended from the adjusted trial balance columns to the debit column of the balance sheet pair of columns. Likewise, Revenue is an income statement account with a credit balance; notice that it is extended to the income statement credit column. This extension of accounts should occur for every item in the adjusted trial balance. Look at the worksheet, and consider the additional comments that follow.

After all adjusted trial balance amounts have been extended to the appropriate financial statement columns, the income statement columns are subtotaled. If credits exceed debits, the company has more revenues than expenses (e.g., $32,800 vs. $30,200 = $2,600 net income)). Or, an excess of debits over credits would represent a net loss. To complete the worksheet, the amount of net income or loss is entered in the lower portion of the income statement columns in a manner which causes total debits to equal total credits. England Tours had a $2,600 net income, and a debit is needed to balance the income statement pair. An offsetting credit is entered in the lower portion of the retained earnings columns. This credit represents income for the year that must be added to retained earnings to complete the preparation of a formal statement of retained earnings. Within the retained earnings columns, the subtotal indicates that ending retained earnings is $1,600 (noted by the excess of credits ($2,600) over debits ($1,000)); this amount is debited in the retained earnings columns and credited in the balance sheet columns, thereby bringing both sets of columns into balance.

ENGLAND TOURS COMPANY
Worksheet to Prepare Financial Statements
December 31, 20X3

	Trial Balance		Adjustments		Adjusted Trial Balance		Income Statement		Statement of Ret. Earnings		Balance Sheet	
	Debit	Credit	Debit	Credit	Debit	Credit	Debit	Credit	Debit	Credit	Debit	Credit
Cash	$15,500				$15,500						$15,500	
Accounts receivable	4,500				4,500						4,500	
Equipment	45,000				45,000						45,000	
Accounts payable		$ 4,000				$ 4,000						$ 4,000
Unearned revenue		3,000	$ 1,800			1,200						1,200
Notes payable		20,000				20,000						20,000
Capital stock		30,000				30,000						30,000
Revenue		31,000		$ 1,800		32,800		$32,800				
Salaries expense	15,000		2,000		17,000		$17,000					
Advertising expense	5,000				5,000		5,000					
Fuel expense	2,000				2,000		2,000					
Dividends	1,000				1,000				$1,000			
Depreciation expense			5,000		5,000		5,000					
Accum. depreciation				5,000		5,000						5,000
Salaries payable				2,000		2,000						2,000
Interest expense			1,200		1,200		1,200					
Interest payable				1,200		1,200						1,200
	$88,000	$88,000	$10,000	$10,000	$96,200	$96,200	$30,200	$32,800				
Net income							2,600			$2,600		
							$32,800	$32,800	$1,000	$2,600		
Retained earnings									1,600			1,600
									$2,600	$2,600	$65,000	$65,000

The companion website includes a linked animation that presents the development of the worksheet on a step-by-step basis, and may further aid understanding of the worksheet's construction.

ADDITIONAL EXAMPLES The illustration shown assumed England Tours was formed early in 20X3. As such, there was no beginning retained earnings balance. One may wonder how the worksheet would be influenced by a beginning retained earnings balance. The following is an illustration of England's 20X4 worksheet, where the $1,600 ending retained earnings from 20X3 carries over to become the beginning balance for 20X4. The other numbers for 20X4 are all assumed.

20X4 Illustration With Beginning Retained Earnings Balance

ENGLAND TOURS COMPANY Worksheet to Prepare Financial Statements December 31, 20X4												
	Trial Balance		Adjustments		Adjusted Trial Balance		Income Statement		Statement of Ret. Earnings		Balance Sheet	
	Debit	Credit	Debit	Credit	Debit	Credit	Debit	Credit	Debit	Credit	Debit	Credit
Cash	$ 19,900				$ 19,900						$19,900	
Accounts receivable	12,000		$ 3,000		15,000						15,000	
Equipment	45,000				45,000						45,000	
Accum. depreciation		$ 5,000		$ 5,000		$ 10,000						$10,000
Accounts payable		12,300				12,300						12,300
Unearned revenue		4,000				4,000						4,000
Notes payable		15,000				15,000						15,000
Capital stock		30,000				30,000						30,000
Retained earnings, beg.		1,600				1,600				$1,600		
Revenue		45,000		3,000		48,000		$48,000				
Salaries expense	22,000		4,100		26,100		$26,100					
Advertising expense	7,500				7,500		7,500					
Fuel expense	3,700				3,700		3,700					
Legal expense	1,300				1,300		1,300					
Dividends	1,500				1,500				$1,500			
Depreciation expense			5,000		5,000		5,000					
Salaries payable				4,100		4,100						4,100
Interest expense			900		900		900					
Interest payable				900		900						900
	$112,900	$112,900	$13,000	$13,000	$125,900	$125,900	$44,500	$48,000				
Net income							3,500			$3,500		
							$48,000	$48,000	$1,500	$5,100		
Retained earnings, end.									3,600			3,600
									$5,100	$5,100	$79,900	$79,900

One may also be curious to see how a net loss situation would be handled in the worksheet. The next illustration is for England's 20X5 worksheet. It is assumed that England lost $1,000 in 20X5. Notice how the expenses of $39,600 exceed revenues of $38,600 as evident in the income statement columns. The $1,000 balancing amount is reflected as a credit in the income statement and a debit to the retained earnings column.

20X5 Illustration With Net Loss

	Trial Balance		Adjustments		Adjusted Trial Balance		Income Statement		Statement of Ret. Earnings		Balance Sheet	
ENGLAND TOURS COMPANY Worksheet to Prepare Financial Statements December 31, 20X5												
	Debit	Credit	Debit	Credit	Debit	Credit	Debit	Credit	Debit	Credit	Debit	Credit
Cash	$ 18,500				$ 18,500						$18,500	
Accounts receivable	9,000				9,000						9,000	
Equipment	45,000				45,000						45,000	
Accum. depreciation		$ 10,000		$5,000		$ 15,000						$15,000
Accounts payable		9,700				9,700						9,700
Unearned revenue		2,100	$ 900			1,200						1,200
Notes payable		12,000				12,000						12,000
Capital stock		30,000				30,000						30,000
Retained earnings, beg.		3,600				3,600				$3,600		
Revenue		37,700		900		38,600		$38,600				
Salaries expense	19,900		2,100		22,000		$22,000					
Advertising expense	6,800				6,800		6,800					
Fuel expense	4,300				4,300		4,300					
Legal expense	900				900		900					
Dividends	700				700				$ 700			
Depreciation expense			5,000		5,000		5,000					
Salaries payable				2,100		2,100						2,100
Interest expense			600		600		600					
Interest payable				600		600						600
	$105,100	$105,100	$8,600	$8,600	$112,800	$112,800	$39,600	$38,600				
Net loss								1,000	1,000			
							$39,600	$39,600	$1,700	$3,600		
Retained earnings, end.									1,900			1,900
									$3,600	$3,600	$72,500	$72,500

The Accounting Cycle and Closing Process

Reflecting on the accounting processes thus far described reveals the following typical steps:

- transactions are recorded in the journal

- journal entries are posted to appropriate ledger accounts

- a trial balance is constructed

- adjusting entries are prepared and posted

- an adjusted trial balance is prepared

- formal financial statements are produced (perhaps with the assistance of a worksheet)

It appears that the **accounting cycle** is completed by capturing transaction and event information and moving it through an orderly process that results in the production of useful financial statements. Importantly, one is left with substantial records that document each transaction (the journal) and each account's activity (the ledger). It is no wonder that the basic elements of this accounting methodology have endured for hundreds of years.

There remains one final process known as the **closing process**. Closing has two objectives:

OBJECTIVE 1: UPDATE RETAINED EARNINGS

Closing is a mechanism to update the Retained Earnings account in the ledger to equal the end-of-period balance. Keep in mind that the recording of revenues, expenses, and dividends do not automatically produce an updating debit or credit to Retained Earnings. As such, the beginning-of-period retained earnings amount remains in the ledger until the closing process "updates" the Retained Earnings account for the impact of the period's operations.

OBJECTIVE 2: RESET TEMPORARY ACCOUNTS

Revenues, expenses, and dividends represent amounts for a period of time; one must "zero out" these accounts at the end of each period (as a result, revenue, expense, and dividend accounts are called **temporary or nominal accounts**). In essence, by zeroing out these accounts, they are reset to begin the next accounting period. In contrast, asset, liability, and equity accounts are called **real accounts**, as their balances are carried forward from period to period. For example, one does not "start over" each period reaccumulating assets like cash and so on; their balances carry forward.

Closing involves a four-step process:

Closing Process
Step One: Close the Revenue account to a unique account called Income Summary, a non-financial statement account used only to facilitate the closing process
Step Two: Close expense accounts to Income Summary
Step Three: Close the Income Summary account to Retained Earnings
Step Four: Close the Dividends account to Retained Earnings

This process results in all revenues and expenses being "corralled" in **Income Summary** (the net of which represents the income or loss for the period). In turn, the income or loss is then swept to Retained Earnings along with the dividends. Recall that beginning retained earnings, plus income, less dividends, equals ending retained earnings; likewise, the closing process updates the beginning retained earnings to move forward to the end-of-period balance.

Following are the closing entries for England Tours for 20X3. Compare the accounts and amounts to those that appeared in the 20X3 adjusted trial balance:

12-31-X3	Revenues		32,800	
	Income Summary			32,800
	To close revenues to Income Summary			
12-31-X3	Income Summary		30,200	
	Salaries Expense			17,000
	Advertising Expense			5,000
	Fuel Expense			2,000
	Depreciation Expense			5,000
	Interest Expense			1,200
	To close expenses to Income Summary			
12-31-X3	Income Summary		2,600	
	Retained Earnings			2,600
	To close Income Summary to retained earnings (balance equals net income)			
12-31-X3	Retained Earnings		1,000	
	Dividends			1,000
	To close dividends			

The effect of the above entries is to update the Retained Earnings account and cause a zero balance to occur in the temporary accounts. The Income Summary account is also "zeroed" out ($32,800 (cr.) = $30,200 (dr.) + $2,600 (dr.)). The following T-accounts reveal the effects of the closing entries:

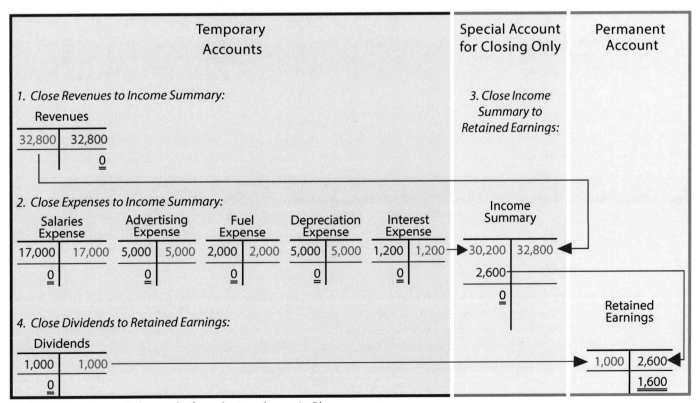

Balances before closing shown in Blue

POST CLOSING TRIAL BALANCE The **post-closing trial balance** reveals the balance of accounts after the closing process, and consists of balance sheet accounts only. The post-closing trial balance is a tool to demonstrate that accounts are in balance; it is not a formal financial statement. All of the revenue, expense, and dividend accounts were zeroed away via closing, and do not appear in the post-closing trial balance.

ENGLAND TOURS COMPANY Trial Balance December 31, 20X3	Debits	Credits
Cash	$15,500	
Accounts receivable	4,500	
Equipment	45,000	
Accumulated depreciation		$ 5,000
Accounts payable		4,000
Salaries payable		2,000
Interest payable		1,200
Notes payable		20,000
Unearned revenue		1,200
Capital stock		30,000
Retained earnings		1,600
	$65,000	$65,000

REVISITING SOFTWARE Many accounting software programs are based on database logic. These powerful tools allow the user to query with few restrictions. As such, one could request financial results for most any period of time (e.g., the 45 days ending October 15, 20XX), even if it related to a period several years ago. In these cases, the notion of closing the accounts becomes far less relevant. Very simply, the computer can mine all transaction data and pull out the accounts and amounts that relate to virtually any requested interval of time.

Reversing Entries

Reversing entries are optional accounting procedures which may sometimes prove useful in simplifying record keeping. A reversing entry is a journal entry to "undo" an adjusting entry. Consider the alternative sets of entries on the following page.

The first example does <u>not</u> utilize reversing entries. An adjusting entry was made to record $2,000 of accrued salaries at the end of 20X3. The next payday occurred on January 15, 20X4, when $5,000 was paid to employees. The entry on that date required a debit to Salaries Payable (for the $2,000 accrued at the end of 20X3) and Salaries Expense (for $3,000 earned by employees during 20X4).

The next example revisits the same facts using reversing entries. The adjusting entry in 20X3 to record $2,000 of accrued salaries is the same. However, the first journal entry of 20X4 simply reverses the adjusting entry. On the following payday, January 15, 20X5, the entire payment of $5,000 is recorded as expense.

Illustration Without Reversing Entries

20X3			
12-31-X3	Salaries Expense (20X3)	2,000	
	Salaries Payable		2,000
	Adjusting entry for accrued salaries due to employees at the end of December		
	Note: closing would "zero-out" all expense accounts at the end of 20X3		
20X4			
01-15-X4	Salaries Payable	2,000	
	Salaries Expense (20X4)	3,000	
	Cash		5,000
	To record payroll, part of which related to prior year service		

Illustration With Reversing Entries

20X3			
12-31-X3	Salaries Expense (20X3)	2,000	
	Salaries Payable		2,000
	Adjusting entry for accrued salaries due to employees at the end of December		
	Note: closing would "zero-out" all expense accounts at the end of 20X3		
20X4			
01-01-X4	Salaries Payable	2,000	
	Salaries Expense (20X4)		2,000
	Reversing entry for accrued salaries		
01-15-X4	Salaries Expense (20X4)	5,000	
	Cash		5,000
	To record payment of salaries		

The net impact with reversing entries still records the correct amount of salary expense for 20X4 ($2,000 credit and $5,000 debit, produces the correct $3,000 net debit to Salaries Expense). It may seem odd to credit an expense account on January 1, because, by itself, it makes no sense. The credit only makes sense when coupled with the subsequent debit on January 15. Notice from the following diagram that both approaches produce the same final results:

Without Reversing Entries: With Reversing Entries:

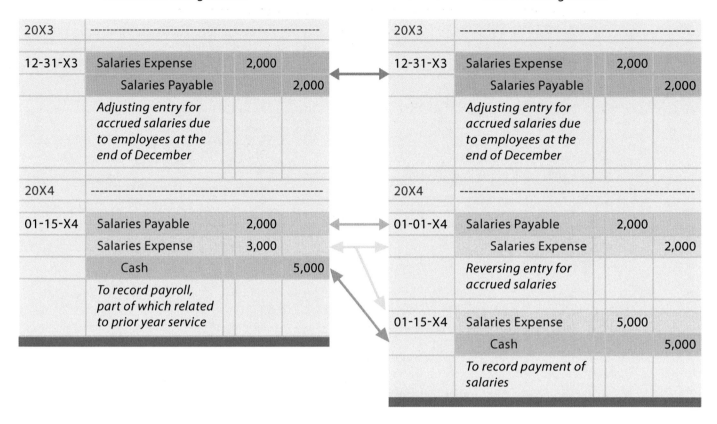

BY COMPARING THE <u>ACCOUNTS</u> AND <u>AMOUNTS</u>, NOTICE THAT THE SAME END RESULT IS PRODUCED!

In practice, reversing entries will simplify the accounting process. For example, on the first payday following the reversing entry, a "normal" journal entry can be made to record the full amount of salaries paid as expense. This eliminates the need to give special consideration to the impact of any prior adjusting entry.

Reversing entries would ordinarily be appropriate for those adjusting entries that involve the recording of accrued revenues and expenses; specifically, those that involve future cash flows. Importantly, whether reversing entries are used or not, the same result is achieved!

Classified Balance Sheets

The balance sheet reveals the assets, liabilities, and equity of a company. In examining a balance sheet, always be mindful that all components listed in a balance sheet are not necessarily at fair value. Some assets are carried at historical cost, and other assets are not reported at all (such as the value of a company's brand name, patents, and other internally developed resources). Nevertheless, careful examination of the balance sheet is essential to analysis of a company's overall financial condition. To facilitate proper analysis, accountants will often divide the balance sheet into categories or classifications. The result is that important groups of accounts can be identified and subtotaled. Such balance sheets are called "classified balance sheets."

ASSETS The asset side of the balance sheet may be divided into as many as five separate sections (when applicable): Current assets; Long-term investments; Property, plant, and equipment; Intangible assets; and Other assets. The contents of each category are determined based upon the following general rules:

- **Current Assets** include cash and those assets that will be converted into cash or consumed in a relatively short period of time; specifically, those assets that will be converted into cash or consumed within one year or the operating cycle, whichever is longer. The **operating cycle** for a particular company is the period of time it takes to convert cash back into cash (i.e., purchase inventory, sell the inventory on account, and collect the receivable); this is usually less than one year. In listing assets within the current section, the most liquid assets should be listed first (i.e., cash, short-term investments, and receivables). These are followed with inventories and prepaid expenses.

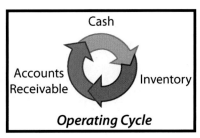

- **Long-term Investments** include land purchased for speculation, funds set aside for a plant expansion program, funds redeemable from insurance policies (e.g., cash surrender value of life insurance), and investments in other entities.

- **Property, Plant, & Equipment** includes the land, buildings, and equipment productively in use by the company.

- **Intangible Assets** lack physical existence, and include items like purchased patents and copyrights, "goodwill" (the amount by which the fair value of an acquired business exceeds that entity's identifiable net assets), rights under a franchise agreement, and similar items.

- **Other Assets** is the section used to report asset accounts that just don't seem to fit elsewhere, such as a special long-term receivable.

LIABILITIES

Just as the asset side of the balance sheet may be divided, so too for the liability section. The liability section is customarily divided into:

- **Current Liabilities** are those obligations that will be liquidated within one year or the operating cycle, whichever is longer. Normally, current liabilities are paid with current assets.

- **Long-term Liabilities** relate to any obligation that is not current, and include bank loans, mortgage notes, certain deferred taxes, and the like. Importantly, some long-term notes may be classified partially as a current liability and partially as a long-term liability. The portion classified as current would be the principal amount to be repaid within the next year (or operating cycle, if longer). Any amounts due after that period of time would be shown as a long-term liability.

EQUITY

The appropriate financial statement presentation for equity depends on the nature of the business organization for which it is prepared. Businesses generally may be organized as sole proprietorships, partnerships, or corporations. The illustrations in this book generally assume that the business is incorporated. Therefore, the equity section consists of:

- **Capital Stock** includes the amounts received from investors for the stock of the company. The investors become the owners of the company, and that ownership interest is represented by shares that can be transferred to others (without further involvement by the company). In actuality, the legalese of stock issues can become quite involved, and one is apt to encounter expanded capital stock related accounts (such as preferred stock, common stock, paid-in-capital in excess of par, and so on). Those advanced issues are covered in subsequent chapters.

- **Retained Earnings** should be familiar, representing the accumulated income less the dividends. In essence, it is the profit that has been retained and plowed back (reinvested) into expansion of the business.

CLASSY COMPANY Balance Sheet December 31, 20X3					
Assets			**Liabilities**		
Current assets			**Current liabilities**		
Cash	$100,000		Accounts payable	$ 80,000	
Short-term investments	50,000		Salaries payable	10,000	
Accounts receivable	75,000		Interest payable	15,000	
Inventories	200,000		Taxes payable	5,000	
Prepaid insurance	25,000	$450,000	Current portion of note	40,000	$150,000
Long-term investments			**Long-term liabilities**		
Stock investments	$ 40,000		Notes payable	$110,000	
Cash value of insurance	10,000	50,000	Bank loan	35,000	
			Mortgage obligation	75,000	
Property, plant, & equipment			Deferred income taxes	80,000	300,000
Land	$ 25,000		Total liabilities		$450,000
Buildings and equipment $150,000					
Less: Accum. depreciation (50,000)	100,000	125,000			
Intangible assets					
Goodwill		275,000	**Stockholders' equity**		
			Capital stock	$300,000	
Other assets			Retained earnings	160,000	
Receivable from employee		10,000	Total stockholders' equity		460,000
Total assets		$910,000	Total liabilities and equity		$910,000

OTHER ENTITY FORMS There is nothing that requires that a business activity be conducted through a corporation. A sole proprietorship is an enterprise owned by one person. If the preceding classified balance sheet illustration was instead being prepared for a sole proprietorship, it would look the same except that the equity section would consist of a single owner's capital account (instead of capital stock and retained earnings). If several persons are involved in a business that is not incorporated, it is likely a partnership. Again, the balance sheet would be unchanged except for the equity section; the equity section would be divided into separate accounts for each partner (representing each partner's residual interest in the business). Recent years have seen a spate of legislation creating variants of these entity forms (limited liability companies/LLC, limited liability partnerships/LLP, etc.), but the overall balance sheet structure is relatively unaffected. The terminology used to describe entity forms and equity capital structure also varies considerably around the world, but there is very little substantive difference in the underlying characteristics or the general appearance and content of the balance sheet.

Financial statements, by themselves, may not tell the whole story. Many important details about a company cannot be described in money on the balance sheet. Notes are used to describe accounting policies, major business events, pending lawsuits, and other facets of operation. The principle of **full disclosure** means that financial statements result in a fair presentation and that all facts which would influence investors' and creditors' judgments about the company are disclosed in the financial statements or related notes. Oftentimes, the notes will be more voluminous than the financial statements themselves.

NOTES TO THE FINANCIAL STATEMENTS

Business Liquidity and the Operating Cycle

Investors and creditors must be mindful of a company's liquidity. **Liquidity** is the ability of a firm to meet its near-term obligations as they come due. Inadequate liquidity can spell doom, even for a company with bright long-term prospects and significant noncash assets.

Working capital is the difference between current assets and current liabilities. The illustration for Classy Company revealed current assets of $450,000 and current liabilities of $150,000. Thus, working capital is $300,000 ($450,000 - $150,000). For obvious reasons, one would hope to find a positive amount of working capital. If not, it may be an indication of financial stress.

WORKING CAPITAL

Of course, care should be taken in drawing blanket conclusions about a firm's condition based solely upon an examination of a single number. Could a firm have negative working capital, and still be in great shape? Yes! For instance, the firm may have a standby letter of credit at a bank that enables it to borrow money as needed to meet near-term obligations. Or, some companies are in great shape even though they have negative working capital. Consider a fast food restaurant that has virtually no receivables (most sales are for cash) and a very low inventory (bread and milk don't store well). The only current assets may consist of cash, nominal inventories, and some prepaid items. Nevertheless, they may have current liabilities in the form of significant accounts payable and short-term debt. How do they survive? The velocity of their cash flow may be very fast, as they hopefully turn large volumes of business at high profit margins. This enables the spinning of enough free cash flow to pay obligations as they come due and have money left over to reinvest in growing other business locations. So, working capital is important to monitor. Just be careful about blanket conclusions based on any single measure.

Is $1,000,000 of working capital a lot? Maybe, maybe not. To a corporate giant, $1,000,000 is but a drop in the bucket and that amount of working capital could signal the end. On the other hand, a "mom and pop" business could be doing grand with far less than $1,000,000. So, it really depends on the ratio of current assets to current liabilities. The **current ratio** is used to express the relative amount of working capital. It is calculated by dividing current assets by current liabilities:

CURRENT RATIO

$$\textbf{Current Ratio} = \frac{\textbf{Current Assets}}{\textbf{Current Liabilities}}$$

Classy Company has a current ratio of 3:1 ($450,000/$150,000). Be advised that ratios can be manipulated. If Classy wished to increase its current ratio, it could just pay off a little debt. For instance, if it paid off $50,000 of accounts payable with cash, then current assets and current liabilities would each decline by $50,000, and the revised current ratio would "improve" to 4:1 (($450,000 -$50,000)/($150,000 - $50,000)).

A company could possess a large amount of inventory that is not easily sold. Thus, the current ratio (which includes inventory) could signal no problem, all the while the company is struggling to pay its bills. A tougher ratio is the **quick ratio**. This ratio provides a more stringent test of debt-paying ability by dividing only a firm's quick assets (cash, short-term investments, and accounts receivable) by current liabilities:

$$\text{Quick Ratio} = \frac{\text{(Cash + Short-term Investments + Accounts Receivable)}}{\text{Current Liabilities}}$$

Classy Company has a quick ratio of 1.5:1 (($100,000 + $50,000 + $75,000)/$150,000).

Chapter 4 Quiz

Q4-1. If the subtotal amounts in the income statement columns of a worksheet reveal debits in excess of credits, then which is indicated?

net income or net loss

Q4-2. The post-closing trial balance would consist of which account types?

income statement accounts or balance sheet accounts

Q4-3. Whether or not a company utilizes reversing entries, identical financial statements should be achieved.

right or wrong

Q4-4. Which should precede the other on a classified balance sheet?

long-term investments or property, plant, & equipment

Q4-5. If a company has a current ratio of 2, and then pays half of its current liabilities from current assets, the current ratio would become:

3 or 4

Fill in the Blanks

Q4-6. The _____ is a large columnar form that assists in the preparation of an entity's financial statements.

Q4-7. Amounts in the adjusted trial balance columns of the worksheet are extended to the _____, _____ or _____ columns of the worksheet.

Q4-8. The _____ account is used only in closing, and summarizes the net income or net loss of a business.

Q4-9. A _____ is the exact opposite of an adjusting entry.

Q4-10. Current assets should be listed on a balance sheet in order of _____.

Q4-11. Working capital is computed by subtracting _____ from _____.

Multiple Choice

Q4-12. The accountant's worksheet:

a. lays the groundwork for formal financial statement preparation.

b. is a fundamental financial statement.

c. provides details necessary for full disclosure and the preparation of footnotes.

d. is prepared at the end of each operating cycle.

Q4-13. After closing all revenue and expense accounts, Norris Company had a debit balance in its Income Summary account of $10,000. The proper entry to record the closing of the Income Summary account would be:

a. Revenue   10,000
     Income Summary   10,000

b. Retained Earnings   10,000
     Income Summary   10,000

c. Income Summary   10,000
     Retained Earnings   10,000

d. Income Summary   10,000
     Expenses   10,000

Q4-14. Which of the following statements about reversing entries is true?

a. Identical account balances are achieved in the subsequent accounting period whether reversing entries are utilized or not.

b. Reversing entries may not be used with accrued revenues.

c. Reversals are generally applied to those adjusting items that do not involve future cash flow.

d. Reversing entries would not be prepared if a company also utilized closing entries.

Q4-15. Shipman Company had accrued salaries of $300 on December 31. The company recorded reversing entries on the following January 1. On the next payday, January 7, the appropriate entry to record the payment of $1,000 in salaries should include:

a. a debit to Salaries Expense of $1,000.

b. a debit to Salaries Expense of $700.

c. a debit to Salaries Expense of $1,300.

d. a debit to Salaries Payable for $300.

Q4-16. On a classified balance sheet, the appropriate ordering of specific classifications is:

a. Current assets; long-term investments; property, plant, and equipment; intangible assets; other assets.

b. Current assets; property, plant, and equipment; long-term investments; intangible assets; other assets.

c. Current assets; intangible assets; property, plant, and equipment; long-term investments; other assets.

d. Current assets; other assets; long-term investments; intangible assets; property, plant, and equipment.

Chapter 4 Problems

Basic Problems

Preparation of an adjusted trial balance	*B-04.01*

Amber Nestor has an eye for quality. She recently formed an art gallery where she allows artists to display their artwork for sale. Customers buy the artwork through the gallery, but payments are actually made payable directly to the originating artist. Artists, in turn, pay Amber a 20% commission that is appropriately reflected as revenue of the gallery.

Following is Amber's trial balance after the first year of operation. This trial balance does not reflect the adjustments that are necessary, as described by the additional information.

AMBER NESTOR ART GALLERY Trial Balance As of December 31, 20X4		
	Debits	**Credits**
Cash	$18,400	
Supplies	6,790	
Display equipment	15,000	
Loan payable		$ 7,500
Capital stock		25,000
Revenues		48,590
Rent expense	11,000	
Salaries expense	24,000	
Interest expense	500	
Utilities expense	5,400	
	$81,090	$81,090

The Display equipment was purchased near the beginning of the year. It has a 3-year life and no salvage value. Its cost should be depreciated equally over its life.

Amber is entitled to receive $17,900 of commissions for art sold. This revenue has not yet been recorded, but it is fully expected that the artists will soon be making payment.

Supplies on hand at year end were counted, and amount to $3,400.

December's rent of $1,000 has not yet been paid.

(a)   Prepare the necessary adjusting entries as of December 31, 20X4.

(b)   Use T-accounts to determine the adjusted balances of the accounts.

(c)   Prepare the adjusted trial balance for Amber Nestor.

Reagan Sakai is in charge of financial management for Land Monitrix. Land Monitrix utilizes satellite technology and sophisticated mapping software to alert its customers to trespassing, illegal dumping, and other encroachments on property these customers own around the globe. Customers typically purchase one-year contracts for this service, and the pricing depends on the number and size of sites monitored.

SPREADSHEET TOOL:

Macros

Mr. Sakai desires to review financial reports -- an income statement, statement of retained earnings, and balance sheet. Prepare these reports from the following adjusted trial balance. Mr. Sakai needs this information for internal review purposes, and does not require a classified balance sheet. The operating data relate to the full year.

LAND MONITRIX CORPORATION Adjusted Trial Balance As of December 31, 20X5		
	Debits	**Credits**
Cash	$ 834,221	
Accounts receivable	345,909	
Prepaid expenses	45,787	
Supplies	66,665	
Satellite equipment	3,009,000	
Accumulated depreciation		$1,222,199
Accounts payable		544,190
Unearned revenues		455,000
Loan payable		1,000,000
Capital stock		560,000
Retained earnings, Jan. 1		228,892
Dividends	50,000	
Revenues		2,373,402
Selling expenses	476,445	
Interest expense	80,000	
Salaries expense	677,667	
Maintenance and supplies expense	222,989	
Depreciation expense	575,000	
	$6,383,683	$6,383,683

Utilize the following worksheet to prepare the income statement, statement of retained earnings, and balance sheet for Himarios Corporation. For this problem, you do not need to prepare a classified balance sheet.

HIMARIOS COMPANY
Worksheet to Prepare Financial Statements
December 31, 20X9

	Trial Balance Debit	Trial Balance Credit	Adjustments Debit	Adjustments Credit	Adjusted Trial Balance Debit	Adjusted Trial Balance Credit	Income Statement Debit	Income Statement Credit	Statement of Ret. Earnings Debit	Statement of Ret. Earnings Credit	Balance Sheet Debit	Balance Sheet Credit
Cash	$ 59,300				$ 59,300						$ 59,300	
Accounts receivable	12,371				12,371						12,371	
Equipment	60,000				60,000						60,000	
Accum. depreciation		$ 12,000		$ 4,000		$ 16,000						$ 16,000
Accounts payable		7,566				7,566						7,566
Unearned revenue		4,000	$ 1,500			2,500						2,500
Notes payable		25,000				25,000						25,000
Capital stock		50,000				50,000						50,000
Retained earnings, beg.		6,343				6,343				$ 6,343		
Service revenue		139,987		1,500		141,487		$141,487				
Salaries expense	108,425		4,300		112,725		$112,725					
Interest expense	2,100				2,100		2,100					
Dividends	2,700				2,700				$ 2,700			
Depreciation expense			4,000		4,000		4,000					
Salaries payable				4,300		4,300						4,300
Rent expense			2,500		2,500		2,500					
Rent payable				2,500		2,500						2,500
	$244,896	$244,896	$12,300	$12,300	$255,696	$255,696	$121,325	$141,487				
Net income							20,162			20,162		
							$141,487	$141,487	$ 2,700	$26,505		
Retained earnings, end.									23,805			23,805
									$26,505	$26,505	$131,671	$131,671

Some of the following accounts are real (permanent) accounts, and some are nominal (temporary) accounts. Identify each account as real or nominal.

Capital Stock	Unearned Revenues
Revenues	Income Summary
Accumulated Depreciation	Equipment
Salaries Expense	Prepaid Rent
Accounts Payable	Interest Payable
Dividends	Retained Earnings
Supplies	Loan Payable
Rent Expense	

Timber Creek prepared the following adjusted trial balance on December 31, 20X3. The company has completed preparation of financial statements and is now ready to prepare closing entries.

TIMBER CREEK Adjusted Trial Balance As of December 31, 20X3		
	Debits	Credits
Cash	$ 35,600	
Accounts receivable	23,700	
Supplies	7,500	
Equipment	325,700	
Accumulated depreciation		$ 40,400
Accounts payable		34,800
Loan payable		100,000
Capital stock		80,000
Retained earnings		70,000
Dividends	20,000	
Revenues		478,400
Rent expense	120,000	
Salaries expense	235,600	
Supplies expense	18,000	
Interest expense	7,400	
Depreciation expense	10,100	
	$803,600	$803,600

(a) Prepare the necessary closing entries.

(b) Use T-accounts to determine the post-closing balances of the accounts.

(c) Prepare the post-closing trial balance.

Flowcharts are often used to document business activity. Rectangles represent "processes" and "documents" are represented by the boxes with a rolling bottom. Rearrange the following flowchart shapes into the correct order, and connect with arrows as appropriate.

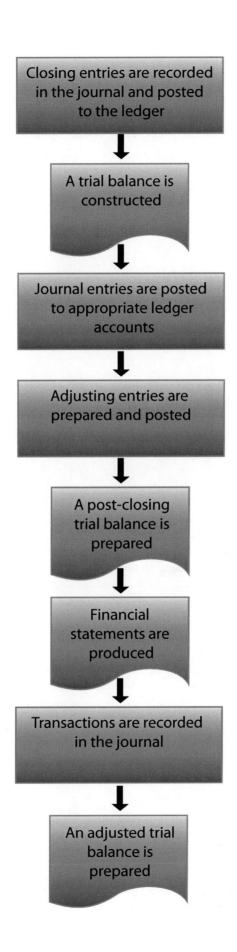

Closing entries are recorded in the journal and posted to the ledger

A trial balance is constructed

Journal entries are posted to appropriate ledger accounts

Adjusting entries are prepared and posted

A post-closing trial balance is prepared

Financial statements are produced

Transactions are recorded in the journal

An adjusted trial balance is prepared

Traditions is an upscale university housing complex providing all the amenities of private townhouse living, and a full service 24-hour cafeteria for busy students. Prior to recording any adjusting entries for 20X4, Traditions has incurred and recorded total salary expense of $875,000 and total rental revenue of $4,800,000.

As of December 31, 20X4, the company owes $15,000 of additional salaries to employees, and accrued rent due from residents amounts to $100,000.

On January 10, 20X5, Traditions paid salaries of $40,000 covering the amount due as of December 31, as well as additional amounts relating to 20X5.

On January 15, 20X5, Traditions received rental payments for $250,0000 covering the rents due as of December 31, 20X4, and additional amounts relating to the first half of January, 20X5.

(a)   Prepare the necessary year-end adjusting entries for salaries and rent.

(b)   Determine the total salaries expense and total rent revenue for 20X4.

(c)   Assuming the company uses reversing entries, prepare necessary reversals for early 20X5.

(d)   Assuming the company used reversing entries, prepare entries for January 10 and 15, 20X5.

(e)   Assuming the company does not use reversing entries, prepare entries for January 10 and 15, 20X5.

(f)   Show how 20X5 salaries expense and rent revenue will be the same, whether reversing entries are used or not.

Liz Ross Corporation prepares a classified balance sheet that includes the following traditional sections:

Current Assets	Other Assets
Long-term Investments	Current Liabilities
Property, Plant & Equipment	Long-term Liabilities
Intangibles	Stockholders' Equity

In which section of the classified balance sheet would the following accounts appear? Some of the accounts may not appear in the balance sheet.

Note Payable (due in 3 months)	Retained Earnings (ending)
Accumulated Depreciation	Rent Expense
Investment in Government Bonds	Unearned Revenues
Accounts Receivable	Income Summary

Accounts Payable	Equipment
Long-term Receivable From Employee	Revenues
Dividends	Prepaid Rent
Capital Stock	Interest Payable
Patent	Retained Earnings (beginning)
Supplies	Loan Payable (due in 5 years)

Current and quick ratios   *B-04.09*

Nkululeko J. Ntshanga owns a manganese ore mining business in South Africa. He is interested in attracting additional investors to obtain financing for planned expansion. Some potential investors have expressed a concern that money is really being sought to address liquidity problems being faced by Nkululeko's company.

To alleviate this concern Nkululeko provided the following complete list of assets and liabilities of the company. The currency unit is the South African Rand. Use this information to determine the company's current assets, current liabilities, working capital, current ratio, and quick ratio. Based on your calculations, does it appear that the company is experiencing liquidity problems?

Accumulated Depreciation	R 4,569,000
Prepaid Rent	45,800
Note Payable (due in 3 months)	100,000
Accounts Receivable	468,000
Accounts Payable	255,000
Patent	3,000,000
Cash	790,000
Supplies	134,800
Unearned Revenues	133,000
Equipment	8,777,600
Interest Payable	45,000
Loan Payable (due in 3 years)	1,500,000

Involved Problems

Berry Corporation prepared the following preliminary trial balance. The trial balance and other information was evaluated by Delton Wiser, CPA. Delton has returned a list of proposed adjustments that are necessary to facilitate preparation of correct financial statements for the year ending December 31, 20X3.

BERRY CORPORATION Trial Balance December 31, 20X3		
	Debits	**Credits**
Cash	$ 30,540	
Accounts receivable	45,000	
Supplies	7,000	
Equipment	244,500	
Accumulated depreciation		$ 46,500
Accounts payable		12,700
Unearned revenue		31,250
Notes payable		80,000
Capital stock		100,000
Retained earnings, Jan. 1		63,200
Dividends	12,000	
Revenues		289,800
Wages expense	214,600	
Utilities expense	8,700	
Selling expense	41,610	
Depreciation expense	12,000	
Interest expense	7,500	
	$623,450	$623,450

Delton discovered that 40% of the unearned revenue appearing in the trial balance had actually been earned as of the end of the year.

A physical count of supplies on hand revealed a year-end balance of only $3,000.

Unpaid and unrecorded invoices for utilities for December amounted to $1,500.

The last payday was December 26. Employees are owed an additional $3,900 that has not been recorded.

Additional depreciation of $3,100 needs to be recorded.

(a) Prepare journal entries relating to the adjustments.

(b) Prepare an adjusted trial balance.

(c) Prepare an income statement and statement of retained earnings for 20X3, and a classified balance sheet as of the end of the year.

(d) Berry's bookkeeper argued with Delton that there was no need to record the adjustments since they have no "net" effect on income. Evaluate whether this observation is true or false, and comment on the appropriateness of this logic.

| Analysis of adjustments by review of trial balances | I-04.02 |

Examine the following trial balances, before and after adjustment:

CHESTERFIELD CORPORATION
Trial Balance and Adjusted Trial Balance
December 31, 20X9

	Trial Balance		Adjusted Trial Balance	
	Debits	**Credits**	**Debits**	**Credits**
Cash	$166,890		$166,890	
Accounts receivable	87,654		107,654	
Supplies	8,992		4,500	
Prepaid rent	6,000		2,000	
Equipment	145,700		145,700	
Accumulated depreciation		$ 37,660		$ 44,660
Accounts payable		13,590		13,590
Wages payable				4,500
Interest payable				1,500
Unearned revenue		18,000		12,000
Notes payable		50,000		50,000
Capital stock		225,000		225,000
Retained earnings, Jan. 1		89,119		89,119
Dividends	40,000		40,000	
Revenues		334,490		360,490
Wages expense	276,123		280,623	
Rent expense	33,000		37,000	
Depreciation expense			7,000	
Supplies expense			4,492	
Interest expense	3,500		5,000	
	$767,859	$767,859	$800,859	$800,859

(a) Determine and record the apparent adjusting entries in journal entry format.

(b) Prepare an income statement for the year ending December 31, 20X9.

(c) Prepare a statement of retained earnings for the year ending December 31, 20X9.

(d) Prepare a classified balance sheet as of December 31, 20X9.

Wild River Rafting provides guided tours of the Rattlesnake River. Most of the company's business activity occurs during the summer season, so the company ends its fiscal year on August 31. Below is the unadjusted trial balance for the year. It is followed by information about necessary adjusting entries.

WILD RIVER RAFTING CORPORATION		
Trial Balance		
August 31, 20X5		
	Debits	**Credits**
Cash	$ 20,700	
Prepaid license	10,000	
Equipment	167,500	
Accumulated depreciation		$ 48,900
Accounts payable		3,100
Loan payable		65,000
Capital stock		55,000
Retained earnings (beginning)		13,200
Dividends	5,000	
Revenues		414,900
Wages expense	303,000	
Advertising expense	42,200	
Bus expense	21,700	
Insurance expense	30,000	
	$600,100	$600,100

The company has not recorded depreciation of $12,000 on rafting equipment.

The prepaid license granted access to the Rattlesnake during 20X5, and is now expired.

The company hires a shuttle bus company. The billing for August amounted to $6,600 and has not been paid or recorded.

The loan has accrued interest of $2,000 that is now due.

(a)   Prepare a worksheet incorporating the necessary adjustments.

(b)   Prepare an income statement and statement of retained earnings for fiscal year 20X5, and a balance sheet as of August 31, 20X5.

(c)   Evaluate the company's financial results, and comment on the dividend.

Auditors frequently discover errors relating to recording and adjusting journal entries, and they must be able to clearly explain the necessary corrections to their clients in a nonconfrontational fashion.

The partners at the audit firm of Kumar & Kumar routinely request feedback from clients at the close of an audit, and have been getting some negative feedback. The comments include "staff lacks diplomacy when pointing out errors" and "inability to clearly explain proposed adjustments."

Karthick Praveen is an audit manager with the firm of Kumar & Kumar, and has been tasked with preparing a training seminar for new staff in how to prepare and present proposed adjustments. Karthick developed the following six illustrations:

ITEM #1

Date	Accounts	Debits	Credits
06-30	Supplies Expense	10,000	
	Cash		10,000
	Purchased computers with a three-year life and no salvage value		

ITEM #2

Date	Accounts	Debits	Credits
04-15	Cash	10,000	
	Revenues		10,000
	Collected customer deposits for future services		
12-31	Revenues	2,500	
	Unearned Revenues		2,500
	Completion of 25% of services provided under Apr. 15 agreement		

ITEM #3

Date	Accounts	Debits	Credits
09-30	Prepaid Insurance	3,000	
	Insurance Expense		3,000
	Purchased for cash a 1-year insurance policy; coverage commences on Oct. 1		

ITEM #4

Date	Accounts	Debits	Credits
01-04	Wages Expense	2,400	
	Cash		2,400
	Paid wages, $1,000 of which was properly accrued at the end of the prior year		

ITEM #5			
Date	**Accounts**	**Debits**	**Credits**
08-01	Advertising Expense	9,000	
	Cash		9,000
	Purchased a 9-month advertising campaign from a local newspaper running from Sept. 1 to May 30		

ITEM #6			
Date	**Accounts**	**Debits**	**Credits**
12-31	Utilities Expense	2,500	
	Utilities Payable		250
	Recorded $2,500 of estimated utilities cost for December		

Divide your class into six teams. Each team is to prepare the necessary adjusting/correcting entry(ies) related to one of the errors and present their solution to the class as though they are auditors making a presentation to their client. For each error, assume that your corrections are as of the calendar year end. Unless shown, assume that no additional entries were recorded during the year related to the item in question.

The goal will be diplomacy and clarity of explanation. At the end of each presentation, by show of hands, measure how many classmates believe the team was able to effectively and correctly explain their proposed correction. At the conclusion of the presentations, discuss elements that went well or poorly.

I-04.05   *The complete accounting cycle*

On January 1, 20X7, Jacqueline Fernandez formed a corporation to purchase wheat harvesting equipment and provide contract support services to farmers throughout the Midwest. Information about the first year of operation follows:

Jan. 1   Investors provided $2,500,000 of cash in exchange for stock of Fernandez Corporation

Jan. 1   Purchased combines and trucks in exchange for $1,000,000 cash and a $3,000,000 note payable

Feb. 7   Purchased $40,000 of supplies on account that will be needed during the upcoming harvest

Mar. 3   Paid wages of $65,400

Apr. 1   Billed customers for services in the amount of $230,000

Apr. 11   Paid $30,000 toward the purchase of February 7

May 1   Purchased a $24,000 insurance policy, recorded as prepaid insurance

June 6   Collected $210,000 on accounts receivable

June 9   Paid wages of $130,600

June 15   Paid $30,200 for fuel costs

June 20   Paid $12,500 for lodging costs incurred by crew

June 30   Paid $120,000 of interest and $80,000 to reduce the balance of the note payable

Aug. 1 Billed customers for services provided in the amount of $812,000

Sept. 3 Collected $715,000 on accounts receivable

Sept. 16 Purchased $25,000 of supplies on account

Sept. 25 Paid $61,200 for fuel costs

Oct. 20 Paid $8,100 for lodging costs incurred by crew

Nov. 3 Paid wages of $125,900

Dec. 15 Collected $100,000 as deposits from customers who contracted for 20X8 harvesting services

Dec. 31 Declared and paid a $25,000 dividend to shareholders

Fernandez Corporation uses the following accounts:

Cash	Retained Earnings
Accounts Receivable	Dividends
Supplies	Revenues
Prepaid Insurance	Wage Expense
Equipment	Fuel Expense
Accumulated Depreciation	Lodging Expense
Accounts Payable	Insurance Expense
Interest Payable	Supplies Expense
Unearned Revenue	Interest Expense
Notes Payable	Depreciation Expense
Capital Stock	Income Summary

(a) Journalize the listed transactions.

(b) Post the transactions to the appropriate general ledger accounts.

(c) Prepare a trial balance as of December 31.

(d) Journalize and post adjusting entries based on the following additional information.

> The equipment had 25-year life, with no salvage value.
>
> Supplies on hand at year end amount to $20,000.
>
> At year end, $115,000 of additional interest is due on the note payable.
>
> The insurance policy covered a 12-month period commencing on May 1.
>
> At year end, Fernandez had provided $30,000 of unbilled services to customers. These services will be billed in early 20X8.

(e) Prepare an adjusted trial balance as of December 31.

(f) Prepare an income statement and statement of retained earnings for 20X7, and a classified balance sheet as of the end of the year.

(g) Journalize and post closing entries.

(h) Prepare a post-closing trial balance as of December 31.

Classified balance sheet

Use this randomly arranged data to prepare a classified balance sheet for Imamani Corporation as of December 31, 20X5. Some of the accounts do not belong in the balance sheet, and 20% of the loan payable matures each June 30.

Capital stock	$ 755,000
Patent	275,000
Accumulated depreciation (equipment)	(477,654)
Building	1,990,776
Land held for speculation	156,098
Dividends	50,000
Cash	182,345
Retained earnings	646,992
Accounts receivable	56,766
Accounts payable	78,011
Income tax expense	123,334
Prepaid insurance	3,883
Accumulated depreciation (building)	(988,777)
Loan payable	1,000,000
Equipment	887,885
Land	278,790
Interest payable	31,117
Inventories	121,008
Cash value of life insurance	25,000

Current and quick ratios from annual reports

Identify three companies with shares of stock that are publicly traded on an organized stock exchange. Obtain their most recent annual reports.

For U.S. companies, those reports are required to be filed with the Securities and Exchange Commission (SEC). The annual filing is known as the 10-K. The SEC website allows you to readily search for and download the filings of specific companies. As an alternative, it has become common practice for public companies to have an investor relations section on their own websites, with links to annual reports.

Using the information included in the balance sheet of the annual report, calculate each company's working capital, current ratio, and quick ratio. Evaluate your calculations and discuss implications.

Frequently, management will comment on liquidity in the MD&A (management's discussion and analysis) section of the annual SEC filing. Is the MD&A discussion consistent with your observations?

Chapter 5:
Special Issues for Merchants

Goals:

Merchandising businesses and related sales recognition issues.
Purchase recognition issues for the merchandising business.
An alternative inventory system: The perpetual method.
Enhancements of the income statement.
The control structure.

principlesofaccounting.com

The discussions in earlier chapters were all based on service businesses like law firms and architects. Service businesses are a large component of an advanced economy. However, a lot of money is also spent in stores or on the internet. Such businesses are generally referred to as "merchants," and their goal is to purchase inventory and resell it at a higher price to customers. This chapter focuses on the merchandising business, where measuring income involves unique considerations, like the computation and presentation of an amount called "gross profit."

Gross profit is the difference between sales and cost of goods sold and is reported on the income statement as an intermediate amount. Observe the income statement for Chair Depot to the right. The gross profit number indicates that the company is selling merchandise for more than cost. The company also incurred other **operating expenses** in the course of business. The presentation of gross profit is important for users of the financial statements. If the gross profit rate is small, the business might have trouble making a profit, even if sales improved. The reverse is true if the gross profit rate is strong; improved sales can markedly improve the bottom-line net income (especially if operating expenses do not change)! Separating gross profit from other components is an important part of reporting.

CHAIR DEPOT Income Statement For the Year Ending December 31, 20X3		
Sales		$200,000
Cost of goods sold		120,000
Gross profit		$ 80,000
Operating expenses		
Advertising	$6,000	
Salaries	9,000	
Rent	5,000	20,000
Net income		$ 60,000

The Sales account is a revenue account used to record sales of merchandise. Sales are initially recorded via one of the following entries, depending on whether the sale is for cash or is a sale on account:

01-05-X5	Cash		4,000	
	Sales			4,000
	Sold merchandise for cash			
01-06-X5	Accounts Receivable		6,000	
	Sales			6,000
	Sold merchandise on account			

SALES RETURNS AND ALLOWANCES

Occasionally, a customer returns merchandise. When that occurs, the following entry should be made:

01-09-X5	Sales Returns and Allowances		1,000	
	Accounts Receivable			1,000
	Customer returned merchandise previously purchased on account			

Notice that the above entry included a debit to Sales Returns and Allowances (rather than canceling the sale). The Sales Returns and Allowances account is a contra-revenue account that is deducted from sales. The calculation of sales less sales returns and allowances is sometimes called "net sales." This approach allows interested parties to easily track the level of sales returns in relation to overall sales. Important information is revealed about the relative level of returns, thereby providing a measure of customer satisfaction or dissatisfaction. Sales returns (on account) are typically documented by the creation of an instrument known as a **credit memorandum**. The credit memorandum indicates that a customer's Account Receivable balance has been credited (reduced) and that payment for the returned goods is not expected. If the transaction involved a cash refund, the only difference in the entry would involve a credit to Cash instead of Accounts Receivable. The calculation of net sales would be unaffected.

The following income statement provides an example showing the presentation of net sales:

CHAIR DEPOT Income Statement For the Year Ending December 31, 20X3		
Sales		$200,000
Less: Sales returns and allowances		10,000
Net sales		$190,000
Cost of goods sold		114,000
Gross profit		$ 76,000
Expenses		
Advertising	$6,000	
Salaries	9,000	
Rent	5,000	20,000
Net income		$ 56,000

Note the use of the word "allowances" in the account title "Sales Returns and Allowances." What is the difference between a return and an allowance? Perhaps a customer's reason for wishing to return an item is because of a minor defect; the customer may be willing to keep the item if the price is reduced. The merchant may give an allowance to induce the customer not to return the item. The entry to record the allowance would ordinarily involve the same accounts as those previously illustrated for the return. However, one could use a separate account for returns and another for allowances.

TRADE DISCOUNTS

Product catalogs often provide a **list price** for an item. Those list prices may bear little relation to the ultimate selling price. A merchant may offer customers a trade discount that involves a reduction from list price. Ultimately, the purchaser is responsible for the **invoice price**, that is, the list price less the negotiated **trade discount**. Trade discounts are not entered in the accounting records. They are not considered to be a part of the sale because the exchange agreement was based on the reduced price.

Remember the general rule that sales are recorded when an exchange takes place. Because the measurement of the sale is based on the exchange price, the amount recorded as a sale is the invoice price. The entries previously shown for a $4,000 sale would also be appropriate if the list price was $5,000, subject to a 20% trade discount.

CREDIT CARDS

In the retail trade, merchants often issue credit cards. Why? Because they induce people to spend, and interest charges that may be assessed can themselves provide a generous source of additional revenue. However, these company-issued cards introduce added costs: customers that don't pay (known as bad debts), maintenance of a credit department, periodic billings, and so forth.

To avoid these issues, many merchants accept other forms of credit cards like Visa and MasterCard. When a merchant accepts these cards, they are usually paid instantly by the credit card company (net of a service charge that is negotiated in the general range of 1% to 3% of the sale). The subsequent billing and collection is handled by the credit card company. Many merchants will record the full amount of the sale as revenue, and then recognize an offsetting expense for the amount charged by the credit card companies.

CASH DISCOUNTS/ SALES DISCOUNTS

Merchants often sell to other businesses. Assume that Barber Shop Supply Company sells equipment and supplies to various barber shops on open account. An open account is a standing agreement to extend credit for purchases. In these settings, the seller would like to be paid promptly after billing and may encourage prompt payment by offering a **cash discount** (also known as a **sales discount**).

To be entitled to the cash discount, the buyer must pay the invoice promptly. The amount of time one has available to pay is expressed in a unique manner, such as 2/10, n/30. These terms mean that a 2% discount is available if the purchaser pays the invoice within 10 days; otherwise, the net amount is expected to be paid within 30 days. Assume that Barber Shop Supply Company sold goods for $1,000, subject to terms of 2/10, n/30. The following entry would be recorded at the time of sale:

05-11-X4	Accounts Receivable	1,000	
	Sales		1,000
	Sold merchandise on account, terms 2/10, n/30		

The invoice that would be issued by Barber Shop Supply follows. Take special note of the invoice date, terms, and invoice amount.

BARBER SHOP SUPPLY
987 Industrial Blvd., Chicago, IL 12345

Bill To: Tomas Mueller

Invoice #88765

Hair Port Landing
111 Style Lane, Suite 15
Dallas, TX 99889

P.O. NUMBER	INVOICE DATE	F.O.B. POINT	TERMS
66554f8	MAY 11, 20X4	Dallas	2/10, n/30

QTY.	PART #	DESCRIPTION	UNIT PRICE	TOTAL
4	A7786	Full Length Mirrors	$ 90	$ 360
1	C8876	Swivel Chair -- Brown Leather	370	370
1	M8776	Barber Pole Motor and Light Kit	140	140
4	T8870	Black Floor Mats	20	80
1	V9076	Small Shop Vacuum	50	50
			Subtotal	$1,000
			Freight	-
	THANK YOU FOR YOUR BUSINESS!		TOTAL	$1,000

If Hair Port Landing pays the invoice in time to receive the discount, a check for $980 would be received by Barber Shop Supply:

Hair Port Landing
111 Style Lane, Suite 15
Dallas, TX 99889

Date: May 19, 20X4

Pay to the order of: BARBER SHOP SUPPLY $980.00

********* NINE-HUNDRED EIGHTY AND NO/100 DOLLARS*************************

First Corner Bank

MEMO   Invoice #88765

Tomas Mueller

The following entry reflects that the customer took advantage of the discount by paying within the 10-day window. Notice that the entry reduces Accounts Receivable for the full invoice amount because the payment satisfied the total obligation. The discount is recognized in a special Sales Discounts account, which is subtracted in calculating net sales (similar to Sales Returns and Allowance).

05-19-X4	Cash	980	
	Sales Discounts	20	
	Accounts Receivable		1,000
	Collected outstanding receivable within discount period, 2% discount granted		

If the customer pays too late to get the discount, then the payment received should be for the full invoice amount, and it would be recorded as follows:

05-29-X4	Cash	1,000	
	Accounts Receivable		1,000
	Collected outstanding receivable outside of the discount period		

Having looked at several of the important and unique issues for recognizing sales transactions of merchandising businesses, it is now time to turn to the accounting for purchasing activities.

Purchase Considerations for Merchandising Businesses

A quick stroll through most any retail store will reveal a substantial investment in **inventory**. Even if a merchant is selling goods at a healthy profit, financial difficulties can creep up if a large part of the inventory remains unsold for a long period of time. Goods go out of style, become obsolete, and so forth. Therefore, a prudent business manager will pay very close attention to inventory content and level. There are many detailed accounting issues that pertain to inventory, and a separate chapter is devoted exclusively to inventory issues. This chapter's introduction is brief, focusing on elements of measurement that are unique to the merchant's accounting for the basic cost of goods.

INVENTORY ACQUISITION

The first phase of the merchandising cycle occurs when the merchant acquires goods to be stocked for resale to customers. The appropriate accounting for this action requires the recording of the purchase. There are two different techniques for recording the purchase; a periodic system or a perpetual system. Generally, the **periodic inventory system** is easier to implement but is less robust than the "real-time" tracking available under a perpetual system. Conversely, the **perpetual inventory system** involves more constant data update and is a far superior business management tool. The following presentation begins with a close examination of the periodic system. Later in the chapter the perpetual system will be described.

PERIODIC INVENTORY SYSTEM

When a purchase occurs and a periodic inventory system is in use, the merchant should record the transaction via the following entry:

07-07-X1	Purchases	3,000	
	Accounts Payable		3,000
	Purchased inventory on account		

The Purchases account is unique to the periodic system. The Purchases account is not an expense or asset, per se. Instead, the account's balance represents total inventory purchased during a period, and this amount must ultimately be apportioned between cost of goods sold on the income statement and inventory on the balance sheet. The apportionment is based upon how much of the purchased goods are resold versus how much remains in ending inventory. Soon, the accounting mechanics of how this occurs will be shown. But, for the moment, simply focus on the concepts portrayed by the following graphic:

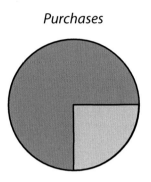
Purchases

Income Statement — Cost of Goods Sold

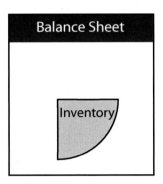
Balance Sheet — Inventory

PURCHASE RETURNS AND ALLOWANCES

Recall the earlier discussion of *sales* returns and allowances. Now examine how a *purchaser* of inventory would handle a return to its vendor/supplier. First, it is a common business practice to contact the supplier before returning goods. Unlike the retail trade, transactions between businesses are not so easily undone. A supplier may require that a customer first obtain an "RMA" or "Return Merchandise Authorization." This indicates a willingness on the part of the supplier to accept the return. When the merchandise is returned to a supplier, a **debit memorandum** may be prepared to indicate that the purchaser is to debit their Accounts Payable account; the corresponding credit is to Purchases Returns and Allowances:

07-19-X1	Accounts Payable	1,000	
	Purchase Returns and Allowances		1,000
	To record return of defective inventory to vendor		

Purchase returns and allowances are subtracted from purchases to calculate the amount of net purchases for a period. The specific calculation of net purchases will be demonstrated after a few more concepts are introduced.

CASH DISCOUNTS/ PURCHASE DISCOUNTS

Recall the previous discussion of cash discounts (sometimes called **purchase discounts** from the purchaser's perspective). Discounts are typically very favorable to the purchaser, as they are designed to encourage early payment. Discount terms vary considerably. Here are some examples:

- 1/15, n/30 -- 1% if paid within 15 days, net due in 30 days

- 1/10, n/eom -- 1% if paid within 10 days, net due end of month

- .5/10, n/60 -- ½% if paid within 10 days, net due in 60 days

While discounts may seem slight, they can represent substantial savings and should usually be taken. Consider the following calendar, assuming a purchase was made on May 31, terms 2/10, n/30. The discount can be taken if payment is made within the "blue shaded" days. The discount cannot be taken during the "yellow shaded" days (of which there are twenty). The bill becomes past due during the "purple shaded" days. What is important to note here is that skipping past the discount period will only achieve a twenty-day deferral of the payment. Consider that a 2% return is "earned" by paying 20 days early. This is indeed a large savings. There are approximately 18 twenty-day periods in a year (365/20), and, at 2% per twenty-day period, this equates to over a 36% annual interest rate equivalent.

			June			
Sunday	Monday	Tuesday	Wednesday	Thursday	Friday	Saturday
May 31 Date of Purchase	1	2	3	4	5	6
7	8	9	10 Last Date for Discount	11	12	13
14	15	16	17	18	19	20
21	22	23	24	25	26	27
28	29	30 Due Date	*July* 1 Past Due	2	3	4

A business should set up its accounting system to timely process, and take advantage of, all reasonable discounts. In a small business setting, this might entail using a system where invoices are filed for payment to match the discount dates. A larger company will usually have an automated payment system where checks are scheduled to process concurrent with invoice discount dates. Very large payments, and global payments, are frequently processed as "wire transfers." This method enables the purchaser to retain use of funds (and the ability to generate investment income on those funds) until the very last minute. This is considered to be a good business practice.

Many vendors will accept a "discounted payment" outside of the discount period. In other words, a purchaser might wait 30, 60, or 90 days and still take the discount! Some vendors are glad to receive the payment and will still grant credit for the discount. Others will return the payment and insist on the full amount due. Is it a good business practice to "bend the terms" of the agreement to take a discount when the supplier will stand for this practice? Is it ethical to "bend the terms" of the agreement? Are these two questions really one and the same?

A fundamental accounting issue is how to account for purchase transactions when discounts are offered. One technique is the **gross method** of recording purchases. This technique records purchases at their total gross or full invoice amount:

GROSS METHOD

11-05-X7	Purchases		5,000	
	Accounts Payable			5,000
	Purchased inventory on account, terms 2/10, n/30			

If payment is made *within* the discount period, the purchase discount is recognized in a separate account. The Purchase Discounts account is similar to Purchases Returns & Allowances, as it is deducted from total purchases to calculate the net purchases for the period:

11-13-X7	Accounts Payable	5,000	
	Purchase Discounts		100
	Cash		4,900
	Paid outstanding payable within discount period, discount taken ($5,000 X 2% = $100)		

If payment is made outside the discount period, the purchaser loses the right to take a discount. Therefore, the full amount of the invoice becomes due and payable. The following entry would be needed to reflect this payment:

11-29-X7	Accounts Payable	5,000	
	Cash		5,000
	Paid outstanding payable outside of the discount period		

NET METHOD Rather than recording purchases under the gross method, a company may elect to record the purchase and payment under a **net method**. With this technique, the initial purchase is again recorded by debiting Purchases and crediting Accounts Payable. However, the amount of the entry is for the invoice amount of the purchase, less the anticipated discount. Assuming the company intends to take the discount, this entry results in recording the net anticipated payment into the accounts.

11-05-X7	Purchases	4,900	
	Accounts Payable		4,900
	Purchased $5,000 of inventory on account, terms 2/10, n/30		

If payment is made *within* the discount period, the entry is quite straightforward because the payable was initially established at the net of discount amount:

11-13-X7	Accounts Payable	4,900	
	Cash		4,900
	Paid accounts payable within discount period		

If payment is made *outside* the discount period, the lost discounts are recorded in a separate account. The Purchase Discounts Lost account is debited to reflect the added cost associated with missing out on the available discount amount:

11-29-X7	Accounts Payable	4,900	
	Purchase Discounts Lost	100	
	Cash		5,000
	Paid outstanding payable outside of the discount period		

In evaluating the gross and net methods, notice that the Purchase Discounts Lost account (used only with the net method) indicates the total amount of discounts missed during a particular period. The presence of this account draws attention to the fact that discounts are not being taken, frequently an unfavorable situation. The Purchase Discounts account (used only with the gross method) identifies the amount of discounts taken, but does not indicate discounts missed, if any. For reporting purposes, purchases discounts are subtracted from purchases to arrive at net purchases, while purchases discounts lost are recorded as an expense following the gross profit number for a particular period.

The following illustration contrasts the gross and net methods for a case where the discount is taken. Notice that $4,900 is accounted for under each method. The gross method reports the $5,000 gross purchase, less the applicable discount. In contrast, the net method only shows the $4,900 purchase amount.

Gross	
Purchases	$5,000
Less: Purchase discounts	100
	$4,900

VS.

Net	
Purchases	$4,900
Plus: Purchase discounts lost	0
	$4,900

The next illustration contrasts the gross and net methods for the case where the discount is lost. Notice that $5,000 is accounted for under each method. The gross method simply reports the $5,000 gross purchase, without any discount. In contrast, the net method shows purchases of $4,900 and an additional $100 expense pertaining to lost discounts.

Gross	
Purchases	$5,000
Less: Purchase discounts	0
	$5,000

VS.

Net	
Purchases	$4,900
Plus: Purchase discounts lost	100
	$5,000

A potentially significant inventory-related cost pertains to freight. The importance of considering this cost in any business transaction is critical. The globalization of commerce, rising energy costs, and the increasing use of overnight delivery via more expensive air transportation all contribute to high freight costs. Freight costs can easily exceed 10% of the value of a transaction. As a result, business negotiations relate not only to matters of product cost, but must also include consideration of freight terms.

Freight agreements are often described by abbreviations that describe the place of delivery, when the risk of loss shifts from the seller to the buyer, and who is to be responsible for the cost of shipping. One very popular abbreviation is F.O.B., which stands for "free on board." Its historical origin related to a seller's duty to place goods on a shipping vessel without charge to the buyer.

International commercial terms ("incoterms") and abbreviations (e.g., FCA, DDU, etc.) have been developed by the International Chamber of Commerce. As a result, great care should be taken to understand the specific nature of various freight agreements that occur in global commerce.

In the U.S., the F.O.B. point is normally understood to represent the place where ownership of goods transfers. Along with shifting ownership comes the responsibility for the purchaser to assume the risk of loss, pay for the goods, and pay freight costs beyond the F.O.B point.

In the illustration at right, notice that money is paid by the seller to the transport company. This is the case where the terms called for F.O.B. Destination -- the seller had to get the goods to the destination. This situation reverses in the next illustration: F.O.B. Shipping Point -- the buyer had to pay to get the goods delivered. The third illustration calls for the buyer to bear the freight cost (F.O.B. Shipping Point). However, the cost is prepaid by the seller as an accommodation. Notice that the buyer then sends payment to the seller to reimburse for the prepaid freight; ultimately the buyer is still bearing the freight cost. Of course, other scenarios are possible. For example, terms could be F.O.B. St. Louis, in which case the seller would pay to get the goods from New York to St. Louis, and the buyer would pay to bring the goods from St. Louis to Los Angeles.

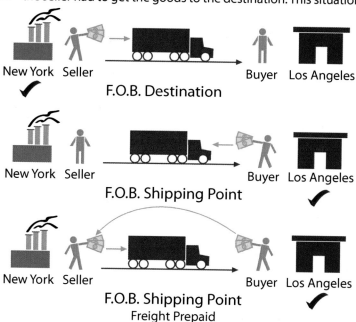

Take a moment and look at the invoice presented earlier in this chapter for Barber Shop Supply. Notice that the seller was in Chicago and the purchaser was in Dallas. Just to the right of the invoice date, note that the terms were F.O.B. Dallas. This means that Barber Shop Supply is responsible for getting the goods to the customer in Dallas. That is why the invoice included $0 for freight; the purchaser was not responsible for the freight cost. Had the terms been F.O.B. Chicago, then Hair Port Landing would have to bear the freight cost.

Next are presented appropriate journal entries to deal with alternative scenarios.

- If goods are sold **F.O.B. destination**, the seller is responsible for costs incurred in moving the goods to their destination. Freight cost incurred by the seller is called freight-out and is reported as a selling expense that is subtracted from gross profit in calculating net income.

Seller's entry:

05-11-X4	Accounts Receivable	7,000	
	Freight-out	400	
	Cash		400
	Sales		7,000
	Sold merchandise on account for $7,000, terms F.O.B. destination, and paid the freight bill of $400		

Purchaser's entry:

05-11-X4	Purchases	7,000	
	Accounts Payable		7,000
	Purchased $7,000 of inventory, terms F.O.B. destination		

- If goods are sold **F.O.B. shipping point**, the purchaser is responsible for paying freight costs incurred in transporting the merchandise from the point of shipment to its destination. Freight cost incurred by a purchaser is called freight-in, and is added to purchases in calculating net purchases:

Seller's entry:

06-06-X4	Accounts Receivable	8,000	
	Sales		8,000
	Sold merchandise on account for $8,000, terms F.O.B. shipping point		

Purchaser's entry:

06-06-X4	Purchases	8,000	
	Freight-in	1,500	
	Cash		1,500
	Accounts Payable		8,000
	Purchased $8,000 of inventory, terms F.O.B. shipping point, and paid the shipping freight bill of $1,500		

- If goods are sold F.O.B. shipping point, freight prepaid, the seller prepays the trucking company as an accommodation to the purchaser. This prepaid freight increases the accounts receivable of the seller. That is, the seller expects payment for the merchandise and a reimbursement for the freight. The purchaser would record this transaction by debiting Purchases for the amount of the purchase, debiting Freight-In for the amount of the freight, and crediting Accounts Payable for the combined amount due to the seller.

Seller's entry:

03-10-X8	Accounts Receivable	10,400	
	Cash		400
	Sales		10,000
	Sold merchandise on account for $10,000, terms F.O.B. shipping point, $400 freight prepaid		

Purchaser's entry:

03-10-X8	Purchases	10,000	
	Freight-in	400	
	Accounts Payable		10,400
	Purchased merchandise on account for $10,000, terms F.O.B. shipping point, $400 freight prepaid		

Cash discounts for prompt payment are not usually available on freight charges. For example, if there was a 2% discount on the above purchase, it would amount to $200 ($10,000 X 2%), NOT $208 ($10,400 X 2%).

CALCULATION OF NET PURCHASES

A number of new accounts have been introduced in this chapter. Purchases, Purchase Returns and Allowances, Purchase Discounts, and Freight-in have all been illustrated. Each of these accounts is necessary to calculate the "net purchases" during a period. Assume total purchases of $400,000 during the period. This would be based on the total invoice amount for all goods purchased during the period, as identified from the Purchases account in the ledger. The cost of the purchases is increased for the freight-in costs. Purchase discounts and purchase returns and allowances are subtracted. The result is "net purchases" of $420,000. Net purchases reflect the actual costs that were deemed to be ordinary and necessary to bring the goods to their location for resale to an end customer.

Add:	Purchases		$400,000
	Freight-in		40,000
			$440,000
Less:	Purchase discounts	$ 6,000	
	Purchase returns & allowances	14,000	20,000
	Net purchases		$420,000

Importantly, storage costs, insurance, interest and other similar costs are considered to be period costs that are not attached to the product. Instead, those ongoing costs are simply expensed in the period incurred as operating expenses of the business.

COST OF GOODS SOLD The cost of all purchases must ultimately be allocated between cost of goods sold and inventory, depending on the portion of the purchased goods that have been resold to end customers. This allocation must also give consideration to any beginning inventory that was carried over from prior periods.

Beginning inventory	$115,000	*From end of prior period*
Plus: Net purchases	420,000	*From calculations*
Goods available for sale	$535,000	
Less: Ending inventory	91,000	*From physical count*
Cost of goods sold	$444,000	

Very simply, goods that remain unsold at the end of an accounting period should not be "expensed" as cost of goods sold. Therefore, the calculation of **cost of goods sold** requires an assessment of total goods available for sale, from which ending inventory is subtracted. With a periodic system, the ending inventory is determined by a physical count. In that process, the goods held are actually counted and assigned cost based on a consistent method. The actual methods for assigning cost to ending inventory is the subject of considerable discussion in the inventory chapter. Understanding the allocation of costs to ending inventory and cost of goods sold is very important and is worthy of additional emphasis. Consider the following diagram:

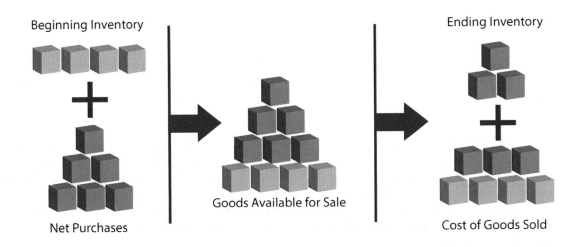

The beginning inventory is equal to the prior year's ending inventory, as determined by reference to the prior year's ending balance sheet. The net purchases is extracted from this year's ledger (i.e., the balances of Purchases, Freight-in, Purchase Discounts, and Purchase Returns & Allowances). Goods available for sale is the sum of beginning inventory and net purchases. **Goods available for sale** is not an account, per se; it is merely a defined result from adding two amounts together. The total cost incurred (i.e., cost of goods available for sale) must be "allocated" according to its nature at the end of the year. The cost of goods still held are assigned to inventory (an asset), and the remainder is attributed to cost of goods sold (an expense).

There is a lot of activity to consider: net sales, net purchases, cost of sales, gross profit, etc.! A detailed income statement can provide the necessary organization to present all of the data in an understandable format. Study the following detailed income statement.

DETAILED INCOME STATEMENT

BILL'S SPORTING GOODS
Detailed Income Statement
For the Year Ending December 31, 20X5

Revenues			
Sales			$750,000
Less: Sales discounts		$ 7,000	
Sales returns & allow.		3,000	10,000
Net sales			$740,000
Cost of goods sold			
Beginning inventory, Jan. 1		$115,000	
Add: Purchases	$400,000		
Freight-in	40,000		
	$440,000		
Less: Purchase discounts	$ 6,000		
Purchase returns & allow.	14,000	20,000	
Net purchases		420,000	
Goods available for sale		$535,000	
Less: Ending inventory, Dec. 31		91,000	
Cost of goods sold			444,000
Gross profit			$296,000
Expenses			
Advertising		$ 60,000	
Freight-out		32,000	
Depreciation		18,000	
Utilities		29,000	
Salaries		134,000	
Rent		12,000	285,000
Net income			$ 11,000

Sales		$750,000
Less: Sales discounts	$7,000	
Sales returns & allow.	3,000	10,000
Net sales		$740,000

Add: Purchases		$400,000
Freight-in		40,000
		$440,000
Less: Purchase discounts	$ 6,000	
Purchase returns & allow.	14,000	20,000
Net purchases		$420,000

Beginning Inventory, Jan. 1	$115,000
Net purchases	420,000
Goods available for sale	$535,000
Less: Ending inventory, Dec. 31	91,000
Cost of goods sold	$444,000

Net sales	$740,000
Cost of goods sold	444,000
Gross profit	$296,000

In reviewing the above income statement, be sure to notice (1) the calculation of net sales, (2) the inclusion of details about the calculation of net purchases (including the treatment of freight-in), (3) the calculation of cost of goods sold and presentation of gross profit, and (4) that freight-out is a selling expense included among the various expenses subtracted from gross profit. Be aware that the income statement for a merchandising company may not present all of this detail. Depending on the materiality of the individual line items, it may be sufficient to only present line items for the key elements, like net sales, cost of sales, gross profit, various expense accounts, and net income.

CLOSING ENTRIES

Because of all the new income statement-related accounts that were introduced for the merchandising concern, it is helpful to revisit the closing process. Recall the objective of closing; to transfer the net income to retained earnings and to reset the income statement accounts to zero in preparation for the next accounting period. As a result, all income statement accounts with a credit balance must be debited and vice versa. The closing entries for Bill's Sporting Goods follow. Several items are highlighted in these journal entries and are discussed further in the next paragraph.

These closing entries are a bit more complex than that from the earlier chapter. In particular, note that the closing includes all of the new accounts like purchases, discounts, etc. In addition, it is important to update the inventory records. It may be confusing to see Inventory being debited and credited in the closing process. After all, isn't Inventory a balance sheet (real) account? And, aren't the temporary accounts the only ones closed? Why then is Inventory included in the closing? The answer is that Inventory must be updated to reflect the ending balance on hand.

Remember that the periodic system resulted in a debit to Purchases, not Inventory. Further, as goods are sold, no entry is made to reduce Inventory. Therefore, the Inventory account would continue to carry the beginning of year balance throughout the year. As a result, Inventory must be updated at the time of closing. These entries accomplish that objective by crediting/removing the beginning balance and debiting/establishing the ending balance. Note that these entries also cause the Income Summary account to be reduced by the cost of sales amount (beginning inventory + net purchases - ending inventory).

12-31-X5	Sales		750,000	
	Purchase Discounts		6,000	
	Purchase Returns & Allowances		14,000	
	Inventory		91,000	
	Income Summary			861,000
	To close income statement accounts with a credit balance, and establish ending inventory balance			
12-31-X5	Income Summary		850,000	
	Sales Discounts			7,000
	Sales Returns & Allowances			3,000
	Purchases			400,000
	Freight-in			40,000
	Advertising Expense			60,000
	Freight-out			32,000
	Depreciation Expense			18,000
	Utilities Expense			29,000
	Salaries Expense			134,000
	Rent Expense			12,000
	Inventory			115,000
	To close income statement accounts with a debit balance, and remove the beginning inventory balance			
12-31-X5	Income Summary		11,000	
	Retained Earnings			11,000
	To close Income Summary to retained earnings (note that the balance is equal to the net income)			

Alternative Inventory System

The periodic system only required the recording of inventory purchases to a Purchases account; inventory records were updated only during the closing process based on the results of a physical count. No attempt is made to adjust inventory records at the time of actual purchase and sale transactions. The weakness of the periodic system is that it provides no real-time data about the levels of inventory or gross profit. If inventory is significant, the lack of up-to-date inventory data can be very costly.

Managers need to know what is selling, and what is not selling, in order to optimize business success. That is why many successful merchants use sophisticated computer systems to implement perpetual inventory management. Bar code scanners at a retail checkout not only facilitate speedy transactions but may also be linked to an accounting information system. With a high-performance perpetual system, each purchase or sale results in an immediate update of the inventory and cost of sales data in the accounting system. The following entries are appropriate to record the purchase and subsequent resale of an inventory item:

Entry to record purchase of inventory:

12-12-X1	Inventory	3,000	
	Accounts Payable		3,000
	Purchased $3,000 of inventory on account		

Entries to record sale of inventory:

12-21-X1	Accounts Receivable	5,000	
	Sales		5,000
	Sold merchandise on account		
12-21-X1	Cost of Goods Sold	3,000	
	Inventory		3,000
	To record the cost of merchandise sold		

With the perpetual system, the Purchases account is not needed. The Inventory account and Cost of Goods Sold account are constantly being adjusted as transactions occur. Freight-in is added to the Inventory account. Discounts and returns reduce the Inventory account. Therefore, the determination of cost of goods sold is by reference to the account's general ledger balance, rather than needing to resort to the calculations illustrated for the periodic system.

If the perpetual system looks simpler, don't be deceived. Consider that it is no easy task to determine the cost of each item of inventory as it is sold, and that is required with a perpetual system. In a large retail environment, that is almost impossible without a sophisticated computer system. Nevertheless, such systems have become commonplace with the decline in the cost of computers.

One final point should be noted. No matter how good the computer system, differences between the computer record and physical quantity of inventory on hand will arise. Differences are created by theft, spoilage, waste, errors, and so forth. Therefore, merchants must occasionally undertake a physical count and adjust the Inventory accounts to reflect what is actually on hand.

Income Statement Enhancements

Accountants must always be cognizant of the capacity of financial statement users to review and absorb reports. Sometimes, the accountant may decide that a simplified presentation is sufficient. In those cases, the income statement may be presented in a "single-step" format.

This very simple approach reports all revenues (and gains) together, and the aggregated expenses (and losses) are tallied and subtracted to arrive at income. A **single-step income statement** is shown below:

HUNTER COMPANY Income Statement For the Year Ending December 31, 20X9		
Revenues		
Net sales		$653,000
Expenses and losses		
Cost of goods sold	$283,000	
Selling expenses	142,000	
General & administrative	170,000	
Loss on sale of land	2,000	
Interest expense	7,000	604,000
Income before tax		$ 49,000
Income tax expense		10,000
Net income		$ 39,000

Caution should be used when examining a single-step presentation. One should look at more than the bottom-line net income, and be certain to discern the components that make up income. For example, a company's core operations could be very weak, but the income could be good because of a non-recurring gain from the sale of assets. Tearing away such "masking" effects are a strong argument in favor of a more complex multiple-step approach.

A **multiple-step income statement** divides business operating results into separate categories or steps, and enhances the financial statement user's ability to understand the intricacy of an entity's operations. Often, companies will wish to further divide the expense items according to their nature: selling expenses (costs associated with the sale of merchandise) or general and administrative (costs incurred in the management of the business). Some costs must be allocated between the two categories; like depreciation of the corporate headquarters wherein both sales and administrative activities are conducted.

A business may, from time to time, have incidental or peripheral transactions that contribute to income. For example, a business might sell land at a gain. Or, a fire might produce a loss. These gains and losses are often reported separately from the ongoing measures of revenues and expenses. A subsequent chapter includes coverage of additional special reporting for other unique situations, like discontinued operations.

Likewise, many businesses break out the financing costs (i.e., interest expense) from the other expense components. This tends to separate the operating impacts from the cost of capital needed to produce those operating results. This is not to suggest that interest is not a real cost.

Instead, the company has made decisions about borrowing money ("leverage"), and breaking out the interest cost separately allows users to have a better perspective of how well the borrowing decisions are working. Investors want to know if enough extra income is being produced to cover the added financing costs associated with growth through debt financing.

HUNTER COMPANY Income Statement For the Year Ending December 31, 20X9				
Revenues				
Sales				$660,000
Less: Sales discounts			$ 5,000	
Sales returns & allowances			2,000	7,000
Net sales				$653,000
Cost of goods sold				
Beginning inventory, Jan. 1			$120,000	
Add: Purchases		$230,000		
Freight-in		10,000		
		$240,000		
Less: Purchase discounts	$2,400			
Purchase returns & allowances	3,600	6,000		
Net purchases			234,000	
Goods available for sale			$354,000	
Less: Ending inventory, Dec. 31			71,000	
Cost of goods sold				283,000
Gross profit				$370,000
Selling expenses				
Advertising		$ 70,000		
Freight-out		4,000		
Depreciation		28,000		
Utilities		11,000		
Salaries		29,000	$142,000	
General and administrative				
Salaries		$ 63,000		
Depreciation		17,000		
Utilities		22,000		
Insurance		44,000		
Rent		24,000	170,000	
Other				
Loss on sale of land		$ 2,000		
Interest expense		7,000	9,000	321,000
Income before tax				$ 49,000
Income tax expense				10,000
Net income				$ 39,000

Not to be overlooked in the determination of income is the amount of any tax that must be paid. Businesses are subject to many taxes, not the least of which is income tax, which must be paid, and is usually based on complex formulas related to the amount of business income or value added in production. As a result, it is customary to present income before tax, then the amount of tax, and finally the net income.

ANALYSIS OF A DETAILED INCOME STATEMENT

No matter which income statement format is used, detailed data is of no value if it is not carefully evaluated. One should monitor not only absolute dollar amounts, but should also pay close attention to ratios and percentages. It is typical to monitor the gross profit margin and the net profit on sales:

Gross Profit Margin = Gross Profit/Net Sales

$370,000/$653,000 = 56.66% for Hunter

Net Profit on Sales = Net Income/Net Sales

$39,000/$653,000 = 5.97% for Hunter

There are countless variations of these calculations, but they all highlight the issue of evaluating trends in performance separate and apart from absolute dollar amounts. Be aware that margins can be tricky. For example, suppose Liu's Janitorial Supply sold plastic trash cans. During Year 1, sales of cans were $3,000,000, and these units cost $2,700,000. During Year 2, oil prices dropped significantly. Oil is a critical component in plastics, and Liu passed along cost savings to his customers. Liu's Year 2 sales were $1,000,000, and the cost of goods sold was $700,000. Liu was very disappointed in the sales drop. However, he should not despair, as his gross profit was $300,000 in each year, and the gross profit margin soared during Year 2. The gross profit margin in Year 1 was 10% ($300,000/$3,000,000), and the gross profit margin in Year 2 was 30% ($300,000/$1,000,000). Despite the plunge in sales, Liu may actually be better off. Although this is a dramatic example to make the point, even the slightest shift in business circumstances can change the relative relationships between revenues and costs. A smart manager or investor will always keep a keen eye on business trends revealed by the shifting of gross profit and net profit percentages over time.

GLOBAL ISSUES IN INCOME REPORTING

International financial reporting standards and practices do not prescribe a detailed format for the income statement. Thus, the concepts of "multiple-step" and "single-step" presentations are not as relevant. Instead, the global perspective focuses on reporting of revenues, financing costs, profit shares from ventures/investments, tax expense, and profit or loss. Further, expenses may be classified according to either nature or function.

Classification by "nature" means that a company would elect to categorize and present information relating to utilities expense, salaries expense, advertising expense, insurance expense, and the like. Alternatively, classification by "function" means that a company would instead classify expenses according to their purpose: manufacturing, administrative, sales, and so on. If a functional classification scheme is used in the income statement, then supplemental disclosures ordinarily provide additional detail about the underlying nature of costs incurred by the organization.

In addition, global accounting rules are sometimes more permissive than U.S. rules when it comes to recording gains or losses that are based upon changing values of long-term assets like land and buildings. Thus, a company that is reporting globally might prepare an additional statement that reconciles net income to this broader concept of income measurement. The statement is sometimes called a statement of recognized income and expense.

An organization should carefully define various measures to safeguard its assets, check the reliability and accuracy of accounting information, ensure compliance with management policies, and evaluate operating performance and efficiency. The internal control structure depends on the accounting system, the control environment, and the control procedures. The control environment is the combined effect of a firm's policies and attitudes toward control implementation. Control procedures are specifically integrated into the accounting system and relate to the following:

- One important control is limited access to assets. This control feature assures that only authorized and responsible employees can obtain access to key assets. For example, a supplies stock area may be accessible only to department supervisors.

- Separation of duties is another important control. Activities like transaction authorization, transaction recording, and asset custody should be performed by different employees. Separating functions reduces the possibility of errors (because of cross-checking of accounting records to assets on hand, etc.) and fraud (because of the need for collusion among employees).

- A number of accountability procedures can be implemented to improve the degree of internal control:

  ¤ Duty authorization is a control feature which requires that certain functions be performed by a specific person (e.g., customer returns of merchandise for credit can be approved only by a sales manager).

  ¤ Prenumbered documents allow ready identification of missing items. For example, checks are usually prenumbered so that missing checks can be identified rapidly.

  ¤ Independent verification of records is another control procedure. Examples include comparing cash in a point of sale terminal with the sales recorded on that register and periodic reconciliation of bank accounts.

- A company may engage an accounting firm or CPA to provide an independent review of the company's accounting records and internal controls. The accountant may offer suggestions for improvement and test the established system to determine if it is functioning as planned.

In designing and implementing an internal control system, careful attention should be paid to the costs and benefits of the system. It is folly to develop a system which costs more to establish and maintain than it is worth to the company.

RETAIL CONTROLS

The basic elements of control are common to most businesses. However, the merchandiser must pay special attention to several unique considerations. Foremost is asset control. Obviously, the retailer has a huge investment in inventory, and that inventory is not easily "isolated." As a result, theft and spoilage are all too common. Retailers should go to great lengths to protect against these costly events.

Think, for a moment, about walking through an electronics retail store. Upon entering the front door, one may first notice "architecturally pleasing" barricades (like planter boxes or posts) to prevent crash entry. Next is a doorman (guard), who perhaps oversees separate entrances and exits, and is responsible for matching receipts to goods leaving the store. An alarm may sound if a hidden inventory sensor has not been deactivated at check out.

A quick glance up may reveal cameras. The most expensive items are display only; to buy these items a claim ticket is presented at a caged area. Only authorized employees can enter that area. At check out, point-of-sale terminals must be accessed with a key that is assigned to an employee. The terminal tracks who processed the sale. In addition, an employee may look inside a box or bag that contains a customer's purchased items, picture IDs are examined, and so forth. In general, the goal is simple -- make sure that only purchased merchandise gets out of the store. Several times daily, the cash drawers in the terminals will be pulled (replaced with another) and their contents audited. Daily bank runs (maybe via armored courier) will occur to make sure that funds are quickly and safely deposited in the bank. These controls are visible at the "front end" of the business.

PURCHASING CYCLE

Purchasing cycle controls are invisible to the customer, but equally as important. And, these purchasing controls are pervasive in other non-merchandising businesses as well. There is no single correct process, but the following concepts should be considered:

- Purchases should be initiated only by appropriate supervisory personnel, in accord with budgets or other authorizing plans.

- The purchasing action should be undertaken by trained purchasing personnel who know how to negotiate the best terms (with full understanding of freight issues, discount issues, and so forth).

- Purchasing departments should have strong procedural rules, including prohibitions against employees receiving "gifts" and limitations on dealings with related parties.

- Large purchases should be preceded by solicitation of bids from multiple vendors.

- A purchase order should be prepared to initiate the actual order.

- When goods are received, the receiving department should not accept them without inspection, including matching the goods to an open purchase order to make sure that what is being delivered was in fact ordered.

- The receiving department should prepare a receiving report, indicating that goods have been received in good order.

- When an invoice ("bill") is received, it should be carefully matched to the original purchase order and receiving report. The bill should be scheduled for payment in time to take advantage of available discounts. It is important to only pay for goods that were ordered and received. In a large organization, the person preparing the payment has likely never seen the goods; hence the importance of complete documentation.

- Before payment is released, an independent supervisor should make one last review of all the documents.

In an automated environment many of these processes and documents will be generated and preserved electronically. However, the underlying controls are of equal importance.

CONTROL SYSTEMS

Accountants spend much of their time dealing with issues that are complex, like designing and testing the control environment. For example, an auditor does not just look at a bunch of transactions to see if the debits and credits are correct. Instead, the control environment will be studied and tested to see if it is working as planned. If it is, then the "system" should be producing correct financial data, and much less time can be devoted to actually focusing on specific transactions.

Chapter 5 Quiz

Q5-1. Sales returns and allowances and sales discounts are known as:

contra-revenue accounts   or   expense accounts

Q5-2. The Purchase Discounts Lost account would be utilized under the:

gross method   or   net method

Q5-3. Net purchases equals gross purchases plus freight-in minus purchase discounts and purchase returns and allowances.

true   or   false

Q5-4. Modern computers have greatly increased the ability of firms to apply the:

periodic inventory system   or   perpetual inventory system

Q5-5. Which of the following income statement formats is justified on the grounds of simplicity and ease of understanding?

single-step approach   or   multiple-step approach

Q5-6. Once a return or allowance is authorized, the seller documents the transaction on a form known as a _____.

Q5-7. A _____ might be expressed as 2/10, n/30.

Q5-8. Under the net method of recording purchases, a missed discount would be recorded to the Purchase Discounts Lost account with a _____ at the time of _____.

Q5-9. An income statement approach which presents accounts by association (i.e., sales and cost of goods sold, etc.) is termed the _____ format.

Q5-10. A company's _____ represents the combined effect of many factors on implementing, evaluating, and improving the effectiveness of specified firm policies.

Q5-11. Important forms such as checks, sales invoices, and purchase orders are usually serially _____.

Multiple Choice

Q5-12. Purchasers of merchandise may be dissatisfied with the quality of goods purchased on account and return the goods to the seller with an indication that payment will not be forthcoming. In this case, the document prepared by the purchaser is called:

a. a debit memorandum.

c. a receiving report.

b. a credit memorandum.

d. an invoice.

Q5-13. Bergstrom accepted the return of merchandise by a customer. The merchandise had been sold on account, and payment had not been received on the date of return. The returned goods retailed for $400 but cost Bergstrom only $300. The appropriate journal entry for Bergstrom is:

a. Accounts Receivable   400

     Sales Returns & Allowances   400

c. Sales   400

     Purchases   300

     Accounts Receivable   100

b. Sales Returns & Allowances   400

     Accounts Receivable   400

d. Sales Returns & Allowances   400

     Purchases   300

     Accounts Receivable   100

Q5-14. Lux had net purchases of $50,000, ending inventory of $25,000, net sales of $100,000, and gross profit of $32,000. How much was Lux's beginning inventory?

a. $7,000

c. $93,000

b. $43,000

d. $143,000

Q5-15. Dodd Company utilizes the periodic inventory accounting system. Dodd had beginning inventory of $59,000, ending inventory of $37,000, and net purchases of $123,000. Which of the following components should be included in the year-end closing entries prepared by Dodd?

a. Purchases   123,000

     Inventory   123,000

c. Income Summary   59,000

     Inventory   59,000

b. Income Summary   37,000

     Inventory   37,000

d. All of the above

Q5-16. A multiple-step income statement is thought to be more beneficial to financial statement users because of the revelation of important relationships. Which of the following is not separately identified on a multiple-step income statement?

a. Gross profit

c. Income taxes

b. Net income

d. Total costs and expenses

Chapter 5 Problems

Basic Problems

Harold Frieze owns Euro Lighting, a lighting products store that specializes in energy efficient and aesthetically pleasing fixtures. Sales have grown rapidly due to recent consumer interest in reducing energy consumption for economic and environmental reasons.

Increased sales have brought new challenges. First, the "modern" styling of the fixtures looks great in the store, but consumers often find they clash with other fixtures once they take them home. This has brought about a high rate of return. Harold accepts returns of undamaged goods with original packaging.

Second, many of the fixtures are rather technical and require care when installing. Customers frequently damage the products (and packaging) when attempting to do an installation. Harold does not accept such goods for return, but has established a policy of refunding a portion of the purchase price as an "allowance" for customers who complain of such problems.

(a) Prepare a journal entry for each of the following scenarios.

> A customer purchased a lighting fixture for cash of €350
>
> A customer purchased a lighting fixture on account for €500
>
> A customer returned a lighting fixture for a cash refund of €275
>
> A customer returned a fixture for a credit on account of €600
>
> A complaining customer received a €100 allowance in cash
>
> A complaining customer received a €70 credit on account
>
> A customer paid their balance on account of €475

(b) Calculate Euro Lighting's net sales and gross profit based on the following information, and show how such information would appear on the upper portion of the income statement for the year ending December 31, 20X3.

> Gross sales, €760,000
>
> Sales returns and allowances, €42,500
>
> Cost of goods sold, €312,000

College Bookstore is facing increased competition from online resellers and electronic media. To combat eroding sales, management adopted new discounting policies as follows:

Students are offered a trade discount based on the number of books purchased:

Each student purchasing one book gets 0% discount.

Each student purchasing two books gets a 10% discount.

Each student purchasing three books gets a 20% discount.

Each student purchasing four or more books gets a 30% discount.

Students are now offered credit terms at the time of purchase. If the student pays within 30 days of the date of purchase, he or she receives a 3% cash discount.

(a) Calculate the amount of the sale that should be recorded by College Bookstore for each of the following transactions. How much should ultimately be collected for each transaction?

Student A, 3 books, $425 list price, purchased on August 11, paid on August 19

Student B, 2 books, $210 list price, purchased on August 18, paid on October 4.

Student C, 1 book, $90 list price, purchased on Sept. 3, paid on Sept. 3.

Student D, 7 books, $1,205 list price, purchased on August 5, paid on Sept. 20.

(b) Demonstrate the appropriate journal entry to record the sale and subsequent collection from students A and B.

B-05.03   *Purchase transactions, business papers, net vs. gross*

Shirley Williams Apparel Store purchases clothing merchandise on account from various vendors. Below is an invoice from Terra Wear.

TERRA WEAR
ACTION SPORT CLOTHING
HIGH POINT, CO

BILL TO: SHIRLEY WILLIAMS APPAREL STORE	INVOICE #3778
DENVER SPORTS CENTER, #1234	
DENVER, CO	

DELIVERY DATE	INVOICE DATE	F.O.B. POINT	TERMS
MAY 5, 20X1	MAY 5, 20X1	DENVER	1/10,N/30

QTY.	DESCRIPTION	UNIT PRICE	TOTAL
70	WORK OUT WONDER SPORT COLLECTION	$125	$8,750
30	SUN FUN - FUN WEAR	35	$1,050
10	FALL COLOR COLLECTION	60	$600
THANK YOU FOR YOUR BUSINESS!		TOTAL	$10,400

(a) Prepare Shirley's journal entries for each of the following transactions, assuming use of a periodic inventory system and the "gross method" of recording:

>   To record the invoice on May 5.
>
>   To record the return of the Fall Color collection on May 7.
>
>   To record the payment of the balance due if payment occurred on May 10.
>
>   To record the payment of the balance due if payment occurred on May 20.

(b) Repeat requirement (a) assuming Shirley uses the periodic inventory system and the "net method" of recording.

Sales and freight cost	B-05.04

Gerloff Supply sells cables, connectors, and other basic wiring components to audio video dealers across the country. Dealers with "preferred status" receive a 20% discount off of list price. All sales are on account, and payment terms are 2/10, n/30.

Sales of $1,000 and up (large orders) will ship F.O.B. destination. Orders less than $1,000 (small orders) are always F.O.B. shipping point. However, Gerloff will prepay freight on small orders by "preferred dealers." Otherwise, small orders are shipped freight collect by the common carrier making the delivery. In no event may a customer apply the cash discount terms to freight charges.

Prepare journal entries to record the sale and subsequent collection for each of the following transactions:

Transaction	Customer Status	List Price	Freight Cost	Date of Sale	Date of Payment
1	Preferred	$1,500	$125	3-Jun	9-Jun
2	Regular	300	30	7-Jun	20-Jun
3	Preferred	700	45	9-Jun	20-Jun
4	Regular	2,000	200	10-Jun	17-Jun
5	Regular	1,800	230	12-Jun	29-Jun
6	Preferred	2,400	180	15-Jun	27-Jun

Purchases and freight cost	B-05.05

Gunnison Creamery produces a variety of specialty ice creams and buys ingredients from many suppliers. Each supplier seems to have unique policies about discounts and freight terms. Gunnison Creamery records all purchases "gross" and uses a periodic inventory system.

Gunnison recently hired a new bookkeeper and needs your help to develop a template of sample journal entries for different scenarios. For purposes of preparing the template, assume that the purchase is $1,000 and freight is $100.

Scenario	Cash Discount	Freight Terms	Discount Condition
1	2/10, n/30	F.O.B. Shipping point/freight prepaid	taken
2	2/10, n/30	F.O.B. Shipping point/freight prepaid	missed
3	2/10, n/30	F.O.B. Destination/freight prepaid	taken
4	2/10, n/30	F.O.B. Destination/freight prepaid	missed
5	2/10, n/30	F.O.B. Shipping point/freight collect	taken
6	2/10, n/30	F.O.B. Shipping point/freight collect	missed

The first scenario is done as an example on the preprinted worksheet, and the electronic spreadsheet version expedites your solution by including a journal pick list of the following accounts:

Cash

Purchases

Accounts Payable

Purchase Discounts

Freight-in

B-05.06   *Calculating values for a merchandising income statement*

SPREADSHEET TOOL:

Solver/ Goal Seek function

Partial information follows about net sales, net purchases, cost of goods sold, gross profit, total expenses, and net income for Slabaugh Company. Compute the missing values.

Net Sales

Sales	$800,000
Sales discounts	20,000
Sales returns and allowances	?
Net sales	735,000

Net Purchases

Purchases	$400,000
Freight-in	20,000
Purchase discounts	?
Purchase returns and allowances	2,500
Net purchases	413,500

Cost of Goods Sold

Beginning inventory	$ 85,400
Ending inventory	74,500
Cost of goods sold	?

Gross Profit

Gross profit	?

Total Expenses

Rent	$ 36,000
Salaries	145,700
Utilities	12,300
Freight-out	?
Other	24,100
Total expenses	242,200

Net Income

Net income	?

Preparing a merchandising income statement	*B-05.07*

Pitkin Health Care Products provides the following alphabetic list of accounts and their respective balances. All accounts have normal balances, and income statement account balances are for the year ending December 31, 20X4. A physical count of merchandise inventory on hand at year end revealed a balance of $277,390.

Use this information to prepare a comprehensive income statement.

Accounts payable	$ 93,789	Note Payable	$250,000
Accounts receivable	82,890	Purchase discounts	1,788
Accumulated depreciation	166,554	Purchase returns & allowances	6,665
Beginning inventory, Jan. 1	244,956	Purchases	433,443
Capital stock	144,000	Rent expense	42,335
Cash	25,442	Retained earnings, Jan. 1	24,327
Depreciation expense	65,990	Salaries expense	233,998
Dividends	12,000	Salaries payable	9,955
Equipment	324,556	Sales	977,932
Freight-in	43,441	Sales discounts	8,817
Freight-out	3,566	Sales returns and allowances	13,998
Insurance expense	8,700	Utilities expense	18,887
Marketing expense	111,991		

Interiors With Oohs and Aahs sells custom home décor. Following is the corporation's income statement. Use this statement to prepare closing entries. No dividends were declared during the period.

INTERIORS WITH OOHS AND AAHS Income Statement For the Year Ending December 31, 20X4			
Revenues			
Sales			$887,654
Less: Sales discounts		$ 4,667	
Sales returns & allowances		9,880	14,547
Net sales			$873,107
Cost of goods sold			
Beginning inventory, Jan. 1		$182,343	
Add: Purchases	$593,356		
Freight-in	21,090		
	$614,446		
Less: Purchase discounts	$ 3,501		
Purchase returns & allowances	19,009	22,510	
Net purchases		591,936	
Goods available for sale		$774,279	
Less: Ending inventory, Dec. 31		199,055	
Cost of goods sold			575,224
Gross profit			$297,883
Expenses			
Salaries		$188,000	
Insurance		9,152	
Utilities		7,760	
Freight-out		2,434	
Depreciation		13,773	221,119
Net income			$ 76,764

J & S Pet Supplies uses a perpetual inventory system. Prepare journal entries necessary to record the purchase (for $22 on account) and resale (for $39 cash) of a 50 pound bag of dog chow.

Stober's Lawn Sprinkler Company sells irrigation equipment. Below is information necessary to prepare Stober's income statement for the year ending December 31, 20X7. Stober attributes 60% of the rent and utilities to selling functions, and the remainder to general and administrative activities. Seventy percent of the salaries are devoted to sales. Prepare an income statement in both single-step and multiple-step formats.

Advertising expense	$ 33,998
Cost of goods sold	466,773
Rent expense	144,000
Salaries expense	166,321
Net sales	972,299
Income tax expense	30,000
Utilities expense	26,997
Interest expense	18,500

Morton Corporation and Skyline Corporation each sell playground equipment. Morton Corporation's strategy is to focus on selling quality units at the best possible prices, while attempting to minimize selling, general, and administrative expenses (SG&A). Skyline Corporation has concluded that many customers will differentiate more on brand than quality, and is promoting its inferior goods with a significant marketing campaign.

Study each company's income statement below, and calculate the respective proportion of sales returns, the gross profit margin, and the net profit on sales. Both companies are subject to a 25% tax rate. Assuming no change in SG&A, which company would experience the biggest increase in profit from a 10% increase in net sales? Which company would experience the biggest decline in profit from a 10% decrease in net sales?

MORTON CORPORATION
Income Statement
For the Year Ending December 31, 20X6

Net sales		
Gross sales	$945,876	
Less: Sales returns	18,918	$926,958
Cost of goods sold		709,407
Gross profit		$217,551
Selling expenses	$ 45,000	
General and administrative expenses	120,000	165,000
Income before taxes		$ 52,551
Income tax expense (25%)		13,138
Net income		$ 39,413

SKYLINE CORPORATION
Income Statement
For the Year Ending December 31, 20X6

Net sales		
Gross sales	$985,876	
Less: Sales returns	58,918	$926,958
Cost of goods sold		417,131
Gross profit		$509,827
Selling expenses	$337,276	
General and administrative expenses	120,000	457,276
Income before taxes		$ 52,551
Income tax expense (25%)		13,138
Net income		$ 39,413

B-05.12   *Control structure*

Seaside Village is a retirement community, and many residents work together on a local charitable auction to raise money to support community endeavors. Basically, volunteers solicit residents and local merchants to donate items for the auction. The night of the auction, volunteers bring their donated items for display on tables placed around the floor of the town's school gymnasium. Virtually the whole town turns out to bid on items that are up for sale. The lucky purchaser makes payment at a collection booth that is staffed by two of the volunteers. At the end of the evening, the buyers collect their items. A volunteer takes the money home to count. The money is deposited to the charity's bank account on the following day.

Following last year's auction, many complaints were heard. One merchant complained that he had donated an expensive LCD television, but it was not offered for sale at the auction. One of the buyers complained that the item she paid for was not to be found at the end of the evening. Another donor complained that he needed a receipt for tax purposes, and another person complained that some people were making up receipts for donations that were never made.

The charity's board is considering expanded controls for next year's event, and is considering ten specific proposals received from various volunteers. Which five of these proposals are the most valid strengthening of the control structure?

1. Donors will be sent a thank you letter, which will include a paragraph asking them to confirm that their donated item was present at the auction.

2. Proceeds should be counted and recorded by two or more people immediately following the auction, and taken directly to the bank for deposit in the night depository.

3. The person taking the money to the bank will be required to perform a bank reconciliation at the end of the month to verify the deposit's posting.

4. All volunteers should be emailed a blank receipt form. Volunteers are encouraged to reprint a generous supply and be sure to issue one to each donor.

5. Prenumbered receipt books (with carbon copy film) should be used for donated items, and a log should be maintained of who received a receipt book. The receipts should be reconciled to donated items.

6. A paid receipt prepared by collection booth volunteers must be presented by a purchaser before being allowed to leave the gym with an item of merchandise.

7. An advertisement will be run in the local paper asking for support of the upcoming auction. The advertisement will include instructions to donors reminding them to always ask for a receipt for their gift, and encouraging them to call in to a special phone number to register to be eligible for a special prize drawing for donors!

8. Only one person at a time will be allowed in the collection booth. Each collection booth volunteer will be limited to a one-hour shift. No volunteer is to remove funds from the booth.

9. The charity's president will be required to perform an audit of the books and records related to the annual event. The president must issue a written audit report.

10. Donated items must be taken to a local storage facility upon receipt. A warehouse custodian volunteer will log the items, and another volunteer will be authorized to lock and unlock the warehouse.

Involved Problems

Comprehensive merchandising entries	I-05.01

Tic Toc Clock Shop reported the following merchandising-related transactions during June. Tic Tock Clock Shop records all purchases "gross," and credit terms are precisely followed on both purchases and sales. Prepare journal entries to record each transaction.

3-Jun	Purchased $4,000 of clocks on account from Swiss Time, F.O.B. destination, terms 1/10, n/30.
5-Jun	Sold a $1,500 clock to Janci Holgren on account, terms 2/10, n/eom. The customer picked up the clock from the shop.
9-Jun	Paid the amount due for the purchase of June 3.
11-Jun	Purchased $8,000 of clocks on account from Melbourne Clockworks, F.O.B. shipping point, terms 2/10, n/30. Freight charges of $460 were prepaid by Melbourne and added to the invoice. No discount is permitted on the freight charges.
19-Jun	Sold a $3,500 clock on account, terms 2/10, n/eom. Tic Toc sold the clock F.O.B. destination, and paid the freight charges of $330.
23-Jun	The customer of June 19 called to report that the clock was received damaged. An agreement was reached to reduce the invoice by 20%.
27-Jun	Paid Melbourne Clockworks for the purchase of June 11.
27-Jun	Janci Holgren paid for the purchase of June 5.
28-Jun	The customer of June 19 paid the balance due.

Ahson Tariq is director of operations for CTC which specializes in global merchandising of the world's finest cotton fibers. It is common practice for CTC to purchase cotton in bulk from regional growers, and then apply grading and measurement techniques to the fiber. Substandard fibers are subject to return or purchase price adjustment. CTC has negotiated credit terms with all suppliers of 1/10, n/30. Following are summary statements about June's purchases.

Purchased cotton for 80,000,000 Pakistan Rupees (PKR), on account.

Returned cotton for credit on account, PKR 3,000,000.

Agreed with suppliers to purchase price allowances, PKR 5,000,000.

Made payment of PKR 60,000,000 on open accounts within discount period and received PKR 600,000 purchase discounts.

Made payment of PKR 12,000,000 on open accounts outside of discount period and lost PKR 120,000 purchase discounts.

Additional information for June follows:

Net sales, PKR 97,000,000

Beginning inventory, PKR 6,000,000

Ending inventory, PKR 5,000,000

Freight-in, PKR 2,200,000

Freight-out, PKR 1,700,000

Rent expense, PKR 3,500,000

Salaries expense, PKR 2,400,000

(a)   Prepare summary journal entries for the purchase related transactions using the "gross" method.

(b)   Prepare summary journal entries for the purchase related transactions using the "net" method.

(c)   Prepare an income statement for June assuming use of the entries recorded in part (a).

(d)   Prepare an income statement for June assuming use of the entries recorded in part (b).

Hanna Sports is a retailer that specializes in athletic equipment. The corporate strategy is to focus on towns with a population of less than 25,000 people, thereby avoiding head-to-head competition with large retail chains. Following is Hanna's adjusted trial balance for the year 20X7. Hanna's ending inventory is $525,525.

HANNA SPORTS CORPORATION
Adjusted Trial Balance
As of December 31, 20X7

	Debits	Credits
Cash	$ 644,909	
Accounts receivable	333,654	
Inventory, Jan. 1	433,477	
Equipment	488,765	
Accumulated depreciation		$144,895
Accounts payable		111,888
Loan payable		500,900
Capital stock		250,000
Retained earnings, Jan. 1		322,433
Dividends	25,000	
Sales		3,665,667
Sales discounts	23,112	
Sales returns and allowances	144,367	
Purchases	2,198,560	
Purchase discounts		114,432
Purchase returns and allowances		26,341
Freight-in	73,091	
Selling expenses	185,312	
Rent expense	262,000	
Interest expense	60,400	
Salaries expense	200,700	
Depreciation expense	63,209	
	$5,136,556	$5,136,556

(a) Prepare a comprehensive income statement.

(b) Prepare closing entries.

Perpetual inventory vs. periodic inventory   *I-05.04*

Big Swing Sales is a rapidly growing speciality advertising company that distributes golf balls printed with personalized corporate logos. Heretofore, the company has used a manual periodic inventory system. However, the company is evaluating installation of an automated inventory tracking system that can be integrated with a perpetual inventory module in the company's accounting software package that is presently under development.

The company's information technology staff is working on the basic software development for this task, and is needing some help understanding the mechanics of periodic vs. perpetual inventory accounting techniques.

(a) Develop journal entries for each of the following representative transactions to show how they would be handled with a periodic (gross and net) vs. perpetual system (gross and net).

#1 Purchased $55,000 of balls on account, F.O.B. destination, terms 2/10, n/30.

#2 Paid the amount due for the preceding purchase within the discount period.

#3 Sold golf balls for $80,000 on account, F.O.B. shipping point, freight-collect, terms 1/10, n/30. The balls had a net cost of $39,300.

(b) Using the representative transactions, show how cost of goods sold is measured under the alternative systems. Assume Big Swing had a beginning inventory of $21,000.

I-05.05   *Single-step and multiple-step income statements, profit margins*

Synandre Montaque is the CEO of Montaque Corporation. The company recently held a webcast to announce preliminary results for the year ending December 31, 20X5. The webcast began with an opening statement by Synandre, followed by a question and answer session from analysts and investors who utilized a call-in Q&A phone line. Following is the transcript of the session:

Synandre   Ladies and gentleman, thank you for participating today. There has been recent speculation that Montaque Corporation's 20X5 reported results will fall short of previously announced guidance. I wish to allay that fear by today offering some preliminary information about 20X5's results. Our official results will be released on February 19, when our independent auditors issue their final report.

Synandre   With that having been said, I am very pleased that we will be reporting record gross sales of $5,675,000,000 for the reporting period. Our gross profit margin continues at a very favorable 44%, and our bottom line net income will equal the targeted 4% of net sales goal. With that good news, I will be pleased to answer your questions.

Caller #1   Congratulations on those very good results. I did note that you referred to gross sales as record-setting. But, there have been reports of product failures resulting in a very high rate of return. Can you respond to that issue?

Synandre   That is very plainly bunk; a rumor being spread by our competition. We continue to gain market share across all areas. Our sales returns and allowances will come in at only 3% of gross sales. Now, to be clear, we did offer improved credit terms to our key customers this year, and our sales discounts will amount to 1.5% of gross sales.

Caller #2   You began the year with inventory of $425,000,000, and indicated that you desired to trim that level. Did you accomplish that goal?

Synandre	No. I am sorry to report that business conditions have required us to further increase our inventory levels by 30%. However, this has resulted, we believe, in improved customer satisfaction with our product availability.
Caller #3	Your competitors have reported significant increases in freight costs. Did you experience similar problems?
Synandre	We have been very fortunate to negotiate favorable terms on purchases. Our freight-in cost of $55,000,000 was more than offset by purchase discounts of $34,444,000 and purchase returns and allowances of $61,225,000.
Caller #4	How have recent tax law changes impacted the company?
Synandre	While tax law changes have been grabbing headlines, our global tax strategy remains intact, and our total tax expense for the year will be at the $100,000,000 level.
Caller #5	You have yet to comment on SG&A. Can you give those numbers some color?
Synandre	I really cannot give you the specifics just yet, but I can give you some general guidance. First, as you know, we carefully control SG&A. Our historic pattern shows that that our total operating expenses break down as 60% selling, 35% general and administrative, and 5% interest cost. We will match this historic pattern, even though we spent $250,710,000 on advertising. The other selling expense categories of salaries / depreciation / utilities will allocate on a 60 / 10 / 30 ratio.
Caller #6	You are losing me here . . . I follow your selling expense, but how about general and administrative costs?
Synandre	Ok, you guys are really pressing me for the details. All I can tell you at this point is that the general and administrative costs will consist of three categories: salaries / depreciation / utilities. These will allocate out on a 50 / 30 / 20 basis. I cannot yet give you the specific amounts. With that, it is time to close this webcast. Thank you for your attention. We look forward to providing you with detailed income statements in the next few weeks. Good day.

Assume you are a financial analyst. Your assignment is to a review the above transcript and prepare a report for your clients that includes a preliminary view of how you think the income statement will appear, when issued. Prepare both a multiple-step and single-step income statement for their review.

Team-based study of controls	*I-05.06*

Form a team with four other classmates. This problem requires your team to visit a business that is willing to share some information about its control procedures, so try to form teams such that at least one team member has a contact or relationship that will facilitate the business visit.

Visit the business and discuss its general control environment and control procedures. Inquire about how such procedures were created, and the necessity for such controls. Determine if any specific problems prompted the implementation of any unique controls. Finally, each team member should focus on one of the following control dimensions and identify an example of how it is utilized by the entity:

Member #1   Limited access to assets -- identify some entity-owned asset that is protected by limited access. Prepare a brief report to share with your class about the nature of the protected asset, how it is protected, and why.

Member #2   Separation of duties -- identify some accounting task or transaction that requires multiple parties to complete. Prepare a brief report to share with your class about the nature of the task or transaction, and how the involvement of multiple parties reduces the risk of error or irregularity.

Member #3   Duty authorization -- identify some activity that requires specific management action to authorize. What prevents this activity without appropriate authorization? Prepare a brief report to share with your class about the nature of the activity and the system for authorization.

Member #4   Prenumbered documents -- identify some document type that is prenumbered. How are the "numbers" utilized for control purposes? Prepare a brief report to share with your class about how prenumbering of the particular document aids in the control environment of the business.

Member #5   Independent verification -- identify a verification process within the entity. What is verified and why? Prepare a brief report to share with your class about the verification procedure and its importance.

Hint: Provide, in advance, a copy of this assignment to the person(s) you will be meeting with at the business. This makes for a more meaningful and efficient visit.

Chapter 6:
Cash and Highly-Liquid Investments

Goals:

The composition of cash and how cash is presented on the
    balance sheet.

Cash management and controls for receipts and disbursements.

Reconciliation of bank accounts.

The correct operation of a petty cash system.

Accounting for highly-liquid short-term investments.

principlesofaccounting.com

What exactly is **cash**? This may seem like a foolish question until one considers the possibilities. Cash includes coins and currency. But what about items like undeposited checks, certificates of deposit, and similar items? Generalizing, cash includes those items that are acceptable to a bank for deposit and are free from restrictions (i.e., available for use in satisfying current debts). Cash typically includes coins, currency, funds on deposit with a bank, checks, and money orders.

Items like postdated checks, certificates of deposit, IOUs, stamps, and travel advances are not classified as cash. These would customarily be classified in accounts such as receivables, short-term investments, supplies, or prepaid expenses. The existence of **compensating balances** (amounts that must be left on deposit and not withdrawn) should be disclosed and, if significant, reported separately from cash.

Separate treatment is also given to "sinking funds" (monies that must be set aside to satisfy debts) and restricted foreign currency holdings (that cannot easily be transferred or converted into another currency). These unique categories of funds may be reported in the long-term investments category. Some companies will report "cash and **cash equivalents**":

Cash and cash equivalents (See note 1) $15,187,156

Note 1: Cash equivalents are defined as short-term, highly-liquid investments with original maturities of 90 days or less.

Cash equivalents arise when companies place their cash in very short-term financial instruments that are deemed to be highly secure and will convert back into cash within 90 days (e.g., short-term government-issued treasury bills). These financial instruments are usually very marketable in the event the company has an immediate need for cash.

Cash Management

It is very important to ensure that sufficient cash is available to meet obligations and that idle cash is appropriately invested. One function of the company "treasurer" is to examine the cash flows of the business, and pinpoint anticipated periods of excess or deficit cash flows. A detailed cash budget is often maintained and updated on a regular basis. The **cash budget** is a major component of a cash planning system and represents the overall plan that depicts cash inflows and outflows for a stated period of time. A future chapter provides an in-depth look at cash budgeting.

Although cash shortages may seem to be a sign of weakness or mismanagement, this is not always the case. Successful companies may need cash for new business locations, added inventory levels, growing receivables, and so forth. Careful cash planning must occur to sustain growth.

STRATEGIES TO ENHANCE CASH FLOWS

As a business looks to improve cash management or add to the available cash supply, a number of options are available. Some of these solutions are "external" and some are "internal" in nature.

External solutions include:

Issuing additional shares of stock -- This solution allows a company to obtain cash without a fixed obligation to repay. Unfortunately, the existing shareholders do incur a detriment, because the added share count dilutes the ownership proportions. In essence, existing shareholders are selling off part of the business.

Borrowing additional funds -- This solution brings no shareholder dilution, but borrowed funds must be repaid along with interest. Thus, the business cost and risk is increased. Many companies will pay a fee to establish a standing line of credit that enables them to borrow as needed.

Internal solutions include:

Accelerate cash collections -- If customers pay more quickly, a significant source of cash is found. Simple tools include electronic payment, credit cards, and cash discounts for prompt payment.

Postponement of cash outflows -- Companies may delay payment as long as possible. Paying via check sent through the mail allows use of the "float" to preserve cash on hand. However, one needs to know that it is illegal to issue a check when there are insufficient funds in the bank to cover that item.

Cash control -- Internal control for cash is based on the same general control features introduced in the previous chapter; access to cash should be limited to a few authorized personnel, incompatible duties should be separated, and accountability features (like prenumbered checks, etc.) should be developed.

- Control of receipts from cash sales should begin at the point of sale and continue through to deposit at the bank. Specifically, point-of-sale terminals should be used, actual cash on hand at the end of the day should be compared to register reports, and daily bank deposits should be made.

- Control of receipts by mail begins with the person opening the mail. They should prepare a listing of checks received and forward the list to the accounting department. The checks are forwarded to a cashier who prepares a daily bank deposit. The accounting department enters the information from the listing of checks into the accounting records and compares the listing to a copy of the deposit slip prepared by the cashier.

- Controls over cash disbursements include procedures that allow only authorized payments and maintenance of proper separation of duties. Control features include making disbursements by check, performance of periodic bank reconciliations, proper utilization of petty cash systems, and verification of supporting documentation before disbursing funds.

Proper bank reconciliation and petty cash systems are discussed in following sections.

Bank Reconciliation

One of the most common cash control procedures is the **bank reconciliation**. In business, every bank statement should be promptly reconciled by a person not otherwise involved in the cash receipts and disbursements functions. The reconciliation is needed to identify errors, irregularities, and adjustments for the Cash account. Having an independent person prepare the reconciliation helps establish separation of duties and deters fraud by requiring collusion for unauthorized actions.

There are many different formats for the reconciliation process, but they all accomplish the same objective. The reconciliation compares the amount of cash shown on the monthly **bank statement** (the document received from a bank which summarizes deposits and other credits, and checks and other debits) with the amount of cash reported in the general ledger. These two balances will frequently differ as shown in the following illustration:

Bank Statement

Lake City National Bank		
212 Golden Street P.O. Box 6458 Lake City, XX 12345	Statement date: July 1, 20X3 - July 31, 20X3	
	Statement for:	The Tackle Shack 445 Main Street Lake City, XX 12345
		Account # 76-7888-0987

CHECKING SUMMARY		
Previous statement balance on 06-30-X3		46,543.89
Total of 4 deposits	+	31,209.11
Total of 16 withdrawals	-	27,077.77
Interest earnings	+	119.34
Service charges	-	55.00
New balance		50,739.57

General Ledger

Cash				
Date	**Description**	**Debit**	**Credit**	**Balance**
July 22, 20X3	Journal page 7	$ 375.62		$44,234.61
July 24, 20X3	Journal page 7	2,779.59		41,455.02
July 24, 20X3	Journal page 7	9.31		41,445.71
July 25, 20X3	Journal page 7		$3,909.65	45,355.36
July 25, 20X3	Journal page 7	30.30		45,325.06
July 30, 20X3	Journal page 7	109.00		45,216.06
July 30, 20X3	Journal page 7	1,196.69		44,019.37
July 30, 20X3	Journal page 8	50.00		43,969.37
July 31, 20X3	Journal page 8		3,565.93	47,535.30

Differences are caused by items reflected on company records but not yet recorded by the bank. Examples include **deposits in transit** (a receipt entered on company records but not processed by the bank) and **outstanding checks** (checks written which have not cleared the bank). Other differences relate to items noted on the bank statement but not recorded by the company. Examples include non-sufficient funds (**NSF**) checks ("hot" checks previously deposited but which have been returned for nonpayment), bank service charges, notes receivable (like an account receivable, but more "formalized") collected by the bank on behalf of a company, and interest earnings.

The following format is typical of one used in the reconciliation process. Note that the balance per the bank statement is reconciled to the "correct" amount of cash; likewise, the balance per company records is reconciled to the "correct" amount. These amounts must agree. Once the correct adjusted cash balance is satisfactorily calculated, journal entries must be prepared for all items identified in the reconciliation of the ending balance per company records to the correct cash balance. These entries serve to record the transactions and events which impact cash but have not been previously journalized (e.g., NSF checks, bank service charges, interest income, and so on).

Ending balance per bank statement	$50,739.57
Add: Deposits in transit (and similar receipts entered on company records but not yet reported on the bank statement)	XX,XXX.XX
Deduct: Outstanding checks (and similar disbursements entered on company records but not reported on the bank statement)	X,XXX.XX
Correct cash balance	$XX,XXX.XX

Must equal

Ending balance per company records	$47,535.30	Requires a debit to adjust Cash account ◄
Add: Interest (and similar receipts reported on the bank statement but not entered on company records)	XX,XXX.XX	
Deduct: NSF checks (and similar disbursements reported on the bank statement but not entered on company records)	X,XXX.XX	Requires a credit to adjust Cash account ◄
Correct cash balance	$XX,XXX.XX	

EXAMPLE

The following pages include a detailed illustration of the bank reconciliation process. Begin by carefully reviewing the bank statement for The Tackle Shop found on the next page. Then look at the company's check register spreadsheet that follows. Information found on that spreadsheet would correlate precisely to activity in the company's Cash account within the general ledger.

The following additional information must also be considered:

- Check #5454 was written in June but did not clear the bank until July 2. There were no other outstanding checks, and no deposits in transit at the end of June.

- The EFT (electronic funds transfer) on July 11 relates to the monthly utility bill; the Tackle Shop has authorized the utility to draft its account directly each month.

- The Tackle Shop is optimistic that they will recover the full amount, including the service charge, on the NSF check that was given to them during the month.

- The bank collected a $5,000 note for The Tackle Shop, plus 9% interest ($5,450).

- The Tackle Shop's credit card clearing company remitted funds on July 25; the Tackle Shop received an email notification of this posting and simultaneously journalized this cash receipt in the accounting records.

- The Tackle Shop made the deposit of $3,565.93 late in the day on July 31, 20X3.

- The ending cash balance, per the company general ledger, was $47,535.30.

Be aware that conducting a successful bank reconciliation requires careful attention to every detail. After examining the bank statement, check register, and additional information, proceed to verify each component within (1) the balance per bank statement to the correct cash balance and (2) the balance per company records to the correct cash balance.

**Lake City
National Bank**
212 Golden Street
P.O. Box 6458
Lake City, XX 12345

Statement date: July 1, 20X3 through July 31, 20X3

Statement for: The Tackle Shack

445 Main Street

Lake City, XX 12345

Account # 76-7888-0987

CHECKING SUMMARY

Previous statement balance on 06-30-X3		46,543.89
Total of 4 deposits	+	31,209.11
Total of 16 withdrawals	-	27,077.77
Interest earnings	+	119.34
Service charges	-	55.00
New balance		50,739.57

CHECKS AND OTHER DEBITS

Check	Date Paid	Amount	Check	Date Paid	Amount
5454	2-Jul	4,456.09	*5465*	16-Jul	85.58
5457	3-Jul	245.00	5466	19-Jul	1,199.19
5458	3-Jul	12.34	5467	23-Jul	76.14
5459	10-Jul	66.14	5468	23-Jul	375.62
5460	5-Jul	11,998.20	5469	30-Jul	2,779.59
5461	9-Jul	3,000.00	5470	27-Jul	9.31
5463	16-Jul	2,119.44	*5472*	31-Jul	109.00

	Date Paid	Amount
Electronic funds transfer	11-Jul	109.07
NSF returned check	17-Jul	437.06
NSF fee	31-Jul	25.00
Monthly service fee	31-Jul	30.00

DEPOSITS AND OTHER CREDITS

	Date Posted	Amount
Customer deposit at main location	10-Jul	12,994.36
Customer deposit at River Branch location	17-Jul	8,855.10
Collection item -- note receivable	25-Jul	5,450.00
Credit card posting - transaction 07e79849657	25-Jul	3,909.65
Interest earnings	31-Jul	119.34

Spreadsheet					▢◻✕
F 25		*fx*	=F24-D25+E25		
A	B	C	D	E	F
	DATE	PARTY	REF #	CHECK	DEPOSIT	Balance

	DATE	PARTY	REF #	CHECK	DEPOSIT	Balance
1	DATE	PARTY	REF #	CHECK	DEPOSIT	Balance
2						
3	07-01-X3		BALANCE			$42,087.80
4	07-01-X3	Bailey	5457	$ 245.00		41,842.80
5	07-02-X3	Boyatzis	5458	12.34		41,830.46
6	07-03-X3	Smith	5459	66.14		41,764.32
7	07-05-X3	Blaize	5460	11,998.20		29,766.12
8	07-08-X3	Paronto	5461	3,000.00		26,766.12
9	07-08-X3	Void	5462			26,766.12
10	07-09-X3	Deposit			$ 12,994.36	39,760.48
11	07-15-X3	Sanchez	5463	2,119.44		37,641.04
12	07-15-X3	Bauer	5464	525.00		37,116.04
13	07-15-X3	Cameron	5465	85.58		37,030.46
14	07-17-X3	Deposit			8,855.10	45,885.56
15	07-19-X3	Hartman	5466	1,199.19		44,686.37
16	07-21-X3	Ashkanasy	5467	76.14		44,610.23
17	07-22-X3	Forest	5468	375.62		44,234.61
18	07-24-X3	Augier	5469	2,779.59		41,455.02
19	07-24-X3	Arbaugh	5470	9.31		41,445.71
20	07-25-X3	Credit Card			3,909.65	45,355.36
21	07-25-X3	Bento	5471	30.30		45,325.06
22	07-30-X3	Peterson	5472	109.00		45,216.06
23	07-30-X3	Taggart	5473	1,196.69		44,019.37
24	07-30-X3	Klimoski	5474	50.00		43,969.37
25	07-31-X3	Deposit			3,565.93	47,535.30
26				$23,877.54	$29,325.04	

Below is the July reconciliation of the *balance per bank statement to the correct cash balance*.

Ending balance per bank statement		$50,739.57	
Add: Deposits in transit		3,565.93	
Deduct: Outstanding checks			
#5464	$ 525.00		
#5471	30.30		
#5473	1,196.69		
#5474	50.00	(1801.99)	
Correct cash balance		$52,503.51	

The reconciliation of the *balance per company records to the correct cash balance* is presented below. This reconciliation will trigger various adjustments to the Cash account in the company ledger.

Ending balance per company records			$47,535.30	
Add: Customer note collection		$5,450.00		
Interest earnings		119.34	5,569.34	
Deduct: EFT for utilities		$ 109.07		
NSF check returned		437.06		
NSF fee		25.00		
Service charges		30.00	(601.13)	
Correct cash balance			$52,503.51	

The identified items necessitated increasing cash by $4,968.21 ($52,503.51 correct balance, less the balance per company records of $47,535.30). Note that the $462.06 debit to Accounts Receivable indicates that The Tackle Shop is going to attempt to collect on the NSF check and related charge. The interest income of $569.34 reflects that posted by the bank ($119.34) plus the $450 on the collected note.

07-31-X3	Cash		4,968.21	
	Utilities Expense		109.07	
	Accounts Receivable		462.06	
	Miscellaneous Expense		30.00	
	Notes Receivable			5,000.00
	Interest Income			569.34
	To record adjustments from bank reconciliation			

This reconciliation example demonstrates the importance of the process, without which accounting records would soon become unreliable.

DEBIT CARDS

Another example of an item that could impact the bank statement but not yet be recorded on company records relates to the use of bank "**debit cards**." A bank debit card transaction is equivalent to an electronically generated check but it results in an almost immediate withdrawal of funds. Such withdrawals would be listed on the bank statement individually.

Great care is necessary to record each debit card transaction into the accounting records, and appropriate approval and documentation can be problematic. When debit cards are used, the reconciliation process is often complicated because additional withdrawals will be discovered on the bank statement that still need to be recorded on the company records.

PROOF OF CASH

Many businesses prepare a reconciliation just like that illustrated. However, this approach leaves one gaping hole in the control process. What if the bank statement included a $5,000 check to an employee near the beginning of the month, and a $5,000 deposit by that employee near the end of the month (and these amounts were not recorded on the company records)? In other words, the employee took out an unauthorized "loan" for a while. The reconciliation would not reveal this unauthorized activity because the ending balances are correct and in agreement. To overcome this deficiency, some companies will reconcile not only the beginning and ending balances, but also the total checks per the bank statement to the total disbursements per the company records, and the total deposits per the bank statement to the total receipts on the company accounts. If a problem exists, the totals on the bank statement will exceed the totals per the company records for both receipts and disbursements. This added reconciliation technique is termed a **proof of cash**. It is highly recommended where the volume of transactions and amount of money involved is very large.

Also illegal is "kiting" which occurs when one opens numerous bank accounts at various locations and then proceeds to write checks on one account and deposit them to another. In turn, checks are written on that account, and deposited to yet another bank. And, over and over and over. Each of the bank accounts may appear to have money; but, it is illusionary because there are numerous checks "floating" about that will hit and reduce the accounts. Somewhere in the process the perpetrator makes a cash withdrawal and then vanishes. That is why one will often see bank notices that deposited funds cannot be withdrawn for several days. Such restrictions are intended to make sure that a deposit clears the bank on which it is drawn before releasing those funds. Kiting is complex and illegal. Enhanced electronic clearing procedures adopted by banks have made kiting far more difficult to accomplish.

Petty Cash

Petty cash, also known as imprest cash, is a fund established for making small payments that are impractical to pay by check. Examples include postage due, reimbursement to employees for small purchases of office supplies, and numerous similar items. The establishment of a petty cash system begins by making out a check to cash, cashing it, and placing the cash in a petty cash box:

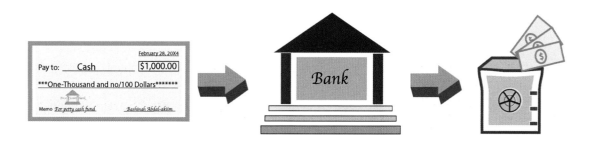

A petty cash custodian should be designated to safeguard and make payments from this fund. At the time the fund is established, the following journal entry is needed. This journal entry, in essence, subdivides the petty cash portion of available funds into a separate account.

01-31-X4	Petty Cash		1,000	
	Cash			1,000
	To establish a $1,000 petty cash fund			

Policies should be established regarding appropriate expenditures that can be paid from petty cash. When a disbursement is made from the fund, a receipt should be placed in the petty cash box. The receipt should set forth the amount and nature of expenditure. The receipts are known as petty cash vouchers. At any point in time, the receipts plus the remaining cash should equal the balance of the petty cash fund (i.e., the amount of cash originally placed in the fund).

As expenditures occur, cash in the box will be depleted. Eventually the fund will require replenishment. A check for cash is prepared in an amount to bring the fund back up to the original level. The check is cashed and the proceeds are placed in the petty cash box. At the same time, receipts are removed from the petty cash box and formally recorded as expenses.

REPLENISH PETTY CASH

The journal entry for this action involves debits to appropriate expense accounts as represented by the receipts, and a credit to Cash for the amount of the replenishment. Notice that the Petty Cash account is not impacted -- it was originally established as a base amount, and its balance has not been changed by virtue of this activity.

02-28-X4	Supplies Expense	390	
	Fuel Expense	155	
	Miscellaneous Expense	70	
	Cash		615
	To replenish petty cash; receipts on hand totaled $615 related to office supplies ($390), gasoline ($155), coffee and drinks ($70). Remaining cash in the fund was $385, bringing the total to $1,000 ($615 + $385).		

Occasional errors may cause the petty cash fund to be out of balance. The sum of the cash and receipts will differ from the correct Petty Cash balance. This might be the result of simple mistakes, such as math errors in making change, or perhaps someone failed to provide a receipt for an appropriate expenditure. Whatever the cause, the available cash must be brought back to the appropriate level.

CASH SHORT AND OVER

The journal entry to record full replenishment may require an additional debit (for shortages) or credit (for overages) to Cash Short (Over). In the following entry, $635 is placed back into the fund, even though receipts amount to only $615. The difference is debited to Cash Short (Over):

02-28-X4	Supplies Expense	390	
	Fuel Expense	155	
	Miscellaneous Expense	70	
	Cash Short (Over)	20	
	Cash		635
	To replenish petty cash; receipts on hand totaled $615 related to office supplies ($390), gasoline ($155), coffee and drinks ($70). Remaining cash in the fund was $365, bringing the total to $980 ($615 + $365); a $20 shortage was noted and replenished.		

The Cash Short (Over) account is an income statement type account. It is also applicable to situations other than petty cash. For example, a retailer will compare daily cash sales to the actual cash found in the cash register drawers. If a surplus or shortage is discovered, the difference will be recorded in Cash Short (Over); a debit balance indicates a shortage (expense), while a credit represents an overage (revenue).

INCREASING THE BASE FUND

As a company grows, it may find a need to increase the base size of its petty cash fund. The entry to increase the fund would be identical to the first entry illustrated; that is, the amount added to the base amount of the fund would be debited to Petty Cash and credited to Cash. Otherwise, take note that the only entry to the Petty Cash account occurred when the fund was established.

Short-Term Investments

A business may invest cash in stocks of other corporations. Or, a company may buy other types of corporate or government securities. If these investments are acquired for long-term purposes, or perhaps to establish some form of control over another entity, the investments are classified as noncurrent assets. The accounting rules for those types of investments are covered in subsequent chapters. But, when the investments are acquired with the simple intent of generating profits by reselling the investment in the very near future, such investments are classified as current assets (following cash on the balance sheet).

Such investments are initially recorded at cost (including brokerage fees). However, the value of these items may fluctuate. Subsequent to initial acquisition, short-term investments are to be reported at their fair value. The fluctuation in value is reported in the income statement. This approach is often called "mark-to-market" or **fair value** accounting. Fair value is defined as the price that would be received from the sale of an asset in an orderly transaction between market participants.

EXAMPLE

Assume that Webster Company's management was seeing a pickup in their business activity and believed that a similar uptick was occurring for its competitors as well. One of its competitors, Merriam Corporation, was a public company, and its stock was trading at $10 per share. Webster had excess cash earning very low rates of interest and decided to invest in Merriam with the intent of selling the investment in the very near future for a quick profit. The following entry was needed on March 3, 20X6, the day Webster bought stock of Merriam:

03-03-X6	Short-Term Investments	50,000	
	Cash		50,000
	To record the purchase of 5,000 shares of Merriam stock at $10 per share		

Next, assume that financial statements were being prepared on March 31. Despite Webster's plans for a quick profit, the stock declined to $9 per share by March 31. Webster still believes in the future of this investment and is holding all 5,000 shares. But, accounting rules require that the investment "be written down" to current value, with a corresponding charge against income. The charge against income is recorded in an account called Unrealized Loss on Investments:

03-31-X6	Unrealized Loss on Investments	5,000	
	Short-Term Investments		5,000
	To record a $1 per share decrease in the value of 5,000 shares of Merriam stock		

Notice that the loss is characterized as "unrealized." This term is used to describe an event that is being recorded ("recognized") in the financial statements, even though the final cash consequence has not yet been determined. Hence, the term "unrealized."

During April, the stock of Merriam bounced up $3 per share to $12. At the end of April, another entry is needed if financial statements are again being prepared:

04-30-X6	Short-Term Investments	15,000	
	Unrealized Gain on Investments		15,000
	To record a $3 per share increase in the value of 5,000 shares of Merriam stock		

Notice that the three journal entries now have the investment valued at $60,000 ($50,000 - $5,000 + $15,000). This is equal to market value ($12 X 5,000 = $60,000). The income statement for March includes a loss of $5,000, but April shows a gain of $15,000. Cumulatively, the income statements show a total gain of $10,000 ($5,000 loss + $15,000 gain). This cumulative gain corresponds to the total increase in value of the original $50,000 investment.

The preceding illustration assumed a single investment. However, the treatment would be the same even if there was a portfolio of many investments. That is, each and every investment would be adjusted to fair value.

RATIONALE FOR FAIR VALUE

The fair value approach is in stark contrast to the historical cost approach. The rationale is that the market value for short-term investments is readily determinable, and the periodic fluctuations have a definite economic impact that should be reported. Given the intent to dispose of the investments in the near future, the belief is that the changes in value likely have a corresponding effect on the ultimate cash flows of the company. As a result, the accounting rules recognize those changes as they happen.

A VALUATION ADJUSTMENT ACCOUNT

As an alternative to directly adjusting the Short-Term Investments account, some companies may maintain a separate Valuation Adjustment account that is added to or subtracted from the Short-Term Investments account. The results are the same; the reason for using the alternative approach is to provide additional information that may be needed for more complex accounting and tax purposes. One such purpose is to determine the "taxable gain or loss" on sale. Tax rules generally require comparing the sales price to the original cost (tax rules sometimes differ from accounting rules, and the fair value approach used for accounting is normally not acceptable for tax purposes). There are also more involved accounting rules relating to measurement of the "realized" gains and losses when the securities are, in fact, sold. Those rules are ordinarily the subject of more advanced courses.

DIVIDENDS AND INTEREST

Since short-term investments are turned over rather quickly, the amount of interest and dividends received on those investments is probably not very significant. However, any dividends or interest received is reported as income and included in the income statement:

09-15-X5	Cash	5,000	
	Dividend Income		5,000
	To record receipt of dividend on investment		

The presence or absence of dividends or interest does not change the basic fair value approach for the Short-Term Investments account.

DERIVATIVES

There are an endless array of more exotic investment options. Among these are commodity futures, interest rate swap agreements, options related agreements, and so on. These investments are generally referred to as **derivatives**, because their value is based upon or derived from something else (e.g., a cotton futures contract takes its value from cotton, etc.). The underlying accounting approach follows that for short-term investments. That is, such instruments are initially measured at fair value, and changes in fair value are recorded in income as they happen.

Chapter 6 Quiz

Q6-1. The items reported in the Cash account on the balance sheet must be acceptable to a bank for deposit and free from restrictions for use in satisfying current debts.

true   or   false

Q6-2. The accounting department should have exclusive control over the functions of cash collection, bank deposits, recording appropriate journal entries, and preparing the periodic bank reconciliation.

true   or   false

Q6-3. The reconciliation of the cash balance per company records to the correct adjusted cash balance would indicate the need for journal entries.

true   or   false

Q6-4. The initial recording of short-term investments is at cost, including brokerage fees.

true   or   false

Q6-5. Only decreases in value are recognized for short-term investments.

true   or   false

Q6-6. _____ includes coins, currency, and money orders, but not checks that become payable on a future date (known as _____).

Q6-7. The _____ is a major component of a cash planning system, and represents the overall plan of activity that depicts cash inflows and outflows for a stated period of time.

Q6-8. The bank reconciliation is based on the Cash account and a document called a _____.

Q6-9. A short-term investment should be classified in the _____ section of the balance sheet.

Q6-10. Short-term investments should be measured and reported at _____ value.

Q6-11. Unrealized gains and losses on short-term investments impact _____ .

Multiple Choice

Q6-12. The Cash account on the balance sheet should not include which of the following items:

a. Travel advances to employees

b. Currency

c. Money orders

d. Deposits in transit

Q6-13. When reconciling the ending cash balance per the bank statement to the correct adjusted cash balance, how would deposits in transit be handled?

a. Added to the balance per the bank statement.

b. Subtracted from the balance per the bank statement.

c. Added to the balance per company records.

d. Ignored.

Q6-14. Malory Company provides the following information about the month-end bank reconciliation:

Ending cash per bank statement	$1,367
Ending cash per company records	7,383
Monthly bank service charge	25
Deposits in transit at month-end	8,345
Outstanding checks at month-end	2,399
Customer check returned NSF	45

a. $4,914

b. $7,268

c. $7,313

d. $7,383

Q6-15. Short-term investments owned by a company are:

a. reported on the balance sheet as a current asset.

b. reported on the balance sheet as a noncurrent asset.

c. reported on the balance sheet as a contra-equity account.

d. reported on the balance sheet as a reduction of liabilities.

Q6-16. During its first year of operation, Lenton Company acquired three short-term investments. Investment A cost $50,000 and had a year-end market value of $60,000. Investment B cost $35,000 and had a year-end market value of $17,000. Investment C cost $26,000 and had a year-end market value of $24,000. The journal entry to record the decline in market value would include:

a. a debit to Unrealized Loss on Short-Term Investments.

b. a credit to Unrealized Gain on Short-Term Investments.

c. a debit to Short-Term Investments.

d. At least two of the above.

Chapter 6 Problems

Basic Problems

Composition of cash	B-06.01

Review the following items and decide if each would be more appropriately classified as:

Cash   Cash equivalent   Neither cash nor cash equivalent

(a)   Currency in the petty cash box

(b)   Postage stamps in a file cabinet

(c)   The balance on deposit in a regular checking account

(d)   An advance to an employee for travel costs to be incurred

(e)   A certificate of deposit maturing in 2 years

(f)   A 30-day certificate of deposit

(g)   An investment in a government treasury security maturing in 2 years

(h)   A 90-day government treasury security

(i)   A post-dated check accepted from a customer

(j)   Amounts due from customers

(k)   Amounts paid to suppliers by check, but the supplier has not yet cashed the check

Cash management	B-06.02

Arctic Blast has developed a cold treatment process for killing home-invading ants and termites. Its pesticide-free process provides a highly attractive alternative to sprays and poisons. The business is growing quite rapidly, and it is investing heavily in new equipment. Frank Miller is Arctic's treasurer, and he is preparing a cash budget. The budget reveals that the company can anticipate periods of cash flow difficulties as they attempt to finance ever increasing amounts of receivables, inventories, and equipment.

Frank is evaluating the merits of eight alternative cash management strategies. Each has a potential downside that Frank must consider. Match each item in the "strategy" list with one of the "hazards."

Strategy
_____

Borrowing money

Attempting to accelerate customer collections

Delaying payments

Writing checks against future receipts not yet deposited

Slowing expansion plans

Establishing bank overdraft protection or a line of credit

Issuing additional capital stock

Planning full utilization of cash flows, with no reserves

Hazard

May necessitate offering of a discount

May result in unnecessary financing costs

May dilute ownership of existing shareholders

May alienate key suppliers

May result in unexpected shortfall

May be an illegal strategy

May give competitors an advantage

May result in risk of financial failure

B-06.03   *Preparation of a basic bank reconciliation*

Dine-Corp International publishes ratings and reviews of the world's finest restaurants. Following are facts you need to prepare Dine-Corp's March bank reconciliation:

Balance per company records at end of month	$ 72,644.12
Bank service charge for the month	44.00
NSF check returned with bank statement	1,440.66
Note collected by the bank during the month	45,000.00
Outstanding checks at month end	31,553.57
Interest on note collected during the month	4,500.00
Balance per bank at end of month	144,223.99
Deposit in transit at month end	7,989.04

B-06.04   *Journal entries from bank reconciliation*

Daniel Scott is an audit manager with the accounting firm of Nelson & Riley, CPAs. As part of the routine audit procedures for one of the firm's clients, Daniel instructed Wanda Mullins, a newly hired staff auditor, to obtain a bank statement directly from the client's bank and prepare an independent reconciliation of the Cash account. Wanda did a great job and presented Daniel with the following reconciliation. Daniel has now forwarded this document directly to you, with a request that you prepare proposed adjusting entries that need to be recorded by the client.

Ending balance per bank statement		$67,700.98	
Add: Deposits in transit		13,444.12	
Deduct: Outstanding checks			
#12221	$16,887.34		
#12327	8,550.50		
#12329	132.74	(25,570.58)	
Correct cash balance		$55,574.52	

Ending balance per company records		$52,148.55	
Add: Payment from customer via ETF*	$3,445.99		
Interest earnings	566.88	4,012.87	
Deduct: Reject customer credit card/charge back	$ 466.90		
Service charges	120.00	(586.90)	
Correct cash balance		$55,574.52	

* This payment has yet to be recorded as revenue by the company.

Petty cash   B-06.05

Biscay Bay Boats established a petty cash fund for minor day-to-day expenses. Following are activities related to this fund. Prepare the necessary journal entries for petty cash.

(1)   Established a $500 petty cash fund by writing a check to "cash," cashing the check, and placing the proceeds in a petty cash box entrusted to Herman Jones as custodian.

(2)   At the end of the month, the petty cash fund contained remaining cash of $127, and receipts for $65 postage, $123 office supplies, and $180 gasoline for company vehicles. Herman is not sure why the fund is short $5. A check payable to cash in the amount of $373 was prepared, and the funds were placed into the box.

(3)   At the end of the next month, the petty cash fund contained remaining cash of $35, and receipts for $265 postage, $160 office supplies, and $40 gasoline for company vehicles. A check payable to cash in the amount of $715 was prepared, and the funds were placed into the box. This amount reimburses the fund and increases its balance to $750.

Piven Mining Corporation holds significant limestone deposits. One of its key customers, Kuai Oil, produces crude oil from shale deposits. This production process requires limestone, and Piven is seeing a large increase in order flow from Kuai and other shale companies. Piven's management believes Kuai's stock is undervalued, and has decided to invest excess cash in the stock of Kuai Oil. The intent of this investment is for short-term investment purposes only. Following are detailed facts about the Kuai investment. You should prepare journal entries to record the investment, and necessary end-of-month adjusting entries to reflect changes for each month.

May 7	Purchased 500,000 shares of Kuai Oil at $7 per share.
May 31	The fair value of Kuai's stock was $9 per share.
June 30	The fair value of Kuai's stock was $5 per share.
July 15	Received a dividend from Kuai of $0.10 per share.
July 31	The fair value of Kuai's stock was $8 per share.

Involved Problems

Various contractual arrangements entered into by Nusbaum Company require it to maintain a minimum balance of cash and cash equivalents of $1,000,000. The company's balance is dipping near that level, and the CFO is considering strategies to avoid a shortfall.

Evaluate the following ideas and assess the relative merits and costs of each.

The company has a 1-year certificate of deposit, and it is earning 5% interest. The bank has offered to swap this CD for a 1-month CD bearing a 4.5% interest rate.

The company holds significant investments in "trading" securities. These investments have typically yielded about 8% per year. The company can sell these securities and convert the proceeds to cash.

The company carries several million dollars of accounts payable, terms 2/10, n/30. The company always takes the discount, but can delay payment to preserve cash.

The company can begin to offer cash discounts of 1/10, n/30 on its receivables, and anticipates that this would greatly speed cash collections.

The company maintains a significant investment in postage stamps and travel advances. The company can buy postage "as needed" via an internet linked postage meter, and the company can do away with travel advances and provide key employees with a company credit card to use for travel costs.

The company is considering establishing a line of credit that enables it to borrow, on demand, up to $5,000,000 in cash. The bank will charge a $12,500 annual fee for making this credit line available to the company. Any borrowed funds will accrue interest at the established London Interbank Offered Rate (LIBOR) plus 1%.

Manahan Corporation received its August 31 bank statement showing total funds on deposit of $288,090.09. This amount was $149,158.22 in excess of the balance in the general ledger Cash account. Additional information consists of the following:

> The company has a 1-year, $100,000, certificate of deposit. This amount is included in the total funds listed on the bank statement. Manahan classifies this security in a separate investment account in its general ledger.

> Interest earned on the CD was $475 during the month. This interest is free for withdrawal and is automatically posted to the regular checking account. Manahan's first notification of the amount of interest for the month is via the bank statement, and the interest income has not yet been recorded in the general ledger Cash account.

> Manahan Corporation received a $50,000 draft for an oil and gas lease from XTX Exploration. This draft was presented to the bank in early July. Drafts are not cash until the maker (XTX) honors them (at their option), and this process can take as long as several weeks. The bank statement included notification that XTX had honored and funded the draft in mid August. This is the first notification to Manahan of actual funding, and Manahan has not previously recorded this transaction.

> Manahan made a deposit late in the afternoon of August 31. The amount of the deposit was $3,666.04, but this amount did not appear on the August 31 bank statement. The bank has a sign in its lobby that says "Deposits after 3 pm will be processed on the next business day."

> Manahan has authorized automatic payments to its utility company for monthly charges. Withdrawals of $1,445.99 appear in the bank statement for such utilities. This is the first notification to Manahan, and Manahan has not previously recorded this transaction.

> Late in August, Manahan did an online authorization for a credit card company payment. Due to a timing issue, the bank statement does not yet reflect the payment for $4,446.09. Manahan has appropriately recorded the reduction in cash in the general ledger.

> Manahan prepared a $3,000 payment to Sims via check #12234. Due to a bookkeeping error, Sims reported that it had not received payment. Manahan issued a $3,000 replacement check #12257. Both checks cleared the bank in August, and Sims has admitted its error. Sims will be returning $3,000 to Manahan.

> The bank statement included monthly service charges of $125. Manahan has not previously recorded these charges.

> At the end of July, three checks were outstanding (#12170, $245.55; #12200, $1,889.66; and #12202, $75). At the end of August, three checks were outstanding (#12170, $245.55; #12290, $1,333.07, and #12291, $1,117.54).

> A review of deposits clearing the bank revealed that Manahan had recorded a $2,000.22 deposit as $2,222.22 in the general ledger Cash and Revenue accounts.

(a)   Prepare Manahan's bank reconciliation as of August 31, 20X5.

(b)   What is the correct balance for Cash in the August 31 balance sheet?

(c)   Prepare the journal entry suggested by the reconciliation.

Following is the September 30, 20X4 bank reconciliation for the Quiet Moose Lodge. You are also provided with the October check register and bank statement. Utilize this information to prepare October's bank reconciliation and related adjusting entry. You may assume that any discrepancies between the check register and bank statement relate to recording errors in the accounts of the Quiet Moose, and not the bank.

Ending balance per bank statement			$18,344.07
Add: Deposits in transit			2,505.55
Deduct: Outstanding checks			
#3444		$ 175.00	
#3446		1,908.09	(2,083.09)
Correct cash balance			$18,766.53

Ending balance per company records		$18,696.53
Add: Interest earnings		80.00
Deduct: Service charges		(10.00)
Correct cash balance		$18,766.53

Spreadsheet   ⬒ ⬚ ✖

fx

	A	B	C	D	E	F
1	DATE	PARTY	REF #	CHECK	DEPOSIT	Balance
2						
3	10-01-X4		BALANCE			$18,766.53
4	10-02-X4	Gomez	3448	$ 145.99		18,620.54
5	10-05-X4	Deposit			$ 3,400.00	22,020.54
6	10-07-X4	Bryers	3449	387.97		21,632.57
7	10-07-X4	Morton	3450	1,204.67		20,427.90
8	10-07-X4	Lee	3451	4,664.50		15,763.40
9	10-10-X4	Morici	3452	43.23		15,720.17
10	10-10-X4	LaCorx	3453	2,990.44		12,729.73
11	10-11-X4	Benson	3454	1,100.31		11,629.42
12	10-12-X4	Void	3455			11,629.42
13	10-13-X4	Morgan	3456	695.77		10,933.65
14	10-13-X4	Russell	3457	788.87		10,144.78
15	10-14-X4	Deposit			3,476.88	13,621.66
16	10-17-X4	Lowen	3458	3,664.34		9,957.32
17	10-19-X4	Post Office	3459	45.45		9,911.87
18	10-20-X4	Nguen	3460	677.21		9,234.66
19	10-30-X4	Behn	3461	499.00		8,735.66
20	10-31-X4	Deposit			8,131.21	16,866.87
21				$16,907.75	$15,008.09	

MOUNTAIN HOME BANK

121 Main Street

P.O. Box 5566

Statement date: October 1, 20X4 through October 31, 20X4

Statement for: Quiet Moose Lodge

13 River Street

Patawa Township

Account # 474784

CHECKING SUMMARY

Previous statement balance on 09-30-X4		18,344.07
Total of 5 deposits	+	19,339.09
Total of 14 withdrawals	-	14,887.45
Interest earnings	+	65.66
Service charges	-	35.00
New balance		22,826.37

CHECKS AND OTHER DEBITS

Check	Date Paid	Amount	Check	Date Paid	Amount
3446	3-Oct	1908.09	3454	12-Oct	1100.31
3448	5-Oct	145.99	*3456*	13-Oct	695.77
3449	7-Oct	387.97	3457	14-Oct	788.87
3450	7-Oct	1204.67	3458	18-Oct	3664.34
3452	10-Oct	43.23	3459	20-Oct	54.45
3453	11-Oct	2990.44	3460	21-Oct	677.21

	Date Paid	Amount
Electronic funds transfer - Patawa Water Co-op	25-Oct	237.34
NSF returned check - maker, Stacey	28-Oct	988.77
NSF fee	28-Oct	25.00
Monthly service fee	31-Oct	10.00

DEPOSITS AND OTHER CREDITS

	Date Posted	Amount
Customer deposit	1-Oct	2505.55
Customer deposit	5-Oct	3400.00
Collection item -- note receivable ($6500 + interest)	11-Oct	6774.33
Customer deposit	14-Oct	3476.88
Credit card sales posting	28-Oct	3182.33
Interest earnings	31-Oct	65.66

Team-based study of petty cash with business papers

I-06.04

This problem provides a tangible, team exercise pertaining to the correct operation of a petty cash fund. Begin by forming a nine-person team consisting of four employees, a banker, a petty cash custodian, a treasurer, an accountant, and an auditor. Refer to the problem section of the website for additional instructions and copies of the corresponding business papers.

SPREADSHEET TOOL:

Pivot tables

Pulaski Mining Corporation occasionally acquires short-term investments. On August 1, 20X7, Pulaski acquired stock investments in four different companies: Aztec Zinc (cost of $125,000), Morton Construction (cost of $75,000), Particle Drilling (cost of $80,000), and Astraview Navigation (cost of $20,000). The company's stockbroker emailed the following listing of investment values at the end of August, September, and October. These data were imported into a spreadsheet as follows. You are to prepare the journal entries needed to record the initial investment in this portfolio, as well as end of month adjusting entries for August, September, and October. The electronic spreadsheet on the website includes a pivot table that will aid your compilation of data necessary to solve this problem. It is found immediately after the data on the excel spreadsheet version of the problem.

Spreadsheet			🗕🗖✕
		fx	
	A	B	C	D
1	Company	Month	Market Value	
2				
3	Aztec Zinc	August	$130,000	
4	Aztec Zinc	September	145,000	
5	Aztec Zinc	October	142,000	
6	Morton Construction	August	70,000	
7	Morton Construction	September	61,000	
8	Morton Construction	October	58,000	
9	Particle Drilling	August	89,000	
10	Particle Drilling	September	109,000	
11	Particle Drilling	October	101,000	
12	Astraview Navigation	August	20,000	
13	Astraview Navigation	September	22,000	
14	Astraview Navigation	October	16,000	
15				
16				
17	PIVOT TABLE		Company	Astraview Navigation ▼
18				
19			Sum of Market Value	
20			Month	Total
21			August	20000
22			Grand Total	20000
23				

This problem requires you to select three stocks for a hypothetical short-term investment portfolio. Assume you invest $100,000 in each company at beginning of "day one."

Prepare a daily journal entry at the end of each day for five consecutive business days to properly account for the change in value of your investment portfolio. Numerous internet sites or the business section of most newspapers should allow you to readily track the changes in value of your stocks! Keep detailed notes to document the changes in value of your investments, and have a classmate audit your journal entries.

Chapter 7:
Accounts Receivable

Goals:

The costs and benefits of selling on credit.
Accounting considerations for uncollectible receivables.
The allowance method of accounting for uncollectibles.
Notes receivable and interest, including dishonored obligations.

principlesofaccounting.com

Receivables arise from a variety of claims against customers and others, and are generally classified as current or noncurrent based on expectations about the amount of time it will take to collect them. The majority of receivables are classified as **trade receivables**, which arise from the sale of products or services to customers. Such trade receivables are carried in the **Accounts Receivable** account. **Nontrade receivables** arise from other transactions like advances to employees and utility company deposits.

CREDIT SALES

Purchases of inventory and supplies will often be made on account. Likewise, sales to customers may directly (by the vendor offering credit) or indirectly (through a bank or credit card company) entail the extension of credit. While the availability of credit facilitates many business transactions, it is also costly. Credit providers must conduct investigations of credit worthiness and monitor collection activities. In addition, the creditor must forego alternative uses of money while credit is extended. Occasionally, a borrower may refuse or is unable to pay. Depending on the nature of the credit relationship, some credit costs may be offset by interest charges. And, merchants frequently note that the availability of credit entices customers to make a purchase decision.

CREDIT CARDS

Banks and financial services companies have developed credit cards that are widely accepted by many merchants, and eliminate the necessity of those merchants maintaining separate credit departments. Popular examples include MasterCard, Visa, and American Express. These credit card companies earn money from these cards by charging merchant fees (usually a formula-based percentage of sales) and assess interest and other charges against the users. Nevertheless, merchants tend to welcome their use because collection is virtually assured and very timely (oftentimes same day funding of the transaction is made by the credit card company). In addition, the added transaction cost is offset by a reduction in the internal costs associated with maintaining a credit department.

The accounting for credit card sales depends on the nature of the card. Some bank card-based transactions are essentially regarded as cash sales since funding is immediate. Assume that Rayyan Company sold merchandise to a customer for $1,000. The customer paid with a bank card, and the bank charged a 2% fee. Rayyan Company should record the following entry:

01-09-X3	Cash		980	
	Service Charge		20	
	Sales			1,000
	Sold merchandise on "bank card;" same day funding, net of fee of 2% assessed by bank			

Other card sales may involve delayed collection, and are initially recorded as credit sales:

01-09-X3	Accounts Receivable		1,000	
	Sales			1,000
	Sold merchandise on "non bank card"			

When collection occurs on January 25, notice that the following entry includes a provision for the service charge. The estimated service charge could (or perhaps should) have been recorded at the time of the sale on January 9, but the exact amount might not have been known. Rather than recording an estimate, and adjusting it later, this illustration is based on the simpler approach of not recording the charge until collection occurs.

01-25-X3	Cash		980	
	Service Charge		20	
	Accounts Receivable			1,000
	Collected amount due from credit card company; net of fee of 2%			

Accounting for Uncollectible Receivables

Unfortunately, some sales on account may not be collected. Customers go broke, become unhappy and refuse to pay, or may generally lack the ethics to complete their half of the bargain. Of course, a company does have legal recourse to try to collect such accounts, but those often fail. As a result, it becomes necessary to establish an accounting process for measuring and reporting these uncollectible items. Uncollectible accounts are frequently called "bad debts."

DIRECT WRITE-OFF METHOD

A simple method to account for uncollectible accounts is the **direct write-off** approach. Under this technique, a specific account receivable is removed from the accounting records *at the time it is finally determined to be uncollectible*. The appropriate entry for the direct write-off approach is as follows:

02-10-X7	Uncollectible Accounts Expense	500	
	Accounts Receivable		500
	To record the write-off of an uncollectible account from Jones		

Notice that the preceding entry reduces the receivables balance for the item that is uncollectible. The offsetting debit is to an expense account: Uncollectible Accounts Expense.

While the direct write-off method is simple, it is only acceptable in those cases where bad debts are immaterial in amount. In accounting, an item is deemed material if it is large enough to affect the judgment of an informed financial statement user. Accounting expediency sometimes permits "incorrect approaches" when the effect is not material.

Recall the discussion of non bank credit card charges above; there, the service charge expense was recorded subsequent to the sale, and it was suggested that the approach was lacking but acceptable given the small amounts involved. Materiality considerations permitted a departure from the best approach. But, what is material? It is a matter of judgment, relating only to the conclusion that the choice among alternatives really has very little bearing on the reported outcomes.

Consider why the direct write-off method is not to be used in those cases where bad debts are material; what is "wrong" with the method? One important accounting principle is the notion of matching. That is, costs related to the production of revenue are reported during the same time period as the related revenue (i.e., "matched").

With the direct write-off method, many accounting periods may come and go before an account is finally determined to be uncollectible and written off. As a result, revenues from credit sales are recognized in one period, but the costs of uncollectible accounts related to those sales are not recognized until another subsequent period (producing an unacceptable mismatch of revenues and expenses).

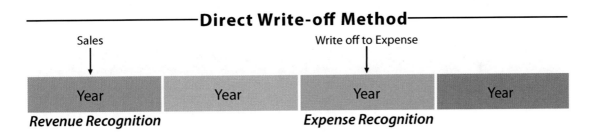

To compensate for this problem, accountants have developed "allowance methods" to account for uncollectible accounts. Importantly, an allowance method must be used except in those cases where bad debts are not material (and for tax purposes where tax rules often stipulate that a direct write-off approach is to be used). Allowance methods will result in the recording of an estimated bad debts expense in the same period as the related credit sales, and result in a fairer balance sheet valuation for outstanding receivables. As will soon be shown, the actual write-off in a subsequent period will generally not impact income.

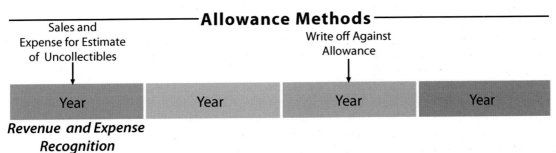

Allowance Methods for Uncollectibles

Having established that an **allowance method for uncollectibles** is preferable (indeed, required in many cases), it is time to focus on the details. Begin with a consideration of the balance sheet. Suppose that Ito Company has total accounts receivable of $425,000 at the end of the year, and is in the process or preparing a balance sheet. Obviously, the $425,000 would be reported as a current asset. But, what if it is estimated that $25,500 of this amount may ultimately prove to be uncollectible? Thus, a more correct balance sheet presentation would show the total receivables along with an allowance account (which is a contra asset account) that reduces the receivables to the amount expected to be collected. This anticipated amount is often termed the **net realizable value**.

ITO COMPANY Balance Sheet December 31, 20X3		
Assets		
.....		
Accounts receivable	$425,000	
Less: Allowance for uncollectibles	(25,500)	$399,500
.....		

DETERMINE THE ALLOWANCE ACCOUNT

In the preceding illustration, the $25,500 was simply given as part of the fact situation. But, how would such an amount actually be determined? If Ito Company's management knew which accounts were likely to not be collectible, they would have avoided selling to those customers in the first place. Instead, the $25,500 simply relates to the balance as a whole. It is likely based on past experience, but it is only an estimate. It could have been determined via an aging analysis.

An **aging of accounts receivable** stratifies receivables according to how long they have been outstanding. Percentages based on past history are applied to different strata. These percentages vary by company, but the older the account, the more likely it is to represent a bad account.

Ito's aging may have appeared as follows:

Spreadsheet						☐☐☒
L24			*fx*	=SUM(L20:L23)		
	I	J	K	L	M	N
19	Age	Balance	Estimated % Uncollectible	Estimated Amount Uncollectible		
20	Current	$250,000	1%	$ 2,500		
21	31-60 days	100,000	5%	5,000		
22	61-90 days	50,000	15%	7,500		
23	Over 90 days	25,000	42%	10,500		
24		$425,000		$25,500		
25						

Once the estimated amount for the allowance account is determined, a journal entry will be needed to bring the ledger into agreement. Assume that Ito's ledger revealed an Allowance for Uncollectible Accounts credit balance of $10,000 (prior to performing the above analysis).

As a result of the analysis, it can be seen that a target balance of $25,500 is needed; necessitating the following adjusting entry:

12-31-X5	Uncollectible Accounts Expense	15,500	
	Allowance for Uncollectible Accounts		15,500
	To adjust the allowance account from a $10,000 balance to the target balance of $25,500 ($25,500 - $10,000)		

Carefully study the illustration that follows. In particular take note of two important concepts:

- the amount of the entry is based upon the needed change in the account (i.e., to go from an existing balance to the balance sheet target amount), and

- the debit is to an expense account, reflecting the added cost associated with the additional amount of anticipated bad debts.

Balance Sheet Approaches

Spreadsheet 　⬜⬜❌

	L24		*fx*	=SUM(L20:L23)
	I	J	K	L
19	Age	Balance	Estimated % Uncollectible	Estimated Amount Uncollectible
20	Current	$250,000	1%	$ 2,500
21	31-60 days	100,000	5%	5,000
22	61-90 days	50,000	15%	7,500
23	Over 90 days	25,000	42%	10,500
24		$ 425,000		$25,500
25				

Allowance Account

10,000	Existing Balance
15,500	Expense
(25,500)	"Desired" Balance

WRITING OFF ACCOUNTS

When an allowance method is used, how are individual accounts written off? The following entry would be needed to write off a specific account that is finally deemed uncollectible:

03-15-X3	Allowance for Uncollectible Accounts	5,000	
	Accounts Receivable		5,000
	To record the write-off of an uncollectible account from Aziz		

Notice that the entry reduces both the Allowance account and the related Receivable, and has no impact on the income statement. Further, consider that the write-off has no impact on the net realizable value of receivables, as shown by the following illustration of a $5,000 write-off:

Before Write-off
Net Realizable Value $109,000

Assets

.....

Accounts receivable	$120,000	
Less: Allowance for uncollectibles	(11,000)	
	$109,000	

.....

After Write-off
Net Realizable Value $109,000

Assets

.....

Accounts receivable	$115,000	
Less: Allowance for uncollectibles	(6,000)	
	$109,000	

.....

(-$5,000) → Accounts receivable
(-$5,000) → Less: Allowance for uncollectibles

ACCOUNTS PREVIOUSLY WRITTEN OFF On occasion, a company may collect an account that was previously written off. For example, a customer that was once in dire financial condition may recover, and unexpectedly pay an amount that was previously written off. The entry to record the recovery involves two steps: (1) a reversal of the entry that was made to write off the account, and (2) recording the cash collection on the account:

Reversal of write-off:

06-16-X6	Accounts Receivable	1,000	
	Allowance for Uncollectible Accounts		1,000
	To reestablish an account previously written off via the reversal of the entry recorded at the time of write-off		

Record cash collection:

06-16-X6	Cash	1,000	
	Accounts Receivable		1,000
	To record collection of account receivable		

It may seem incorrect for the Allowance account to be increased because of the above entries; but, the general idea is that another, as yet unidentified, account may prove uncollectible (consistent with the overall estimates in use). If this does not eventually prove to be true, an adjustment of the overall estimation rates may be indicated.

MATCHING ACHIEVED Carefully consider that the allowance methods all result in the recording of estimated bad debts expense during the same time periods as the related credit sales. These approaches satisfy the desired matching of revenues and expenses.

A business must carefully monitor its accounts receivable. This chapter has devoted much attention to accounting for bad debts; but, don't forget that it is more important to try to avoid bad debts by carefully monitoring credit policies. A business should carefully consider the credit history of a potential credit customer, and be certain that good business practices are not abandoned in the zeal to make sales.

MONITORING AND MANAGING ACCOUNTS RECEIVABLE

It is customary to gather this information by getting a credit application from a customer, checking out credit references, obtaining reports from credit reporting agencies, and similar measures. Oftentimes, it becomes necessary to secure payment in advance or receive some other substantial guaranty such as a letter of credit from an independent bank. All of these steps are normal business practices, and no apologies are needed for making inquiries into the creditworthiness of potential customers.

Many countries have very liberal laws that make it difficult to enforce collection on customers who decide not to pay or use "legal maneuvers" to escape their obligations. As a result, businesses must be very careful in selecting parties that are allowed trade credit in the normal course of business.

Equally important is to monitor the rate of collection. Many businesses have substantial money tied up in receivables, and corporate liquidity can be adversely impacted if receivables are not actively managed to insure timely collection. One ratio that is often monitored is the accounts receivable turnover ratio. That number reveals how many times a firm's receivables are converted to cash during the year. It is calculated as net credit sales divided by average net accounts receivable:

$$\textbf{Accounts Receivable Turnover Ratio} = \frac{\textbf{Net Credit Sales}}{\textbf{Average Net Accounts Receivable}}$$

To illustrate these calculations, assume Shoztic Corporation had annual net credit sales of $3,000,000, beginning accounts receivable (net of uncollectibles) of $250,000, and ending accounts receivable (net of uncollectibles) of $350,000. Shoztic's average net accounts receivable is $300,000 (($250,000 + $350,000)/2), and the turnover ratio is "10":

$$10 = \frac{\$3,000,000}{\$300,000}$$

A closely related ratio is the "days outstanding" ratio. It reveals how many days sales are carried in the receivables category:

$$\textbf{Days Outstanding} = \frac{\textbf{365 Days}}{\textbf{Accounts Receivable Turnover Ratio}}$$

For Shoztic, the days outstanding calculation is:

$$36.5 = \frac{365}{10}$$

By themselves, these numbers mean little. But, when compared to industry trends and prior years, they will reveal important signals about how well receivables are being managed. In addition, the calculations may provide an "early warning" sign of potential problems in receivables management and rising bad debt risks.

Analysts carefully monitor the days outstanding numbers for signs of weakening business conditions. One of the first signs of a business downturn is a delay in the payment cycle. These delays tend to have ripple effects; if a company has trouble collecting its receivables, it won't be long before it may have trouble paying its own obligations.

Notes Receivable

A written promise from a client or customer to pay a definite amount of money on a specific future date is called a **note receivable**. Such notes can arise from a variety of circumstances, not the least of which is when credit is extended to a new customer with no formal prior credit history. The lender uses the note to make the loan legal and enforceable. Such notes typically bear interest charges. The **maker** of the note is the party promising to make payment, the **payee** is the party to whom payment will be made, the **principal** is the stated amount of the note, and the **maturity date** is the day the note will be due.

Interest is the charge imposed on the borrower of funds for the use of money. The specific amount of interest depends on the size, rate, and duration of the note. In mathematical form, interest equals Principal X Rate X Time. For example, a $1,000, 60-day note, bearing interest at 12% per year, would result in interest of $20 ($1,000 X 12% X 60/360). In this calculation, notice that the "time" was 60 days out of a 360 day year. Obviously, a year normally has 365 days, so the fraction could have been 60/365. But, for simplicity, it is not uncommon for the interest calculation to be based on a presumed 360-day year or 30-day month. This presumption probably has its roots in early days before electronic calculators, as the resulting interest calculations are much easier. But, with today's technology, there is little practical use for the 360 day year, except that it tends to benefit the creditor by producing a little higher interest amount -- caveat emptor (*Latin for "let the buyer beware"*)! The following illustrations will preserve this approach with the goal of producing nice, round numbers that are easy to follow.

ACCOUNTING FOR NOTES RECEIVABLE To illustrate the accounting for a note receivable, assume that Butchko initially sold $10,000 of merchandise on account to Hewlett. Hewlett later requested more time to pay, and agreed to give a formal three-month note bearing interest at 12% per year. The entry to record the conversion of the account receivable to a formal note is as follows:

06-01-X8	Notes Receivable	10,000	
	Accounts Receivable		10,000
	To record conversion of an account receivable to a note receivable		

At maturity, Butchko's entry to record collection of the **maturity value** would appear as follows:

08-31-X8	Cash	10,300	
	Interest Income		300
	Notes Receivable		10,000
	To record collection of note receivable plus accrued interest of $300 ($10,000 X 12% X 90/360)		

If Hewlett **dishonored the note** at maturity (i.e., refused to pay), then Butchko would prepare the following entry: *DISHONORED NOTE*

08-31-X8	Accounts Receivable	10,300	
	Interest Income		300
	Notes Receivable		10,000
	To record dishonor of note receivable plus accrued interest of $300 ($10,000 X 12% X 90/360)		

The debit to Accounts Receivable reflects the hope of eventually collecting all amounts due, including interest. If Butchko anticipated difficulty collecting the receivable, appropriate allowances would be established in a fashion similar to those illustrated earlier in the chapter.

In the illustrations for Butchko, all of the activity occurred within the same accounting year. However, if Butchko had a June 30 accounting year end, then an adjustment would be needed to reflect accrued interest at year-end. The appropriate entries illustrate this important accrual concept: *NOTES AND ADJUSTING ENTRIES*

Entry to set up note receivable:

06-01-X8	Notes Receivable	10,000	
	Accounts Receivable		10,000
	To record conversion of an account receivable to a note receivable		

Entry to accrue interest at June 30 year end:

06-30-X8	Interest Receivable	100	
	Interest Income		100
	To record accrued interest at June 30 ($10,000 X 12% X 30/360 = $100)		

Entry to record collection of note (including amounts previously accrued at June 30):

08-31-X8	Cash	10,300	
	Interest Income		200
	Interest Receivable		100
	Notes Receivable		10,000
	To record collection of note receivable plus interest of $300 ($10,000 X 12% X 90/360); $100 of the total interest had been previously accrued		

The following drawing should aid one's understanding of these entries:

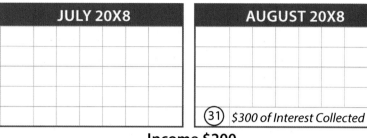

Chapter 7 Quiz

Q7-1.   Advances to employees and deposits with utilities are examples of:

trade receivables   or   nontrade receivables

Q7-2.   When is a sale normally recognized if a customer uses a nonbank credit card?

at the time of sale   or   at the time of collection from the credit card company

Q7-3.   The allowance method of accounting for uncollectible accounts seeks to provide a fair valuation of outstanding receivables on the:

income statement   or   balance sheet

Q7-4.   The numerator used in calculating the accounts receivable turnover ratio is:

total sales   or   net credit sales

Q7-5.   A dishonored note should be:

transferred to accounts receivable   or   written off

Q7-6.   _____ receivables arise from the sale of goods and services to customers on account.

Q7-7.   The _____ is the amount of cash expected to be collected from accounts receivable balances.

Q7-8.   The allowance method places emphasis on the _____ principle.

Q7-9.   The _____ promises to pay a stipulated amount of a note to the payee.

Q7-10.   _____ is the charge imposed on the borrower of funds, and can be computed as _____ X _____ X _____ .

Q7-11.   The maturity value of a note is the amount due on the maturity date and includes _____ plus _____ .

Multiple Choice

Q7-12. Trade accounts receivable:

a. arise from the sale of a company's products or services.

b. are reported in the noncurrent asset section of the balance sheet.

c. include deposits with utilities.

d. generally comprise the minority of the total receivables balance.

Q7-13. Taylor Company uses the direct write-off method of recording uncollectible accounts receivable. Recently, a customer informed Taylor that he would be unable to pay $300 owed to Taylor. Taylor's proper journal entry to reflect this event would be:

a.
Uncollectible Acct. Exp.	300	
Allow. for Uncollectible Acct.		300

b.
Allow. for Uncollectible Acct.	300	
Accounts Receivable		300

c.
Uncollectible Acct. Exp.	300	
Accounts Receivable		300

d.
Sales	300	
Accounts Receivable		300

Q7-14. Lindy Company uses an allowance method to account for bad debts. Lindy estimates that 5% of the outstanding accounts receivable will be uncollectible. At the end of the year, Lindy has outstanding accounts receivable of $750,000, and a debit balance in the Allowance for Uncollectible Accounts of $9,000. Lindy should record uncollectible accounts expense of:

a. $28,500

b. $37,500

c. $46,500

d. $55,500

Q7-15. John Company uses an allowance method for recording uncollectible receivables. John was notified by Paul that payment on a $1,000 receivable would be forthcoming. John had previously written off the receivable from Paul. The proper journal entry for John to record to reinstate the receivable into the accounts is:

a.
Accounts Receivable	1,000	
Allow. for Uncollectible Acct.		1,000

b.
Allow. for Uncollectible Acct.	1,000	
Sales		1,000

c.
Accounts Receivable	1,000	
Sales		1,000

d.
Accounts Receivable	1,000	
Uncollectible Acct. Exp.		1,000

Q7-16. Vivian Howell is the payee of $10,000, 180-day, 8% note. At maturity, the maker failed to pay. How much interest income should Vivian recognize on the dishonored note?

a. $0

b. $400

c. $800

d. $10,800

Chapter 7 Problems

Basic Problems

La Piaza Restaurant has always adhered to a strict cash only policy. Management is, for the first time, considering accepting credit cards and/or extending direct credit to customers. The left side of the following table includes seven factors that management has under consideration as it contemplates its cash/credit policy alternatives. Complete the "check-off" process for each factor/policy. The first factor is completed as an example.

	Cash Only		Direct Extension of Credit		Accept Credit Cards	
	Advantage	Disadvantage	Advantage	Disadvantage	Advantage	Disadvantage
Opportunity to charge/collect additional income in the form of interest		✓	✓			✓
Likely increase in revenues						
Conducting credit background check/ obtaining a credit report						
Significant risk of uncollectible accounts						
Increased accounting cost in the form of periodic billings						
Incurrence of fees on each transaction						
Immediate access to proceeds						

Morrison Mountain Medical Clinic (MMMC) accepts credit card payments from its patients. Following are the batched transactions for June 11.

(1) Total charges on MasterMoney and Wisa credit cards were $21,000. These cards are "bank cards" and MMMC receives daily cash settlement directly to its bank account, net of service charges of 1.5%.

(2) Total charges on USExpress cards were $3,000. This card is not a bank card, and settlement does not occur until approximately two weeks following the date of the transaction. USExpress is known to charge a 4% fee, and this amount is recorded on the day of sale.

Prepare journal entries for the credit card transactions. Be sure to include a separate entry for the eventual collection of the USExpress charges.

Flowers and Fluff frequently receives rush orders for floral deliveries. Some of these orders are on account. Occasionally, customers do not pay for their orders. Flowers and Fluff is a small business and is not too concerned about exactly following generally accepted accounting principles.

Review the two following "open" accounts and determine which should be written off. Flowers and Fluff prefers to use the direct write-off method and routinely reviews all accounts that are more than 90 days past due.

(1) Vince Colioni ordered flowers to be delivered to his girlfriend. Unfortunately, a bee was delivered along with the flowers, and Vince and his girlfriend spent the evening at the emergency room nursing a bad sting. Vince had planned to propose marriage that evening. Vince owes $125 for the flowers. The account is six months past due, and under the circumstances, the owners of Flowers and Fluff have no plans to press Vince for payment.

(2) Rebecca Warren ordered flowers to be delivered to a friend in the hospital. Rebecca owes $60, and the account is four months past due. The owners of Flowers and Fluff just realized that the bill was sent to Warren Rebecca, a different customer. Rebecca Warren has since moved to a distant town, but was last known to be a responsible person. The owners of Flowers and Fluff are now trying to get a new address for Rebecca Warren from her friend that was in the hospital.

(a) When and how might a business choose to ignore GAAP and use the direct write-off method?

(b) What is the U.S. tax code position on the direct write-off method, and how might Flowers and Fluff be simplifying their record keeping issues by using the direct writeoff method? Could a large corporation that must meet financial reporting obligations to shareholders select this simplifying option?

(c) Prepare the journal entry necessary to write off the "bad" account.

(d) How does the existence of "other" questionable accounts potentially produce misleading financial reports?

| *Allowance method: Percentage of receivables* | *B-07.04* |

Pablo's Precision Parts distributes carbon fiber parts for customization of sports cars. The company has a broad customer base, and routinely sells on credit. Annually, the company reviews and updates its allowance for uncollectible accounts. Periodic write-offs against the allowance account are made throughout the year when individual accounts are deemed to be worthless.

Following are relevant facts for the current year:

Prior to recording any year-end adjustments, the total balance of all accounts receivable amounted to $2,300,000.

The existing Allowance for Uncollectible Accounts had a balance of $18,000.

No entry was made during the year to increase Allowance for Uncollectible Accounts, but $40,000 of uncollectible accounts were written off against the allowance during the year.

(a)   What was the beginning-of-year balance for the Allowance for Uncollectible Accounts?

(b)   Prepare a summary journal entry that reflects the $40,000 of write-offs already recorded by Pablo's.

(c)   Assuming that the year-end allowance should equal 3% of outstanding receivables, what end-of-year adjusting entry is needed?

(d)   How will the accounts receivable and allowance appear on the balance sheet?

(e)   How much expense will appear in the annual income statement as uncollectible accounts expense?

| *Allowance method: Aging of accounts* | *B-07.05* |

Wiggins Corporation utilizes an accounting software package that is capable of producing a detailed aging of outstanding accounts receivable. Following is the aging schedule as of December 31, 20X2.

Spreadsheet					⊟◻☒
			fx		
	A	B	C	D	E
1	Age	Amount Outstanding			
2	0 to 30 days	$1,200,000			
3	31 to 60 days	700,000			
4	61 to 120 days	200,000			
5	Over 120 days	25,000			
6					

Casper Wiggins has owned and operated Wiggins Corporation for many years and has a very good sense of the probability of collection of outstanding receivables, based on an aging analysis. The following table reveals the likelihood of collection:

	A	B	fx		
			C	D	E
1	Age	Probability of Collection			
2	0 to 30 days	98%			
3	31 to 60 days	90%			
4	61 to 120 days	75%			
5	Over 120 days	50%			
6					

Spreadsheet

(a)   Prepare an aging analysis, and show how accounts receivable and the related allowance for uncollectibles should appear on the balance sheet at December 31.

(b)   Prepare the necessary journal entry to update the allowance for uncollectibles, assuming the balance prior to preparing the aging was a $15,000 credit.

(c)   Prepare the necessary journal entry to update the allowance for uncollectibles, assuming the balance prior to preparing the aging was a $5,000 debit. How could the allowance account have contained a debit balance?

B-07.06   *Critical thinking about account balances*

Morrison Supply sells pressured air devices that assist patients with breathing disorders during sleep. These devices are delivered to patients immediately upon completion of a diagnostics exam, and are subsequently billed to insurance companies. Insurance companies sometime refuse to pay and/or only agree to a reduced price. Patients are then responsible for any amount denied by the insurance company, but are often unable or unwilling to pay. Because clinical standards of cleanliness must be maintained, Morrison is unable to accept returns for resale to others.

Morrison is reluctant to litigate to collect unpaid amounts. As a result, Morrison experiences a high rate of uncollectible accounts, and prepares a monthly adjusting entry for uncollectibles.

January was Morrison's first month of operations. Monthly sales, write-offs, and ending receivables balances for the first quarter of 20X7 follow:

MONTH	SALES	ACTUAL WRITE-OFFS	ENDING GROSS RECEIVABLES	ENDING ALLOWANCE BALANCE
January	$630,000	$ 80,000	$400,000	$70,000
February	$480,000	$ 90,000	$650,000	$150,000
March	$590,000	$125,000	$900,000	$210,000

(a)   Prepare monthly journal entries to summarize sales on account, the recording of the provision for uncollectibles, and the actual write-offs, and collections.

(b)   Morrison's CFO attended a trade group conference, and learned providers of this service in other cities have begun offering a 10% cash discount if the patient will pay the full amount themselves. The patient then deals directly with their insurance carrier for reimbursement. What are your thoughts on this policy?

(c)   Morrison Supply is contemplating issuing shares of stock to a group of outside investors. The CEO has requested the CFO to adjust the allowance balances to reflect a lower rate of uncollectibles. What might be the motivation behind this request, and how should the CFO respond?

Allowance method: Write-off of accounts	*B-07.07*

Wang Corporation follows generally accepted accounting principles in accounting for uncollectibles. Wang received notification from a bankruptcy court that its customer, Timber Creek, had been adjudicated and released from all claims presently pending against it by Wang Corporation.

Frank Wang, owner of Wang Corporation, was not at all pleased with this decision. Frank had anticipated recovering at least $50,000 from Timber Creek, and that balance remained in the Accounts Receivable accounts of Wang Corporation. Because Wang Corporation has no further remedies for collection, Frank directed the accounting department to prepare a journal entry to write off the account of Timber Creek.

(a)   Prepare the journal entry to write off the Timber Creek account.

(b)   Explain why the actual write-off will not result in a reduction of Wang Corporation's income.

(c)   Suppose Timber Creek recovered from its bankruptcy and eventually voluntarily paid the $50,000 "owed" to Wang. Prepare Wang's journal entries to record the unexpected recovery.

Monitoring receivables: Analysis and ratios	*B-07.08*

Supreme Vacuum uses television advertising blitzes to generate consumer interest in its highly-touted floor cleaners. Customers are directed to a website for more information. Once on the website, customers are constantly confronted with a "video game" where they can use icon-like vacuums to suck up coupons that float on and off their browser windows. At check out, customers are able to clean the contents of their imaginary vacuums and select one of the coupons to apply against their purchase.

The best coupon is a no-money-down, four equal monthly payments coupon. "Magically", every customer will find at least one of these coupons. Virtually all customers will use this coupon in making their final purchases. As a result, Supreme carries a substantial balance in accounts receivable. It is imperative that Supreme manage credit risk, and careful attention is paid to the "accounts receivable turnover ratio" and the "days outstanding."

During 20X5, net credit sales were $6,000,000. The sales were evenly spread throughout the year.

The beginning-of-year net realizable value of accounts receivable was $2,150,000 and the end-of-year balance was $2,650,000.

(a)   Calculate the "accounts receivable turnover ratio" and the "days outstanding."

(b)   Evaluate the information from part (a), and determine if Supreme's customer base is in compliance with the four equal monthly payments agreement.

(c)   In addition to the facts above, suppose Supreme ran a major holiday sales campaign in December of 20X5. This campaign promised no payments until 20X6! This campaign generated an additional $3,000,000 in credit sales (and resulted in an end-of-year receivable balance of $5,650,000). Can Supreme record these sales under generally accepted accounting principles, and what is the impact on the ratios (compared to the values you computed in part (a))?

B-07.09   *Notes receivable terminology*

A "Note" is a written promise to pay a definite amount of money on a specific future date. Explicit terminology is used to describe various attributes of a note.

Match the following terms to their correct description.

(1)   Payee

(2)   Principal

(3)   Dishonor

(4)   Maker

(5)   Interest

(6)   Maturity

(a)   Stated amount of the note

(b)   Party to whom payment will be made

(c)   Party promising to make payment

(d)   Charge imposed on the borrower of funds for the use of money

(e)   Date the note will be due

(f)   Refusing to pay a note at maturity

B-07.10   *Notes receivable interest calculations*

Vinay Sanja was interviewing for a job at the State Bank of India. The bank requires all job applicants to take a competency test on basic money mathematics. Vinay has completed the interest calculations portion of the exam. Following are his questions and answers. Vinay must correctly answer in at least 3 cases to be eligible for the job. Evaluate and correct Vinay's answers. Does he qualify for the job?

(a) Assume the bank holds a 400,000 Indian Rupee (INR) note receivable dated June 1, 20X1. This note matures on August 31, 20X1. This note is written to assume a 360 day year and 30 day months. The annual interest rate is stated at 10%. What is the maturity value of the note, including interest?

Answer: 400,000 X 10% X 60/360 =

6,666.67

400,000 + 6,666.67 = 406,666.67

(b) Assume the bank holds a INR 400,000 note receivable dated June 1, 20X1. This note matures on August 31, 20X1. This note is written to assume a 365 day year, and actual days outstanding are used in all calculations. The annual interest rate is stated at 10%. What is the maturity value of the note, including interest?

Answer: 400,000 X 10% X 92/365 =

10,082.19

(c) Assume the bank holds a INR 1,000,000 note receivable dated October 1, 20X5. This note matures on September 30, 20X6. This note is written to assume a 360 day year and 30 day months. The annual interest rate is stated at 8%. How much interest income should the bank record for its accounting year ending December 31, 20X5?

Answer: Zero, the note is not due until 20X6

(d) Assume the bank holds a INR 1,000,000 note receivable dated October 1, 20X5. This note matures on September 30, 20X6. This note is written to assume a 360 day year and 30 day months. The annual interest rate is stated at 8%. How much interest income should the bank record for its accounting year ending December 31, 20X6?

Answer: 1,000,000 X 8% X 270/360 =

600,000

Accounting for notes receivable   *B-07.11*

Prepare journal entries for each of the following transactions:

On December 1, 20X5, Musaka received a 10%, 1-year, note receivable from Lambert. This note was issued in payment for a $24,000 outstanding account receivable.

On December 31, 20X5, Musaka recorded an end-of-year adjusting entry to record accrued interest on the note receivable.

On November 30, 20X6, Lambert paid Musaka the full amount due on the note receivable.

How would the November 30 entry differ if Lambert defaulted on the payment?

Involved Problems

Rocks Shoes is a three-year old company that started out producing specialty shoes for rock climbing and mountaineering. The shoe's unique styling has made them a hit with climbing enthusiasts, and the company is now growing rapidly. Rocks needs additional capital to expand its manufacturing capacity, and it plans to sell additional shares of stock to raise money.

During its first three years in operation, Rocks used the direct-write off method to account for uncollectible accounts.

Information about sales, write-offs, and the company's income follows:

	Sales	Write-offs	Net Income
Year 1	$ 2,400,000	$ -	$100,000
Year 2	6,300,000	24,000	300,000
Year 3	12,900,000	111,000	550,000

Rocks is required to have audited financial statements prior to offering its shares of stock for sale. This will require the company to recompute its income under generally accepted accounting principles for each of the three prior years. The only item that requires adjustment is the treatment of uncollectible accounts.

Rocks estimates that the allowance for uncollectible accounts balance should have been $75,000, $250,000, and $500,000, respectively, at the end of Years 1, 2, and 3.

(a)   Prepare the journal entries that were used by Rocks for each year under the direct write-off method.

(b)   Why does GAAP require an allowance method for uncollectibles?

(c)   Prepare the journal entries that would have been made each year had the allowance method been used. Be sure to include entries to both establish the allowance and record the write offs.

(d)   How much is the corrected net income for each year? Will the reduction in income potentially impact the amount of capital that can be raised?

Myssie Cardenas was recently hired as the chief financial officer for Barajas Corporation. At the time Myssie was hired, the company had just completed the accounting cycle for the year ending December 31, 20X7.

Myssie began her new job by reviewing the following information about sales and receivables activity during the year:

Beginning accounts receivable	$ 1,500,000
Beginning allowance for uncollectibles	40,000
Sales on account	6,000,000
Collections on account	4,800,000
Sales discounts	68,000
Accounts written-off	33,000
Additions to allowance for uncollectible accounts	59,320

(a)   Based on her review, Myssie prepared some handwritten notes in journal entry form summarizing the above sales, collections, discounts, write-offs, and additions to the allowance. She wanted to compare her entries to what had actually been recorded by the company. How should her summary entries appear?

(b)   After completing her review, Myssie concluded that, as of the end of 20X8, the company should provide an Allowance for Uncollectible Accounts at a end-of-year balance equal to 3% of total gross receivables. Prepare summary journal entries for 20X8 to capture the following information and to update the allowance account from its beginning-of-year balance (see part (a) to determine the beginning balance).

Sales on account	6,600,000
Collections on account	5,900,000
Sales discounts	88,000
Accounts written-off	53,000

Journal entries and analysis of receivables and allowances	**I-07.03**

Wangming Lu Energy Company builds specially designed blades for generators used in wind energy farming operations. The company started the year with the following accounts receivable position:

Accounts receivable	$10,500,000	
Less: Allowance for uncollectibles	(320,500)	$10,179,500

During the year, customer Windy Point Power Company was devastated by an unusually severe storm. At that time, Wangming concluded that it was highly unlikely that Windy Point would ever be able to pay its outstanding balance of $150,000. This account was written off against the allowance account. Much later in the year, Windy Point was rescued by a group of investors who offered to pay $90,000 toward the unpaid balance provided Wangming would permanently forgive the other $60,000 and resume selling product to Windy Point. Wangming agreed and has since resumed doing business with Windy Point.

During the year, sales on account amounted to $25,689,000. Collections on account totaled $21,300,500 (excluding the Windy Point collection).

Also during the year, accounts written off (not including the Windy Point transaction) were $123,000. At year's end, a detailed analysis of accounts receivable was performed, and it was concluded that the allowance account should contain a balance of $475,000.

(a) Prepare summary journal entries:

> To record the write-off of the Windy Point receivable
>
> To restore the portion of the Windy Point receivable that was collected
>
> To record the collection of the Windy Point receivable
>
> To record sales on account
>
> To record collections on account
>
> To record the write-off of accounts
>
> To establish the correct balance in the allowance for uncollectibles

(b) Prepare a table including column headings for Accounts Receivable, Allowance for Uncollectibles, Net Realizable Value, and Uncollectible Accounts Expense. Show how each entry from part (a) impacts these components. The first one is done as an example on the preprinted worksheet.

I-07.04   *Aging of accounts receivables*

SPREADSHEET TOOL:

Using the sort routine

Walt's manufactures and sells customized work clothes and uniforms. Following is a list of accounts receivable as of December 31, 2019.

Customer	Date of Sale	Amount
Air There Freight	December 11, 2019	12,300
Aurora	November 12, 2019	5,000
Batesville	August 18, 2019	14,805
CarMan	December 9, 2019	21,900
Clinic Quick	August 15, 2018	16,040
Delorres River Guides	September 19, 2019	8,990
Elonzo's Restaurant	December 17, 2019	11,789
Hospital Supply	December 4, 2019	135,100
Inidigo	November 29, 2019	16,500
Meridan Oil	May 20, 2019	11,786
Museum of Art	December 21, 2019	255,000
Novellus	February 16, 2019	18,780
Norman's	December 23, 2019	10,000
Robert Ricketts	December 14, 2019	3,550
Sanchez Systems	October 25, 2019	22,310
Security by the Hour	December 13, 2019	40,900
Stop Shop	December 27, 2019	34,700
Target Time	February 3, 2019	14,440
Uvlade Ranch	December 7, 2019	3,700
Xhi	October 20, 2019	15,100
Zebra Sports	December 3, 2019	144,000

(a)   Sort the receivables list by age category and determine the estimated balance of uncollectible accounts. Walt's believes the following rates of noncollection will occur: 1% of receivables up to 30 days, 3% for 31 to 90 days, 10% for 91 to 180 days, and 40% of accounts over 180 days.

(b)   If the balance of Allowance for Uncollectible Accounts contained $15,000 (credit), what adjusting entry is needed to reflect the analysis from part (a)?

(c)   If the balance of Allowance for Uncollectible Accounts contained $15,000 (debit), what adjusting entry is needed to reflect the analysis from part (a)?

(d)   How is it possible that the allowance account could contain a debit balance, as in part (c)?

Team-based analysis of receivables	*I-07.05*

Many "publicly held" companies are required to prepare and file financial statements with the U.S. Securities and Exchange Commission (SEC). The annual report filed with the SEC is known as the 10-K. Such reports are available for download from the SEC website (www.sec.gov). The SEC website has a searchable database accessed from the SEC home page (A more advanced search is accessed under "Filings" then "Search for Company Filings).

Form a group of 4 or 5 students. Each member of the group should obtain a recent 10-K for a specific company of choice, and calculate the receivables turnover ratio (you may have to substitute "total sales" for "net credit sales," depending on the amount of available information) and the days outstanding. In addition, find any commentary or information about the company's provision for uncollectible accounts. After each member has gathered information for his or her specific company, the group should meet and prepare a summary report that "rank orders" the companies based on their respective receivables turnover ratios. Discuss the industry characteristics of each business, and determine if this seems to influence the amount of trade credit and uncollectible accounts.

Comprehensive notes receivable	*I-07.06*

Zhejiang Corporation sells customized stage lighting equipment for use in the entertainment industry. Zhejiang has a broad dealer network. One dealer, Min Chen, obtained a large contract with a ship builder to install an elaborate stage lighting system produced by Zhejiang. The new cruise ship was being promoted as the Broadway on the Water and promised to offer the world's finest theatrical performances at sea.

In 20X2, Zhejiang sold the lighting equipment to Min Chen for RMB 30,000,000. Terms were 20% cash payment and the balance in 75 days. The extended payment terms were necessary because Min Chen needed to collect from the ship builder before being able to pay Zhejiang.

Unfortunately, Min Chen experienced difficulties. It seems the floor of the stage was equipped with a sophisticated leveling system that caused it to move in counter-motion to the ship's rocking while at sea. This feature provided entertainers with a stable stage on which to perform. However, this attribute was not considered in the design of the lighting equipment. As a result, when the ship rocked, the beams from the lights moved all about on the stage. No one was happy, and the cruise ship delayed payment to Min Chen. Min Chen was not able to pay Zhejiang. All parties believed some resolution and payment would eventually occur, but the timing was uncertain.

(a)   Prepare Zhejiang's journal entry to record the initial sale and down payment. Be sure to also record the cost of goods sold (assume the lighting equipment cost Zhejiang RMB 22,000,000 and the company uses a perpetual inventory system).

(b) After 75 days, Min Chen paid an additional RMB 4,000,000 and executed a 180- day, 6%, promissory note for the unpaid balance. Prepare Zhejiang's entry.

(c) Zhejiang's accounting year ended 60 days following the execution of the promissory note. Prepare the end-of-year adjusting entry.

(d) After 180 days following the execution of the promissory note, all matters had been resolved, and Min Chen paid the full amount due on the promissory note. Prepare Zhejiang's journal entry.

(e) Why did Zhejiang obtain a promissory note from Min Chen in lieu of the open account receivable?

(f) Suppose the technical problems had been resolved early in 20X3 by Zhejiang contributing RMB 500,000 toward the cost of a gyroscopic lighting control system that eliminated the motion problem. How would this affect Zhejiang's profitability? Technically, when should this cost have been recognized?

Chapter 8:
Inventory

Goals:

The correct components to include in inventory.
Inventory costing methods.
The perpetual system for valuing inventory.
Lower of cost or net realizable value inventory adjustments.
Two inventory estimation techniques: the gross profit and retail methods.
Inventory management and monitoring, and the impact of errors.

principlesofaccounting.com

Inventory for a merchandising business consists of the goods available for resale to customers. However, retailers are not the only businesses that maintain inventory. Manufacturers also have inventories related to the goods they produce. Goods completed and awaiting sale are termed "finished goods" inventory. A manufacturer may also have "work in process" inventory consisting of goods being manufactured but not yet completed. And, a third category of inventory is "raw material," consisting of goods to be used in the manufacture of products.

Inventories are typically classified as current assets on the balance sheet. Managerial accounting courses cover the specifics of accounting for manufactured inventory. This chapter will focus on the general principles of inventory accounting that are applicable to most enterprises.

Recall from the merchandising chapter the discussion of freight charges. In that chapter, F.O.B. terms were introduced, and the focus was on which party would bear the cost of freight. But, F.O.B. terms also determine when goods are (or are not) included in inventory. Technically, goods in transit belong to the party holding legal ownership. Ownership depends on the F.O.B. terms. Goods sold F.O.B. destination do not belong to the purchaser until they arrive at their final destination. Goods sold F.O.B. shipping point become property of the purchaser once shipped by the seller. Therefore, when determining the amount of inventory owned at year end, **goods in transit** must be considered in light of the F.O.B. terms. In the case of F.O.B. shipping point, for instance, a buyer would need to include as inventory the goods that are being transported but not yet received. In the diagram, the buyer or seller shown in green would "inventory" the goods in transit.

GOODS TO INCLUDE

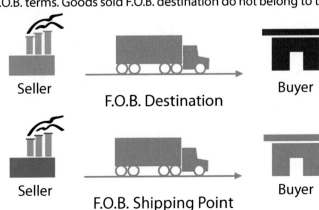

Seller   F.O.B. Destination   Buyer

Seller   F.O.B. Shipping Point   Buyer

Another inventory-related problem area pertains to goods on **consignment**. Consigned goods describe products that are in the physical custody of one party, but actually belong to another party. Thus, the party holding physical possession is not the legal owner. The person with physical possession is known as the consignee. The consignee is responsible for taking care of the goods and trying to sell them to an end customer.

The consignor is the party holding legal ownership/title to the consigned goods. Consigned goods should be included in the inventory of the consignor.

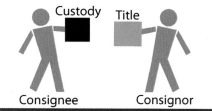

Consignments arise when the owner desires to place inventory in the hands of a sales agent, but the sales agent does not want to pay for those goods unless resold to an end customer. For example, auto parts manufacturers produce many types of parts that are very specialized and expensive. A retail auto parts store

Consigned Goods Belong In the Inventory of the Consignor

may not be able to afford to stock every variety. In addition, there is the real risk of ending up with numerous obsolete units. But, the manufacturer desperately needs these units in the retail channel. As a result, the parts manufacturer may consign their inventory to auto parts retailers.

Conceptually, it is fairly simple to understand the accounting for consigned goods. Practically, there is a significant record keeping challenge. When examining a company's inventory on hand, special care must be taken to identify both goods consigned out to others (which are to be included in inventory) and goods consigned in (which are not to be included in inventory). When the consignee sells consigned goods to an end user, the consignee would keep a portion of the sales price, and remit the balance to the consignor. All of this activity requires an accounting system capable of identifying consigned units, tracking their movement, and knowing when they are actually sold.

Inventory Costing Methods

The value of a company's shares of stock often moves significantly with information about earnings. Why begin a discussion of inventory with this observation? The reason is that inventory measurement bears directly on the determination of income! The slightest adjustment to inventory will cause a corresponding change in an entity's reported income.

Recall from earlier chapters this basic formulation:

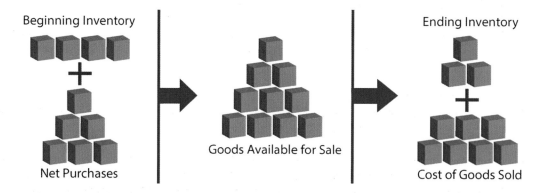

Notice that the goods available for sale are "allocated" to ending inventory and cost of goods sold. In the graphic, the inventory appears as physical units. But, in a company's accounting records, this flow must be translated into units of money. The following graphic illustrates this allocation process.

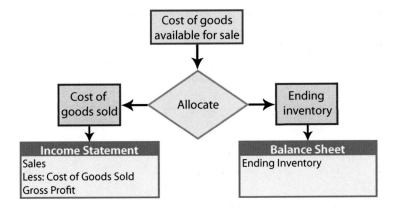

Observe that if $1 less is allocated to ending inventory, then $1 more flows into cost of goods sold (and vice versa). Further, as cost of goods sold is increased or decreased, there is an opposite effect on gross profit. Thus, a critical factor in determining income is the allocation of the cost of goods available for sale between ending inventory and cost of goods sold:

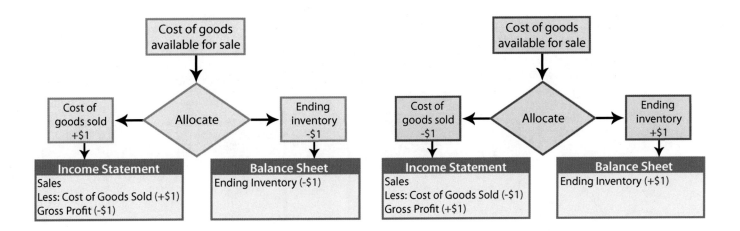

In earlier chapters, the assigned cost of inventory was always given. Not much was said about how that cost was determined. To now delve deeper, consider a general rule: Inventory should include all costs that are "ordinary and necessary" to put the goods "in place" and "in condition" for resale.

This means that inventory cost would include the invoice price, freight-in, and similar items relating to the general rule. Conversely, "carrying costs" like interest charges (if money was borrowed to buy the inventory), storage costs, and insurance on goods held awaiting sale would not be included in inventory accounts; instead those costs would be expensed as incurred. Likewise, freight-out and sales commissions would be expensed as a selling cost rather than being included with inventory.

Once the unit cost of inventory is determined via the preceding logic, specific costing methods must be adopted. In other words, each unit of inventory will not have the exact same cost, and an assumption must be implemented to maintain a systematic approach to assigning costs to units on hand (and to units sold).

To solidify this point, consider a simple example. Mueller Hardware has a nail storage barrel. The barrel was filled three times. The first filling consisted of 100 pounds costing $1.01 per pound. The second filling consisted of 80 pounds costing $1.10 per pound. The final restocking was 90 pounds at $1.30 per pound. The barrel was never allowed to empty completely and customers have picked all around in the barrel as they bought nails. It is hard to say exactly which nails are "physically" still in the barrel. As one might expect, some of the nails are probably from the first filling, some from the second, and some from the final. At the end of the accounting period, Mueller weighs the barrel and decides that 120 pounds of nails are on hand.

What is the cost of the ending inventory? Remember, this question bears directly on the determination of income!

To deal with this very common accounting question, a company must adopt an inventory costing method (and that method must be applied consistently from year to year). The methods from which to choose are varied, generally consisting of one of the following:

- First-in, first-out (FIFO)

- Last-in, first-out (LIFO)

- Weighted-average

Each of these methods entails certain **cost-flow assumptions**. Importantly, the assumptions bear no relation to the physical flow of goods; they are merely used to assign costs to inventory units. (Note: FIFO and LIFO are pronounced with a long "i" and long "o" vowel sound.) Another method that will be discussed shortly is the specific identification method. As its name suggests, the specific identification method does not depend on a cost flow assumption.

FIRST-IN, FIRST-OUT

With **first-in, first-out**, the oldest cost (i.e., the first in) is matched against revenue and assigned to cost of goods sold. Conversely, the most recent purchases are assigned to units in ending inventory. For Mueller's nails, the FIFO calculations would look like this:

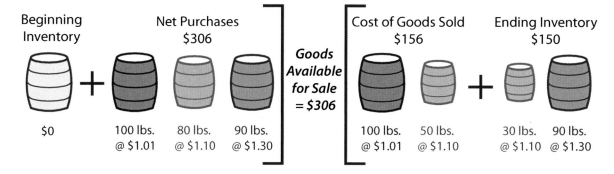

LAST-IN, FIRST-OUT

Last-in, first-out is just the reverse of FIFO; recent costs are assigned to goods sold while the oldest costs remain in inventory:

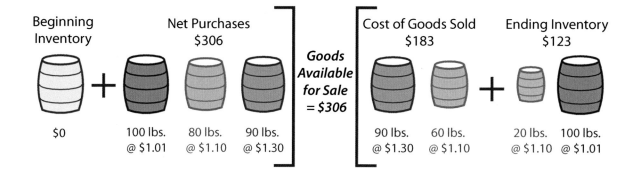

WEIGHTED AVERAGE

The weighted-average method relies on average unit cost to calculate cost of units sold and ending inventory. Average cost is determined by dividing total cost of goods available for sale by total units available for sale. Mueller Hardware paid $306 for 270 pounds, producing an average cost of $1.13333 per pound ($306/270). The ending inventory consisted of 120 pounds, or $136 (120 X $1.13333 average price per pound). The cost of goods sold was $170 (150 pounds X $1.13333 average price per pound):

Beginning Inventory | Net Purchases $306 | Goods Available for Sale = $306 | Cost of Goods Sold $170 | Ending Inventory $136

$0 — 100 lbs. @ $1.01 — 80 lbs. @ $1.10 — 90 lbs. @ $1.30

150 lbs. @ $1.13333 average

120 lbs. @ $1.13333 average

Examine each of the following comparative illustrations noting how the cost of beginning inventory and purchases flow to ending inventory and cost of goods sold.

IMPACT OF BEGINNING INVENTORY

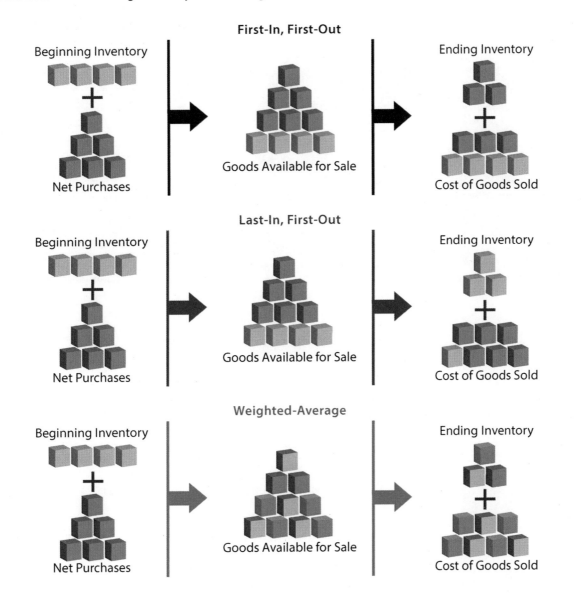

First-In, First-Out

Beginning Inventory + Net Purchases → Goods Available for Sale → Ending Inventory + Cost of Goods Sold

Last-In, First-Out

Beginning Inventory + Net Purchases → Goods Available for Sale → Ending Inventory + Cost of Goods Sold

Weighted-Average

Beginning Inventory + Net Purchases → Goods Available for Sale → Ending Inventory + Cost of Goods Sold

Accountants usually adopt the FIFO, LIFO, or Weighted-Average cost flow assumption. The actual physical flow of the inventory may or may not bear a resemblance to the adopted cost flow assumption. In the following illustration, assume that Gonzales Chemical Company had a beginning inventory balance that consisted of 4,000 units costing $12 per unit. Purchases and sales are shown in the schedule. Assume that Gonzales conducted a physical count of inventory and confirmed that 5,000 units were actually on hand at the end of the year.

DETAILED EXAMPLE

Date	Purchases	Sales	Units on Hand
01-Jan			4,000
05-Mar	6,000 units @ $16 each		10,000
17-Apr		7,000 units @ $22 each	3,000
07-Sep	8,000 units @ $17 each		11,000
11-Nov		6,000 units @ $25 each	5,000

Based on the information in the schedule, Gonzales will report sales of $304,000. This amount is the result of selling 7,000 units at $22 ($154,000) and 6,000 units at $25 ($150,000). The dollar amount of sales will be reported in the income statement, along with cost of goods sold and gross profit. How much is cost of goods sold and gross profit? The answer will depend on the cost flow assumption.

FIFO

If Gonzales uses FIFO, ending inventory, cost of goods sold, and the resulting financial statements are as follows:

Beginning Inventory	+	Net Purchases	=	Cost of goods available for sale	=	Ending Inventory	+	Cost of goods sold
$48,000		$232,000		$280,000		$85,000		$195,000
4,000 @ $12 each				4,000 @ $12 each				4,000 @ $12 each
		6,000 @ $16 each		6,000 @ $16 each				6,000 @ $16 each
		8,000 @ $17 each		8,000 @ $17 each		5,000 @ $17 each		3,000 @ $17 each

GONZALES CHEMICAL COMPANY
Income Statement
For the Year Ending December 31, 20XX

Revenues

Net sales		$304,000
Cost of goods sold		
Beginning inventory, Jan. 1	$ 48,000	
Net purchases	232,000	
Cost of goods available for sale	$280,000	
Less: Ending inventory, Dec. 31	85,000	
Cost of goods sold		195,000
Gross profit		$109,000

....

GONZALES CHEMICAL COMPANY
Balance Sheet
December 31, 20XX

Assets

....	
Inventory	85,000
....	

LIFO

If Gonzales uses LIFO, ending inventory, cost of goods sold, and the resulting financial statements are as follows:

Beginning Inventory	+	Net Purchases	=	Cost of goods available for sale	=	Ending Inventory	+	Cost of goods sold
$48,000		$232,000		$280,000		$64,000		$216,000
4,000 @ $12 each				4,000 @ $12 each		4,000 @ $12 each		
		6,000 @ $16 each		6,000 @ $16 each		1,000 @ $16 each		5,000 @ $16 each
		8,000 @ $17 each		8,000 @ $17 each				8,000 @ $17 each

GONZALES CHEMICAL COMPANY
Income Statement
For the Year Ending December 31, 20XX

Revenues

Net sales		$304,000
Cost of goods sold		
Beginning inventory, Jan. 1	$ 48,000	
Net purchases	232,000	
Cost of goods available for sale	$280,000	
Less: Ending inventory, Dec. 31	64,000	
Cost of goods sold		216,000
Gross profit		$ 88,000
....		

GONZALES CHEMICAL COMPANY
Balance Sheet
December 31, 20XX

Assets

....	
Inventory	64,000
....	

If Gonzales uses the **weighted-average** method, ending inventory and cost of goods sold calculations are as follows:

WEIGHTED AVERAGE

Cost of goods available for sale	$280,000
Divided by units (4,000 + 6,000 + 8,000)	18,000
Average unit cost (Note: Do not round calculation)	$15.5555 per unit
Ending inventory (5,000 units @ $15.5555)	$77,778
Cost of goods sold (13,000 units @ $15.5555)	$202,222

These calculations support the following financial statement components.

Income Statement	
Net sales	$304,000
Cost of goods sold	202,222
Gross profit	$101,778
....	

Balance Sheet	
Assets	
....	
Inventory	77,778
....	

The following table reveals that the amount of gross profit and ending inventory can appear quite different, depending on the inventory method selected:

COMPARING METHODS

	First-in, First-out	Last-in, First-out	Weighted Average
Sales	$304,000	$304,000	$304,000
Cost of Goods Sold	195,000	216,000	202,222
Gross Profit	$109,000	$ 88,000	$101,778
Ending Inventory	$ 85,000	$ 64,000	$ 77,778

The preceding results are consistent with a general rule that LIFO produces the lowest income (assuming rising prices, as was evident in the Gonzales example), FIFO the highest, and weighted average an amount in between. Because LIFO tends to depress profits, one may wonder why a company would select this option; the answer is sometimes driven by income tax considerations. Lower income produces a lower tax bill, thus companies will tend to prefer the LIFO choice. Usually, financial accounting methods do not have to conform to methods chosen for tax purposes. However, in the U.S., LIFO "conformity rules" generally require that LIFO be used for financial reporting if it is used for tax purposes. In many countries LIFO is not permitted for tax or accounting purposes, and there is discussion about the U.S. perhaps adopting this global approach.

Accounting theorists may argue that financial statement presentations are enhanced by LIFO because it matches recently incurred costs with the recently generated revenues. Others maintain that FIFO is better because recent costs are reported in inventory on the balance sheet. Whichever method is used, it is important to note that the inventory method must be clearly communicated in the financial statements and related notes. LIFO companies frequently augment their reports with supplemental data about what inventory cost would be if FIFO were used instead. Consistency in method of application should be maintained. This does not mean that changes cannot occur; however, changes should only be made if financial reporting is deemed to be improved.

SPECIFIC ID   The **specific identification** method requires a business to identify each unit of merchandise with the unit's cost and retain that identification until the inventory is sold. Once a specific inventory item is sold, the cost of the unit is assigned to cost of goods sold. Specific identification requires tedious record keeping and is typically only used for inventories of uniquely identifiable goods that have a fairly high per-unit cost (e.g., automobiles, fine jewelry, and so forth).

To illustrate, assume Classic Cars began the year with 5 units in stock. Classic has a detailed list, by serial number, of each car and its cost. The aggregate cost of the cars is $125,000. During the year, 100 additional cars are acquired at an aggregate cost of $3,000,000. Each car is unique and had a different unit cost. The year ended with only 3 cars in inventory. Under specific identification, it would be necessary to examine the 3 cars, determine their serial numbers, and find the exact cost for each of those units. If that aggregated to $225,000, then ending inventory would be reported at that amount. One may further assume that the cost of the units sold is $2,900,000, which can be calculated as cost of goods available for sale minus ending inventory. The cost of goods sold could be verified by summing up the individual cost for each unit sold.

Perpetual Inventory Systems

The preceding illustrations were based on the periodic inventory system. In other words, the ending inventory was counted and costs were assigned only at the end of the period. A more robust system is the perpetual system. With a perpetual system, a running count of goods on hand is maintained at all times. Modern information systems facilitate detailed perpetual cost tracking for those goods.

PERPETUAL FIFO   The following table reveals the FIFO application of the perpetual inventory system for Gonzales. Note that there is considerable detail in tracking inventory using a perpetual approach. Careful study is needed to discern exactly what is occurring on each date. For example, look at April 17 and note that 3,000 units remain after selling 7,000 units. This is determined by looking at the preceding balance data on March 5 (consisting of 10,000 total units (4,000 + 6,000)), and removing 7,000 units as follows: all of the 4,000 unit layer, and 3,000 of the 6,000 unit layer. Remember, this is the FIFO application, so the layers are peeled away based on the chronological order of their creation. In essence, each purchase and sale transaction impacts the residual composition of the layers associated with the item of inventory. Observe that the financial statement results are the same as under the periodic FIFO approach introduced earlier. This is anticipated because the beginning inventory and early purchases are peeled away and charged to cost of goods sold in the same order, whether the associated calculations are done "as you go" (perpetual) or "at the end of the period" (periodic).

Date	Purchases	Sales	Cost of Goods Sold	Balance
01-Jan				4,000 X $12 = $ 48,000
05-Mar				4,000 X $12 = $ 48,000
	6,000 X $16 = $ 96,000			6,000 X $16 = $ 96,000
				$144,000
17-Apr		7,000 X $22 = $154,000	4,000 X $12 = $48,000	
			3,000 X $16 = $48,000	3,000 X $16 = $ 48,000
			$96,000	
07-Sep				3,000 X $16 = $ 48,000
	8,000 X $17 = $136,000			8,000 X $17 = $136,000
				$184,000
11-Nov		6,000 X $25 = $150,000	3,000 X $16 = $48,000	
			3,000 X $17 = $51,000	5,000 X $17 = $ 85,000
			$99,000	
31-Dec				5,000 X $17 = $ 85,000

The table above provides information needed to record purchase and sale information. Specifically, Inventory is debited as purchases occur and credited as sales occur. The journal entries are below. The resulting ledger accounts and financial statements are shown on the following page:

JOURNAL ENTRIES

03-05-XX	Inventory	96,000	
	Accounts Payable		96,000
	Purchased inventory on account (6,000 X $16)		
04-17-XX	Accounts Receivable	154,000	
	Sales		154,000
	Sold merchandise on account (7,000 X $22)		
04-17-XX	Cost of Goods Sold	96,000	
	Inventory		96,000
	To record the cost of merchandise sold		
09-07-XX	Inventory	136,000	
	Accounts Payable		136,000
	Purchased inventory on account (8,000 X $17)		
11-11-XX	Accounts Receivable	150,000	
	Sales		150,000
	Sold merchandise on account (6,000 X $25)		
11-11-XX	Cost of Goods Sold	99,000	
	Inventory		99,000
	To record the cost of merchandise sold		

Inventory

Date	Description	Debit	Credit	Balance
Jan. 1, 20XX	Balance forward			$ 48,000
Mar. 5, 20XX	Purchase transaction	$ 96,000		144,000
Apr. 17, 20XX	Sale transaction		$ 96,000	48,000
Sep. 7, 20XX	Purchase transaction	136,000		184,000
Nov. 11, 20XX	Sale transaction		99,000	(85,000)

GONZALES CHEMICAL COMPANY
Balance Sheet
December 31, 20XX

Assets

...

Inventory $ 85,000

...

Sales

Date	Description	Debit	Credit	Balance
Jan. 1, 20XX	Balance forward			$ -
Apr. 17, 20XX	Sale transaction		$154,000	154,000
Nov. 11, 20XX	Sale transaction		150,000	(304,000)

GONZALES CHEMICAL COMPANY
Income Statement
For Year Ending December 31, 20XX

Net sales $304,000
Cost of goods sold   195,000
Gross profit $109,000

...

Cost of Goods Sold

Date	Description	Debit	Credit	Balance
Jan. 1, 20XX	Balance forward			$ -
Apr. 17, 20XX	Sale transaction	$ 96,000		96,000
Nov. 11, 20XX	Sale transaction	99,000		(195,000)

PERPETUAL LIFO   The following table, ledgers, and financial statements reveal the application of perpetual LIFO. Note that the results usually differ from the periodic LIFO approach. The journal entries are not repeated here but would be the same as with FIFO; only the amounts would change.

Date	Purchases	Sales	Cost of Goods Sold	Balance
01-Jan				4,000 X $12 = $ 48,000
05-Mar				4,000 X $12 = $ 48,000
	6,000 X $16 = $ 96,000			6,000 X $16 = $ 96,000
				$144,000
17-Apr		7,000 X $22 = $154,000	6,000 X $16 = $ 96,000	
			1,000 X $12 = $ 12,000	3,000 X $12 = $ 36,000
			$108,000	
07-Sep				3,000 X $12 = $ 36,000
	8,000 X $17 = $136,000			8,000 X $17 = $136,000
				$172,000
11-Nov		6,000 X $25 = $150,000	6,000 X $17 = $102,000	3,000 X $12 = $ 36,000
				2,000 X $17 = $ 34,000
				$70,000
31-Dec				3,000 X $12 = $ 36,000
				2,000 X $17 = $ 34,000
				$ 70,000

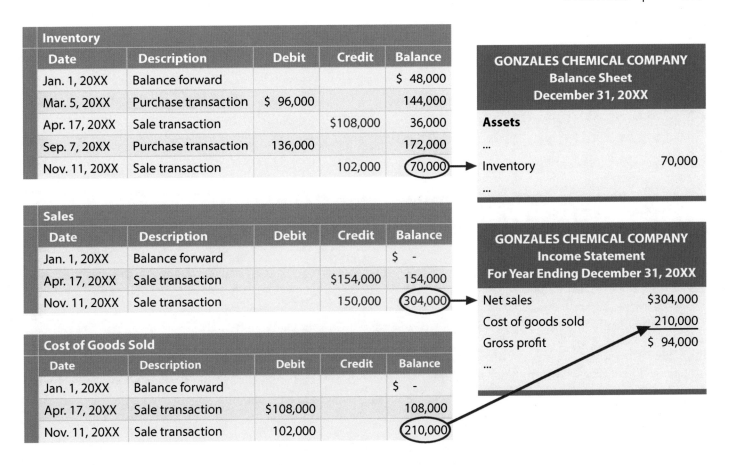

The average method can be applied on a perpetual basis, earning it the name **moving average**. This technique is involved, as a new average unit cost must be computed with each purchase transaction. The following table, ledgers, and financial statements reveal the application of moving average.

Date	Purchases	Sales	Cost of Goods Sold	Balance
01-Jan				4,000 X $12 = $ 48,000
05-Mar				4,000 X $12 = $ 48,000
	6,000 X $16 = $ 96,000			6,000 X $16 = $ 96,000
				$144,000
				($144,000/10,000 units= $14.40 per unit)
17-Apr		7,000 X $22 = $154,000	7,000 X $14.40 = $100,800	3,000 X $14.40 = $ 43,200
07-Sep				3,000 X $14.40 = $ 43,200
	8,000 X $17 = $136,000			8,000 X $17 = $136,000
				$179,200
				($179,200/11,000 units= $16.2909 per unit)
11-Nov		6,000 X $25 = $150,000	6,000 X $16.2909 =$97,745	5,000 X $16.2909 = $ 81,455
31-Dec				5,000 X $16.2909 = $ 81,455

Inventory				
Date	Description	Debit	Credit	Balance
Jan. 1, 20XX	Balance forward			$ 48,000
Mar. 5, 20XX	Purchase transaction	$ 96,000		144,000
Apr. 17, 20XX	Sale transaction		$100,800	43,200
Sep. 7, 20XX	Purchase transaction	136,000		179,200
Nov. 11, 20XX	Sale transaction		97,745	81,445

GONZALES CHEMICAL COMPANY
Balance Sheet
December 31, 20XX

Assets

...

Inventory   81,445

...

Sales				
Date	Description	Debit	Credit	Balance
Jan. 1, 20XX	Balance forward			$ -
Apr. 17, 20XX	Sale transaction		$154,000	154,000
Nov. 11, 20XX	Sale transaction		150,000	304,000

GONZALES CHEMICAL COMPANY
Income Statement
For Year Ending December 31, 20XX

Net sales	$304,000
Cost of goods sold	198,545
Gross profit	$105,455

...

Cost of Goods Sold				
Date	Description	Debit	Credit	Balance
Jan. 1, 20XX	Balance forward			$ -
Apr. 17, 20XX	Sale transaction	$100,800		100,800
Nov. 11, 20XX	Sale transaction	97,745		198,545

As with the periodic system, observe that the perpetual system also produced the lowest gross profit via LIFO, the highest with FIFO, and the moving-average fell in between.

Lower of Cost or Net Realizable Value

Although every attempt is made to prepare and present financial data that are free from bias, accountants do employ a degree of conservatism. **Conservatism** dictates that accountants avoid overstatement of assets and income. Conversely, liabilities would tend to be presented at higher amounts in the face of uncertainty. This is not a hardened rule, just a general principle of measurement.

In the case of inventory, a company may find itself holding inventory that has an uncertain future; meaning the company does not know if or when it will sell. Obsolescence, over supply, defects, major price declines, and similar problems can contribute to uncertainty about the "realization" (conversion to cash) for inventory items. Therefore, accountants evaluate inventory and employ **lower of cost or net realizable value** considerations. This simply means that if inventory is carried on the accounting records at greater than its **net realizable value** (NRV), a write-down from the recorded cost to the lower NRV would be made. In essence, the Inventory account would be credited, and a Loss for Decline in NRV would be the offsetting debit. This debit would be reported in the income statement as a charge against (reduction in) income.

APPLICATION   NRV, in the context of inventory, is the estimated selling price in the normal course of business, less reasonably predictable costs of completion, disposal, and transportation. Obviously, these measurements can be somewhat subjective, and may require the exercise of judgment in their determination. It is also important to note that a company using LIFO or the retail method (as described in the next section of this chapter) would not use the lower of cost or NRV method, but would instead value inventory at lower of cost or "market." Substitution of the word "market" entails subtle technical distinctions, the details of which are usually covered in more advanced accounting classes.

It is noteworthy that the lower of cost or NRV adjustments can be made for each item in inventory, or for the aggregate of all the inventory. In the latter case, the good offsets the bad, and a write-down is only needed if the overall value is less than the overall cost. In any event, once a write-down is deemed necessary, the loss should be recognized in income and inventory should be reduced. Once reduced, the Inventory account becomes the new basis for valuation and reporting purposes going forward. Unlike international reporting standards, U.S. GAAP does not permit a write-up of write-downs reported in a prior year, even if the value of the inventory has recovered.

Inventory Estimation Techniques

Whether a company uses a periodic or perpetual inventory system, a **physical inventory** (i.e., physical count) of goods on hand should occur from time to time. The quantities determined via the physical count are presumed to be correct, and any differences should result in an adjustment of the accounting records. Sometimes, however, a physical count may not be possible or is not cost effective, and estimates are employed.

One such estimation technique is the **gross profit method**. This method might be used to estimate inventory on hand for purposes of preparing monthly or quarterly financial statements, and certainly would come into play if a fire or other catastrophe destroyed the inventory. Very simply, a company's normal gross profit rate (i.e., gross profit as a percentage of sales) would be used to estimate the amount of gross profit and cost of sales. Assume that Tiki's inventory was destroyed by fire. Sales for the year, prior to the date of the fire were $1,000,000, and Tiki usually sells goods at a 40% gross profit rate. Therefore, Tiki can readily estimate that cost of goods sold was $600,000. Tiki's beginning of year inventory was $500,000, and $800,000 in purchases had occurred prior to the date of the fire. The inventory destroyed by fire can be estimated via the gross profit method, as shown.

GROSS PROFIT METHOD

	A	B	C	D	E	F
1						
2	Sales	100%	$1,000,000			
3	Cost of goods sold	*Step 1: Determine relative percentages* — 60%	600,000	*Step 2: Solve for cost of goods sold*		
4	Gross profit	40%	$ 400,000			
5						
6						
7						
8	Beginning inventory		$ 500,000			
9	Purchases	*Step 3: Fill in known values*	800,000			
10	Cost of goods available for sale		$1,300,000			
11	Less: Cost of goods sold		600,000			
12	Ending inventory presumed lost in fire		$ 700,000			
13						

RETAIL METHOD

A method that is widely used by merchandising firms to value or estimate ending inventory is the **retail method**. This method would only work where a category of inventory has a consistent mark-up. The cost-to-retail percentage is multiplied times ending inventory at retail. Ending inventory at retail can be determined by a physical count of goods on hand, at their retail value. Or, sales might be subtracted from goods available for sale at retail.

Crock Buster sells pots that cost $7.50 for $10. This yields a cost-to-retail percentage of 75%. The beginning inventory totaled $200,000 (at cost), purchases were $300,000 (at cost), and sales totaled $460,000 (at retail).

The only "givens" are highlighted in yellow. These three data points are manipulated by the cost-to-retail percentage to solve for ending inventory cost of $155,000. Be careful to note when the percentage factors are divided and when they are multiplied.

Spreadsheet					▢▢✕
	A	B	C	D	E
1		At Cost (75% of Retail)		At Retail	
2	Beginning inventory	$200,000	÷ 0.75 ➜	$266,667	
3	Purchases	300,000	÷ 0.75 ➜	400,000	
4	Cost of goods available for sale	$500,000		$666,667	
5	Sales	345,000	← 0.75 ×	460,000	
6	Ending inventory	$155,000		$206,667	
7					

Inventory Management

The best run companies will minimize their investment in inventory. Inventory is costly and involves the potential for loss and spoilage. In the alternative, being out of stock may result in lost customers, so a delicate balance must be maintained. Careful attention must be paid to the inventory levels. One ratio that is often used to monitor inventory is the Inventory Turnover Ratio. This ratio shows the number of times that a firm's inventory balance was turned ("sold") during a year. It is calculated by dividing cost of sales by the average inventory level:

$$\textbf{Inventory Turnover Ratio} = \frac{\textbf{Cost of Goods Sold}}{\textbf{Average Inventory}}$$

If a company's average inventory was $1,000,000, and the annual cost of goods sold was $8,000,000, one would deduce that inventory turned over 8 times (approximately once every 45 days). This could be good or bad depending on the particular business; if the company was a baker it would be very bad news, but a lumber yard might view this as good. So, general assessments are not in order. What is important is to monitor the turnover against other companies in the same line of business, and against prior years' results for the same company. A declining turnover rate might indicate poor management, slow moving goods, or a worsening economy. In making such comparisons, one must be clever enough to recognize that the choice of inventory method affects the results.

In the process of maintaining inventory records and the physical count of goods on hand, errors may occur. It is quite easy to overlook goods on hand, count goods twice, or simply make mathematical mistakes. It is vital that accountants and business owners fully understand the effects of inventory errors and grasp the need to be careful to get these numbers as correct as possible. A general rule is that overstatements of ending inventory cause overstatements of income, while understatements of ending inventory cause understatements of income. For instance, compare the following correct and incorrect scenario, where the only difference is an overstatement of ending inventory by $1,000 (note that this general rule is only valid when purchases are correctly recorded):

	Correct		**Incorrect**
Beginning inventory	$ 5,000		$ 5,000
Purchases	11,000		11,000
Cost of goods available for sale	$16,000		$16,000
Ending inventory	4,000	*Overstated*	5,000
Cost of goods sold	$12,000		$11,000
Sales	$25,000		$25,000
Cost of goods sold	12,000		11,000
Gross profit	$13,000	*Overstates*	$14,000

Had the above inventory error been an understatement ($3,000 instead of the correct $4,000), then the ripple effect would have caused an understatement of income by $1,000.

Inventory errors tend to be counterbalancing. That is, one year's ending inventory error becomes the next year's beginning inventory error. The general rule of thumb is that overstatements of beginning inventory cause that year's income to be understated, and vice versa. Examine the following table where the only error relates to beginning inventory balances:

	Correct		**Incorrect**
Beginning inventory	$ 4,000	*Overstated*	$ 5,000
Purchases	11,000		11,000
Cost of goods available for sale	$15,000		$16,000
Ending inventory	3,000		3,000
Cost of goods sold	$12,000		$13,000
Sales	$25,000		$25,000
Cost of goods sold	12,000		13,000
Gross profit	$13,000	*Understates*	$12,000

Hence, if the above illustrations related to two consecutive years, the total income would be correct ($13,000 + $13,000 = $14,000 + $12,000). However, the amount for each year is critically flawed.

Chapter 8 Quiz

Goals Achievement

Q8-1. Under the weighted-average inventory method, the average unit cost of inventory is determined by dividing the sum of the individual purchase prices by the number of purchases which occurred during the year.

right or wrong

Q8-2. During a time of rising prices, the LIFO technique causes inventory on the balance sheet to bear what relationship to its fair value?

greater than or less than

Q8-3. In determining inventory's lower of cost or net realizable value, NRV is defined as:

sales price less selling costs or replacement cost

Q8-4. Under the gross profit method, ending inventory is determined by multiplying net purchases by the estimated gross profit percentage.

true or false

Q8-5. The impact of inventory errors on income tends to be counter-balanced by offsetting errors in the following accounting period.

right or wrong

Fill in the Blanks

Q8-6. The _____ is the legal owner of goods on consignment.

Q8-7. The _____ method of costing inventory requires a business to identify each unit of merchandise with the unit's cost, and retain that identification until the inventory is sold.

Q8-8. _____ requires that accounting and valuation methods of application be used on a regular basis from year to year.

Q8-9. Under the perpetual system, when inventory is sold, the _____ account is debited and _____ is credited. The _____ account, which is used with a periodic system, is not used with the perpetual system.

Q8-10. The _____ method estimates inventory on the basis of a company's gross profit rate.

Q8-11. Understating beginning inventory would cause income for that year to be _____.

Q8-12. Inventory accounts should be classified in which section of a balance sheet?

a. Current assets

c. Property, plant, and equipment

b. Investments

d. Intangible assets

Q8-13. Hefty Company wants to know the effect of different inventory methods on financial statements. Given below is information about beginning inventory and purchases for the current year.

January 2	Beginning Inventory	500 units at $3.00
April 7	Purchased	1,100 units at $3.20
June 30	Purchased	400 units at $4.00
December 7	Purchased	1,600 units at $4.40

Sales during the year were 2,700 units at $5.00. If Hefty used the first-in, first-out method, ending inventory would be:

a. $2,780

c. $9,700

b. $3,960

d. $10,880

Q8-14. Hefty Company wants to know the effect of different inventory methods on financial statements. Given below is information about beginning inventory and purchases for the current year.

January 2	Beginning Inventory	500 units at $3.00
April 7	Purchased	1,100 units at $3.20
June 30	Purchased	400 units at $4.00
December 7	Purchased	1,600 units at $4.40

Sales during the year were 2,700 units at $5.00. If Hefty used the weighted-average method, gross profit would be:

a. $3,255

c. $10,245

b. $3,415

d. $13,500

Q8-15. An inventory pricing procedure in which the oldest costs incurred rarely have an effect on the ending inventory valuation is:

a. FIFO

c. Retail

b. LIFO

d. Weighted-average

Q8-16. Gerber Department Store utilizes the retail inventory method. Gerber's beginning inventory cost $140,000 and retailed for $280,000. Purchases for the period amounted to $390,000 and were priced to sell at twice that amount. Sales for the period, all at normal retail, were $600,000. How much is the cost of Gerber's estimated ending inventory?

a. $115,000

c. $230,000

b. $150,000

d. $300,000

Chapter 8 Problems

Basic Problems

C & L Coach buys luxury cars from manufacturers and then "saws them in half" and adds a number of components to upgrade and stretch them into exotic limousines. Examine the following items and decide if each should be included in inventory. If so, should the item be shown as raw materials, work in process, or finished goods?

	Inventory		Category		
	Yes	No	Raw Material	Work in Process	Finished Goods
Finished stretch limos awaiting sale	✔				✔
Limos under production that have been ordered by specific customers and a deposit made					
Finished limos shipped to dealers, terms FOB shipping point					
Luxury cars ordered from a manufacturer and in transit, FOB destination					
Sheet metal in the company's warehouse					
Wiring produced in China, in transit on a ship in the Pacific Ocean, terms FOB Shanghai					
Leather installed on a limo currently under production					
LCD monitors installed in a finished limo awaiting shipment to a customer					
Finished and sold limo returned to the factory for repair under warranty					

Sid Breman Art Gallery operates a retail store in Florida. All art displayed in the gallery is available for purchase. Much of the art is owned by the gallery. However, there are also works on display that belong to other artists. When the consigned art is sold, Sid remits 75% of the proceeds to the creator and retains a 25% commission. Art belonging to the gallery is marked to sell at 200% of cost.

SPREADSHEET TOOL:

Check boxes

Following is a complete list of art on display in the gallery, along with the retail selling price.

NAME	SELLING PRICE	OWNERSHIP
See Shining Sea	$ 2,500	Gallery
Mermaids	1,800	Artist
Big Fish	910	Gallery
Shells At Dawn	3,000	Gallery
Sand Forever	1,090	Gallery
Development!	4,200	Artist
Taking a Chance	20,000	Gallery
Tides and Moons	500	Gallery
Mystery Sea	1,200	Gallery
On the Beach	1,650	Artist
Too Much Sun	4,775	Artist
Spring Break	5,000	Artist
Inland	7,880	Gallery
Alligators Return	19,720	Artist
Frost and Farm	14,300	Gallery

(a) Identify if Sid Breman Art Gallery is the consignor or the consignee. Should the consigned inventory be reported on the balance sheet of the gallery? What special accounting/control challenges are presented by the existence of consigned inventory?

(b) Determine the correct inventory valuation to be reported by the gallery.

(c) Prepare a compound journal entry to reflect the sale of a consigned art item for $1,000 cash. Assume Sid reports only the commission as a revenue, and reflects the amount due to the artist as a payable.

Elizabeth Egbert owns a galvanizing plant. Customers bring in their fabricated steel products (like light poles, towers, trailers, etc.), and Egbert dips them into a heated vat of molten zinc. The zinc bonds to the metal and produces a highly durable corrosion resistant product.

Egbert's primary inventory is molten zinc purchased from suppliers in large blocks of solid material. These blocks are immersed in the heated vat and will melt together with the zinc already in the pool. Egbert generally keeps the vat relatively full, and it is never allowed to cool.

Egbert started the year 20X8 with 500,000 pounds of zinc in the pool. During the year Egbert purchased 2,800,000 pounds of zinc. At year's end, the pool contained 520,000 pounds of zinc.

(a)   How much zinc was used during 20X8?

(b)   Accountants frequently refer to "goods available for sale." Is this concept the same as ending inventory? How much zinc, in pounds, was "available for sale?"

(c)   If the beginning inventory cost $1.25 per pound, and purchases during 20X8 cost $1.50 per pound, how much is the "cost of goods available for sale"?

(d)   In preparing financial statements for 20X8, to what financial statement elements will the amount you calculated in part (c) be allocated?

(e)   If Egbert uses FIFO, how much should be attributed to ending inventory and how much to cost of goods sold?

(f)   If Egbert uses LIFO, how much should be attributed to ending inventory and how much to cost of goods sold?

(g)   What will be the difference in profitability between choosing the FIFO and LIFO methods? Does it seem reasonable that the choice of accounting method can change the reported profit?

B-08.04   *Basic "periodic" calculations for inventory, FIFO, LIFO, average cost*

Patti Devine owns Devine Decorating. One of her most popular items is the Remind-a-Chime digital clock. This programmable clock issues "voice-based" reminders of important events like birthdays, anniversaries, etc.

Following is the Remind-a-Chime inventory activity for January. The clocks on hand at January 1 had a unit cost of $140.

Date	Purchases	Sales	Units on Hand
1-Jan			40
5-Jan	60 units @ $150 each		100
16-Jan		70 units @ $255 each	30
23-Jan	90 units @ $170 each		120
28-Jan		55 units @ $295 each	65

(a)   If Devine uses the first-in, first-out (FIFO) inventory method (periodic approach), what values would be assigned to ending inventory and cost of goods sold? How much is gross profit?

(b)   If Devine uses the last-in, first-out (LIFO) inventory method (periodic approach), what values would be assigned to ending inventory and cost of goods sold? How much is gross profit?

(c)   If Devine uses the weighted-average inventory method (periodic approach), what values would be assigned to ending inventory and cost of goods sold? How much is gross profit?

Tom Pryor is conducting an audit of the computerized inventory system used by Zix Corporation. Tom has inserted hypothetical data into the computer program that tracks inventory on a perpetual basis. Below are the hypotheical data inserted by Tom:

Transaction	Units	Cost per unit
Beginning inventory	10	$10
Purchase, day 1	5	$11
Sale, day 2	6	
Purchase, day 3	8	$12
Sale, day 4	9	

The computer program returned the following ending inventory values:

FIFO perpetual, $96

LIFO perpetual, $80

Moving average, $88

Which of the three values appears to be incorrect, and what "error" might be causing this condition?

B. J. Stewart Furniture Company had the following transactions relating to the purchase and sale of leather sofas. There was no beginning inventory.

Purchased 100 units on account at $1,000 per unit

Sold 75 units for cash at $2,000 per unit

Customers returned 3 defective units for cash refunds

Stewart returned the 3 defective units to its supplier for credit on account

(a)   Assuming Stewart uses a periodic inventory system, what journal entries would be needed to record the preceding activity?

(b)   Assuming Stewart uses a periodic inventory system, show the calculation of gross profit. You may assume that Stewart conducted a physical count of ending inventory and confirmed that 25 were still on hand.

(c)   Assuming Stewart uses a perpetual inventory system, what journal entries would be needed to record the preceding activity?

(d)   Assuming Stewart uses a perpetual inventory system, show the calculation of gross profit. If Stewart uses a perpetual system, would there be any need to perform a periodic physical count of leather sofas on hand?

Park Place Luxury Autos uses the specific identification method to value its inventory. Below is a listing of automobiles that were either in beginning inventory or acquired during the year:

Automobile	Date Acquired	Cost
Bentley	Beginning inventory	$120,000
Rolls Royce	Beginning inventory	160,000
Cadillac	January	40,000
Lexus	March	50,000
Land Rover	June	60,000
Jaguar	July	42,000
Porsche	September	75,000
Mercedes	November	85,000
BMW	December	64,000
Infiniti	December	39,000

Park Place uses the specific identification method. Total sales during the year were $600,000. Automobiles in ending inventory were the Rolls Royce, Lexus, Jaguar, and BMW. Determine the ending inventory, cost of goods sold, and gross profit for Park Place.

Doyle's Art buys and sells paintings from emerging artists. The values of the works are prone to fluctuate considerably based on the ever changing stature of a particular artist. Following is a listing of 6 paintings, along with their costs, estimated selling prices, and expected selling costs (inclusive of commissions and shipping).

Painting	Cost	Estimated Selling Price	Estimated Selling Expense
Fire on Hill	$1,000	$1,400	$400
Horses in Aspen Grove	2,500	800	100
Baby's First Smile	3,000	6,000	500
Endless War	2,000	2,200	300
Rain Drop on Cactus	1,500	2,500	400
Election Day Upset	2,300	1,600	200

(a) What unit value should be attached to each painting, assuming item-by-item application of the lower of cost or net realizable value rule?

(b) Assuming an item-by-item application of the lower of cost or net realizable value rule, what journal entry is needed to reduce *Election Day Upset*?

(c) As a general rule, is the item-by-item approach required? Is the item-by-item approach the most "conservative?"

(d) If an item of inventory is written down, but subsequently recovers in value during a subsequent year, can it be written back up?

Gross profit estimation technique

Aurora Wedding Gowns was burglarized in May of 20X5. It is unclear how many dresses were stolen. Aurora and its insurance company are currently working to estimate the dollar value of the stolen goods in order to reach a financial settlement under the existing property insurance policy.

Aurora's tax return prepared at the end of 20X4 revealed that the company ended 20X4 with a total inventory of $189,000. Aurora uses the same inventory accounting methods for tax and accounting purposes.

The insurance company has contacted Aurora's suppliers and confirmed Aurora's claim that purchases for 20X5, prior to the date of the burglary, were $376,000. All inventory was purchased FOB destination.

20X5 sales taxes collected by Aurora and remitted to the state, prior to the date of the theft, were $48,000. The sales tax rate is 6% of sales.

An inventory was taken immediately after the burglary, and the cost of dresses in stock was $123,000.

Aurora consistently sells dresses at a gross profit margin of 45%.

Use the gross profit method to estimate the dollar value of stolen dresses.

Retail inventory techniques

The Quilting Pad is a retail store that sells materials for custom quilts. The store has a quilting room where quilters gather to sew and visit.

The store's inventory consists of bolts of fabrics, spools of thread, and trays of various batting and backing material. Customers generally select what they need and pay for what they use. The retail price of goods is clearly marked on the bolts, spools, and trays. The Quilting Pad has virtually no problem with theft or shortages of inventory.

It is virtually impossible to track inventory in any detailed fashion. The store simply marks up all goods by a constant percentage. The mark up formula has been consistently applied to all items in inventory for many years.

The Quilting Pad uses the retail inventory technique. Following is information for 20X7:

	A	B	C	D
Spreadsheet				
1				
2	Beginning inventory at cost	$ 46,800		
3	Beginning inventory at retail	78,000		
4	Cost of purchases of inventory during the year	230,000		
5				

At the end of the year, the Quilting Pad's inventory was physically counted, and it was determined that $100,000 was the retail value of goods on hand.

Apply the retail method to estimate the sales and gross profit for 20X7.

Bell Computers assembles and sells notebook computers. The company is attempting to better manage cash flow and reduce inventory. The most recent strategy has been to require major vendors to establish warehouses adjacent to Bell's factory locations. Bell then buys components from vendors as needed for same day delivery.

During 20X2, Bell had beginning inventory of $23,000,000 and cost of goods sold of $168,000,000. Inventory at the end of 20X2 was $33,000,000. During 20X3, cost of goods sold was $440,000,000. Inventory at the end of 20X3 was $55,000,000.

(a) What is the relationship between cash flow and inventory?

(b) One of Bell's product managers was very disappointed with the continuing increase in inventory from the beginning of 20X2 through the end of 20X3. He felt his directives to better manage inventory were not being followed. Prepare an inventory turnover ratio analysis for 20X2 and 20X3. Based on your analysis, is the company better managing inventory levels? How is it possible that the ratios are improving at the same time that inventory levels are expanding?

Citrin Corporation reported the following information related to 20X7 and 20X8:

	20X7	20X8
Beginning inventory	$ 634,400	$ 530,400
Purchases	1,899,990	2,450,500
Cost of goods available for sale	$2,534,390	$2,980,900
Less: Ending inventory	530,400	480,000
Cost of goods sold	$2,003,990	$2,500,900
Sales	$3,003,990	$4,500,900
Cost of goods sold	2,003,990	2,500,900
Gross profit	$1,000,000	$2,000,000

The 20X7 ending inventory value used in the above presentation erroneously failed to include $200,000 of goods purchased FOB shipping point. The purchase and related accounts payable were correctly recorded by Citrin Corporation. Citrin Corporation uses a periodic inventory system.

(a) Prepare a corrected presentation of the above data.

(b) Prepare a corrected presentation of the above data, but this time assume that the company had also failed to record the purchase before 20X8 (in addition to omitting the $200,000 from 20X7 ending inventory).

(c) In part (a), does the error matter, given that the combined gross profit for both years is $3,000,000 under both the incorrect and correct presentation?

(d) In part (b), does the error matter, given that the gross profit for each year is the same under both the incorrect and correct presentation?

Involved Problems

Track Rack is a software development company that specializes in developing information systems to account for inventory. The company maintains an attractive website, which is one of its primary marketing vehicles. The marketing department has suggested adding a "frequently asked questions" section to the website. The section is intended to focus on general inventory accounting concepts. By so doing, visitors will come to the website to learn about inventory accounting. Based on a visitor's pattern of clicks, pop-up ads will be triggered featuring specific software solutions that may be suitable to help the visitor with accounting issues he or she faces.

The marketing department personnel prepared the following list of "questions" they felt would trigger interest in a particular software product. An inexperienced staffer drafted the proposed "answers." Your job is to review the FAQs below, and suggest necessary corrections or clarifications related to each proposed answer.

QUESTION Are "finished goods" synonymous with "cost of goods sold?"

ANSWER For a manufacturer, inventory may consist of crude goods, work in process, and finished goods categories. Finished goods are completed units awaiting sale. Cost of goods sold is the cost assigned to goods that have been sold and delivered to customers.

QUESTION How does the negotiation of freight terms impact total inventory?

ANSWER Goods that are purchased F.O.B. destination are not included in inventory until received. Goods that are sold F.O.B. destination are transferred out of inventory on the day shipped.

QUESTION Are consigned goods included in inventory?

ANSWER Consigned goods remain in the inventory of the consignee, and should not be reported on the books of the consignor.

QUESTION Is "inventory" also called "cost of goods available for sale"?

ANSWER Cost of goods available for sale is not the same as inventory. Cost of goods available for sale relates to a period of time and the amount is probably never actually on hand all at once. It is calculated as ending inventory plus purchases.

QUESTION How does LIFO result in cash savings during a period of rising prices?

ANSWER LIFO generally results in a higher income level during a period of rising prices. More income equates to more cash!

QUESTION Will a periodic and perpetual system give me the same results?

ANSWER Never. The perpetual recalculation of inventory balances gives a different result than is achieved under a periodic application of FIFO, LIFO, and average costing techniques.

QUESTION It seems like the "gross profit" method is much simpler than FIFO, LIFO, or average costing. Can I use it as my primary inventory valuation technique?

ANSWER Yes. The gross profit method is an acceptable alternative to one of the other mentioned inventory costing methods.

QUESTION   How can I use the retail inventory technique to estimate inventory theft?

ANSWER   You cannot. Retail inventory techniques are used to assign costs to retail inventory on hand. It is unreasonable to expect an accounting method to determine the cost of inventory that no longer exists.

QUESTION   What's the big deal if I undercount ending inventory? The goods are still there so there is no real problem, right?

ANSWER   That's right. Even if you miscount, there is no economic effect. After all, the goods are still on hand. The numbers don't really matter in this case.

I-08.02   *Periodic inventory - application of methods*

Adriaan Taylor Corporation is a newly formed entity that engages in the purchase and resale of amphibious tour vehicles. Purchases for the first year of operation were as follows:

Date	Purchases
7-Jan	50 units @ $15,000 each
15-Mar	70 units @ $16,000 each
16-Jun	30 units @ $16,500 each
3-Aug	90 units @ $17,000 each
11-Oct	25 units @ $17,200 each

Sales for this first year of operation amounted to 210 units and totaled $4,250,000.

(a)   If Adriaan Taylor uses the first-in, first-out (FIFO) inventory method (periodic approach), what values would be assigned to ending inventory and cost of goods sold? How much is gross profit?

(b)   If Adriaan Taylor uses the last-in, first-out (LIFO) inventory method (periodic approach), what values would be assigned to ending inventory and cost of goods sold? How much is gross profit?

(c)   If Adriaan Taylor uses the weighted-average inventory method (periodic approach), what values would be assigned to ending inventory and cost of goods sold? How much is gross profit?

(d)   Which of the above techniques produces the highest profit? Which of the above techniques reports the most "current" cost on a balance sheet? Which of the above techniques report the most "current" cost in measuring income? Which of the above techniques results in the lowest income tax obligation?

I-08.03   *Perpetual inventory - application of methods*

Ali Naeem was recently placed in charge of inventory accounting for Sialkot Surgical Supply. This company is located in Pakistan and deals in surgical supplies for global export. The company has been using the last-in, first-out inventory method applied on a perpetual basis. The company's export trade is denominated and settled in dollars, and that currency is used within the company's ledger.

Ali's responsibility is to bring Sialkot Surgical's inventory accounting into conformity with international accounting standards that have been embraced by the Institute of Chartered Accountants of Pakistan. As a result of his research, Ali was surprised to learn that LIFO does not have global acceptance and it is not a GAAP method in his country.

Below is January's preliminary inventory schedule for surgical clamps. This schedule was prepared on a LIFO basis.

Date	Purchases	Sales	Cost of Goods Sold	Balance
01-Jan				5,000 X $20 = $100,000
05-Jan				5,000 X $20 = $100,000
	7,000 X $21 = $147,000			7,000 X $21 = $147,000
				$247,000
12-Jan		9,000 @ $35 = $315,000	7,000 X $21 = $147,000	
			2,000 X $20 = $ 40,000	3,000 X $20 = $ 60,000
			$187,000	
17-Jan				3,000 X $20 = $ 60,000
	4,000 X $22 = $ 88,000			4,000 X $22 = $ 88,000
				$148,000
26-Jan		3,000 @ $37 = $111,000	3,000 X $22 = $66,000	3,000 X $20 = $ 60,000
				1,000 X $22 = $ 22,000
				$ 82,000
31-Jan				3,000 X $20 = $ 60,000
				1,000 X $22 = $ 22,000
				$ 82,000

(a) Examine Sialkot's LIFO inventory schedule, and redo the presentation assuming perpetual FIFO. For this problem, you may assume that the beginning inventory would be the same as under LIFO.

(b) Examine Sialkot's LIFO inventory schedule, and redo the presentation assuming a moving average method. For this problem, you may assume that the beginning inventory would be the same as under LIFO.

(c) Prepare journal entries necessary to reflect the FIFO perpetual application.

(d) Show that the Inventory account balance resulting from part (c) agrees with the schedule from part (a). If Ali applied FIFO on a periodic basis, rather than a perpetual basis, would the same results occur?

(e) By applying FIFO, rather than LIFO, will Sialkot Surgical's income be increased or decreased?

(f) Do you suspect that global divergence in accounting practices can contribute to difficulties in cross-border financing and global trade?

Form a six-member team, evaluate the following fact situation, and complete the indicated requirements.

Lynne Pastor is chief financial officer for Lots of Advertising. The company has received an exclusive contract to distribute a unique parking lot striping machine that imprints advertising messages in parking lot stripes. Lots of Advertising is planning for rapid growth and needs to raise expansion capital. Lynne has identified a long-term source of financing on very favorable terms, but the following stipulations must be met:

Gross Profit Percentage for the first year	Must exceed 50%
Inventory Turnover for the first year (for this calculation assume year-end inventory is the "average" level)	Must exceed 1.4
Current ratio at year's end	Must exceed 3:1

The financing agreement requires that Lots of Advertising use FIFO, LIFO, or the weighted-average cost method, applied on a periodic basis. It is anticipated that year-end current assets, excluding inventory, will total $5,500,000. Current liabilities will be $4,750,000. For purposes of your analysis, you may assume that inventory purchases do not change current liabilities (e.g., they will be financed via the long-term source of capital).

Projected first-year sales of the new machine are 16,000 units at $5,000 per unit. Physical purchases are anticipated according to the following schedule:

Date	Purchases
1st quarter	4,000 units @ $2,000 each
2nd quarter	6,000 units @ $2,200 each
3rd quarter	8,000 units @ $2,400 each
4th quarter	10,000 units @ $2,600 each

(a) First Team Member -- Assuming FIFO, identify if the lender conditions are anticipated to be met.

(b) Second Team Member -- Obtain the first team member's results. If all lender conditions were not met, determine if a change in planned 4th quarter purchases could be accomplished that would allow all conditions to be met.

(c) Third Team Member -- Assuming LIFO, identify if the lender conditions are anticipated to be met.

(d) Fourth Team Member -- Obtain the third team member's results. If all lender conditions were not met, determine if a change in planned 4th quarter purchases could be accomplished that would allow all conditions to be met.

(e) Fifth Team Member -- Assuming the weighted-average inventory method, identify if the lender conditions are anticipated to be met.

(f) Sixth Team Member -- Obtain the fifth team member's results. If all lender conditions were not met, determine if a change in planned 4th quarter purchases could be accomplished that would allow all conditions to be met.

(g) Entire Team -- Discuss your findings. In particular, decide if the choice of inventory method impacts financial statement results and measures. Further, analyze the degree to which the scheduling of purchases impacts the various measures. Discuss whether it is reasonable for inventory accounting methods and the specific scheduling of purchases to impact the reported results and financial position.

Inventory estimates, errors, and adjustments	I-08.05

Joyce Cathey owns Southwest Golf Shop. She has reviewed the following preliminary financial data prepared for the year ending December 31, 20X8:

Sales	$500,000
Cost of goods sold	260,000
Gross profit	240,000
Operating expenses	200,000
Income before tax	40,000

Joyce has determined that the above data were based on assumptions that beginning-of-year inventory was $230,000 and end-of-year inventory was $265,000. The company uses a periodic inventory system.

Joyce has owned the golf shop for many years and is surprised and disappointed with these financial results. Accordingly, she has conducted an extensive review of the accounting for selected transactions. Her review turned up the following errors:

A spreadsheet of beginning inventory included 35 Zing golf bags at a cost of $20 each. These particular bags were the nicest in the store, and the unit cost was actually $200. The error was the result of incorrect data entry into the spreadsheet.

The ending inventory value was the result of a physical count on December 31, 20X8. The count failed to include 2,400 imprinted logo golf balls that were in the custody of employees who were going to be giving them away as promotional items at a New Year's Day parade on January 1, 20X9. These balls cost $1.50 each.

The company experienced a theft loss during 20X8. The theft consisted of 6 sets of Caldaway golf clubs that normally sell for $1,000 each, and provide a gross profit margin of 45%. The insurance company purchased replacement goods and delivered them to Southwest Golf Shop. These club sets were included in the year end physical inventory and valued at $1,000 each.

In 20X8, the company consigned golf apparel with a retail value of $30,000 to a vendor at a local golf tournament. The cost to retail percentage on apparel is 60%. At the conclusion of the tournament, the vendor returned $12,000 (at retail) of goods and $18,000 in cash. The agreement was that Southwest Golf Shop would pay the vendor a commission equal to 15% of the gross profit margin on sales. The commission has not yet been calculated or paid.

At year end, the company had 10 units of the Big Face driver in stock. The drivers had a unit cost of $300 and were included in the year end inventory at $3,000 total. The manufacturer of Big Face has just announced a new driver, the Square Face. These units will render the Big Face mostly obsolete. Even though the manufacturer will continue to offer Big Face for sale at a dealer cost of $300, it is anticipated the customers will now be willing to pay no more than $200 retail for the item.

Determine the correct income statement and inventory values. Will Joyce be pleased with the revised results?

Chapter 9:
Long-Term Investments

Goals:

How nature and intent influences the accounting for investments.

Accounting for "trading" and "available-for-sale" debt security investments.

Accounting for securities that are to be "held-to-maturity."

Special accounting for certain investments that require use of the "equity method."

Investments that result in consolidated financial statements.

principlesofaccounting.com

Nature and Intent-Based Accounting

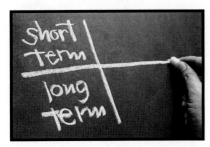

Recall from Chapter 6 that highly-liquid investments made with the intent of reselling them in the near future are classified on the balance sheet as current assets. They are reported at fair market value, and the changes in value are measured and included in the operating income of each period. This chapter will examine other investments, many of which may be acquired with the intent of holding them for an extended period. The specific accounting treatment for these longer-term investments varies based on the nature and intent of the investment.

DEBT

Sometimes one company may invest in debt securities issued by another company. One type of debt security is a "bond" (as in the popular term "stocks and bonds"). A bond payable is a mere "promise" (i.e., bond) to "pay" (i.e., payable). Thus, the issuer of a bond payable receives money today from an investor in exchange for a promise to repay the money, plus interest, over the future. In a later chapter, bonds payable will be examined from the issuer's perspective. In this chapter, the preliminary examination of bonds will be from the investor's perspective.

Bonds may be purchased for short-term "trading" purposes, in which case they are accounted for at fair value like other highly-liquid securities (as illustrated in Chapter 6). At other times, bonds are purchased as "available-for-sale," meaning that there is an intent to hold but a willingness to sell. This category is reported at fair value on the balance sheet, but with a unique income statement reporting aspect. Many bond investments are acquired with the intent of holding them to a scheduled maturity (i.e., final payment date). This latter category is known as a "held-to-maturity" investment, and is afforded a special accounting treatment generally known as the amortized cost approach.

EQUITY

Alternatively one company may acquire an ownership interest in the equity of another company (e.g., by investing in shares of the other company's stock). The reason for such an investment may be as simple as trying to profit from an increase in the stock price of the other company, or to receive periodic dividends paid by the other company. At other times, the acquirer may desire to obtain control of the other company, usually by buying more than 50% of the stock. In this case, the acquirer (sometimes known as the parent) must include the accounts of the acquired subsidiary in with their own through a process called consolidation. Yet another situation is the acquisition of a substantial amount of the stock of another but without obtaining control. This situation generally arises when the ownership level rises above 20%, but stays below 50%. In these cases, the investor is deemed to have the ability to significantly influence the investee company. Accounting rules specify the "equity method" of accounting for such investments.

The following table summarizes the methods one will be familiar with by the conclusion of this chapter:

Type of Investment	Basic Accounting Approach*	Guidelines for Assessment
INVESTMENTS IN DEBT SECURITIES		
Trading	Fair Value Gains and Losses to Operating Income	Intent to buy/sell for short-term profits
Available-for-Sale	Fair Value Gains and Losses to Other Comprehensive Income	Default Debt Category
Held-to-Maturity	Amortized Cost	Intent to buy and hold until fixed maturity date
INVESTMENTS IN EQUITY SECURITIES		
Significant Influence	Equity Method of Accounting	Stock investments generally ranging from 20-50%
Control	Consolidation	Stock investments generally exceeding 50%
Other (to benefit from price changes and dividends)	Fair Value Gains and Losses to Operating Income	Default Equity Category

* These approaches apply to investments that continue to be held. When any type of investment is sold, the "realized" gain or loss is included in operating income.

FAIR VALUE OPTION

Companies may also elect to measure certain financial assets (and liabilities) at fair value. This option essentially allows for a company to bypass the above table (other than where consolidation or equity method accounting is warranted) and instead measure an investment at fair value. When fair value accounting is elected, the unrealized gains and losses are reported in operating income, similar to the approach used for short-term investments illustrated in Chapter 6. This relatively new accounting option is indicative of a continuing evolution by the Financial Accounting Standards Board toward value-based accounting in lieu of traditional historical cost-based approaches. Importantly, the decision to apply the fair value option to a particular investment is irrevocable.

Debt Securities

As highlighted in the preceding table, the accounting for investments in debt securities will generally follow one of three broad approaches. One of these categories is that of trading securities. The accounting model for trading securities is straight-forward and was actually introduced in an earlier chapter. Therefore, only a brief paragraph is needed to review that method.

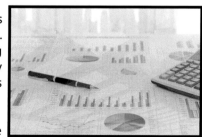

TRADING

Investments in debt that securities that are undertaken to try to capture gains from near-term price fluctuations are to be classified as **Trading Securities**. The accounting model is identical to the approach described in Chapter 6 for short-term investments. In other words, the investment in the debt security will be reported at each balance sheet date at its then current market value. Changes in market value from period to period are reported as unrealized gains and losses in each period's income statement. Consider reviewing the discussion from Chapter 6, imagining that the "example" was instead based on investments in Merriam Company's debt (rather than stock as shown) that fluctuated in value from $45,000 to $60,000.

The accounting for investments in **available-for-sale** debt is similar to the accounting for trading securities. In both cases, the investment asset account will be reflected at fair value. But, there is one significant difference pertaining to the recognition of the changes in value. For trading securities, the changes in value are recorded in operating income. However, for available-for-sale securities, the changes in value go into a special account called Unrealized Gain/Loss - Other Comprehensive Income.

AVAILABLE-FOR-SALE

Other comprehensive income (OCI) is somewhat unique. Begin by recognizing that the accounting profession embraces the **all-inclusive approach** to measuring income. This essentially means that all transactions and events make their way through net income. This has not always been the case; once only operational items were included in the income statement (a **current operating** concept of income).

OCI

Despite the all-inclusive approach, there are a few circumstances where accounting rules provide for special treatment. Such is the case with Unrealized Gain/Loss - OCI. The changes in value on available-for-sale debt securities are recognized, not in operating income as with trading securities, but instead in this unique account. There are two reporting options for OCI. Some companies report OCI within a broader statement of comprehensive income, while others prepare a separate schedule reconciling net income to total comprehensive income.

Assume that Webster acquired an investment in Merriam Corporation debt. The intent was not for trading purposes. The investment was classified as available-for-sale.

EXAMPLE

The following entry was needed on March 3, 20X6, the day Webster bought Merriam's debt:

03-03-X6	Available-for-Sale Debt Securities		50,000	
	Cash			50,000
	To record the purchase of Merriam debt			

Next, assume that financial statements were being prepared on March 31. By that date, Merriam's debt had declined in value. Accounting rules require that the investment "be written down" to current value, with a corresponding charge against OCI. The charge is recorded as follows:

03-31-X6	Unrealized Gain/Loss - OCI		5,000	
	Available-for-Sale Debt Securities			5,000
	To record a $5,000 decrease in the value of Merriam debt			

This charge reduces other comprehensive income. But, net income is not reduced. The rationale is that the net income is not affected by temporary fluctuations in market value, given the intent to hold the investment for a longer term. During April, the debt's market value improved to $60,000. Webster's adjustment is:

04-30-X6	Available-for-Sale Debt Securities	15,000	
	Unrealized Gain/Loss - OCI		15,000
	To record an increase in the value of Merriam debt		

Notice that the three journal entries now have the available-for-sale securities valued at $60,000 ($50,000 - $5,000 + $15,000). This is equal to market value. The OCI has been adjusted for a total of $10,000 in credits ($5,000 debit and $15,000 credit). This cumulative credit corresponds to the total increase in value of the original $50,000 investment. As an alternative to directly adjusting the Available-for-Sale Debt Securities account, some companies may maintain a separate Valuation Adjustments account that is added to or subtracted from the Available-for-Sale Debt Securities account. The results are the same; the reasons for using the alternative approach are to provide additional information that may be needed for more complex accounting and tax purposes.

INTEREST INCOME

Interest income received on available-for-sale debt securities is included in net income:

04-15-X6	Cash	100	
	Interest Income		100
	To record receipt of interest on available-for-sale debt security investment		

ON THE INCOME STATEMENT

Assume that Webster's operations produced a $10,000 net income for April. The lower portion of the resulting statement of comprehensive income would appear as follows:

WEBSTER COMPANY
Statement of Comprehensive Income
For the Month Ending April 30, 20X6

.....	.....
Interest income	100
Net income	$10,000
Unrealized gain - other comprehensive income	15,000
Comprehensive income	$25,000

ON THE BALANCE SHEET

The preceding events would result in the following balance sheet presentations of available-for-sale securities at March 31 and April 30. To simplify the illustration, the only accounts that are assumed to change during April relate to the fluctuation in value of Merriam's debt and an assumed increase in cash and retained earnings because of the $10,000 net income. In reviewing the following illustrations, note that available-for-sale securities are customarily classified in the Long-term Investments section of the balance sheet. And, take note that the accumulated OCI is appended to stockholders' equity.

WEBSTER COMPANY
Balance Sheet
March 31, 20X6

Assets				Liabilities			
Current assets				**Current liabilities**			
Cash		$160,000		Accounts payable		$ 80,000	
Accounts receivable		75,000		Salaries payable		10,000	
Inventories		200,000		Interest payable		20,000	
Prepaid insurance		25,000	$460,000	Current portion of notes payable		40,000	$150,000
Long-term investments				**Long-term liabilities**			
Available-for-sale debt securities			45,000	Notes payable		$190,000	
				Mortgage liability		110,000	300,000
Property, plant, & equipment				Total liabilities			$450,000
Land		$ 25,000					
Buildings and equipment	$150,000			**Stockholders' equity**			
Less: Accum. depreciation	(50,000)	100,000	125,000	Capital stock		$300,000	
				Retained earnings		170,000	
Intangible assets				Accumulated other comprehensive			
Goodwill			275,000	income/loss		(5,000)	
Other assets			10,000	Total stockholders' equity			465,000
Total assets			$915,000	Total liabilities and equity			$915,000

WEBSTER COMPANY
Balance Sheet
April 30, 20X6

Assets				Liabilities			
Current assets				**Current liabilities**			
Cash		$170,000		Accounts payable		$ 80,000	
Accounts receivable		75,000		Salaries payable		10,000	
Inventories		200,000		Interest payable		20,000	
Prepaid insurance		25,000	$470,000	Current portion of notes payable		40,000	$150,000
Long-term investments				**Long-term liabilities**			
Available-for-sale debt securities			60,000	Notes payable		$190,000	
				Mortgage liability		110,000	300,000
Property, plant, & equipment				Total liabilities			$450,000
Land		$ 25,000					
Buildings and equipment	$150,000			**Stockholders' equity**			
Less: Accum. depreciation	(50,000)	100,000	125,000	Capital stock		$300,000	
				Retained earnings		180,000	
Intangible assets				Accumulated other comprehensive			
Goodwill			275,000	income/loss		10,000	
Other assets			10,000	Total stockholders' equity			490,000
Total assets			$940,000	Total liabilities and equity			$940,000

Held-to-Maturity Securities

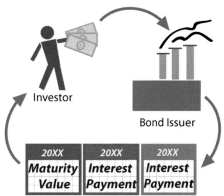

Investor

Bond Issuer

20XX	20XX	20XX
Maturity Value	**Interest Payment**	**Interest Payment**

It was noted earlier that certain types of financial instruments have a fixed maturity date; the most typical of such instruments are "bonds." The **held-to-maturity** securities are normally accounted for by the **amortized cost method**.

To elaborate, if an individual wishes to borrow money he or she would typically approach a bank or other lender. But, a corporate giant's borrowing needs may exceed the lending capacity of any single bank or lender. Therefore, the large corporate borrower may instead issue "bonds," thereby splitting a large loan into many small units.

For example, a bond issuer may borrow $500,000,000 by issuing 500,000 individual bonds with a face amount of $1,000 each (500,000 X $1,000 = $500,000,000). If an individual wished to loan some money to that corporate giant, he or she could do so by simply buying ("investing in") one or more of the bonds.

The specifics of bonds will be covered in greater detail in a subsequent chapter, where bonds are examined from the issuer's perspective (i.e., borrower). For now, bonds will be considered from the investor perspective. Each bond has a "face value" (e.g., $1,000) that corresponds to the amount of principal to be paid at maturity, a contract or stated interest rate (e.g., 5% -- meaning that the bond pays interest each year equal to 5% of the face amount), and a term (e.g., 10 years -- meaning the bond matures 10 years from the designated issue date). In other words, a $1,000, 5%, 10-year bond would pay $50 per year for 10 years (as interest), and then pay $1,000 at the stated maturity date.

THE ISSUE PRICE

How much would one pay for a 5%, 10-year bond: Exactly $1,000, more than $1,000, or less than $1,000? The answer to this question depends on many factors, including the credit-worthiness of the issuer, the remaining time to maturity, and the overall market conditions. If the "going rate" of interest for other bonds was 8%, one would likely avoid this 5% bond (or, only buy it if it were issued at a deep discount). On the other hand, the 5% rate might look pretty good if the "going rate" was 3% for other similar bonds (in which case one might actually pay a premium to get the bond).

So, bonds might have an **issue price** that is at **face value** (also known as **par**), or above (at a premium) or below (at a discount) face. The price of a bond is typically stated as percentage of face; for example 103 would mean 103% of face, or $1,030. The specific calculations that are used to determine the price one would pay for a particular bond are revealed in a subsequent chapter.

BONDS PURCHASED AT PAR

An Investment in Bonds account (at the purchase price plus brokerage fees and other incidental acquisition costs) is established at the time of purchase. Premiums and discounts on bond investments are not recorded in separate accounts:

01-01-X3	Investment in Bonds	5,000	
	Cash		5,000
	To record the purchase of five $1,000, 5%, 3-year bonds at par -- interest payable semiannually		

The above entry reflects a bond purchase as described, while the following entry reflects the correct accounting for the receipt of the first interest payment after 6 months.

06-30-X3	Cash	125	
	Interest Income		125
	To record the receipt of an interest payment ($5,000 par X .05 interest X 6/12 months)		

The entry that is recorded on June 30 would be repeated with each subsequent interest payment, continuing through the final interest payment on December 31, 20X5. In addition, at maturity, when the bond principal is repaid, the investor would also make this final accounting entry:

12-31-X5	Cash	5,000	
	Investment in Bonds		5,000
	To record the redemption of bond at maturity		

When bonds are purchased at a **premium**, the investor pays more than the face value up front. However, the bond's maturity value is unchanged; thus, the amount due at maturity is less than the initial issue price! This may seem unfair, but consider that the investor is likely generating higher annual interest receipts than on other available bonds. Assume the same facts as for the preceding bond illustration, but this time imagine that the market rate of interest was something less than 5%. Now, the 5% bonds would be very attractive, and entice investors to pay a premium:

BONDS PURCHASED AT A PREMIUM

01-01-X3	Investment in Bonds	5,300	
	Cash		5,300
	To record the purchase of five $1,000, 5%, 3-year bonds at 106 -- interest payable semiannually		

The above entry assumes the investor paid 106% of par ($5,000 X 106% = $5,300). However, remember that only $5,000 will be repaid at maturity. Thus, the investor will be "out" $300 over the life of the bond. Thus, accrual accounting dictates that this $300 "cost" be amortized ("recognized over the life of the bond") as a reduction of the interest income:

06-30-X3	Cash	125	
	Interest Income		75
	Investment in Bonds		50
	To record the receipt of an interest payment ($5,000 par X .05 interest X 6/12 months = $125; $300 premium X 6 months/36 months = $50 amortization)		

The preceding entry can be confusing and bears additional explanation. Even though $125 was received, only $75 is being recorded as interest income. The other $50 is treated as a return of the initial investment; it corresponds to the premium amortization ($300 premium allocated evenly over the life of the bond: $300 X (6 months/36 months)). The premium amortization is credited against the Investment in Bonds account. This process of premium amortization would be repeated with each interest payment. Therefore, after three years, the Investment in Bonds account would be reduced to $5,000 ($5,300 - ($50 amortization X 6 semiannual interest recordings)).

This method of tracking amortized cost is called the **straight-line method**. There is another conceptually superior approach to amortization, called the effective-interest method, which will be revealed in later chapters. However, it is a bit more complex and the straight-line method presented here is acceptable so long as its results are not materially different than would result under the effective-interest method.

In addition, at maturity, when the bond principal is repaid, the investor would make this final accounting entry:

12-31-X5	Cash		5,000	
	Investment in Bonds			5,000
	To record the redemption of bond investment at maturity			

In an attempt to make sense of the preceding, perhaps it is helpful to reflect on just the "cash out" and the "cash in." How much cash did the investor pay out? It was $5,300; the amount of the initial investment. How much cash did the investor get back? It was $5,750; $125 every 6 months for 3 years and $5,000 at maturity. What is the difference? It is $450 ($5,750 - $5,300). This is equal to the income recognized via the journal entries ($75 every 6 months, for 3 years). At its very essence, accounting measures the change in money as income. Bond accounting is no exception, although it is sometimes illusive to see. The following "amortization" table reveals certain facts about the bond investment accounting, and is worth studying closely. Be sure to "tie" the amounts in the table to the illustrated journal entries.

Spreadsheet								□◻⊠
	I3			fx	=I2-G3			
	A	B	C	D	E	F	G	H	I
1	Date		Cash Received		Interest Income		Premium Amortization		Investment in Bonds
2	01-01-X3		$ (5,300)	cr					$ 5,300
3	06-30-X3		125	dr	$ 75	cr	$ 50	cr	5,250
4	12-31-X3		125	dr	75	cr	50	cr	5,200
5	06-30-X4		125	dr	75	cr	50	cr	5,150
6	12-31-X4		125	dr	75	cr	50	cr	5,100
7	06-30-X5		125	dr	75	cr	50	cr	5,050
8	12-31-X5		125	dr	75	cr	50	cr	5,000
9	12-31-X5		5,000	dr	---	cr	---	cr	---
10			$ 450	=	$ 450		$ 300		
11									
12									

Cash Invested
$5,300

Interest Income $450

1st Half 20X3	1st Half 20X4	1st Half 20X5
$75	$75	$75
2nd Half 20X3	2nd Half 20X4	2nd Half 20X5
$75	$75	$75

Cash Returned
$5,750

Sometimes, complex transactions are easier to understand when one simply thinks about the balance sheet impact. For example, on December 31 20X4, Cash is increased $125, but the Investment in Bonds account is decreased by $50 (dropping from $5,150 to $5,100). Thus, total assets increased by a net of $75. The balance sheet remains in balance because the corresponding $75 of interest income causes a corresponding increase in retained earnings.

The discount scenario is very similar to the premium, but "in reverse." When bonds are purchased at a **discount**, the investor pays less than the face value up front. However, the bond's maturity value is unchanged; thus, the amount due at maturity is more than the initial issue price! This may seem like a bargain, but consider that the investor is likely getting lower annual interest receipts than is available on other bonds.

BONDS PURCHASED AT A DISCOUNT

Assume the same facts as for the previous bond illustration, except imagine that the market rate of interest was something more than 5%. Now, the 5% bonds would not be very attractive, and investors would only be willing to buy them at a discount:

01-01-X3	Investment in Bonds	4,850	
	Cash		4,850
	To record the purchase of five $1,000, 5%, 3-year bonds at 97 -- interest payable semiannually		

The above entry assumes the investor paid 97% of par ($5,000 X 97% = $4,850). However, remember that a full $5,000 will be repaid at maturity. Thus, the investor will get an additional $150 over the life of the bond. Accrual accounting dictates that this $150 "benefit" be recognized over the life of the bond as an increase in interest income:

06-30-X3	Cash	125	
	Investment in Bonds	25	
	Interest Income		150
	To record the receipt of an interest payment ($5,000 par X .05 interest X 6/12 months = $125; $150 discount X 6 months/36 months = $25 amortization)		

The preceding entry would be repeated at each interest payment date. Again, further explanation may prove helpful. In addition to the $125 received, another $25 of interest income is recorded. The other $25 is added to the Investment in Bonds account, as it corresponds to the discount amortization ($150 discount allocated evenly over the life of the bond: $150 X (6 months/36 months)=$25).

This process of discount amortization would be repeated with each interest payment. Therefore, after three years, the Investment in Bonds account would be increased to $5,000 ($4,850 + ($25 amortization X 6 semiannual interest recordings)). This example again uses the straight-line method of amortization since the amount of interest is the same each period. The alternative effective-interest method demonstrated later in the book would be required if the results would be materially different.

When the bond principal is repaid at maturity, the investor would also make this final entry:

12-31-X5	Cash	5,000	
	Investment in Bonds		5,000
	To record the redemption of bond investment at maturity		

Consider the "cash out" and the "cash in." How much cash did the investor pay out? It was $4,850; the amount of the initial investment. How much cash did the investor get back? It is the same as it was in the premium illustration: $5,750 ($125 every 6 months for 3 years and $5,000 at maturity). What is the difference? It is $900 ($5,750 - $4,850). This is equal to the income recognized ($150 every 6 months, for 3 years).

Be sure to "tie" the amounts in the following amortization table to the related entries.

Spreadsheet								□◻☒
	I3			fx	=I2+G3			
	A	B	C	D	E	F	G	H	I
1	Date		Cash Received		Interest Income		Discount Amortization		Investment in Bonds
2	01-01-X3		$ (4,850)	cr					$ 4,850
3	06-30-X3		125	dr	$ 150	cr	$ 25	dr	4,875
4	12-31-X3		125	dr	150	cr	25	dr	4,900
5	06-30-X4		125	dr	150	cr	25	dr	4,925
6	12-31-X4		125	dr	150	cr	25	dr	4,950
7	06-30-X5		125	dr	150	cr	25	dr	4,975
8	12-31-X5		125	dr	150	cr	25	dr	5,000
9	12-31-X5		5,000	dr	---	cr	---	dr	---
10			$ 900	=	$ 900		$ 150		
11									
12									

Cash Invested
$4,850

Interest Income $900

1st Half 20X3	1st Half 20X4	1st Half 20X5
$150	$150	$150
2nd Half 20X3	2nd Half 20X4	2nd Half 20X5
$150	$150	$150

Cash Returned
$5,750

What is the balance sheet impact on June 30, 20X5? Cash increased by $125, and the Investment in Bonds account increased $25. Thus, total assets increased by $150. The balance sheet remains in balance because the corresponding $150 of interest income causes a corresponding increase in retained earnings.

Equity Securities

The table from the opening portion of this chapter distinguished between investments in debt securities and investments in equity securities. Attention is now turned to the specific details of accounting for investments in equity securities. Equity securities infer an ownership claim to the investor, and include investments in capital stock as well as options to acquire stock. The accounting method for an investment in equity securities primarily depends on the level of investment.

Most investments in equity securities are relatively small, giving the investor less than a 20% ownership stake. These investments are ordinarily insufficient to give the investor the right to control or significantly influence the investee company. The purposes for such smaller investments varies; suffice it to say that the end goal is usually to profit from price appreciation and dividends. Such investments may be short- or long-term in nature.

Short-term investments in equity securities were covered in Chapter 6, and that presentation is equally applicable to long-term investments. That is to say, the manner of accounting for short-term and long-term investments (those "generally below the 20% level") does not vary. The investment is reported on the balance sheet at fair value, and changes in value are booked in income each period. The only notable difference is that the short-term investments would be presented in the current asset section of a balance sheet, while the longer-term investments would be positioned within the long-term investments category.

An investor may acquire enough ownership in the stock of another company to permit the exercise of "significant influence" over the **investee** company. For example, the investor has some direction over corporate policy and can sway the election of the board of directors and other matters of corporate governance and decision making. Generally, this is deemed to occur when one company owns more than 20% of the stock of the other. However, the ultimate decision about the existence of **significant influence** remains a matter of judgment based on an assessment of all facts and circumstances.

THE EQUITY METHOD

Once significant influence is present, generally accepted accounting principles require that the investment be accounted for under the **equity method.** Market-value adjustments are usually not utilized when the equity method is employed. In global circles, the term "associate investment" might be used to describe equity method investments.

With the equity method, the accounting for an investment tracks the "equity" of the investee. That is, when the investee makes money (and experiences a corresponding increase in equity), the investor will record its share of that profit (and vice-versa for a loss). The initial accounting commences by recording the investment at cost:

04-01-X3	Investment	50,000	
	Cash		50,000
	To record the purchase of 5,000 shares of Legg stock at $10 per share. Legg has 20,000 shares outstanding, and the investment in 25% of Legg (5,000/20,000 = 25%) is sufficient to give the investor significant influence		

Next, assume that Legg reports income for the three-month period ending June 30, 20X3, in the amount of $10,000. The investor would simultaneously record its "share" of this reported income as follows:

06-30-X3	Investment	2,500	
	Investment Income		2,500
	To record investor's share of Legg's reported income (25% X $10,000)		

Importantly, this entry causes the Investment account to increase by the investor's share of the investee's increase in its own equity (i.e., Legg's equity increased $10,000, and the entry causes the investor's Investment account to increase by $2,500), thus the name "equity method." Notice, too, that the credit causes the investor to recognize income of $2,500, again corresponding to its share of Legg's reported income for the period. Of course, a loss would be reported in the opposite fashion.

When Legg pays out dividends (and decreases its equity), the investor will need to reduce its Investment account as shown below.

07-01-X3	Cash	1,000	
	Investment		1,000
	To record the receipt of $1,000 in dividends from Legg -- Legg declared and paid a total of $4,000 ($4,000 X 25% = $1,000)		

The above entry is based on the assumption that Legg declared and paid a $4,000 dividend. This treats dividends as a return of the investment (not income, because the income is recorded as it is earned rather than when distributed). In the case of dividends, consider that the investee's equity reduction is met with a corresponding proportionate reduction of the Investment account on the books of the investor.

Investments Requiring Consolidation

A casual review of business news won't take long to reveal a story about one business buying another. Such acquisitions are common and number in the thousands annually. There are many reasons for these transactions, and this helps to explain their frequency. One business may acquire another to eliminate a competitor, to gain access to critical technology, to insure a supply chain, to expand distribution networks, to reach a new customer base, and so forth.

These transactions can be simple or complex, but generally involve the acquirer buying a majority of the stock of the target company. This majority position enables the acquirer to exercise control over the other company. Control is ordinarily established once ownership jumps over 50%, but management contracts and other similar arrangements may allow control to occur at other levels.

ECONOMIC
ENTITY
CONCEPT AND
CONTROL

A controlled company may continue to operate and maintain its own legal existence. Assume Premier Tools Company bought 100% of the stock of Sledge Hammer Company. Sledge (now a "subsidiary" of Premier the "parent") will continue to operate and maintain its own legal existence. It will merely be under new ownership. Even though it is a separate legal entity, it is viewed by accountants as part of a larger "economic entity."

The intertwining of ownership means that Parent and Sub are "one" as it relates to economic performance and outcomes. Therefore, accounting rules require that parent companies "consolidate" their financial reports and include all the assets, liabilities, and operating results of all controlled subsidiaries. For example, the financial statements of a conglomerate like General Electric are actually a consolidated picture of many separate companies controlled by GE.

ACCOUNTING
ISSUES

Assume that Premier's "separate" (before consolidating) balance sheet immediately after purchasing 100% of Sledge's stock appears below. Notice the highlighted Investment in Sledge account. This asset reflects ownership of all of the stock of Sledge and that Premier paid $400,000 for this investment.

Importantly, the $400,000 flowed from Premier to the former owners of Sledge (not directly to Sledge). Sledge has a new owner, but is otherwise unaffected by the transaction. Sledge's balance sheet appears at the top of the facing page. Notice that Sledge's total equity is highlighted to call attention to its reported balance of $300,000.

PREMIER TOOLS COMPANY
Balance Sheet
March 31, 20X3

Assets			Liabilities		
Current assets			**Current liabilities**		
Cash	$100,000		Accounts payable	$ 80,000	
Trading securities	70,000		Salaries payable	10,000	
Accounts receivable	80,000		Interest payable	10,000	$ 100,000
Inventories	200,000	$ 450,000			
			Long-term liabilities		
Long-term investments			Notes payable	$190,000	
Investment in Sledge		400,000	Mortgage liability	110,000	300,000
					$ 400,000
Property, plant, & equipment					
Land	$ 25,000				
Buildings and equipment (net)	100,000	125,000	**Stockholders' equity**		
			Capital stock	$300,000	
Intangible assets			Retained earnings	500,000	800,000
Patent		225,000			
Total assets		$1,200,000	Total liabilities and equity		$1,200,000

SLEDGE HAMMER COMPANY
Balance Sheet
March 31, 20X3

Assets			Liabilities		
Current assets			**Current liabilities**		
Cash	$ 50,000		Accounts payable	$ 80,000	
Accounts receivable	30,000		Salaries payable	20,000	$100,000
Inventories	20,000	$100,000			
			Long-term liabilities		
			Notes payable		50,000
Property, plant, & equipment					$150,000
Land	$ 75,000		**Stockholders' equity**		
Buildings and equipment (net)	275,000	350,000	Capital stock	$100,000	
			Retained earnings	200,000	300,000
Total assets		$450,000	Total liabilities and equity		$450,000

It may seem odd that Premier's investment is reported at $400,000, while Sledge's equity is only $300,000. However, this would actually be quite common. Consider what Premier got for its $400,000. Premier became the sole owner of Sledge, which has assets that are reported on Sledge's books at $450,000, and liabilities that are reported at $150,000. The resulting net book value ($450,000 - $150,000 = $300,000) corresponds to Sledge's total stockholders' equity. Premier paid $100,000 in excess of book value ($400,000 - $300,000). This excess is often called "acquisition differential" (the excess of the fair value over the net book value).

Acquisition differential can be explained by many factors. Remember that assets and liabilities are not necessarily reported at fair value. For example, the cost of land held by Sledge may differ from its current value. Assume Sledge's land is worth $110,000, or $35,000 more than its carrying value of $75,000. That would explain part of the acquisition differential. Assume that all other identifiable assets and liabilities are carried at fair value. What about the other $65,000 of acquisition differential ($100,000 total differential minus $35,000 attributable to land)?

GOODWILL

The remaining $65,000 is due to goodwill. Whenever one business buys another and pays more than the fair value of all the identifiable pieces, the excess is termed **goodwill**.

Goodwill only arises from the acquisition of one business by another. Many companies may have implicit goodwill, but it is not recorded until it arises from an actual acquisition transaction.

Why would someone be willing to pay for goodwill? There are many possible scenarios, but suffice it to say that many businesses are worth more than their identifiable pieces.

A rental store with a favorable location and established customer base is perhaps worth more than its facilities and equipment. A law firm is hopefully worth more than its desks, books, and computers. Consider the value of a quality business reputation that has been established for years.

PROCESS

The process of **consolidation** can become complex, but the basic principles are not. Shown on the next page is the consolidated balance sheet for Premier and its subsidiary. Note that the Investment in Sledge account is absent. It has been replaced with the assets and liabilities of Sledge! But, the assets and liabilities are not necessarily the simple sum of the amounts reported by the parent and subsidiary.

For example, the $135,000 Land account reflects the parent's land plus the fair value of the subsidiary's land ($25,000 + $110,000). Notice that the amount attributable to the land is not $25,000 (from the parent's books) plus $75,000 (from subsidiary's books). Instead, the consolidated amounts reflect the reported amounts for the parent's assets (and liabilities) plus the values of the subsidiary's assets (and liabilities) as implicit in the acquisition price.

Also, note that consolidated equity amounts match Premier's separate balance sheet. This result is expected since Premier's separate accounts include the ownership of Sledge via the Investment in Sledge account (which has now been replaced by the actual assets and liabilities of Sledge).

PREMIER TOOLS AND CONSOLIDATED SUBSIDIARY					
Balance Sheet					
March 31, 20X3					
Assets			**Liabilities**		
Current assets			**Current liabilities**		
Cash	$150,000		Accounts payable	$160,000	
Trading securities	70,000		Salaries payable	30,000	
Accounts receivable	110,000		Interest payable	10,000	$ 200,000
Inventories	220,000	$ 550,000			
			Long-term liabilities		
Property, plant, & equipment			Notes payable	$240,000	
Land	$135,000		Mortgage liability	110,000	350,000
Buildings and equipment (net)	375,000	510,000			$ 550,000
Intangible assets			**Stockholders' equity**		
Patent	$225,000		Capital stock	$300,000	
Goodwill	65,000	290,000	Retained earnings	500,000	800,000
Total assets		$1,350,000	Total liabilities and equity		$1,350,000

INCOME STATEMENT

Be aware that the income statements of the parent and sub will be consolidated post-acquisition. In future periods, the consolidated income statement will reflect the revenues and expenses of both the parent and sub added together. This process is ordinarily straightforward. But, an occasional wrinkle will arise.

For instance, if the parent paid a premium in the acquisition for depreciable assets and/or inventory, the amount of consolidated depreciation expense and/or cost of goods sold may need to be tweaked to reflect alternative amounts based on values included in the consolidated balance sheet. And, if the parent and sub have done business with one another, adjustments will be needed to avoid reporting intercompany transactions. Internal transactions between affiliates should not be reported as actual sales.

WORKSHEET An orderly worksheet can be used to demonstrate preparation of the consolidated balance sheet. This is shown on the top of the facing page. Amounts from both Premier's and Sledge's balance sheets are incorporated into the first two data columns. These values are the carrying amounts for assets and liabilities taken directly from the separate accounting records of each company.

The Debit/Credit columns reflect a "worksheet only" entry that will be used to process the elimination of the $400,000 Investment account against the $300,000 equity of the subsidiary ($200,000 capital stock and $100,000 retained earnings). The "acquisition differential" is then allocated to land ($35,000 to increase to fair value) and goodwill ($65,000). Adding across all of the columns produces the consolidated amounts that correspond to the values shown in the consolidated balance sheet.

Consolidating Spreadsheet

	A	B	C	D	E	F
1	Accounts	Premier	Sledge	Debit	Credit	Consolidated
2	Cash	100,000	50,000			150,000
3	Trading securities	70,000				70,000
4	Accounts receivable	80,000	30,000			110,000
5	Inventories	200,000	20,000			220,000
6	Investments in Sledge	400,000			400,000	
7	Land	25,000	75,000	35,000		135,000
8	Buildings and equipment (net)	100,000	275,000			375,000
9	Patent	225,000				225,000
10	Goodwill			65,000		65,000
11	Accounts payable	(80,000)	(80,000)			(160,000)
12	Salaries payable	(10,000)	(20,000)			(30,000)
13	Interest payable	(10,000)				(10,000)
14	Notes payable	(190,000)	(50,000)			(240,000)
15	Mortgage liability	(110,000)				(110,000)
16	Capital stock	(300,000)	(100,000)	100,000		(300,000)
17	Retained earnings	(500,000)	(200,000)	200,000		(500,000)
18						

In summary, understand that the consolidated balance sheet on the date of the acquisition encompasses the assets (excluding the investment account), liabilities, and equity of the parent at their dollar amounts reflected on the parent's books, along with the assets (including goodwill) and liabilities of the sub adjusted to their fair values.

In the event one of the affiliated companies owes money to the other (i.e., there are intercompany payables/receivables), great care must be taken to also eliminate those accounts from consolidated reports. It would be highly inappropriate to show amounts that are in essence owed to yourself as an asset!

Chapter 9 Quiz

Q9-1. Which type of investment security is eligible for "Available-for-Sale" accounting treatment?:

debt or equity

Q9-2. Presently, the accounting profession purports to use which conceptual approach to measuring income:

current operating or all inclusive

Q9-3. Dividends received on investments are reported as income.

true or false

Q9-4. The equity method involves journal entries at the time the investee's earnings are announced, as well as when:

dividends are paid or market value declines

Q9-5. When consolidating, which of the following accounts would be eliminated from the consolidated presentation:

Goodwill or Investment in Subsidiary

Fill in the Blanks

Q9-6. The _____ method is used to account for held-to-maturity investments.

Q9-7. The _____ approach to measuring income is generally employed in modern financial reporting.

Q9-8. Bond investment _____ amortization causes investment income to be increased beyond the amount of cash received.

Q9-9. The equity method focuses principally on changes in the investee's _____, rather than on changes in the market value of the investee's stock.

Q9-10. Consolidation is required for greater than 50% owned _____.

Q9-11. If the parent and sub have done business with one another, adjustments will be needed to avoid reporting _____ transactions.

Multiple Choice

Q9-12. Ace Corporation has a long-term investment in the common stock of another entity. The investment does <u>not</u> render the investor with the ability to exercise significant influence or control over the investee. A journal entry to record a $10,000 decline in market value below cost would necessarily involve:

a. a debit to Unrealized Gain/Loss

c. a debit to Long-Term Investment.

b. a credit to Unrealized Gain/Loss

d. a debit to Investment Revenue.

Q9-13. On June 1, Pennell Corporation purchased $100,000 of 9%, 5-year bonds. The bonds are dated June 1, 20X1. The bonds were issued at 96, and pay interest on December 1 and June 1. The entry to record the investment in bonds is:

a. Investment in Bonds 100,000
      Cash   100,000

c. Investment in Bonds 104,000
      Cash   104,000

b. Investment in Bonds 96,000
      Cash   96,000

d. Investment in Bonds 96,000
      Interest Income   4,000
      Cash   100,000

Q9-14. On January 1, 20X2, Miller Corporation purchased $100,000 of 5%, 10-year bonds dated January 1, 20X2, at 98. Interest is paid on June 30 and December 31 of each year. Assuming use of the straight-line amortization method, the proper amount to report for Investment in Bonds at December 31, 20X3 is:

a. $98,000

c. $100,000

b. $98,400

d. $101,600

Q9-15. Investor Corporation owns 30% of Investee Corporation. Investee had net earnings of $100,000 during the year and paid dividends of $30,000. Investor's Investment in Investee account contained a $70,000 balance at the beginning of the year. What would be the correct balance of this account at the end of the year?

a. $70,000

c. $100,000

b. $91,000

d. $140,000

Q9-16. Mega Corporation owns 100% of Wolf Corporation's stock. Mega paid $1,000,000 for its investment. At the time of the initial investment, Wolf had total stockholders' equity of $600,000. All of Wolf's assets and liabilities were carried at amounts that equaled their fair value, except for a building that was undervalued by $100,000. How much goodwill would you anticipate finding in the consolidated balance sheet?

a. $0

c. $300,000

b. $100,000

d. $400,000

Chapter 9 Problems

Basic Problems

Classification of investments	B-09.01

Determine the "type" and "basic accounting" approach for each of the following categories of investments. You may find this problem easier to complete by using the pick lists on the excel version of this problem.

SPREADSHEET TOOL:

Creating a drop down list

	Type	Basic Accounting
Debt Investments:		
Investment in debt with a plan to hold until a particular future event of payoff		
Investment in debt with the goal of a near-term profit		
Investments in debt other than one of the above two types		
Equity Investments:		
Investment in equity generally over 20% but not giving control		
Investment in equity usually over 50%		
Relatively permanent investments in equity other than one of the above two types		

Your randomized choices for "*type*" are:	Your randomized choices for "*basic accounting*" are:
Control	Fair Value - gains/losses to operating income
Available-for-Sale	Fair Value - gains/losses to other comprehensive income
Held-to-Maturity	Equity Method
Trading	Consolidation
Significant Influence	Amortized Cost
Long-term investment	

This problem requires you to carefully reread and think about the book's brief discussion on emerging trends in fair value reporting. As you do so, edit the following incorrect comments to make them correct. The first one is done as an example on the preprinted worksheet.

> The Securities and Exchange Commission is increasingly issuing standards focused on fair value accounting.

> The fair value standards contemplate revaluing all categories of assets and liabilities.

> The fair value standards pertain to financial assets, but not financial liabilities.

> The fair value measurements are mandatory.

> The fair value standards represent a narrowing of the opportunities to depart from the historical cost tradition.

Micro Detect Corporation was sued for securities fraud. It was alleged that the company deliberately overstated net income by failing to appropriately recognize losses on its trading securities. Following is the transcript of the testimony given by one of Micro Detect's expert witnesses, Professor Winston, in response to questioning by the company's attorney. Examine the testimony, and determine if any statement made by the professor is patently untrue. Develop a list of questions that an attorney for the plaintiff would want to use to cross examine the professor. Non-GAAP statements in the following testimony may be assumed to be correct; focus only on the assertions about accounting methods.

QUESTION   Professor, did Micro Detect realize a loss on its trading securities during the time period in question?

ANSWER   Absolutely not. The company continues to hold the securities that have declined in value. Realization would only occur when the securities are sold. Micro Detect has never sold any securities at less than their cost.

QUESTION   Would you mind telling the jury how these so-called "trading securities" should be accounted for?

ANSWER   Unsold trading securities should be valued at fair value, you know, and this is exactly what the company did.

QUESTION   So, then, it is your testimony that the assets in question were correctly valued?

ANSWER   Yes.

QUESTION   Now, I suspect that on cross-examination, the plaintiff's attorney is going to try to make a

LONG-TERM INVESTMENTS | 253

big deal about how the company kept the balance sheet in balance, so to speak. Let's go ahead and anticipate their questioning and try to clarify now. Please explain to the jury the process that Micro Detect used to keep the balance sheet in balance.

ANSWER   OK. When assets go down, something else must go down to offset, or keep the books in balance. There is an equation: assets = liabilities + equity. In this case, the company decreased equity to offset the decreased trading security value.

QUESTION   I see. So the company correctly valued assets and total equity.

ANSWER   Yes.

QUESTION   And this decrease in equity, can you tell the jury more about how the company recorded that?

ANSWER   Equity sometimes contains an account known as "accumulated other comprehensive income." There are various alternative mechanisms for reporting this account, and its changes.

QUESTION   So, equity was decreased and the company's net income was not impacted?

ANSWER   Right, the profession uses a "current operating approach" to measuring income. Things that are not related to day-to-day operations go directly to other comprehensive income and thereby reduce equity.

QUESTION   And, so, "other comprehensive income" is used to record these types of transactions and events that are not otherwise considered to be part of the company's net income?

ANSWER   Right.

Accounting for available-for-sale investments   *B-09.04*

Winsloe Corporation obtained an investment in the debt of Southern Rail. Although Winsloe has no immediate plans to trade the investment for near-term profits, Winsloe is equally unlikely to hold the debt until it finally matures. Southern Rail faces an uncertain future and the market value of its debt tends to be volatile. Following is a description of the activity related to the investment in Southern Rail:

Aug. 5   Purchased debt of Southern Rail for $90,000.

Aug. 31   The fair market value of the Southern Rail debt was $100,000.

Sept. 30   The fair market value of the Southern Rail debt was $85,000.

Oct. 15   Received an interest payment on the Southern Rail debt of $2,500.

Oct. 31   The fair market value of the Southern Rail debt was $95,000.

(a)   What method should be used to account for this investment? Does management intent influence this decision? If the investment were obtained with the objective of near-term trading for profit, what would be done differently?

(b)   Prepare journal entries for the activity pertaining to the investment in Southern Rail debt.

Beckwith Boots invested $100,000 in 5-year bonds issued by Ace Brick Company. The bonds were purchased at par on January 1, 20X1, and bear interest at a rate of 8% per annum, payable semiannually.

(a)   Prepare the journal entry to record the initial investment on January, 20X1.

(b)   Prepare the journal entry that Beckwith would record on each interest date.

(c)   Prepare the journal entry that Beckwith would record at maturity of the bonds.

(d)   How much cash flowed "in" and "out" on this investment, and how does the difference compare to total interest income that was recognized?

Devol Computing invested in $100,000 face amount of 6-year bonds issued by Horton Micro Chip Company on January 1, 20X1. The bonds were purchased at 103, and bear interest at a stated rate of 8% per annum, payable semiannually.

(a)   Prepare the journal entry to record the initial investment on January, 20X1.

(b)   Prepare the journal entry that Devol would record on each interest date.

(c)   Prepare the journal entry that Devol would record at maturity of the bonds.

(d)   How much cash flowed "in" and "out" on this investment, and how does the difference compare to total interest income that was recognized?

Petersen Stores invested in $100,000 face amount of 4-year bonds issued by Erik Food Supply Company on January 1, 20X1. The bonds were purchased at 98, and bear interest at a stated rate of 8% per annum, payable semiannually.

(a)   Prepare the journal entry to record the initial investment on January, 20X1.

(b)   Prepare the journal entry that Petersen would record on each interest date.

(c)   Prepare the journal entry that Petersen would record at maturity of the bonds.

(d)   How much cash flowed "in" and "out" on this investment, and how does the difference compare to total interest income that was recognized?

Accounting for equity method investments	B-09.08

Davis Steel Company acquired 30% of the stock of Reginald Metals Company. Davis acquired this investment for purposes of being able to exert significant influence over the strategic plans and operations of Reginald. Following are events pertaining to this investment:

June 1   Purchased 30,000 shares of Reginald for $28 per share.

June 30   The fair value of Reginald's stock was $31 per share, and the company reported June income of $80,000.

July 15   The fair value of Reginald's stock was $30 per share, and the company declared and paid a dividend of $0.50 per share.

July 31   The fair value of Reginald's stock was $29 per share, and the company reported July income of $60,000.

(a)   What method should be used to account for this investment?

(b)   Prepare journal entries to account for the activity pertaining to the investment in Reginald Metals.

(c)   If the investment in Reginald Metals was insufficient to allow Davis to exert significant influence, how would the accounting approach differ?

Basic consolidated balance sheet	B-09.09

Packed Powder Corporation bought all of the stock of Snowfall Corporation from its existing shareholders on June 30, 20X4. Packed Powder paid Snowfall's shareholders a total of $2,000,000, which happened to be exactly equal to the recorded stockholders' equity of Snowfall. Further, the recorded values for each of the assets and liabilities of Snowfall were approximately equal to their estimated fair values. Following is a listing of the separate assets and liabilities of each company, immediately following the acquisition:

Consolidating Spreadsheet				▢◲☒
	A	B	C	D
1	Accounts	Packed Powder	Snowfall	Consolidated
2	Cash	$ 450,000	$ 60,000	
3	Accounts receivable	400,000	185,000	
4	Inventory	1,250,000	125,000	
5	Investment in Snowfall	2,000,000		
6	Land	850,000	380,000	
7	Buildings and equipment (net)	1,300,000	1,700,000	-
8		$6,250,000	$2,450,000	$ -
9				
10	Accounts payable	$ 760,000	$ 150,000	
11	Notes payable	2,400,000	300,000	
12	Common stock	500,000	400,000	
13	Retained earnings	2,590,000	1,600,000	-
14		$6,250,000	$2,450,000	$ -

Complete the "Consolidated" column to show how these accounts would appear in the consolidated balance sheet for Packed Powder and its subsidiary.

Parrot Corporation bought all of the stock of Sparrow Corporation from its existing shareholders on January 1, 20X6. Parrot paid Sparrow's shareholders a total of $5,000,000, which was $2,000,000 in excess of the recorded stockholders' equity of Sparrow. Further, the recorded values for each of the assets and liabilities of Sparrow were approximately equal to their estimated fair values, with the exception of land which had a fair value of $800,000. Any additional acquisition differential not assigned to land is attributable to goodwill. Following is a listing of the separate assets and liabilities of each company, immediately following the acquisition. The accounts of Sparrow are reported at their book value and do not reflect any acquisition differential allocation.

Consolidating Spreadsheet			▭◻☒
A	B	C	D
1	Accounts	Parrot	Sparrow	Consolidated
2	Cash	$1,450,000	$ 160,000	
3	Accounts receivable	430,000	335,000	
4	Inventory	850,000	725,000	
5	Investment in Sparrow	5,000,000		
6	Land	550,000	500,000	
7	Buildings and equipment (net)	1,700,000	2,530,000	-
8		$9,980,000	$4,250,000	$ -
9				
10	Accounts payable	$ 460,000	$ 450,000	
11	Notes payable	1,700,000	800,000	
12	Common stock	2,530,000	1,000,000	
13	Retained earnings	5,290,000	2,000,000	-
14		$9,980,000	$4,250,000	$ -

Complete the "Consolidated" column to show how these accounts would appear in the consolidated balance sheet for Parrot and its subsidiary. You will need to add an additional row for the goodwill.

Involved Problems

Bitnec Corporation acquired three separate investments at the beginning of the year. Information about each acquisition, the dividends/interest received during the year, income, and year-end stock/debt price, follows:

INITIAL INVESTMENT

Purchased 50,000 shares of Lynch Corporation at $11 per share. This investment was made with the intent of near-term trading profits. Lynch Corporation has 5,000,000 shares outstanding.

Purchased $200,000 of Graham Corporation debt for $200,000. This investment was generally considered to be long-term with no particular plans for near-term trading, although it is unlikely Bitnec will hold the investment until maturity.

Purchased 40% of the shares of Buffet Corporation at $30 per share. This investment was generally considered to be long-term with plans to exert significant influence. Buffet Corporation has 1,500,000 shares outstanding.

DIVIDENDS/INTEREST

Lynch Corporation declared and paid dividends of $0.50 per share.

Graham Corporation paid interest on outstanding debt, including $10,000 to Bitnec.

Buffet Corporation declared and paid dividends of $0.25 per share.

NET INCOME

Lynch Corporation reported net income of $4,000,000 for the year.

Graham Corporation reported net income of $7,000,000 for the year.

Buffet Corporation reported net income of $1,200,000 for the year.

YEAR END STOCK PRICE

Lynch Corporation's closing stock price at the end of the year was $13 per share.

Due to deteriorating finances, the value of Graham's debt held by Bitnec plunged to $150,000.

Buffet Corporation's closing stock price at the end of the year was $33 per share.

(a) Prepare journal entries, as necessary, to account for the initial investment, dividend, and year-end stock price for the investment in Lynch Corporation.

(b) Prepare journal entries, as necessary, to account for the initial investment, interest and year-end debt value for the investment in Graham Corporation securities.

(c) Prepare journal entries, as necessary, to account for the initial investment, dividend and year-end stock price for the investment in Buffet Corporation.

Bonds and amortization table	*I-09.02*

Season Corporation had excess cash on hand on January 1, 20X1 and invested in three separate bond issues on that date. Each bond investment had a maturity date of December 31, 20X6 and a maturity value of $100,000. The bond issues each pay interest on June 30 and December 31 of each year, and it is intended that these investments be held to maturity. Additional information about each investment follows:

Spring Company bonds were purchased at par and pay 7% annual interest.

Summer Company bonds were purchased for $95,168.33 and pay 6% annual interest.

Fall Company bonds were purchased for $104,831.67 and pay 8% annual interest.

(a) Prepare a table showing the accounting implications for the Spring Company bonds. Include columns for the date, cash flows, amount of interest income to record on each payment date, and the resulting bond investment account balance (the blank worksheets should be helpful in allowing you to complete this problem expeditiously).

(b) Prepare a table showing the accounting implications for the Summer Company bonds. Include columns for the date, cash flows, amount of interest income to record on each payment date, discount amortization, and the resulting bond investment account balance (the blank worksheets should be helpful in allowing you to complete this problem expeditiously).

(c) Prepare a table showing the accounting implications for the Fall Company bonds. Include columns for the date, cash flows, amount of interest income to record on each payment date, premium amortization, and the resulting bond investment account balance (the blank worksheets should be helpful in allowing you to complete this problem expeditiously).

(d) Examine the interest rates, and comment on why some bonds were available for purchase at par, while others involved a discount or premium.

I-09.03   *Bond investment accounting*

Season Corporation had excess cash on hand on January 1, 20X1 and invested in three separate bond issues on that date. Each bond investment had a maturity date of December 31, 20X6 and a maturity value of $100,000. The bond issues each pay interest on June 30 and December 31 of each year, and it is intended that these investments be held to maturity. Additional information about each investment follows:

Spring Company bonds were purchased at par and pay 7% annual interest.

Summer Company bonds were purchased for $95,168.33 and pay 6% annual interest.

Fall Company bonds were purchased for $104,831.67 and pay 8% annual interest.

(a) Prepare journal entries for the Spring Company bonds to record the initial investment, a periodic interest payment, and the maturity.

(b) Prepare journal entries for the Summer Company bonds to record the initial investment, a periodic interest payment, and the maturity.

(c) Prepare journal entries for the Fall Company bonds to record the initial investment, a periodic interest payment, and the maturity.

Coastal Pine Corporation acquired 40% of the stock of Delta Shipping. Coastal Pine's investment is a long-term strategic investment. Coastal Pine anticipates that its investment will permit it to elect certain board members and otherwise exercise influence over the plans and policies implemented by Delta.

Coastal Pine paid $20,000,000 for its 40% interest. The acquisition occurred on January 1, 20X4. On that date, Delta Shipping had total stockholders' equity of $50,000,000. During 20X4, Delta earned $13,000,000 and paid $3,000,000 in dividends. Both companies have December 31 year ends.

(a)   Prepare Coastal's entries to account for the activity pertaining to the investment in Delta Shipping.

(b)   Calculate the change in Delta's total equity during the year, and compare this to the change in Coastal's Investment in Delta account. Are they correlated, and does this help explain the term "equity" method of accounting?

Princeton Corporation purchased all of the stock of Stanford Corporation on July 1. Princeton paid $3,000,000 for this investment. Stanford's buildings had a fair value of $1,550,000. All other assets and liabilities of Stanford had fair values that were equivalent to their recorded amounts. Any excess acquisition differential is attributable to goodwill. The separate balance sheets of Princeton and Stanford follow. Prepare the consolidated balance sheet that would be reported to Princeton's shareholders.

PRINCETON CORPORATION
Balance Sheet
July 1, 20X5

Assets			Liabilities		
Current assets			**Current liabilities**		
Cash	$565,000		Accounts payable	$ 237,775	
Accounts receivable	233,789		Salaries payable	125,400	$ 363,175
Inventories	255,909	$1,054,698			
			Long-term liabilities		
Long-term investments			Loan payable		2,500,000
Investment in Stanford		3,000,000	Total liabilities		$2,863,175
Property, plant, & equipment					
Land	$378,790				
Building (net)	861,919		**Stockholders' equity**		
Equipment (net)	476,136	1,716,845	Capital stock	$2,300,000	
			Retained earnings	1,148,368	3,448,368
Intangible assets					
Patent		540,000			
Total assets		$6,311,543	Total liabilities and equity		$6,311,543

STANFORD CORPORATION **Balance Sheet** **July 1, 20X5**					
Assets			**Liabilities**		
Current assets			**Current liabilities**		
Cash	$ 34,545		Accounts payable	$118,998	
Accounts receivable	180,800		Salaries payable	23,441	$ 142,439
Inventories	343,687	$ 559,032			
			Long-term liabilities		
			Loan payable		632,179
Property, plant, & equipment					$ 774,618
Land	$137,776				
Buildings (net)	688,099		**Stockholders' equity**		
Equipment (net)	657,887	1,483,762	Capital stock	$800,000	
			Retained earnings	468,176	1,268,176
Total assets		$2,042,794	Total liabilities and equity		$2,042,794

I-09.06 *Team-based consideration of investment accounting*

Beginning and end-of-year balance sheets for Jensen Corporation follow. Next is the income statement for 20X6. No investments were sold during the year; however, stock in Delta Corporation was acquired on August 15, 20X6. Dividends of $50,000 were received on each of the investments in Alpha and Beta. Interest of $51,000 (cash portion) was received on the Gamma bonds and interest of $20,000 was earned on the Delta debt.

(a)   Form a four-person team. Assign each team member to one of the investments - Alpha, Beta, Delta, or Gamma.

(b)   Team members should examine the financial reports that follow, and prepare an explanation of the activity and accounting for their specifically assigned investment.

(c)   Then, the team should meet and each member present his or her explanation to the remainder of the group.

JENSEN CORPORATION
Balance Sheet
January 1, 20X6

Assets

Current assets

Cash	$ 34,500	
Accounts receivable	145,667	
Short-term investments (Alpha stock)	500,000	$ 680,167

Long-term investments

Equity method investment (Beta)	$800,000	
Investment in Bonds (Gamma)	842,000	1,642,000

Property, plant, & equipment

Equipment (net)	1,455,008

Total assets	$3,777,175

Liabilities

Current liabilities

Accounts payable	$ 56,000	
Utilities payable	18,690	$ 74,690

Long-term liabilities

Loan payable	660,500
Total liabilities	$ 735,190

Stockholders' equity

Capital stock	$2,601,585	
Retained earnings	440,400	
Total stockholders' equity		3,041,985
Total liabilities and equity		$3,777,175

JENSEN CORPORATION
Balance Sheet
December 31, 20X6

Assets

Current assets

Cash	$ 78,689	
Accounts receivable	83,442	
Short-term investments (Alpha stock)	510,000	$ 672,131

Long-term investments

Equity method investment (Beta)	$830,000	
Available-for-sale debt (Delta)	675,000	
Investment in Bonds (Gamma)	844,000	2,349,000

Property, plant, & equipment

Equipment (net)	1,215,000

Total assets	$4,236,131

Liabilities

Current liabilities

Accounts payable	$ 272,806	
Utilities payable	19,435	$ 292,241

Long-term liabilities

Loan payable	645,000
Total liabilities	$ 937,241

Stockholders' equity

Capital stock	$2,601,585	
Retained earnings	722,305	
Accum. other comp. income/loss	(25,000)	
Total stockholders' equity		3,298,890
Total liabilities and equity		$4,236,131

JENSEN CORPORATION
Statement of Comprehensive Income
For the Year Ending December 31, 20X6

Revenues			
Net sales			$2,000,900
Expenses			
Cost of goods sold		$800,500	
Selling		244,700	
General & administrative expenses		695,000	
Interest expense		40,000	
Investment income			
Interest income	$73,000		
Equity method income	80,000		
Unrealized gain/trading securities	10,000		
Dividend income	50,000	(213,000)	1,567,200
Income before tax			$ 433,700
Income tax expense			151,795
Net income			$ 281,905
Unrealized loss - other comprehensive income			(25,000)
Comprehensive income			$ 256,905

Chapter 10:
Property, Plant, & Equipment

Goals:

Measurement of costs assigned to property, plant, and equipment.

Principles relating to service life and depreciation.

Depreciation concepts and terminology.

The straight-line, units-of-output, and double-declining balance depreciation methods.

Unique features of depreciation under tax codes.

Equipment leases and the accounting implications.

principlesofaccounting.com

What Costs are Included in Property, Plant, & Equipment?

Property, Plant, & Equipment is a separate category on a classified balance sheet. It typically follows Long-term Investments and is oftentimes referred to as "PP&E." Items appropriately included in this section are the physical assets *deployed* in the productive operation of the business, like land, buildings, and equipment. Note that idle facilities and land held for speculation are more appropriately listed in some other category on the balance sheet, such as Long-term Investments.

Within the PP&E section, items are customarily listed according to expected life. Land is listed first, followed by buildings, then equipment. For some businesses, the amount of Property, Plant, & Equipment can be substantial. This is the case for firms that have large investments in manufacturing operations or significant real estate holdings. Other service or intellectual-based businesses may actually have very little to show within this balance sheet category.

Below is an example of a typical PP&E section on the balance sheet:

Property, Plant, & Equipment			
Land		$1,000,000	
Buildings	$ 2,300,000		
Less: Accumulated depreciation	(1,500,000)	800,000	
Equipment	$ 4,000,000		
Less: Accumulated depreciation	(1,800,000)	2,200,000	$4,000,000

In the alternative, many companies relegate the preceding level of detail into a note accompanying the financial statements, and instead just report a single number for "property, plant, and equipment, net of accumulated depreciation" on the face of the balance sheet.

COST ASSIGNMENT The correct amount of cost to allocate to a productive asset is based on those expenditures that are ordinary and necessary to get the item in place and in condition for its intended use. Such amounts include the purchase price (less any negotiated discounts), permits, freight, ordinary installation, initial setup/calibration/programming, and other normal costs associated with getting the item ready to use. These costs are termed **capital expenditures** and are assigned to an asset account. In contrast, other expenditures may arise that are not "ordinary and necessary," or benefit only the immediate period. These costs should be expensed as incurred. An example is repair of abnormal damage caused during installation of equipment.

Assume that Pechlat purchased a new lathe. The lathe had a list price of $90,000, but Pechlat negotiated a 10% discount. In addition, Pechlat agreed to pay freight and installation of $5,000. During installation the lathe's spindle was bent and had to be replaced for $2,000. The journal entry to record this transaction is:

03-17-X4	Equipment		86,000	
	Repair Expense		2,000	
	Cash			88,000
	Paid for equipment (($90,000 X .90) + $5,000), and repair cost			

INTEREST AND TRAINING COST Interest paid to finance the *purchase* of property, plant, and equipment is expensed. An exception is interest incurred on funds borrowed to finance *construction* of plant and equipment. Such interest related to the *period of time during which active construction is ongoing* is capitalized. Interest capitalization rules are quite complex, and are typically covered in intermediate accounting courses.

The acquisition of new machinery is oftentimes accompanied by employee training regarding correct operating procedures. The normal rule is that training costs are expensed. The logic is that the training attaches to the employee not the machine, and the employee is not owned by the company. On rare occasion, justification for capitalization of very specialized training costs (where the training is company specific and benefits many periods) is made, but this is the exception rather than the rule.

LAND When acquiring land, certain costs are ordinary and necessary and should be assigned to Land. These costs include the cost of the land, title fees, legal fees, survey costs, and zoning fees. Also included are site preparation costs like grading and draining, or the cost to raze an old structure. All of these costs may be considered ordinary and necessary to get the land ready for its intended use. Some costs are **land improvements**. This asset category includes the cost of parking lots, landscaping, irrigation systems, and similar expenditures. Why separate land and land improvement costs? The answer to this question will become clear when depreciation is considered. Land is considered to have an indefinite life and is not depreciated. Alternatively, parking lots, irrigation systems, and so forth do wear out and must be depreciated.

LUMP-SUM ACQUISITION A company may buy an existing facility consisting of land, buildings, and equipment. The negotiated price is usually a "turnkey" deal for all the components. While the **lump-sum purchase** price for the package of assets is readily determinable, assigning costs to the individual components can become problematic. Yet, for accounting purposes, it is necessary to allocate the total purchase price to the individual assets acquired. This may require a proportional allocation of the purchase price to the individual components.

To illustrate, assume Dibitanzl acquired a manufacturing facility from Malloy for $2,000,000. Assume that the facility consisted of land, building, and equipment. If Dibitanzl had acquired the land separately, its estimated value would be $500,000. The estimated value of the building is $750,000. Finally, the equipment would cost $1,250,000 if purchased independent of the "package." The sum of the values of the components comes to $2,500,000 ($500,000 + $750,000 + $1,250,000). Yet, the actual purchase price was only 80% of this amount ($2,500,000 X 80% = $2,000,000). The accounting task is to allocate the actual cost of $2,000,000 to the three separate pieces, as shown by the following:

Purchase Price Allocation			
	Estimated Values	vs.	Cost Assignment
Land	$ 500,000	X 80% =	$ 400,000
Building	750,000	X 80% =	600,000
Equipment	1,250,000	X 80% =	1,000,000
Total	$2,500,000		$2,000,000

The preceding allocation process proportionately assigns cost based on value, as shown by this illustration:

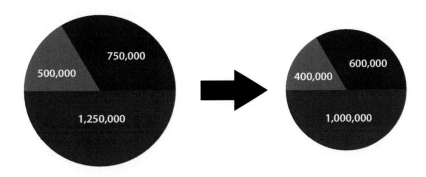

The above calculations form the basis for the following entry:

05-12-X7	Land		400,000	
	Building		600,000	
	Equipment		1,000,000	
	Cash			2,000,000
	Purchased land, building, and equipment			

It is important to note that the preceding allocation approach would not be used if the asset package constituted a "business." Those procedures were briefly addressed in the previous chapter.

JUDGMENT

Accounting may seem to be mechanical. However, there is a need for the exercise of judgment. Professional judgment was required to estimate the value of the components for purposes of making the preceding entry. Such judgments are oftentimes an inescapable part of the accounting process. Note that different estimates of value would have caused a different proportion of the $2,000,000 to be assigned to each item.

Does the allocation really matter? It is actually very important because the amount assigned to land will not be depreciated. Amounts assigned to building and equipment will be depreciated at different rates. Thus, the future pattern of depreciation expense (and therefore income) will be altered by this initial allocation. Investors pay close attention to income, and proper judgment becomes an important element of the accounting process.

MATERIALITY

Many expenditures are for long-lived assets of relatively minor value. Examples include trash cans, telephones, and so forth. Should those expenditures be capitalized and depreciated over their useful life? Or, does the cost of record keeping exceed the benefit? Many businesses simply choose to expense small costs as incurred. The reason is **materiality**; no matter which way one accounts for the cost, it is not apt to bear on anyone's decision-making process about the company. This again highlights the degree to which professional judgment comes into play in the accounting process.

Service Life and Cost Allocation

People will casually speak of depreciation as a decline in value or "using-up" of an asset. However, in accounting jargon, the term is meant to refer to the allocation of an asset's cost to the accounting periods benefited. It is <u>not</u> an attempt to value the asset. Thus, it is often said that depreciation is a process of "allocation" not "valuation." Once an asset's cost is determined, it next becomes necessary to determine the accounting periods benefited (i.e., **service life**).

Determining the service life of an asset is an essential first step in calculating the amount of depreciation attributable to a specific period. Several factors must be considered:

Physical deterioration -- "Wear and tear" will eventually cause most assets to simply wear out and become useless. Thus, physical deterioration serves to establish an outer limit on the service life of an asset.

Obsolescence -- The shortening of service life due to technological advances that cause an asset to become out of date and less desirable.

Inadequacy -- An economic determinant of service life which is relevant when an asset is no longer fast enough or large enough to fill the competitive and productive needs of a company.

Factors such as these must be considered in determining the service life of a particular asset. In some cases, all three factors come into play. In other cases, one factor alone may control the determination of service life. Importantly, service life can be completely different from physical life. For example, computers are often replaced even though still physically functional. Recognize that some assets have an indefinite (or permanent) life. One prominent example is land. Accordingly, it is not considered to be a depreciable asset.

Depreciation Concepts

Once the cost and service life of an asset are determined, it is time to move on to the choice of depreciation method. The depreciation method is simply the pattern by which the cost is allocated to each of the periods involved in the service life. There are many methods from which to choose. Three popular methods are:

*   straight-line

*   units-of-output, and

*   double-declining balance

Why so many choices? To explain, begin by assuming that a $100 asset is to be depreciated over four years. Under the straight-line approach, depreciation expense is simply $25 per year (shown in burgundy on the top of the facing page). This may seem very logical if the asset is used uniformly over the four-year period. But, what if maintenance costs (shown in green) are also considered? As an asset ages, it is not uncommon for maintenance costs to expand. Assume the first-year maintenance is $0 and rises each year as shown. Combining the two costs together reveals an increase in total cost, even though the usage is deemed to be constant.

With accelerated depreciation (shown on the bottom of the facing page), the combined amount of depreciation and maintenance provides a level measure of total cost. This may achieve a better matching of total costs and benefits in this particular scenario. Does this mean that accelerated depreciation is better? Not necessarily. Facts can vary, and the point is to show why multiple methods exist and can be justified.

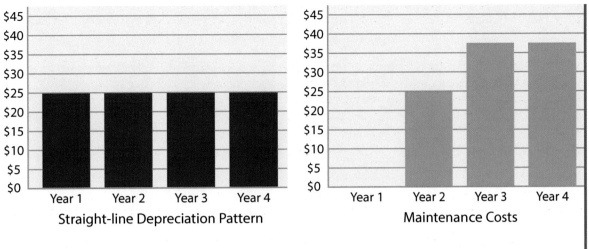

Straight-line Depreciation Pattern

Maintenance Costs

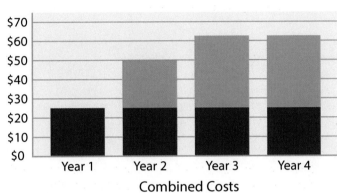

Combined Costs

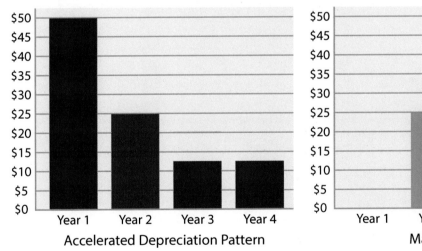

Accelerated Depreciation Pattern

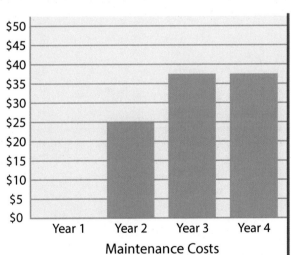

Maintenance Costs

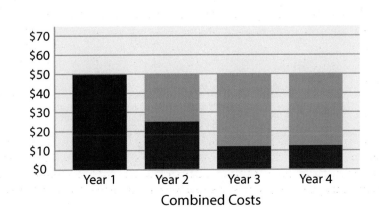

Combined Costs

SOME IMPORTANT TERMINOLOGY

In any discipline, precision is enhanced by adopting terminology that has very specific meaning. Accounting for Property, Plant, & Equipment is no exception. An exact understanding of the following terms is paramount:

- *Cost:* The dollar amount assigned to a particular asset, usually the ordinary and necessary amount expended to get an asset in place and in condition for its intended use.

- *Service life:* The useful life of an asset to an enterprise, usually relating to the anticipated period of productive use of the item.

- *Salvage value:* Also called **residual value**. This is the amount expected to be realized at the end of an asset's service life; for example, the anticipated future sales proceeds for used equipment.

- *Depreciable base:* The cost minus the salvage value. **Depreciable base** is the amount of cost that will be allocated to the service life.

- *Book value:* Also called net book value. This refers to the balance sheet amount at a point in time that reveals the cost minus the amount of accumulated depreciation (book value has other meanings when used in other contexts, so this definition is limited to its use in the context of PP&E).

Below is an illustration relating these terms to the financial statement presentation for a building:

			Book Value
Buildings	*Cost* →	$ 2,300,000	
Less: Accumulated depreciation		(1,500,000)	800,000

Service Life:	Usually found in the notes to the financial statements. ASSUME: 20 years for this example.
Salvage Value:	Used in calculations, but usually not disclosed in the financial statements. ASSUME: $300,000 for this example.
Depreciable Base:	Used in depreciation calculations, but usually not disclosed in the financial statements; cost minus salvage value. Calculated as $2,000,000 for this example:

Cost	$2,300,000
Less: Assumed salvage value	(300,000)
Depreciable base	$2,000,000

In the preceding illustration, assuming straight-line depreciation, what is the asset's age? The $2,000,0000 depreciable base ($2,300,000 - $300,000) is evenly spread over 20 years. This produces annual depreciation of $100,000. As a result, the accumulated depreciation of $1,500,000 suggests an age of 15 years (15 X $100,000).

Depreciation Methods

There are many possible depreciation methods, but straight-line and double-declining balance are the most popular. In addition, the units-of-output method is uniquely suited to certain types of assets. The following discussion covers each of these methods. Intermediate accounting courses typically introduce additional techniques that are sometimes appropriate.

Under the **straight-line** approach the annual depreciation is calculated by dividing the depreciable base by the service life. To illustrate assume that an asset has a $100,000 cost, $10,000 salvage value, and a four-year life. The following schedule reveals the annual depreciation expense, the resulting accumulated depreciation at the end of each year, and the related calculations.

THE STRAIGHT-LINE METHOD

	Depreciation Expense	Accumulated Depreciation at End of Year	Annual Expense Calculation
Year 1	$22,500	$22,500	($100,000 - $10,000)/4
Year 2	$22,500	$45,000	($100,000 - $10,000)/4
Year 3	$22,500	$67,500	($100,000 - $10,000)/4
Year 4	$22,500	$90,000	($100,000 - $10,000)/4

For each of the above years, the journal entry to record depreciation is as follows:

12-31-XX	Depreciation Expense		22,500	
	Accumulated Depreciation			22,500
	To record annual depreciation expense			

The applicable depreciation expense would be included in each year's income statement (except in a manufacturing environment where some depreciation may be assigned to the manufactured inventory, as explained in managerial accounting courses.) The appropriate balance sheet presentation would appear as follows (end of year 3 in this case):

Equipment	$100,000	
Less: Accumulated depreciation on equipment	(67,500)	32,500

Assets may be acquired at other than the beginning of an accounting period. Some companies simply assume that these assets are acquired at the beginning or end of the period. Other companies will calculate depreciation for partial periods. With the straight-line method the partial-period depreciation is simply a fraction of the annual amount. For example, an asset acquired on the first day of April would be used for only nine months during the first calendar year. Therefore, Year 1 depreciation would be 9/12 of the annual amount. Following is the depreciation table for the asset, this time assuming an April 1st acquisition date:

FRACTIONAL PERIOD DEPRECIATION (SL)

	Depreciation Expense	Accumulated Depreciation at End of Year	Annual Expense Calculation
Year 1	$16,875	$16,875	(($100,000 - $10,000)/4) X 9/12
Year 2	$22,500	$39,375	($100,000 - $10,000)/4
Year 3	$22,500	$61,875	($100,000 - $10,000)/4
Year 4	$22,500	$84,375	($100,000 - $10,000)/4
Year 5	$ 5,625	Not applicable - assumed disposed on March 31	(($100,000 - $10,000)/4) X 3/12

SPREADSHEET SOFTWARE (SL) Computer-based spreadsheets usually include built-in depreciation functions. Below is a screen shot showing the straight-line method. Data are entered in the query form, and the routine returns the formula and annual depreciation value to the selected cell of the worksheet.

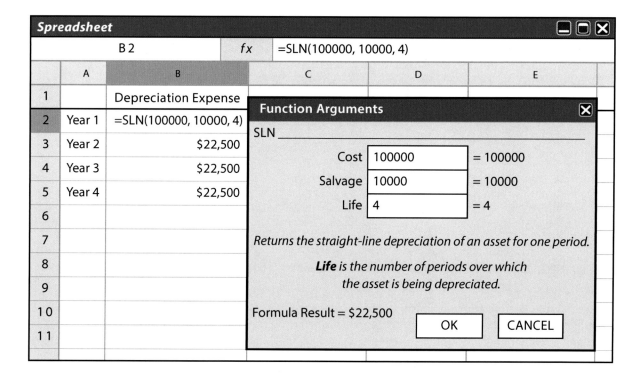

THE UNITS-OF-OUTPUT METHOD The **units-of-output** method involves calculations that are quite similar to the straight-line method, but it allocates the depreciable base over the units of output rather than years of use. It is logical to use this approach in those situations where the life is best measured by identifiable units of machine "consumption." For example, perhaps the engine of a corporate jet has an estimated life of 50,000 hours. Or, a printing machine may produce an expected 4,000,000 copies. In cases like these, the accountant may opt for the units-of-output method.

To illustrate, assume Dat Nguyen Painting Corporation purchased an air filtration system that has a life of 8,000 hours. The filter cost $100,000 and has a $10,000 salvage value. Nguyen anticipates that the filter will be used 1,000 hours during the first year, 3,000 hours during the second, 2,000 during the third, and 2,000 during the fourth. Accordingly, the anticipated depreciation schedule would appear as follows (if actual usage varies, the schedule would be adjusted for the changing estimates using principles that are discussed later in this chapter):

	Depreciation Expense	Accumulated Depreciation at End of Year	Annual Expense Calculation
Year 1	$11,250	$11,250	(1,000 hours/8,000 hours) X ($100,000 - $10,000)
Year 2	$33,750	$45,000	(3,000 hours/8,000 hours) X ($100,000 - $10,000)
Year 3	$22,500	$67,500	(2,000 hours/8,000 hours) X ($100,000 - $10,000)
Year 4	$22,500	$90,000	(2,000 hours/8,000 hours) X ($100,000 - $10,000)

The form of journal entry and balance sheet account presentation are just like the straight-line illustration, but with the revised amounts from this table.

As one of several **accelerated depreciation** methods, **double-declining balance** (DDB) results in relatively large amounts of depreciation in early years of asset life and smaller amounts in later years. This method can be justified if the quality of service produced by an asset declines over time, or if repair and maintenance costs will rise over time to offset the declining depreciation amount.

THE DOUBLE-DECLINING BALANCE METHOD

With this method, 200% of the straight-line rate is multiplied times the remaining book value of an asset (as of the beginning of a particular year) to determine depreciation for a particular year. As time passes, book value and annual depreciation decrease. To illustrate, again utilize the example of the $100,000 asset, with a four-year life, and $10,000 salvage value. Depreciation for each of the four years would appear as follows:

	Depreciation Expense	Accumulated Depreciation at End of Year	Annual Expense Calculation
Year 1	$50,000	$50,000	$100,000 X 50%
Year 2	$25,000	$75,000	($100,000 - $50,000) X 50%
Year 3	$12,500	$87,500	($100,000 - $75,000) X 50%
Year 4	$ 2,500	$90,000	see following discussion

The amounts in the above table deserve additional commentary. Year 1 expense equals the cost times twice the straight-line rate (four-year life = 25% straight-line rate; 25% X 2 = 50% rate). Year 2 is the 50% rate applied to the beginning of year book value. Year 3 is calculated in a similar fashion.

Note that salvage value was ignored in the preliminary years' calculations. For Year 4, however, the calculated amount (($100,000 - $87,500) X 50% = $6,250) would cause the lifetime depreciation to exceed the $90,000 depreciable base. Thus, in Year 4, only $2,500 is taken as expense. This gives rise to an important general rule for DDB: *salvage value is initially ignored, but once accumulated depreciation reaches the amount of the depreciable base, then depreciation ceases.* In the example, only $2,500 was needed in Year 4 to bring the aggregate depreciation up to the $90,000 level.

An asset may have no salvage value. The mathematics of DDB will never fully depreciate such assets (since one is only depreciating a percentage of the remaining balance, the remaining balance would never go to zero). In these cases, accountants typically change to the straight-line method near the end of an asset's useful life to "finish off" the depreciation of the asset's cost.

SPREADSHEET SOFTWARE (DDB) DDB is also calculable from spreadsheet depreciation functions. Below is a routine that returns the $12,500 annual depreciation value for Year 3.

	A	B	C	D	E
1		Depreciation Expense			
2	Year 1	$50,000			
3	Year 2	$25,000			
4	Year 3	=DDB(100000, 10000, 4, 3)			
5	Year 4	$2,500			

B 2   *fx*   =DDB(100000, 10000, 4, 3)

Function Arguments

DDB

Cost	100000	= 100000
Salvage	10000	= 10000
Life	4	= 4
Period	3	= 3

Returns the depreciation of an asset for a specified period using the double-declining balance method.

Formula Result = $12,500

OK   CANCEL

FRACTIONAL PERIOD DEPRECIATION (DDB) Under DDB, fractional years involve a very simple adaptation. The first partial year will be a fraction of the annual amount, and all subsequent years will be the normal calculation (twice the straight-line rate times the beginning of year book value). If the example asset was purchased on April 1st of Year 1, the following calculations result:

	Depreciation Expense	Accumulated Depreciation at End of Year	Annual Expense Calculation
Year 1	$37,500	$37,500	$100,000 X 50% X 9/12
Year 2	$31,250	$68,750	($100,000 - $37,500) X 50%
Year 3	$15,625	$84,375	($100,000 - $68,750) X 50%
Year 4	$ 5,625	$90,000	($100,000 - $84,375) X 50% Limited to depreciable base
Year 5	$ 0	Not applicable - assumed disposed on March 31	$0

ALTERNATIVES TO DDB 150% and 125% **declining balance methods** are quite similar to DDB, but the rate is 150% or 125% of the straight-line rate (instead of 200% as with DDB).

Obviously, the initial assumption about useful life and residual value is only an estimate. Time and new information may suggest that the initial assumptions need to be revised, especially if the initial estimates prove to be materially off course. It is well accepted that **changes in estimates** do not require restating the prior period financial statements; after all, an estimate is just that, and the financial statements of prior periods were presumably based on the best information available at the time. Therefore, such revisions are made prospectively (over the future) so that the remaining depreciable base is spread over the remaining life.

To illustrate, reconsider the straight-line method. Assume that two years have passed for the $100,000 asset that was initially believed to have a four-year life and $10,000 salvage value. As of the beginning of Year 3, new information suggests that the asset will have a total life of seven years (three more than originally thought), and a $5,000 salvage value. As a result, the revised remaining depreciable base (as of the beginning of Year 3) will be spread over the remaining five years, as follows:

	Depreciation Expense	Accumulated Depreciation at End of Year	Annual Expense Calculation
Year 1	$22,500	$22,500	($100,000 - $10,000)/4
Year 2	$22,500	$45,000	($100,000 - $10,000)/4
Year 3	$10,000	$55,000	($100,000 - $45,000 - $5,000)/5
Year 4	$10,000	$65,000	($100,000 - $45,000 - $5,000)/5
Year 5	$10,000	$75,000	($100,000 - $45,000 - $5,000)/5
Year 6	$10,000	$85,000	($100,000 - $45,000 - $5,000)/5
Year 7	$10,000	$95,000	($100,000 - $45,000 - $5,000)/5

Depreciation for Years 3 through 7 is based on spreading the "revised" depreciable base over the last five years of remaining life. The "revised" depreciable base is $50,000. It is computed as the original cost, minus the previous depreciation ($45,000), and minus the revised salvage value ($5,000).

International accounting and reporting standards include provisions that permit companies to revalue items of PP&E to fair value. When applied, all assets in the same class must be revalued annually. Such balance sheet adjustments are offset with a corresponding change in the entity's capital accounts. These revaluations pose additional complications because they result in continuous alterations of the amount of depreciation.

Tax Laws

It is important to note that tax methods and financial accounting methods are not always the same. This is certainly true when it comes to the subject of depreciation. For example, when the economy "slows down" governments will often try to stimulate economic investment activity by providing special incentives that are realized through rapid depreciation for tax purposes (even immediate write-off in some cases). The depreciation causes a decrease in taxable income and a company's tax obligation. This feature can provide significant incentives for capital investment.

The history of tax laws is marked by many changes to the depreciation rates and methods. As a result, it is difficult to generalize; but, one depreciation technique is known as the **Modified Accelerated Cost Recovery System** (MACRS, pronounced "makers"). MACRS provides for a general depreciation system and an alternative system. Within those systems are general provisions relating to the 200% declining balance, 150% declining balance, and straight-line techniques.

Further, tax systems will typically stipulate the useful life of an asset rather than leave it to the imagination of the taxpayer. Tax codes tend to be very complete in identifying assets and their lives. Tax codes tend to be "favorable" to taxpayers, and commonly result in depreciation occurring at a faster rate than under generally accepted accounting principles.

Is it bothersome that a company would use one accounting method for financial reporting and another for tax? Consider that accounting rules are about measuring economic activity of a business and require a proper scheme for assigning revenues and costs to time periods. Meanwhile, tax codes must be followed and are often changed to meet the revenue or social objectives of the government. As a result, temporary (and sometimes not so temporary) differences will arise between accounting and tax measurements. Records of these differences must be maintained, making the accounting task all the more challenging for a complex business organization.

Equipment Leases

Many businesses acquire needed assets via a **lease** arrangement. With a lease arrangement, the **lessee** pays money to the **lessor** for the right to use an asset for a stated period of time. In a strict legal context, the lessor remains the owner of the property. However, the accounting for such transactions looks through the legal form, and is instead based upon the economic substance of the agreement.

For leases generally exceeding one year the applicable accounting rules dictate that the lessee account for a leased asset as though it has been purchased. The lessee records the leased right as an item of property, plant, and equipment, which is then depreciated over its useful life to the lessee. The lessee must also record a liability reflecting the obligation to make continuing payments under the lease agreement, similar to the accounting for a note payable. Such transactions are termed **financing leases**. Note that the basic accounting outcome is as though the lease agreement represents the purchase of an asset, with a corresponding obligation to pay it off over time (the same basic approach as if the asset were purchased on credit). Short-term leases are known as **operating leases**. Rent is simply recorded as rent expense as incurred and the underlying asset is not reported on the books of the lessee.

Why all the trouble over lease accounting? Think about an industry that relies heavily on financing lease agreements, like the commercial airlines. One can see the importance of reporting the aircraft and the fixed commitment to pay for them. To exclude them from the financial statements would fail to represent the true nature of the business operation.

Chapter 10 Quiz

Q10-1. Incidental expenditures incurred when purchasing equipment (like freight, installation, and brokerage fees) that are ordinary and necessary for the acquisition should be:

expensed as incurred or included in an asset's cost

Q10-2. Depreciation is a process of:

valuation or allocation

Q10-3. Under the units-of-output depreciation method, the depreciable base is divided by the service life:

stated in years or stated in output

Q10-4. The process to adjust depreciation for a change in service life entails spreading the remaining depreciable base over the remaining useful life.

true or false

Q10-5. Under which type of lease does the lessee obtain the rights to use leased property for a limited period of time and treat amounts paid as expense?

operating lease or financing lease

Q10-6. A _____ purchase occurs when a package of assets are acquired for a single purchase price amount.

Q10-7. In determining an asset's useful life, consideration must be given to three factors: _____, _____, and _____.

Q10-8. Cost minus residual value is known as _____ , whereas cost minus accumulated depreciation is known as _____.

Q10-9. An accelerated depreciation method which involves applying a fixed depreciation rate to the remaining book value of an asset is known as the _____ method.

Q10-10. Tax laws permit asset cost to be charged against specific years via use of the _____.

Q10-11. A lease is an arrangement that allows one party, the _____, to use the assets of another party, the _____, for a stated period of time.

Multiple Choice

Q10-12. Lancer Corporation purchased a parcel of land as a factory site for $150,000. Construction began immediately on a new building. Costs incurred are as follows:

Architect's fees	$ 25,000
Legal fees for land purchase contract	2,000
Construction costs	250,000

Lancer should record the cost of the new land and building, respectively, at:

a. $150,000 and $275,000

c. $150,000 and $250,000

b. $152,000 and $275,000

d. $152,000 and $250,000

Q10-13. The appropriate journal entry to record machinery depreciation of $1,000 is:

a. Depreciation Expense   1,000
      Accumulated Depreciation   1,000

c. Accumulated Depreciation 1,000
      Depreciation Expense   1,000

b. Depreciation Expense   1,000
      Machine   1,000

d. Accumulated Depreciation 1,000
      Machine   1,000

Q10-14. Realistic Company purchased a new truck on January 1, 20X1. The truck cost $20,000, has a four-year life, and a $4,000 residual value. The company has a December 31 year-end. If Realistic Company depreciates the truck by the straight-line method, how much should Realistic report as the book value of the truck at the end of 20X3?

a. $1,600

c. $8,000

b. $4,000

d. $16,000

Q10-15. A graph is set up with "depreciation expense" on the vertical axis and "time" on the horizontal axis. Assuming linear relationships, how would the lines for straight-line and double-declining-balance depreciation expense, respectively, be drawn on this graph?

a. Vertically and sloping down to the right.

c. Horizontally and sloping down to the right.

b. Vertically and sloping up to the right.

d. Horizontally and sloping up to the right.

Q10-16. Assume that the modified accelerated cost recovery system is used to account for a depreciable asset for tax purposes. In general, which of the following observations is correct?

a. Depreciation amounts will be the same for financial reporting purposes.

c. In the early years of an asset's life, depreciation will be less for tax than for financial reporting purposes.

b. In the early years of an asset's life, depreciation will be greater for tax than for financial reporting purposes.

d. The tax life will exceed the financial reporting life.

Chapter 10 Problems

Basic Problems

Balance sheet presentation of property, plant, and equipment

B-10.01

The following selected account balances were taken from the general ledger of Vance Corporation as of December 31, 20X7. Examine this information and prepare the property, plant, and equipment section of the company's balance sheet. All accounts listed carry a normal balance.

Land	$ 500,000
Buildings	1,650,000
Equipment	2,860,000
Accumulated depreciation: Buildings	472,000
Accumulated depreciation: Equipment	1,333,400
Depreciation expense: Buildings	125,000
Depreciation expense: Equipment	278,111

Determining asset acquisition cost and recording

B-10.02

Sonjay Motors recently purchased a new sign to be erected in front of its dealership. The sign company that produced the sign had a standard price for this item at $25,000, but Sonjay was able to negotiate a 20% discount from standard. In addition, the sign company paid $1,200 of freight costs to deliver the sign to Sonjay. Sonjay hired an electrician for $1,300 to wire the new sign's lighting. In addition, Sonjay rented a crane for $800 and paid an installation crew $1,600 to erect the sign.

The city required Sonjay to pay a one-time sign inspection fee of $500. Furthermore, Sonjay had to obtain an annual permit at a cost of $50 for the first year. During installation, the crew accidentally damaged an adjoining neighbor's landscaping, and Sonjay paid $750 to clean and repair those problems.

Determine the correct cost allocation to the sign, and prepare a journal entry to reflect the total expenditures related to this acquisition.

Identification of capital expenditures

B-10.03

Evaluate the following costs to decide if each is a "capital expenditure," or not. If a capital expenditure, decide in which account the cost should be recorded: Land, Land Improvement, Building, or Equipment. The first item is done as an example.

	Capital		Category			
	Yes	No	Land	Land Improvement	Building	Equipment
Delivery cost of new furniture	✓					✓
Wages paid to guard at office building						
Fees for title insurance on land purchase						
Cost of periodic repainting of parking lot						
Cost of building new sidewalks						
Interest costs on loan to buy equipment						
Computer training class on general commercial software package						
Interest cost on loan during construction period for new building						
Architects fees for new building						
Installation and setup costs on new machinery						
Repair of damage to device broken during initial installation						
Safety violation fines at construction site						
Tap fees for connecting new building to city water system						

B-10.04   *Lump sum purchase price allocation*

CityBank recently held an auction to dispose of various assets it had obtained through foreclosures and other loan settlements. Representatives of Advantage Metals attended the auction to bid on an abandoned manufacturing plant that CityBank included in the sale. The auction website listed the manufacturing plant to include all land, buildings, and equipment. The website indicated that an independent appraisal had been conducted and that land was separately valued at $1,000,000, the building at $2,000,000, and the equipment at $4,000,000. This information is believed to be reasonably accurate and fair.

Advantage Metals wanted the site for a recycling business it planned to start at the location. All of the equipment would be used in this new operation. The minimum bid price was set at $4,900,000. As it turned out, the auction was poorly attended. Advantage was the only bidder on this property and was fortunate to acquire the property at the opening bid minimum.

Determine the correct cost allocation to the land, buildings, and equipment, and prepare a journal entry to reflect this acquisition.

Lease classification   *B-10.05*

Evaluate the following features or comments, and decide if the description would pertain to a financing lease or an operating lease.

	Operating Lease	*Financing Lease*
The lessee reports the leased asset on its balance sheet		✓
Payments are reported fully as rent expense		
Ownership of the property passes to the lessee by the end of the lease term		
The lease term exceeds one year		
Interest expense is measured and reported by the lessee		
Depreciation of the leased asset is not reported by the lessee		
At the inception of the lease, the lessee records both an asset and liability		
The lessee reports a liability for the present value of all future payments anticipated under the lease agreement		
The lessor continues to report the tangible asset covered by the lease on its balance sheet		

On January 1, 20X3, Perkins Printing Corporation purchased a digital press for $1,450,000. It cost an additional $50,000 to deliver, install, and calibrate the press. This machine has a service life of 5 years, at which time it is expected that the device will be scrapped for a $100,000 salvage value.

Perkins uses the straight-line depreciation method.

(a) Prepare a schedule showing annual depreciation expense, accumulated depreciation, and related calculations for each year.

(b) Show how the asset and related accumulated depreciation would appear on a balance sheet at December 31, 20X5.

(c) Prepare journal entries to record the asset's acquisition, annual depreciation for each year, and the asset's eventual sale for $100,000.

On January 1, 20X6, Outback Air purchased a new engine for one of its airplanes used to transport adventurers to remote regions of western Australia. The engine cost $750,000 and has a service life of 10,000 flight hours. Regulations require careful records of usage, and the engines must be replaced or rebuilt at the end of the 10,000 hour service period. Outback simply chooses to sell its used engines and acquire new ones. Used engines are expected to be resold for 1/3 of their original cost.

Outback uses the units-of-output depreciation method.

(a) Assuming that the engine was used as follows, prepare a schedule showing annual depreciation expense, accumulated depreciation, and related calculations for each year.

> 20X6 1,500 hours
>
> 20X7 4,000 hours
>
> 20X8 3,000 hours
>
> 20X9 1,500 hours

(b) Show how the asset and related accumulated depreciation would appear on a balance sheet at December 31, 20X7.

(c) Prepare journal entries to record the asset's acquisition, annual depreciation for each year, and the asset's eventual sale for $250,000.

On January 1, 20X1, Pagoda Pond Construction acquired a small excavator for $85,000. This device had a 4-year service life to Pagoda, at which time it is expected that the equipment will be sold for a $10,000 salvage value.

Pagoda uses the double-declining balance depreciation method.

(a) Prepare a schedule showing annual depreciation expense, accumulated depreciation, and related calculations for each year.

(b) Show how the asset and related accumulated depreciation would appear on a balance sheet at December 31, 20X3.

(c) Prepare journal entries to record the asset's acquisition, annual depreciation for each year, and the asset's eventual sale for $10,000.

Change in estimate for depreciation B-10.09

On January 1, 20X1, Floral Features purchased a delivery truck for $65,000. At the time of purchase, Floral Features anticipated that it would use the truck for 4 years, even though its physical life is 8 years. At the end of the 4-year period, Floral believes it will be able to sell the truck for $35,000. Floral Features uses the straight-line depreciation method.

Gasoline prices increased significantly, and consumers began to buy more efficient vehicles. By early 20X3, it became apparent that the market for used delivery trucks like the one belonging to Floral Features was virtually nonexistent. Accordingly, Floral Features changed its plans and decided it would use the truck for its full 8-year life. At the end of the revised useful life, it is expected that the truck will be worth $2,000 for scrap value.

Prepare a schedule showing annual depreciation expense, accumulated depreciation, and related calculations for each year of the eight year holding period.

Involved Problems

Terminology and concepts I-10.01

Examine the following list of items, and match each to the best corresponding description from the choices list. Each choice should be used only once.

(1) Cost minus salvage value

(2) Cost minus accumulated depreciation

(3) Depreciation is a process of this, rather than valuation

(4) Costs that are added to an asset account

(5) Costs of items added to a land-related account, like paving and landscaping

(6) A bundled purchase of assets

(7) Lessee does not report the asset

(8) Like straight-line, but the denominator is not time

(9) A tax-based allocation of cost that is not GAAP

(10)   Justification for expensing small items

(11)   Included with land cost

(12)   Expensed immediately

(13)   Results in less depreciation each year than the year before

CHOICES:

Materiality	Depreciable base
Book value	Survey and title fees
MACRS	Abnormal damage during installation
Land improvements	Operating lease
Capital expenditures	Allocation
Accelerated depreciation	Units-of-output method
Lump sum purchase	

I-10.02   *Evaluation of property, plant, and equipment*

The accounting firm of Haynes and Haynes was asked by one of its clients to help them properly account for various transactions related to plant and equipment. The client prepared the following list of transactions that occurred during 20X7. Because the client was not sure what to do with these activities, they debited an account called "Suspense" and credited "Cash" for each expenditure. The only exception relates to item #7, for which no entry has been recorded.

You should examine the following activities, and prepare a spreadsheet showing how the costs should be allocated to specific Land, Land Improvement, Building, Equipment, or expense accounts (you may assume that the spreadsheet data are for the year ending December 31, 20X7, and disregard any depreciation implications). The blank worksheet template will expedite your completion of this problem. After you complete the allocation, prepare a suggested correcting journal entry (i.e., debit the various asset/expenses and credit Suspense).

Item 1   Paid $2,500 for 20X7 insurance coverage on equipment

Item 2   Paid $7,500 for trees and shrubs

Item 3   Paid $500 attorney's fees for document preparation related to land purchase

Item 4   Paid $150,000 for land and building. The land was separately valued at $40,000, and the building at $120,000.

Item 5   Paid $1,000 freight costs on purchase of new furniture

Item 6   Paid $300 for staplers, trash cans, and desktop mats

Item 7   Ordered new $50,000 truck, to be delivered and paid for in 20X8

Item 8   Paid $10,000 of interest costs on loan on active building construction project

Item 9   Paid $25,000 to expand parking lot paving

Item 10   Paid $5,000 of interest on loan related to completed in-use office building

---

Depreciation calculations with alternative methods   *I-10.03*

On January 1, 20X2, The GenKota Winery purchased a new bottling system. The system has an expected life of 5 years. The system cost $325,000. Shipping, installation, and set up was an additional $35,000. At the end of the useful life, Julie Hayes, chief accountant for GenKota, expects to dispose of the bottling system for $96,000. She further anticipates total output of 660,000 bottles over the useful life.

(a)   Assuming use of the straight-line depreciation method, prepare a schedule showing annual depreciation expense, accumulated depreciation, and related calculations for each year.

(b)   Assuming use of the units-of-output depreciation method, prepare a schedule showing annual depreciation expense, accumulated depreciation, and related calculations for each year. Actual output, in bottles, was 100,000 (20X2), 130,000 (20X3), 150,000 (20X4), 160,000 (20X5), and 120,000 (20X6).

(c)   Assuming use of the double-declining balance depreciation method, prepare a schedule showing annual depreciation expense, accumulated depreciation, and related calculations for each year.

(d)   Assuming use of the straight-line method, prepare revised depreciation calculations if the useful life estimate was revised at the beginning of 20X4, to anticipate a remaining useful life of 4 additional years (in other words, a total life of 6 years). The revised useful life was accompanied by a change in estimated salvage value to $54,400.

Fractional year depreciation calculations   *I-10.04*

Grant Price is conducting an audit of the property, plant, and equipment records of Wellron Corporation. Grant selected two specific assets for closer inspection. Grant has examined documentation related to each asset's original purchase and compared it to the recorded cost, physically inspected the item to determine that it is still in the possession of the company, and conducted other similar assurance procedures.

The final step in the audit of these accounts is to test the calculations of depreciation expense and accumulated depreciation. Grant has asked you to perform this final procedure for 20X8. Below is a schedule of the two assets, with the depreciation values determined by Wellron. The building was depreciated by the straight-line method, and the truck by the double-declining balance method. Determine if the indicated depreciation values are correct.

Item	Cost	Purchase Date	Service Life	Salvage Value	Depreciation Expense for 20X8	Accumulated Depreciation at 12/31/X8
Building	$1,200,000	July 1, 20X1	25 years	$400,000	$32,000	$256,000
Truck	$ 80,000	Oct. 1, 20X6	8 years	$ 5,000	$13,184	$ 35,449

SPREADSHEET TOOL:

Depreciation functions

Dr. Matt Brown purchased a new digital X-ray machine for his dental practice. The machine cost $275,000 and has a $10,000 salvage value after 7 years.

As shown in the text, spreadsheet software packages, like Microsoft Excel, include built-in functions to calculate depreciation. Use these routines to calculate depreciation for Dr. Brown's X-ray machine for the third year of use. Try this problem with the straight-line (SLN) and double-declining balance (DDB) techniques. The functions are usually accessed via a toolbar pick list or from the *Formulas/Function* operation. Once you know the correct way to structure a function, a quick shortcut is to simply key in the formula (e.g., *SLN(100,10,4)* is the straight-line formula for a $100 asset having a $10 salvage value and 4-year life).

You should print out two copies of your answer; one with the "values" and the other showing the "formulas." Oftentimes, you will want to view all the formulas used in a worksheet. To toggle between showing formulas and values, simply press "CTRL + `" (grave accent).

Form a five-person team. Each team member should identify a public company and obtain its financial reports (available at www.sec.gov, or from the company website). If looking on the SEC website, look under the section for "search for company filings" and select the company's Form 10-K (annual report). Each member should find the company disclosures relative to the accounting for property, plant, and equipment, such as the following example:

Property, plant, and equipment — For financial reporting purposes, depreciation is computed using the straight-line method over the estimated useful lives of the related assets as follows:

Buildings and structures	10-25 years
Machinery and equipment	3-15 years
Furniture and fixtures	3-15 years
Automotive equipment	3 years

Maintenance and repairs are charged to expense as incurred; renewals and betterments that significantly extend the useful life of the asset are capitalized.

Each team member should compile information about company name, depreciation method in use, and estimated useful lives for the selected company. Then, the team should compile a master list for all five companies. Discuss the similarities and differences. How can such information, in conjunction with information about cost and accumulated depreciation balances, be used to judge the relative age of a company's fixed assets? Of what value is such an assessment? In class, consider merging each team's data into a class-wide study to determine the frequency of use of straight-line, double-declining balance, and other methods.

Chapter 11:
Advanced PP&E Issues/Natural Resources/Intangibles

Goals:

The accounting for costs incurred subsequent to asset acquisition.
Appropriate methods to measure and record the disposal of PP&E.
Accounting for asset exchanges.
Rules for recording asset impairments.
Natural resource accounting and depletion concepts.
Intangible asset accounting and amortization concepts.

principlesofaccounting.com

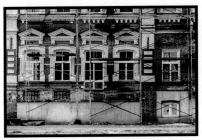

Most items of PP&E require substantial ongoing costs to keep them in good order. The accounting rules for such costs treat them as "capital expenditures" if future economic benefits result from the expenditure. Future economic benefits occur if the service life of an asset is prolonged, the quantity of services expected from an asset is increased, or the quality of services expected from an asset is improved. Expenditures not meeting at least one of these criteria should be accounted for as a **revenue expenditure** and be expensed as incurred. Judgment is required in applying these rules. A literal reading might lead one to believe that routine maintenance would be capitalized. After all, fueling a car does extend its service life. But, that interpretation would miss the intent of the rule. It is implied that routine costs to maintain normal operating condition be expensed as incurred. The capitalization criteria are instead focused on nonrecurring costs.

RESTORE AND IMPROVE

A truck may have an engine that is in need of **replacement**. The replacement of the engine represents a "restoration" of some of the original condition (akin to "undepreciating"). Restoration and improvement type costs are considered to meet the conditions for capitalization because of the enhancement to service life/quality. This entry records the restoration:

05-15-X5	Accumulated Depreciation		16,000	
	Cash			16,000
	Paid $16,000 to replace engine on delivery truck			

Notice that the preceding debit is to Accumulated Depreciation. The effect is to increase the net book value of the asset by reducing its accumulated depreciation on the balance sheet. This approach is perfectly fine for "restoration" expenditures. However, if one is "improving" the asset beyond its original condition (sometimes termed a **betterment**), the costs would instead be capitalized by debiting the asset account directly.

Disposal of PP&E

Over time the productive assets in use by a company may no longer be needed and a decision is made to dispose of those assets. Disposal may occur by abandonment, sale, or exchange. In any case, it is necessary to update depreciation calculations through the date of disposal. Then, and only then, would the asset disposal be recorded.

If the asset is being scrapped (abandoned), the journal entry entails the elimination of the cost of the asset from the books, removal of the related accumulated depreciation, and potentially recording a loss to balance. This loss reflects the net book value that was not previously depreciated:

06-30-X3	Accumulated Depreciation	75,000	
	Loss	25,000	
	Equipment		100,000
	Abandoned equipment costing $100,000. The equipment was 75% depreciated on the date of disposal.		

On the other hand, an asset may be disposed of by sale, in which case the journal entry would need to be modified to include the proceeds of the sale. Assume the above asset was sold for $10,000. The entry would be as follows:

06-30-X3	Accumulated Depreciation	75,000	
	Loss	15,000	
	Cash	10,000	
	Equipment		100,000
	Sold equipment costing $100,000 for $10,000. The equipment was 75% depreciated on the date of sale.		

While the journal entry alone might be sufficient to demonstrate the loss calculation, one might also consider that an asset with a $25,000 net book value is being sold for $10,000. This gives rise to the loss of $15,000.

Conversely, what if this asset were sold for $30,000? In that case, the asset having a $25,000 net book value is converted to $30,000 cash. This triggers a $5,000 gain. Simply stated a $30,000 asset replaces an asset that was reported at $25,000. Following is the entry for that scenario:

06-30-X3	Accumulated Depreciation	75,000	
	Cash	30,000	
	Gain		5,000
	Equipment		100,000
	Sold equipment costing $100,000 for $30,000. The equipment was 75% depreciated on the date of sale.		

Accounting for Asset Exchanges

Sometimes a new car purchase is accompanied by a "trade in" of an old car. This would be a classic **exchange transaction**. In business, equipment is often exchanged (e.g., an old copy machine for a new one). Sometimes land is exchanged. Exchanges can be motivated by tax rules because neither company may be required to recognize a taxable event on the exchange. The result could be quite different if the asset was sold for cash. Whatever the motivation behind the transaction, the accountant is pressed to measure and report the event.

COMMERCIAL SUBSTANCE

Exchanges that have **commercial substance** (future cash flows are expected to change) should be accounted for at fair value. Various scenarios are illustrated in the following examples. Recognize that some exchanges may lack commercial substance. For example, two companies may swap inventory and neither expects a significant change in cash flows because of the trade. Gains are not recorded on exchanges lacking commercial substance and are typically illustrated in more advanced courses.

FAIR VALUE APPROACH

The fair value approach for exchanges having commercial substance will ordinarily result in recognition of a gain or loss because the fair value will typically differ from the recorded book value of a swapped asset. There is deemed to be a culmination of the earnings process when assets are exchanged. In other words, one productive component is liquidated and another is put in its place. The following examples illustrate exchange transactions for scenarios involving both losses and gains.

Example A: Loss Implied

Company A gives an old truck ($1,000,000 cost, $750,000 accumulated depreciation) for a boat. The fair value of the old truck is $150,000 (which is also deemed to be the fair value of the boat).

The boat should be recorded at fair value. Because this amount is less than the net book value of the old truck, a loss is recorded for the difference:

06-30-X3	Accumulated Depreciation (truck)	750,000	
	Loss	100,000	
	Equipment (boat)	150,000	
	Equipment (truck)		1,000,000
	To remove all accounts related to the old truck, set up the new boat at its fair value, and record the balancing loss		

Example B: Gain Implied

Company A gives an old truck ($1,000,000 cost, $750,000 accumulated depreciation) for a boat. The fair value of the old truck is $350,000 (which is also deemed to be the fair value of the boat).

The boat should be recorded at fair value. Because this amount is more than the net book value of the old truck, a gain is recorded for the difference:

06-30-X3	Accumulated Depreciation (truck)	750,000	
	Equipment (boat)	350,000	
	Gain		100,000
	Equipment (truck)		1,000,000
	To remove all accounts related to the old truck, set up the new boat at its fair value, and record the balancing gain		

BOOT

Exchange transactions are oftentimes accompanied by giving or receiving **boot**. Boot is the term used to describe additional monetary consideration that may accompany an exchange transaction. Its presence only slightly modifies the preceding accounting by adding one more account (typically Cash) to the journal entry.

Example C: Boot given

Company A gives an old truck ($1,000,000 cost, $750,000 accumulated depreciation) and $50,000 cash for a boat. The fair value of the old truck is $100,000. The fair value of the boat is $150,000.

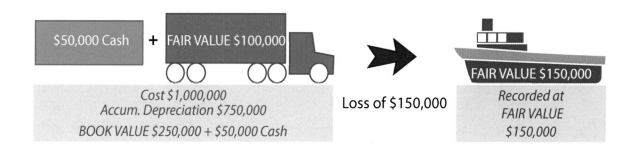

Notice that the following entry has an added credit to Cash reflecting the additional consideration. The loss is $150,000. The loss is the balancing amount, and reflects that $300,000 of consideration (cash ($50,000) and an old item of equipment ($1,000,000 - $750,000 = $250,000)) was swapped for an item worth only $150,000. Had boot been received, Cash would have instead been debited (and a smaller loss, or possibly a gain, would be recorded to balance the entry).

06-30-X3	Accumulated Depreciation (truck)	750,000	
	Loss	150,000	
	Equipment (boat)	150,000	
	Cash		50,000
	Equipment (truck)		1,000,000
	To remove all accounts related to the old truck and cash, set up the new boat at its fair value, and record the balancing loss		

Asset Impairment

When the carrying amount of a long-lived asset (or group of assets) is not recoverable from expected future cash flows, an **impairment** has occurred. The owner of the asset no longer expects to be able to generate returns of cash from the asset sufficient to recapture its recorded net book value. A loss is recognized for the amount needed to reduce the asset to its fair value (i.e., debit loss and credit the asset). The downward revised carrying value will be depreciated over its remaining estimated life.

Measurements of impairment involve subjective components and judgment. These factors should be taken into consideration: significant decrease in market value, physical condition has declined unexpectedly, the asset is no longer used as intended, legal or regulatory issues have impeded the asset, the overall business seems threatened by unsuccessful performance, and so forth. In addition, the specific methods for determining if an impairment has occurred vary globally. While the U.S. approach focuses first on cash recovery, global standards look to a more restrictive fair value test.

Natural Resources

Oil and gas reserves, mineral deposits, thermal energy sources, and standing timber are just a few examples of **natural resource** assets that a firm may own. There are many industry-specific accounting measurements attributable to such assets.

As a general rule, natural resources are initially entered in the accounting records at their direct cost plus logically related items like legal fees, surveying costs, and exploration and development costs. Once the cost basis is properly established, it must be allocated over the periods benefited through a process known as **depletion**. Think of it this way: depletion is to a natural resource as depreciation is to property, plant, and equipment.

DEPLETION The cost of a natural resource (less expected residual value) is divided by the estimated units in the resource deposit; the resulting amount is depletion per unit. If all of the resources extracted during a period are sold, then depletion expense equals depletion per unit times the number of units extracted and sold. If a portion of the extracted resources are unsold resources, then their cost (i.e., number of inventory units times depletion per unit) should be carried on the balance sheet as inventory.

Assume that a mine site is purchased for $9,000,000, and another $3,000,000 is spent on developing the site for production. Assume the site is estimated to contain 5,000,000 tons of the targeted ore. At completion of the operation, the site will be water flooded and sold as a recreational lake site for an estimated $2,000,000. The depletion rate is $2 per ton, as the following calculations show:

Initial cost	$ 9,000,000
Development cost	3,000,000
Less: Estimated residual value	(2,000,000)
Depletable base	$10,000,000
Divided by estimated tons	÷ 5,000,000
Depletion	$2 per ton

If 1,000,000 tons of ore are extracted in a particular year, the assigned cost would be $2,000,000. But where does that cost go? If 750,000 tons are sold and the other 250,000 tons are simply held in inventory of extracted material, then $1,500,000 would go to cost of goods sold and the other $500,000 would go to the balance sheet as inventory. A representative entry follows:

12-31-X8	Inventory	500,000	
	Cost of Goods Sold	1,500,000	
	Natural Resource (or accumulated depletion)		2,000,000
	To record annual depletion charge reflecting assignment of depletion cost to inventory (250,000 X $2) and cost of goods sold (750,000 X $2)		

EQUIPMENT USED TO EXTRACT NATURAL RESOURCES Property, plant, and equipment used to extract natural resources must be depreciated over its useful life. Sometimes the useful life of such PP&E is tied directly to the natural resource life, even though its actual physical life is much longer. For example, if a train track is built into a mine, the track is of no use once the mine closes (even though it could theoretically still carry a train for a much longer period). As a result, the track would be depreciated over the life of the mine. Conversely, the train that runs on the track can be re-located and used elsewhere; as such it would likely be depreciated over the life of the train rather than the life of the mine.

Intangibles

The defining characteristic of an **intangible asset** is the lack of physical existence. Nevertheless, such assets contribute to the earnings capability of a company. Examples include patents, copyrights, trademarks, brands, franchises, and similar items.

A company may develop such items via ongoing business processes. Globally, some internally developed intangibles are recognized where future benefits are clear and measurable. The U.S. is far more restrictive, and self-created intangibles seldom appear on a balance sheet.

On the other hand, intangibles may be purchased from another party. For example, one company may need to utilize technology embedded in a patent right belonging to someone else. When intangibles are purchased, the cost is recorded as an intangible asset. When a purchased intangible has an *identifiable* economic life, its cost is **amortized** over that useful life (amortization is the term to describe the allocation of the cost of an intangible, just as depreciation describes the allocation of the cost of PP&E).

Some intangibles have an *indefinite* life and those items are not amortized. Instead, they are periodically evaluated for impairment. If they are never found to be impaired, they will permanently remain on the balance sheet. The unamortized/unimpaired cost of intangible assets is positioned in a separate balance sheet section immediately following Property, Plant, and Equipment.

Assume that Mercury Pharmaceutical purchased a patent for $50,000, estimating its useful life to be five years. The appropriate entries are:

EXAMPLE

01-01-X1	Patent	50,000	
	Cash		50,000
	Paid $50,000 to purchase a patent		
12-31-XX	Amortization Expense	10,000	
	Patent		10,000
	To record annual amortization expense ($50,000/5 years)		

Unlike PP&E, notice that the preceding annual amortization entry credits the asset account directly. There is usually not a separate accumulated amortization account for intangible assets.

Patents give their owners exclusive rights to use or manufacture a particular product. The cost of obtaining a patent should be amortized over its useful life (not to exceed its legal life of 20 years). The amount included in the Patent account includes the cost of a purchased patent and/or incidental costs related to the registration and protection of a patent.

SOME SPECIFIC INTANGIBLES

Copyrights provide their owners with the exclusive right to produce or sell an artistic or published work. A copyright has a legal life equal to the life of the creator plus 70 years; the economic life is usually shorter. The economic life is the period of time over which the cost of a copyright should be amortized.

Franchises give their owners the right to manufacture or sell certain products or perform certain services on an exclusive or semi-exclusive basis. The cost of a franchise is reported as an intangible asset, and should be amortized over the estimated useful life.

Trademarks/brands/internet domains are another important class of intangible assets. Although these items have fairly short legal lives, they can be renewed over and over. As such, they have indefinite lives.

Goodwill is a unique intangible asset that arises out of a business acquisition. It reflects the excess of the fair value of an acquired entity over the net of the amount assigned to the identifiable assets acquired and liabilities assumed. Such excess may be paid because of the acquired company's outstanding management, earnings record, or other similar features. Goodwill is deemed to have an indefinite life and not normally amortized, but should be evaluated for impairment at least annually.

Goodwill accounting for companies that do not have "public" shareholders is eligible for two simplifications: (1) amounts attributable to selected intangibles (certain customer related intangibles and the value of noncompetition agreements) can be combined with goodwill, and (2) the cost of goodwill may be amortized over a ten-year period.

Chapter 11 Quiz

Goals Achievement

Q11-1. Which of the following expenditures meet at least one of the criteria for capitalization?

repairs   or   betterments

Q11-2. The difference between the book value of an asset and the proceeds received from its sale should be reported as a gain or loss.

true   or   false

Q11-3. Briefly stated, which of the following should not be recognized on exchanges that lack commercial substance?

gains   or   losses

Q11-4. An asset impairment is normally accompanied by a direct charge to:

retained earnings   or   income

Q11-5. The amortization period for intangible assets is generally considered to be the economic life of the property, not to exceed 40 years.

true   or   false

Fill in the Blanks

Q11-6. _____, also known as improvements or extraordinary repairs, generally improve or increase future service potential of an asset.

Q11-7. If a cash sale of an item of depreciable property occurs, and the journal entry to record the sale is balanced by the recording of a debit, then a _____ should be recognized.

Q11-8. For tax purposes, the exchange of similar assets will normally result in no _____ or _____.

Q11-9. _____ is the allocation of natural resource cost to the resources extracted during an accounting period.

Q11-10. Patents, copyrights, and franchises are examples of_____.

Q11-11. _____ occurs when the fair value of an acquired company as an operating entity exceeds the value of its identifiable assets and liabilities.

Q11-12. On January 1, 20X2, Lynn Corporation purchased a machine for $100,000. Lynn paid shipping expenses of $1,000 as well as installation costs of $2,400. The machine was estimated to have a useful life of ten years and an estimated salvage value of $6,000. In January 20X3, additions costing $7,200 were made to the machine. These additions significantly improved the quality of output, but did not change the life or salvage value of the machine. If Lynn records depreciation under the straight-line method, depreciation expense for 20X3 is:

a. $9,740

c. $10,540

b. $10,340

d. $11,140

Q11-13. A machine that cost $18,000, with a book value of $4,000, is sold for $3,400. Which of the following is true concerning the journal entry to record the sale?

a. Accumulated Depreciation is debited for $4,000.

c. Loss on sale of machinery is credited for $600.

b. Machinery is credited for $4,000.

d. Accumulated Depreciation is debited for $14,000.

Q11-14. Equipment costing $3,000 with accumulated depreciation of $2,125 is exchanged for another asset with a fair value of $625. The exchange has commercial substance. How much is the gain or loss on this transaction?

a. A gain of $250 should be recognized.

c. A loss of $500 should be recognized.

b. A loss of $250 should be recognized.

d. No gain or loss should be recognized.

Q11-15. Deep Gold Mining Company recognizes $4 of depletion for each ton of ore mined. This year, 300,000 tons of ore were mined but only 180,000 were sold. The amount of depletion which should be deducted from revenue this year is:

a. $0

c. $720,000

b. $480,000

d. $1,200,000

Q11-16. On January 5, 20X1, a corporation was granted a patent on a product. On January 2, 20X9, to protect its patent, the corporation purchased a patent on a competing idea that was originally issued on January 10, 20X5. Because of its unique nature, the corporation does not feel the competing patent can be used in producing a product. The cost of the competing patent should be:

a. Amortized over a maximum period of 20 years.

c. Amortized over a maximum period of 12 years.

b. Amortized over a maximum period of 13 years.

d. Expensed in 20X9.

Chapter 11 Problems

Basic Problems

B-11.01 *Classification of costs subsequent to acquisition*

Scott Drilling Company owns an oil and gas drilling rig. The company Is continually spending money to repair, maintain, refurbish, and upgrade this unit. Below is a listing of various costs incurred. Indicate, by placing check marks in the appropriate boxes, if each cost is a "capital" or "revenue" expenditure. If a capital item, indicate whether the cost is more likely considered to be a "replacement" or a "betterment."

	Classification:		For Capital Items:	
	Capital	Revenue	Replacement	Betterment
Routine cleaning and repainting		✓		
Replacement of expensive cables and pulleys				
Addition of directional drilling motor				
Safety inspection fee				
Raising and lowering rig at each new drill site				
Interest cost on loan to buy rig				
Installation of additional advanced lighting system technology				
Turntable, deck, and bearings in place of similar worn out unit				
Lubrication of all moving parts				
Welding broken outrigger mount				
Installation of anti-slip flooring on all smooth surface walk ways				

Robinson Corporation recently requested a contractor to prepare a proposal to refurbish the exterior of its office building. Robinson wanted to give its building a "face lift." The contractor provided the following bid document:

ROBINSON CORPORATION BID	
Add extension to front porch approach	$20,000
Install shrubs and trees	2,500
Replace rotting exterior siding material	7,500
Replace burned out exterior light bulbs	500
Total for all work:	$30,500

Assume that Robinson Corporation agreed to the bid, and authorized the work. What journal entry would be appropriate for each of the above expenditures?

Ng's Shrimp Company owns a fishing vessel that originally cost $250,000, with a 20-year life, and no anticipated salvage value. Ng uses the straight-line depreciation method. Review the following three *independent* cases, and prepare the journal entry to reflect the disposition of the boat in each case.

Case 1   After 8 years of ownership, the boat was taken by a storm.

Case 2   After 12 years of ownership, the boat was sold for $175,000.

Case 3   After 15 years of ownership, the boat was sold for $60,000.

Wasson Farming Corporation owned many tractors. The company has usually contracted with a trucking company to haul the tractors to the tractor dealership for repairs. With the aging of the tractors, the company is incurring substantial hauling costs because of the increasing frequency of repairs. The company is considering trading a tractor for a trailer, thereby enabling it to haul tractors without having to hire a trucking company. This exchange transaction would significantly improve the company's cash flow and does have "commercial substance."

The trailer that will be acquired in the exchange has a fair value of $35,000. Wasson owns two tractors that are currently valued at $35,000. One of these two tractors will be exchanged (and no boot will be involved). The owner of Wasson Farming is deciding which tractor to give up, and is interested in learning about the financial statement impact of the exchange. Prepare alternative journal entries, assuming an exchange of Tractor A versus Tractor B. Facts about each tractor follow:

Tractor A   Cost, $100,000; accumulated depreciation $80,000

Tractor B   Cost, $75,000; accumulated depreciation $25,000

Leonard Heinz was recently put in charge of the construction division of McMahan Industries. He has reviewed the plant assets and their related accounting records, and believes certain items are "impaired" and should be charged off to a loss account. Examine the following list and decide if you believe the item is impaired.

	Impaired?	
	Yes	No
An abandoned building is slated for demolition	✔	
Equipment that will continue to be used as planned in the production of profitable projects; however, a forced sale of the equipment would not recover its book value		
Used equipment is no longer in use, but will be sold for more than its book value		
Newly purchased assets for which the company significantly overpaid, and which have costs that will not be recovered from future cash flows		
Actions of competitors have forced McMahan to permanently lower prices, and certain items of equipment continue to be used at full capacity, even though the resulting production is unprofitable and will not recover cost		
The maintenance department failed to properly lubricate the bearings on a crane, and it is now significantly damaged		

McCurdy Oil acquired an existing oil well and all related equipment used in the production of oil. McCurdy paid $2,500,000, of which 20% was attributable to pumps, pipelines, and tanks. The oil well is expected to produce oil as follows:

Year 1	100 barrels per day		Year 4	40 barrels per day
Year 2	80 barrels per day		Year 5	20 barrels per day
Year 3	60 barrels per day			

At the end of the 5th year, McCurdy anticipates selling the oil well and equipment for $1,000,000. Of this amount, $250,000 is expected to be attributable to the equipment.

Assuming the preceding estimates serve as the basis for depletion, calculate depletion cost for the 3rd year. Prepare an approriate journal entry for depletion. In preparing the entry, assume that all oil is sold at the time of its production (i.e., none of the oil remains in inventory).

Amortization of intangibles   *B-11.07*

The general journal of Kevin Berry Industries included the following entries relating to various expenditures during 20X5. Review this information and prepare corresponding entries to record any necessary straight-line amortization or other impairment for the year ending December 31.

GENERAL JOURNAL			
Date	Accounts	Debits	Credits
01-01-X5	Patent	30,000	
	Cash		30,000
	Acquired a patent from an inventor. The patent has a 15-year remaining legal life, but it is expected that Berry will utilize the patent for only 5 years.		
05-15-X5	Research Expense	12,000	
	Cash		12,000
	Incurred costs in research and development activity. It is possible these costs will result in new product with a 48-month life.		
09-01-X5	Inventory	25,000	
	Building	75,000	
	Goodwill	50,000	
	Cash		150,000
	To record purchase of business, expected to be operated successfully for an indefinite number of future years.		
12-20-X5	Copyright	10,000	
	Cash		10,000
	Purchased copyright to a video production, but concluded that it was worthless by year's end.		

Involved Problems

Costs subsequent to acquisition and revised depreciation   *I-11.01*

Tidwell Corporation's accounting staff was unsure how to account for certain expenditures relating to its property, plant, and equipment. As a result, the company has delayed recording entries related to the following transactions. In addition, until these items are resolved, the determination of depreciation expense for the year has been delayed.

Item A The company's delivery truck, originally costing $90,000 and having a 6-year life with no salvage value, was substantially overhauled at a cost of $10,000. This expenditure occurred at the beginning of the year, when the truck was two years old. This action restored the truck to "like-new" condition, and extended the useful life by an additional three years.

Item B At mid-year, the company added a new $65,000 dust handling unit to the heating and ventilation system in its inventory warehouse. This new feature is supposed to reduce dust from the air and provide for a cleaner environment in which to store inventory. The new dust unit has a 10-year physical life, but it is anticipated that it will be scrapped after six and one-half years when the primary heating system is replaced. As of the beginning of the year, the heating and ventilation system had a cost of $240,000 and accumulated depreciation of $100,000.

Item C The company entered into a 5-year contract with Reliable Maintenance Services Company. The agreement provides for Tidwell to make monthly payments of $1,500 for all routine cleaning and maintenance activities on shop equipment. Two months of services had been provided and paid as of the end of the year. As of the beginning of the year, shop equipment had a remaining net book value of $300,000, and a remaining life of three years.

Item D Tidwell entered into a joint agreement with several other companies to mutually acquire an easement on an adjoining tract of land. The easement was needed to provide right-of-way for a future rail transport line extension that will benefit all of the participating companies. Tidwell paid $10,000 for its share of the access easement. The easement is perpetual in nature.

Prepare journal entries for each of the four described expenditures. Then, calculate depreciation, as appropriate, for the expenditure and/or related assets. Assume straight-line depreciation in each case.

I-11.02   *Entries and analysis for asset disposals*

Pierce Corporation recently hired a new manager for its struggling construction division. The manager was given responsibility for streamlining operations and restoring profitability. Selling selected assets is one option under consideration.

Begin by reviewing the following asset listing, and prepare hypothetical entries "as if" each asset were sold for cash at its estimated fair value. Then, determine which asset should be sold if the objective becomes to (a) have the largest immediate accounting gain, (b) have the largest immediate accounting loss, (c) result in the highest avoidance of future depreciation expense in periods subsequent to the period of asset sale, (d) produce the most immediate cash inflow, (e) have the largest total asset position, or (f) have no change in total assets.

	Cost	Accumulated Depreciation	Fair Value
Asset A	$2,500,000	$1,000,000	$3,000,000
Asset B	800,000	100,000	700,000
Asset C	4,600,000	500,000	4,000,000
Asset D	3,250,000	1,250,000	1,250,000

Cousin's Bar-B-Q Restaurant recently remodeled its store. The remodel included obtaining all new kitchen equipment. Much of the older equipment was traded-in as partial consideration toward the purchase of the newer items. Examine each of the following exchanges, and prepare appropriate entries to reflect the trade. Each exchange was deemed to have commercial substance, except for the trade of the smoker oven.

	Cost	Accumulated Depreciation	Cash Given or (Received)	Fair Value of New Item
Sink	$10,000	$ 6,500	$ -	$ 5,000
Cutting table	20,000	8,000	-	10,000
Refrigerator	12,000	10,000	15,000	20,000
Freezer	18,000	4,000	11,000	17,000
Computer	7,500	6,000	(1,000)	5,000
Fire suppressor	9,000	2,000	(2,000)	3,000
Smoker oven	12,500	2,500	-	13,000

Out Back Mining purchased land for $100,000,000. The land is believed to contain significant zinc deposits. Preliminary estimates indicate that 250,000 metric tons will be available for extraction over a ten-year period. The anticipated selling price over the ten-year period is estimated at $1,000 per metric ton. Labor and operating expenses, exclusive of depreciation and depletion, is typically 30% of revenue. At the cessation of mining, $25,000,000 must be spent to restore the mining operations area. The land will then be donated to the area government as a wildlife and natural area.

SPREADSHEET TOOL:

Maximum/ Minimum value functions

The investment in mining equipment will involve $5,000,000 of excavation equipment with no salvage value at the end of the mining operation. This category of equipment will be abandoned at the conclusion of the ten-year period. An additional $10,000,000 will be expended on hauling equipment with a 20-year life and $2,000,000 salvage value. This particular equipment will be relocated to a new mining operation after the zinc mine is closed. The company uses straight-line depreciation for all mining equipment.

(a) Assuming that each year's production is sold during the year of extraction, determine annual income for each year, based upon the following production activity:

Year 1	25,000 tons		Year 6	35,000 tons
Year 2	20,000 tons		Year 7	15,000 tons
Year 3	30,000 tons		Year 8	25,000 tons
Year 4	25,000 tons		Year 9	25,000 tons
Year 5	25,000 tons		Year 10	25,000 tons

Which year had the highest income, and which year had the lowest income? How did the choice of depreciation method impact this outcome?

(b) Assuming that 20% of Year 5's production was unsold at year end, how much of Year 5's depletion would be charged to cost of goods sold and how much to ending inventory?

(c) Disregard part (b), and assume that at the beginning of the 9th year, an additional vein of zinc was discovered that increased the estimated reserves by an additional 50,000 tons. No additional costs will be incurred in extracting this material. How much is the revised "per ton" depletion for the remaining deposits?

I-11.05   *Accounting for various intangibles; amortization and impairment*

Tweedy Pharmaceuticals engaged in the following activities during 20X6. Review each and prepare any entry that is needed to record the item, along with adjusting entries at December 31 to record amortization or impairment (if necessary).

Jan. 1	Spent $80,000 in legal fees to register a patent for an internally developed concept. The patent should benefit the company for at least its full legal life, and perhaps even longer.
July 1	Expended $125,000 to research and develop a process that is protected by confidentially agreements with employees (i.e., "trade secret") who worked on the project.
Oct. 1	Purchased the "MemoryMinder" brand name from a competitor for $500,000 cash. This trademarked brand name will be used indefinitely to promote a memory aiding drug.
Oct. 1	Expended $90,000 to purchase a copyright with a 5-year remaining life. This copyright was purchased because it competed with a Tweedy product having a 3-year remaining life.
Dec. 31	Concluded that $1,000,0000 of goodwill from a business combination arising in 20X5 was no longer of any value to Tweedy.

I-11.06   *Team-based evaluation of R&D accounting (global comparison)*

Form a group of four students, then decide who will do each of the following tasks:

Student A	Explore U.S. generally accepted accounting principles to determine the specific standard that addresses the accounting for research and development costs. Determine the basic principles.
Student B	Explore international generally accepted accounting principles to determine the specific standard that addresses the accounting for research and development costs. Determine the basic principles.
Student C	Identify a U.S. company with significant research and development costs. Determine how those costs were reported, and interact with Student A to determine if U.S. GAAP was applied.
Student D	Identify a non-U.S. company with significant research and development costs. Determine how those costs were reported, and interact with Student B to determine if international GAAP was applied.
Group	Get together and discuss your findings and conclusions. Do inconsistencies in accounting standards from one region to the next potentially inhibit the ability to compare financial results? In light of your observations, does it make sense that there is significant effort being devoted to the development of uniform global accounting standards?

Chapter 12:
Current Liabilities and Employer Obligations

Goals:
The nature and recording of typical current liabilities.
Accounting for notes payable.
The criteria for recognition and/or disclosure of contingent
    liabilities.
Basic accounting for payroll and payroll related taxes.
Other components of employee compensation.

The current liabilities section of the balance sheet contains obligations that are due to be satisfied in the near term, and includes amounts relating to accounts payable, salaries, utilities, taxes, short-term loans, and so forth. This casual description is inadequate for all situations, so accountants have developed a very specific definition to deal with more issues.

Current liabilities are debts that are due to be paid within one year or the operating cycle, whichever is longer. Further, such obligations will typically involve the use of current assets, the creation of another current liability, or the providing of some service.

This enhanced definition is expansive enough to capture less obvious obligations pertaining to items like customer prepayments, amounts collected for and payable to third parties, the portion of long-term debt due within one year or the operating cycle (whichever is longer), accrued liabilities for expenses incurred but not yet paid, and contingent liabilities. However, the definition is not meant to include amounts not yet "incurred." For example, salary to be earned by employees next year is not a current liability (this year) because it has yet to be "incurred." Investors, creditors, and managers should pay close attention to current liabilities as they reflect imminent demands on resources.

THE OPERATING CYCLE

Remember from Chapter 4 that the operating cycle is the length of time it takes to turn cash back into cash. That is, a business starts with cash, buys inventory, sells goods, and eventually collects the sales proceeds in cash. The length of time it takes to do this is the operating cycle. Take careful note of how the operating cycle is included in the above definition of current liabilities: *"one year or the operating cycle, whichever is longer."*

For most businesses, the operating cycle is less than one year, but not always. A furniture manufacturer may have to buy and cure wood before it can be processed into a quality product. This could cause the operating cycle to go beyond one year. If that is the case, then current liabilities might include obligations due in more than one year.

TYPICAL CURRENT OBLIGATIONS

Accounts Payable are the amounts due to suppliers relating to the purchase of goods and services. This is perhaps the simplest and most easily understood current liability. Although an **account payable** may be supported by a written agreement, it is more typically based on an informal working relation where credit has been received with the expectation of making payment in the very near term.

Notes Payable are formal short-term borrowings usually evidenced by specific written promises to pay. Bank borrowings, equipment purchases, and some credit purchases from suppliers involve such instruments. The party who agrees to pay is termed the "maker" of the note. Properly constructed, a **note payable** becomes a negotiable instrument, enabling the holder of the note to transfer it to someone else. Notes payable typically involve interest, and their duration varies. When a note is due in less than one year (or the operating cycle, if longer), it is commonly reported as a current liability.

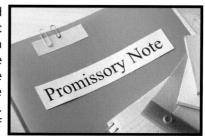

The Current Portion of Long-term Debt is another frequently encountered current obligation. When a note or other debt instrument is of long duration, it is reported as a long-term liability. However, the amount of principal which is to be paid within one year or the operating cycle, whichever is longer, should be separated and classified as a current liability. For example, a $100,000 long-term note may be paid in equal annual increments of $10,000, plus accrued interest. At the end of any given year, the $10,000 principal due during the following year should be reported as a current liability (along with any accrued interest), with the remaining balance shown as a long-term liability.

Accrued Liabilities (sometimes called accrued expenses) include items like accrued salaries and wages, taxes, interest, and so forth. These items relate to expenses that accumulate with the passage of time but will be paid in one lump-sum amount. For example, the cost of employee service accrues gradually with the passage of time. The amount that employees have earned but not been paid is termed accrued salaries and should be reported as a current liability. Likewise, interest on a loan is based on the period of time the debt is outstanding; it is the passage of time that causes the interest payable to accrue. Accrued but unpaid interest is another example of an accrued current liability. The reported accrued liabilities only relate to amounts already accumulated and not to amounts that will arise later.

Prepayments by Customers arise from transactions such as selling magazine subscriptions in advance, selling gift-cards, selling tickets well before a scheduled event, and other similar items where the customer deposits money in advance of receiving the expected good or service. These items represent an obligation on the part of the seller to either return the money or deliver a service in the future. As such, the prepayment is reported as "unearned revenue" within the current liability section of the balance sheet. Recall, from earlier chapters, that the unearned revenue is removed and revenue is recognized as the goods and services are provided.

Collections for Third Parties arise when the recipient of some payment is not the beneficiary of the payment. As such, the recipient has an obligation to turn the money over to another entity. At first, this may seem odd. But, consider sales taxes. The seller of merchandise must collect the sales tax on transactions, but then has a duty to pay those collected amounts to the appropriate taxing entity. Such amounts are appropriately reflected as a current liability until the funds are remitted to the rightful owner.

Obligations to be Refinanced deserve special consideration. A long-term debt may have an upcoming maturity date within the next year. Ordinarily, this note would be moved to the current liability section. However, companies often renew such obligations, in essence, borrowing money to repay the maturing note. Should currently maturing long-term debt that is subject to refinancing be shown as a current or a long-term liability? To resolve this issue, accountants have developed very specific rules. A currently maturing long-term obligation is to be shown as a current liability unless (1) the company intends to renew the debt on a long-term basis and (2) the company has the ability to do so (ordinarily evidenced by a firm agreement with a competent lender).

Notes Payable

Long-term notes will be considered in the next chapter. For the moment, focus on the appropriate accounting for a short-term note. A common scenario would involve the borrowing of money in exchange for the issuance of a promissory note payable. The note will look something like this:

Promissory note

For value received, the undersigned promises to pay to the order of BancZone, Inc.

the sum of: *****Ten-Thousand and no/100 Dollars***** ($10,000.00)

Along with annual interest of 8% on the unpaid balance. This note shall mature and be payable, along with accrued interest, on June 30, 20X8.

January 1, 20X8
Issue Date

Oliva Zavala
Maker signature

The preceding illustration should not be used as a model for constructing a legal document; it is merely an abbreviated form to focus on the accounting issues. A correct legal form would typically be far more expansive and cover numerous things like what happens in the event of default, who pays legal fees if there is a dispute, requirements of demand and notice, and so forth. In the preceding note, Oliva has agreed to pay to BancZone $10,000 plus interest of $400 on June 30, 20X8. The interest represents 8% of $10,000 for half of a year (January 1 through June 30).

The amount borrowed is recorded by debiting Cash and crediting Notes Payable:

01-01-X8	Cash		10,000	
	Note Payable			10,000
	To record note payable, maturity date on June 30, 20X8			

When the note is repaid, the difference between the carrying amount of the note and the cash necessary to repay that note is reported as interest expense. The journal entry follows:

06-30-X8	Interest Expense	400	
	Note Payable	10,000	
	Cash		10,400
	To record repayment of note and interest ($10,000 X 8% X 6/12 = $400)		

Had the above note been created on October 1, the entries would appear as follows:

10-01-X8	Cash	10,000	
	Note Payable		10,000
	To record note payable; maturity date on March 31, 20X9		
12-31-X8	Interest Expense	200	
	Interest Payable		200
	To record accrued interest for 3 months ($10,000 X 8% X 3/12 = $200)		
03-31-X9	Interest Expense	200	
	Interest Payable	200	
	Note Payable	10,000	
	Cash		10,400
	To record repayment of note and interest		

In the preceding entries, notice that interest for three months was accrued at December 31, representing accumulated interest that must be paid at maturity on March 31, 20X9. On March 31, another three months of interest was charged to expense. The cash payment included $400 for interest, half relating to the amount previously accrued in 20X8 and half relating to 20X9.

Next, consider how the preceding amounts would appear in the current liability section of the balance sheet at December 31, 20X8. Observe the inclusion of two separate line items for the note and related interest:

Current Liabilities		
Accounts payable	$90,000	
Salaries payable	2,000	
Taxes payable	3,000	
Customer prepayments	3,000	
Interest payable	200	
Note payable	10,000	$108,200

In examining this illustration, one might wonder about the order in which specific current obligations are to be listed. One scheme is to list them according to their due dates, from the earliest to the latest. Another acceptable alternative is to list them by maturity value, from the largest to the smallest.

Some short-term borrowing agreements may stipulate that a year is assumed to have 360 days, instead of the obvious 365 days. In the old days, before calculators, this could perhaps be justified to ease calculations. In modern days, it may be that a lender is seeking to prey on unsuspecting borrowers. For example, interest on a $100,000, 8% loan for 180 days would be $4,000 assuming a 360-day year ($100,000 X .08 X 180/360), but only $3,945 based on the more correct 365-day year ($100,000 X .08 X 180/365). It becomes apparent that one should be alert to the stated assumptions intrinsic to a loan agreement.

INTEREST CALCULATION

Next, be aware of the "rule of 78s." Some loan agreements stipulate that prepayments will be based on this tricky technique. A year has 12 months, and 12 + 11 + 10 + 9 + ... + 1 = 78; somehow giving rise to the "rule of 78s." Assume that $100,000 is borrowed for 12 months at 8% interest. The annual interest is $8,000, but, if the interest attribution method is based on the "rule of 78s," it is assumed that 12/78 of the total interest is attributable to the first month, 11/78 to the next, and so forth. If the borrower desired to prepay the loan after just two months, that borrower would be very disappointed to learn that 23/78 (12 + 11 = 23) of the total interest was due (23/78 X $8,000 = $2,359). If the interest had been based simply on 2 of 12 months, the amount of interest would only be $1,333 (2/12 X $8,000 = $1,333).

Compounding is another concept that should be understood. So far in this text, simple interest has been used in the illustrated calculations. This merely means that Interest = Loan X Interest Rate X Time. But, at some point, it is fair to assume that the accumulated interest will also start to accrue interest. Some people call this "interest on the interest." In the next chapter, this will be examined in much more detail. For now, just take note that a loan agreement will address this by stating the frequency of compounding, which can occur annually, quarterly, monthly, daily, or continuously (which requires a bit of calculus to compute). The narrower the frequency, the greater the amount of total interest.

One last item to note is that a lender might require interest "up front." The note may be issued with interest included in the face value. For example, $9,000 may be borrowed, but a $10,000 note is established (interest is not separately stated). At maturity, $10,000 is repaid, representing a $9,000 repayment of borrowed amounts and $1,000 interest. Note that the interest rate may appear to be 10% ($1,000 out of $10,000), but the effective rate is much higher ($1,000 for $9,000 = 11.11%).

The journal entry to record a note with interest included in face value (also known as a note issued at discount), is as follows:

01-01-X8	Cash	9,000	
	Discount on Note Payable	1,000	
	Note Payable		10,000
	To record note payable, issued at a discount		

Observe that the $1,000 difference is initially recorded as a discount on note payable. On a balance sheet, the discount would be reported as contra liability. The $1,000 discount would be offset against the $10,000 note payable, resulting in a $9,000 net liability.

Discount amortization transfers the discount to interest expense over the life of the loan. This means that the $1,000 discount should be recorded as interest expense by debiting Interest Expense and crediting Discount on Note Payable. In this way, the $10,000 paid at maturity (credit to Cash) will be entirely offset with a $10,000 reduction in the Note Payable account (debit).

The entries to record at maturity are as follows:

12-31-X8	Interest Expense	1,000	
	Discount on Note Payable		1,000
	To record discount amortization		
	Note Payable	10,000	
	Cash		10,000
	To record repayment of note		

Be aware that discount amortization occurs not only at the date of repayment, but also at the end of an accounting period. If the preceding example had a maturity date at other than the December 31 year-end, the $1,000 of total interest expense would need to be recorded partially in one period and partially in another.

TRUTH IN LENDING

The preceding discussion about unique interest calculations sheds light on the mechanics that lenders can use to tilt the benefit of a lending agreement to their advantage. As a result, statutes have increasingly required fuller disclosure ("truth in lending") and, in some cases, outright limits on certain practices.

Borrowers should be careful to understand the full economics of any agreement, and lenders should understand the laws that define fair practices. Lenders who overcharge interest or violate laws can find themselves legally losing the right to collect amounts loaned.

Contingent Liabilities

Some events may eventually give rise to a liability, but the timing and amount is not presently sure. Such uncertain or potential obligations are known as **contingent liabilities**. There are numerous examples of contingent liabilities. Legal disputes give rise to contingent liabilities, environmental contamination events give rise to contingent liabilities, product warranties give rise to contingent liabilities, and so forth.

Do not confuse these "firm specific" contingent liabilities with general business risks. General business risks include the risk of war, storms, and the like that are presumed to be an unfortunate part of life for which no specific accounting can be made in advance.

ACCOUNTING FOR CONTINGENT LIABILITIES

A subjective assessment of the probability of an unfavorable outcome is required to properly account for most contingencies. Rules specify that contingent liabilities should be recorded in the accounts when it is *probable* that the future event will occur *and* the amount of the liability can be *reasonably estimated*. This means that a loss would be recorded (debit) and a liability established (credit) in advance of the settlement.

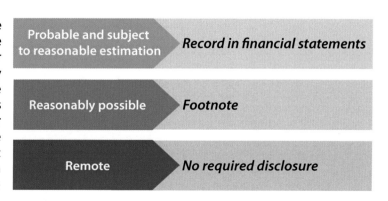

Probable and subject to reasonable estimation → *Record in financial statements*

Reasonably possible → *Footnote*

Remote → *No required disclosure*

An example might be a hazardous waste spill that will require a large outlay to clean up. It is probable that funds will be spent and the amount can likely be estimated. If the estimated loss can only be defined as a range of outcomes, the U.S. approach generally results in recording the low end of the range. International accounting standards focus on recording a liability at the midpoint of the estimated unfavorable outcomes.

On the other hand, if it is only *reasonably possible* that the contingent liability will become a real liability, then a note to the financial statements is required. Likewise, a note is required when it is probable a loss has occurred but the amount simply cannot be estimated. Normally, accounting tends to be very conservative (when in doubt, book the liability), but this is not the case for contingent liabilities. Therefore, one should carefully read the notes to the financial statements before investing or loaning money to a company.

There are sometimes significant risks that are simply not in the liability section of the balance sheet. Most recognized contingencies are those meeting the rather strict criteria of "probable" and "reasonably estimable." One exception occurs for contingencies assumed in a business acquisition. Acquired contingencies are recorded based on an estimate of actual value.

What about *remote* risks, like a frivolous lawsuit? Remote risks need not be disclosed; they are viewed as needless clutter. What about business decision risks, like deciding to reduce insurance coverage because of the high cost of the insurance premiums? GAAP is not very clear on this subject; such disclosures are not required, but are not discouraged. What about contingent assets/gains, like a company's claim against another for patent infringement? Such amounts are almost never recognized before settlement payments are actually received.

TIMING OF EVENTS

If a customer was injured by a defective product in Year 1 (assume the company anticipates a large estimated loss from a related claim), but the company did not receive notice of the event until Year 2 (but before issuing Year 1's financial statements), the event would nevertheless impact Year 1 financial statements. The reason is that the event ("the injury itself") giving rise to the loss arose in Year 1. Conversely, if the injury occurred in Year 2, Year 1's financial statements would not be adjusted no matter how bad the financial effect. However, a note to the financial statements may be needed to explain that a material adverse event arising subsequent to year end has occurred.

WARRANTY COSTS

Product warranties are presumed to give rise to a probable liability that can be estimated. When goods are sold, an estimate of the amount of warranty costs to be incurred on the goods should be recorded as expense, with the offsetting credit to a **Warranty Liability** account. As warranty work is performed, the Warranty Liability is reduced and Cash (or other resources used) is credited. In this manner, the expense is recorded in the same period as the sale (matching principle). Following are illustrative entries for warranties. In reviewing these entries, note the accompanying explanations:

XX-XX-XX	Cash	3,500,000	
	Sales		3,500,000
	To record sales		
XX-XX-XX	Warranty Expense	70,000	
	Warranty Liability		70,000
	To record estimated warranty cost equal to 2% of sales ($3,500,000 X 2%)		
XX-XX-XX	Warranty Liability	80,000	
	Cash		80,000
	Repaired defective products under warranty at a cost of $80,000		

The warranty calculations can require consideration of beginning balances, additional accruals, and warranty work performed. Assume Zeff Company had a beginning-of-year Warranty Liability account balance of $25,000. During the year Zeff sells $3,500,000 worth of goods, eventually expecting to incur warranty costs equal to 2% of sales ($3,500,000 X 2% = $70,000). The 2% rate is an estimate based on the best information available. Such rates vary considerably by company and product. $80,000 was actually spent on warranty work. How much is the end-of-year Warranty Liability? The T-account reveals an ending warranty liability of $15,000.

Warranty Liability			
(Work Performed)	80,000	25,000	*(Beginning Balance)*
		70,000	*(Additional Accruals)*
	80,000	95,000	
		15,000	*(Ending Balance)*

Many costs are similar to warranties. Companies may offer coupons, prizes, rebates, air-miles, free hotel stays, free rentals, and similar items associated with sales activity. Each of these gives rise to the need to provide an estimated liability. While the details may vary, the basic procedures and outcomes are similar to those applied to warranties.

Payroll

Many services are provided to a business by other than employees. These services may include janitorial support, legal services, air conditioner repairs, audits, and so forth. An **independent contractor** is one who performs a designated task or service for a company. The company has the right to control or direct only the result of the work done by an independent contractor. In contrast, an **employee** is defined as a person who works for a specific business and whose activities are directed by that business. The business controls the work that will be done and how it will be done. The distinction is very important, because the payroll tax and record keeping requirements differ for employees and independent contractors. As a general rule, amounts paid to independent contractors do not involve any "tax withholdings" by the payer. However, the payer may need to report the amount paid to the Internal Revenue Service (IRS) on a **Form 1099**, with a copy to the independent contractor. But, the obligation for paying taxes rests with the independent contractor.

The employer's handling of payroll to employees is another matter entirely. Begin by considering the specifics of a paycheck. Paychecks are usually reduced by a variety of taxes, possibly including federal income tax, state income tax, social security taxes, and Medicare/Medicaid. Additional reductions can occur for insurance, retirement savings, charitable contributions, special health and child care deferrals, and other similar items. Employers may also pay costs related to social security, Medicare/Medicaid, unemployment taxes, workers compensation insurance, matching contributions to retirement programs, and other items.

GROSS VS. NET EARNINGS

The total earnings of an employee is the **gross pay**. For hourly employees, it is the number of hours worked multiplied by the hourly rate. For salaried employees, it is the flat amount for the period, such as $3,000 per month. Gross pay might be increased for both hourly and salaried employees based on applicable overtime rules. Employers are well advised to monitor statutes relating to overtime; by law, certain employees must be paid for overtime. Gross earnings less all applicable deductions is the **net pay**.

DEDUCTIONS

Income taxes are required by federal, state (when applicable), and city (when applicable) governments to be withheld and periodically remitted by the employer to the taxing authority. In essence, employers become an agent of the government, serving to collect amounts for the government. Withheld amounts that have yet to be remitted to the government are carried as a current liability on the employer's books (recall the earlier mention of amounts collected for third parties). The level of withholdings is based on the employee's income, the frequency of pay, marital status, and the number of withholding allowances claimed (based on the number of dependents). Employees claim withholding allowances by filing a form **W-4** with their employer.

Social Security/Medicare Taxes are also known as **FICA**. FICA stands for Federal Insurance Contributions Act. This Act establishes a tax that transfers money from workers to aged retirees (and certain other persons who are in the unfortunate position of not being able to fully provide for themselves due to disability, loss of a parent, or other serious problem). The social purpose of the tax is to provide a modest income stream to the beneficiaries. This component is the social security tax. Another component of the Act is the Medicare/Medicaid tax, which provides support for health care costs incurred by retirees (and designated others).

The social security tax is presently a designated percentage of income, up to a certain maximum level of annual income per employee. For illustrative purposes, assume a 6.5% social security tax, on an annual income of $150,000. In the following paycheck stub, note that I. M. Fictitious paid $195 in social security tax for the month (6.5% X $3,000). Since Fictitious has not yet exceeded $150,000 in gross income for the year-to-date, the annual maximum has not been reached. If Fictitious exceeds the annual limit, the tax would cease to be withheld for the remainder of the calendar year. The employee's amount must be matched by the employer. Thus, the burden associated with this tax is actually twice what is apparent to most employees.

The Medicare/Medicaid tax is also a designated percentage of income. Unlike the social security tax, there is no annual maximum. This tax is levied on every dollar of gross income, without regard to an employee's total earnings. In the following illustration, the assumed rate is 1.5% (1.5% X $3,000 = $45). This is another tax the employer must match dollar-for-dollar.

Other Employee Deductions can occur for employee cost sharing in health care insurance programs, employee contributions to various retirement or other savings plans, charitable contributions, contributions to tax-advantaged health and child care savings programs, and so forth. In each case, the employer is acting to collect amounts from the employee, with a resulting fiduciary duty to turn the monies over to another entity. A representative paycheck and the attached stub follows. Examine the check and notice that I. M. Fictitious earned $3,000 during the month but "took home" only $1,819.

Unreal Corporation Payroll Account		Check #	12345
		Date:	July 31, 20XX
Pay to the order of:	I.M. Fictitious		$1,819.⁰⁰
*****ONE-THOUSAND, EIGHT-HUNDRED, NINETEEN AND NO/100 DOLLARS*****			
First Corner Bank			
MEMO July payroll for Fictitious		*Certainly Void*	

Detach below before depositing, and save for your records.

Employee: I.M. Fictitious	Gross Earnings		$3,000.00
Pay period: July 20XX	**Deductions:**		
	Federal Income Tax	$349.00	
	State Income Tax	117.00	
	Social Security Tax	195.00	
	Medicare/Medicaid Tax	45.00	
	Insurance	175.00	
	Retirement Savings Plan	200.00	
	Charity	25.00	
	Health/Child Care Plan	75.00	1,181.00
	Net Pay		$1,819.00

JOURNAL ENTRY FOR PAYROLL

The journal entry to record I.M. Fictitious's pay would be as follows. Carefully match the amounts in the journal entry to the amounts on the paycheck stub.

07-31-XX	Salaries Expense	3,000	
	Federal Income Tax Payable		349
	State Income Tax Payable		117
	Social Security Tax Payable		195
	Medicare/Medicaid Tax Payable		45
	Insurance Payable		175
	Retirement Contribution Payable		200
	Charitable Contribution Payable		25
	Health/Child Plan Payable		75
	Cash		1,819
	To record payroll of Fictitious		

Although not illustrated, as the company remits the withheld amounts to the appropriate entities (i.e., taxes to the government, retirement contributions to an investment trust, etc.), it would debit the related payable and credit Cash.

EMPLOYER COSTS

Recall that the amount of social security and Medicare/Medicaid tax must be matched by employers. In addition, the employer must pay federal and state unemployment taxes. These taxes are levied to provide funds that are paid to workers who are actively seeking but unable to find regular employment.

The bulk of unemployment tax is usually levied at the state level since most states choose to administer their own unemployment programs (which is encouraged by the federal government via a system of credits to the federal tax rate). The specific rates will depend on the particular state of employment and each individual employer's employment history. Employers who rarely lay off or fire employees enjoy a favorable rate, but those who do not maintain a stable labor pool will find their rates adjusted to a higher level.

Like social security, the unemployment tax stops each year once a certain maximum income level is reached. In this text, assume the federal rate is one-half of one percent (0.5%), and the state rate is three percent (3%), on a maximum income of $10,000 per employee. Thus, assume the federal unemployment tax (**FUTA**) is capped at $50 per employee and the state unemployment tax (**SUTA**) is capped at $300.

Many employers will carry **workers compensation insurance**. The rules for this type of insurance vary from state to state. Generally, this type of insurance provides for payments to workers who sustain on-the-job injuries and shields the employer from additional claims. But, for companies that do not carry such insurance, the employer may have an unlimited exposure to claims related to work place injuries. The cost of this insurance can be very high for risky work, like construction.

Employers may provide health care insurance and retirement plan contributions for employees. These amounts can be substantial, perhaps even exceeding the amounts employees contribute on their own behalf. Current law requires employers meeting certain thresholds to provide healthcare insurance to employees or face substantial penalties.

Obviously, the employer's cost of an employee goes well beyond the amount reported on the paycheck. For many companies, the total cost of an employee can be 125% to 150% of the gross earnings. Of course, these added costs should be entered in the accounting records. In preparing the following entry it is assumed that (a) FUTA and SUTA bases had already been exceeded earlier in 20XX (hence the related amounts are zero),

(b) the employer exactly matched employee contributions to insurance and retirement programs, and (c) the employer incurred workers' compensation insurance of $300. Following is the entry for I. M. Fictitious:

07-31-XX	Payroll Tax Expense	240	
	Employee Benefits Expense	675	
	Social Security Tax Payable		195
	Medicare/Medicaid Tax Payable		45
	FUTA Payable		0
	SUTA Payable		0
	Insurance Payable		175
	Workers Compensation Insurance Payable		300
	Retirement Contribution Payable		200
	To record employer portion of payroll taxes and benefits		

ANNUAL REPORTS

Shortly after the conclusion of a calendar year, an employer must review its employee records and prepare a summary wage and tax statement (commonly called a **W-2**). This information is furnished to each employee and the government. It helps employees accurately prepare their own annual federal and state income tax returns and allows the government to verify amounts reported by those individual taxpayers.

ACCURATE PAYROLL SYSTEMS

Accuracy is vital in payroll accounting. Oftentimes, a business may hire an outside firm that specializes in payroll management and accounting. The outside firm manages the payroll, recordkeeping, government compliance, timely processing of tax deposits, and the like.

When a business manages its own payroll, very accurate data must be maintained. Most firms will set up a separate payroll journal or database that tracks information about each employee, as well as in the aggregate. In addition, it is quite common to open a separate payroll bank account into which the gross pay is transferred and from which paychecks and tax payments are disbursed. This system provides an added control to make sure that employee funds are properly maintained, processed, and reconciled.

It is very important to know that the employer's obligation to protect withheld taxes and make certain they are timely remitted to the government is taken very seriously. Employers who fail to do so are subject to harsh penalties for the obvious reason that the funds do not belong to the employer. Likewise, employees who participate in, or are aware of misapplication of such funds can expect serious legal repercussions. The government has made it very simple for employers to remit withheld amounts, as most commercial banks are approved to accept such amounts from employers. Online systems also allow easy funds transfer. The frequency of the required remittance is dependent upon the size of the employer and the total payroll.

Other Components of Employee Compensation

Paid vacations are another element of compensation that many employees receive. In addition to paid vacations, employers may provide for other periods of **compensated absences**. Examples include sick leave, holidays, family emergency time, jury duty time, military reserve time, and so forth. Sometimes, these benefits accumulate with the passage of time, so that the benefit is a function of tenure with the company. To illustrate, a company may stipulate that one half-day of sick leave and one day of vacation time is accrued for each month of employment.

Because the cost of periods of compensated absence can become quite significant, it is imperative that such amounts be correctly measured and reported. Accounting rules provide that companies expense (debit) and provide a liability (credit) for such accumulated costs when specified conditions are present. Those conditions are that the accumulated benefit (1) relates to services already rendered, (2) is a right that vests or accumulates, (3) is probable to be paid to the employee, and (4) can be reasonably estimated. Vacation pay typically meets these conditions for accrual, while other costs depend upon the individual company's policies and history.

PENSION PLANS

It is common for a company to offer some form of retirement plan for its employees. Begin by noting that there are two broad types of **pensions**: defined contribution plans and defined benefit plans. With a **defined contribution plan**, an employer promises to make a periodic contribution (usually a set percentage of the employee's salary with some matching portion also provided by the employee) into a separate pension fund account. After a minimum vesting period, the funds become the property of the employee for his or her benefit once they enter retirement. Prior to withdrawal, the funds might be invested in stocks, bonds, or other approved investments. The employee will receive the full benefit of the funds and the investment returns, usually withdrawing them gradually after retirement.

Defined contribution plans offer an important desirable feature for employers, in that their obligation is known and fixed. Further, the employer ordinarily gets a tax deduction for its contribution, even though the employee does not recognize that contribution as taxable income until amounts are withdrawn from the pension many years later. The company expenses the required periodic contribution as incurred. No further accounting on the corporate books is necessary. The pension assets and obligations are effectively transferred to a separate pension trust, greatly simplifying the recordkeeping of the employer.

In stark contrast are **defined benefit plans**. With these plans the employer's promise becomes more elaborate and its cost far more uncertain. For example, a company may offer annual pension payments equal to 2% per year of service times the final annual salary. So, a person who works 30 years and then retires may be eligible for continuing pay at 60% of his or her annual salary. These plans are fraught with uncertainty. How long will retirees live and draw benefits, how many years will employees work, how much will the annual salary be, and so on?

Actuaries are persons trained and skilled to make assessments about life expectancy and related workforce trends. They prepare estimates that are used by accountants to calculate annual pension expense for a defined benefit plan. Matching concepts expense this cost during the periods of active employee service, rather than periods of retirement. Some or all of the annual expense is funded by a transfer of money into a pension trust fund. Those funds are invested and eventually disbursed to retirees, but the company remains obligated for any shortfalls in the pension trust. If a company has failed to fund all the amounts expensed to date, or if the pension fund is "underfunded" relative to outstanding pension promises made, a pension liability is reported on the balance sheet. But, the bulk of the pension assets and obligations are carried on the books of the separate pension trust fund. Because of reporting complexities and actuarial risks, defined benefit pension plans are becoming less common.

OTHER POST-RETIREMENT BENEFITS

Some companies provide retirees with health care coverage, prescription benefits, and life insurance. Matching principles again dictate that such costs be expensed during the period of time in which the employee is actively working to vest these rights. As a result, companies will expense the estimated cost of post-retirement benefits over many years, creating an offsetting liability on the balance sheet.

Chapter 12 Quiz

Q12-1.   Collections for third parties should be recorded as a current liability.

true   or   false

Q12-2.   A Discount account should be established when interest is included in the face amount of the note.

true   or   false

Q12-3.   The guidelines for the recognition of contingent liabilities reflect that they should be recorded in the accounts when it is probable that the future event will occur and the amount of the liability can be reasonably:

estimated   or   isolated

Q12-4.   Deductions from employee earnings, plus net pay, equals:

gross earnings   or   gross withholdings

Q12-5.   Amounts withheld from employees' paychecks are recorded on the employer's books as a:

liability   or   contra liability

Q12-6.   Sales tax is an example of a collection for a _____ .

Q12-7.   The process of reducing the discount by recognizing interest expense is frequently referred to as _____ .

Q12-8.   The guidelines for recording contingent liabilities into the accounts stipulate that the future event be _____ and the amount of liability be _____ .

Q12-9.   The _____ , commonly called Social Security/Medicare, provides retirement, financial, and medical benefits to aged, disabled, widows, and orphans.

Q12-10. The tax imposed by federal and state governments to financially assist unemployed workers is the _____ .

Q12-11. Employers typically finance retirement plans by making periodic cash payments directly into a _____ .

Multiple Choice

Q12-12. Contingent liabilities should be recorded in the accounts when:

a. It is probable that the future event will occur.

b. The amount of the liability can be reasonably estimated.

c. Both (a) and (b).

d. Either (a) or (b).

Q12-13. The Discount on Notes Payable:

a. Is a contra liability account.

b. Is a contingent liability account.

c. Should be reported as an asset because of its debit balance.

d. Is amortized to reduce interest expense over the life of the note payable.

Q12-14. Landry paid $5,000 cash for warranty service work. If a Warranty Liability account had been previously established, the proper journal entry to record the service work would be:

a. Sales   5,000
         Cash   5,000

b. Warranty Expense   5,000
         Warranty Liability   5,000

c. Warranty Expense   5,000
         Cash   5,000

d. Warranty Liability   5,000
         Cash   5,000

Q12-15. The FICA tax is levied on:

a. Employees only.

b. Employers only.

c. Both employees and employers.

d. Earnings in excess of base amounts.

Q12-16. The gross payroll for Zurich Corporation was $100,000. Federal income tax withheld from employee paychecks amounted to $24,000, state income tax withheld amounted to $3,000, Social Security amounted to $8,500 (both the employee and employer portion), and Medicare amounted to $3,500 (both the employee and employer portion). Furthermore, employees elected to have $1,000 of insurance and charitable contributions withheld from their paychecks. How much was net pay?

a. $34,000

b. $60,000

c. $66,000

d. $72,000

Chapter 12 Problems

Basic Problems

Contemplating the current liability definition   B-12.01

Determining if an obligation is a current liability requires careful consideration of certain conditions. Examine the following five conditions, and determine what other conditions must be met before the obligation would be deemed current (Condition A is done as an example):

	Condition:	Other Conditions to meet:
A	Obligation is due within one year	C, D, or E
B	Obligation is due within the operating cycle	
C	Obligation requires the use of current assets	
D	Obligation results in the creation of another current liability	
E	Obligation to be satisfied by providing services	

Understanding typical current liabilities   B-12.02

Server Planet operates a web hosting company. Examine the following items and prepare the current liability section of the company's December 31, 20X7, balance sheet.

The beginning of year accounts payable was $100,000. Purchases on trade accounts during the year were $650,000, and payments on account were $610,000.

The company incurs substantial costs for electricity to run its servers and air conditioning systems. As of December 31, 20X7, it is estimated that $55,000 of electricity has been used, although the monthly billing for December has not yet been received.

Server Planet sells web hosting plans for as low as $25 per month. However, it requires its customers to prepay in 6-month increments. As of the end of the year, $375,000 had been collected for 20X8 web hosting plans.

Web hosting services are subject to sales taxes, and Server Planet collected $65,000 during the year. All of these amounts have been remitted to taxing authorities, with the exception of $5,000 that is due to be paid in January, 20X8.

The company has total bank loans of $1,500,000. This debt bears interest at 6%, payable monthly. As of December 31, 20X7, all interest had been paid, with the exception of accrued interest for the last half of December.

The company's bank loans ($1,500,000) are all due on June 30, 20X8. However, Server Planet has a firm lending agreement with the bank to renew and extend $1,000,000 of this amount on a 5-year basis. The company intends to exercise this renewal option, but is not yet sure about the final disposition of the remainder.

On October 1, 20X4, Farmer Engineering Services purchased a new laser surveying instrument. Farmer paid $5,000 down and executed the following promissory note:

Promissory note

For value received, the undersigned promises to pay to the order of Laser Equipment Company

the sum of: *****Twenty-Thousand and no/100 Dollars*****   ($20,000.00)

Along with annual interest of 10% on the unpaid balance. This note shall mature and be payable, along with accrued interest, on September 30, 20X5.

October 1, 20X4	J.D. Farmer Farmer Engineering
Issue Date	Maker signature

(a)   Prepare the appropriate journal entry to record the purchase on October 1, 20X4.

(b)   Prepare the appropriate journal entry to record the year-end interest accrual on December 31, 20X4.

(c)   Prepare the appropriate journal entry to record the payment of the note and accrued interest on September 30, 20X5.

On April 1, 20X7, Miller Oil Company purchased a pumping truck. The sole consideration was a $100,000 note due in one year. Interest of $12,000 was included the face amount of the note. If Miller had purchased the truck for cash, the purchase price would have been only $88,000.

(a)   Prepare the appropriate journal entry to record the purchase on April 1, 20X7.

(b)   Prepare the appropriate journal entry to record the year-end discount amortization on December 31, 20X7.

(c)   Prepare the appropriate journal entry to record the payment of the note on March 31, 20X8.

(d)   What was the actual rate of interest on this loan?

Conroy Corporation has borrowed money under two different loans. Conroy's accounting department presented the following calculations to support the interest accrual calculations. Review the calculations and suggest any necessary revisions. What are the financial statement implications associated with the revisions?

The first loan was a one-year loan for $100,000, created on November 1 of the current year. It bears interest at 8%, with interest based on the "rule of 78s."

Calculations: $100,000 X 8% X 2/12 = $1,333.33

The second loan is due on demand and was for $250,000. The loan was originated on November 1 of the current year, and it bears interest at 9%, using a 360-day year assumption.

Calculations: $250,000 X 9% X 2/12 = $3,750.00

Criteria relating to contingent liabilities	B-12.06

The auditing firm of Rossellini and Rossellini was auditing the year-end financial statements of its client, City Center Foods. In the course of the audit, it was discovered that City Center was the defendant in a law suit involving a "food poisoning" case. City Center denies that it sold any tainted food products. City Center's attorney provided a representation letter regarding the ongoing litigation. Following is a portion of the reply received from the attorney:

Dear Ms. Rossellini:

You requested that we furnish you with certain information in connection with your examination of the accounts of City Center Foods, as of December 31, 20X7 . . .

While this firm represents City Center Foods, our engagement has been limited to specific matters involving the ongoing litigation between City Center Foods and Randal Ransom. This response is necessarily limited to those matters. The Company has advised us it does not intend to waive the attorney-client privilege with respect to any information which the Company has furnished to us. Moreover, please be advised that our response to you should not be construed in any way to constitute a waiver of the protection of the attorney work-product privilege with respect to any of our files involving the Company.

In the matter of Randal Ransom v. City Center Foods: On June 30, 20X7, Randal Ransom filed a civil action in Federal District Court for the Eastern District of Texas alleging that he was significantly damaged by consumption of food products sold by City Center Foods. He further alleges that City Center Foods knowingly sold such food products and failed to maintain appropriate refrigeration equipment. Mr. Ransom is requesting specific damages of $1,000,000 and such additional amounts as may be awarded by a jury.

This litigation is in its earliest stages, and discovery is not yet complete. At this stage of litigation, it is impracticable to render an opinion about whether the likelihood of an unfavorable outcome is either "probable" or "remote;" however, the Company believes it has meritorious defenses and is vigorously defending this litigation . . .

Robert Bean, Attorney

(a)   What is a contingent liability?

(b)   What criteria drive the determination of when/how a contingency should be reported?

(c)   How do you believe the litigation described in the attorney's letter should be reported?

Riseva Corporation manufactures and sells energy efficient lighting systems. These systems include a complex dimmer module, and about 10% of all units sold require subsequent repair under the warranty. The average repair cost is $80 per unit.

Riseva began the year with an accrued warranty liability of $250,000. During the year, 50,000 lighting systems were sold. $310,000 was expended on warranty services performed during the year.

Prepare Riseva's journal entries to accrue additional warranty costs relating to current year sales and account for monies expended on actual warranty work performed during the year. How much will appear as warranty expense in the current year income statement, and how much will appear as the warranty liability on the closing balance sheet?

Lawrence Bodine is employed by Baylor Health Systems. During the month of June, Lawrence worked 195 hours. 15 of these hours were overtime, and were required to be paid at 150% of the normal hourly rate. Lawrence's hourly rate is $12.

Lawrence is single, and had $400 of federal income tax withheld from his pay. Baylor is in a state without an income tax.

Lawrence's pay is subject to social security taxes at an (assumed) 6.5% rate and Medicare/Medicaid at an (assumed) 1.5% rate. He has not exceeded the annual base for social security taxes.

Baylor pays for workers' compensation insurance at a 4% rate. None of this cost is paid by the employee.

Baylor provides its employees with health care insurance, and pays 90% of the $500 per employee monthly premium. The other 10% is paid by employees via payroll withholdings.

Lawrence participates in a tax-sheltered deferred savings plan and has 8% of his gross pay withheld each month. Baylor Health Systems provides a 75% matching contribution. In other words, for every dollar that Lawrence saves, Baylor will contribute an additional 75 cents.

Baylor's payroll is subject to federal (0.5%) and state (1.5%) unemployment taxes on each employee's gross pay, up to $8,000 per year. Lawrence had $6,000 of gross earnings in the months prior to June.

Lawrence participates in the Community Chest fund drive each month, via a $25 contribution that is withheld from his pay.

(a) Complete Lawrence's paycheck and the remittance advice (i.e., "paycheck stub"). The blank worksheet will be very helpful for this portion of the assignment.

(b) Prepare journal entries for Lawrence's pay and the related payroll expenses.

(c) What is the total cost to Baylor for Lawrence's services during June?

Wild Man Wilson hosts a television show where he gives investment opinions about companies to call-in-viewers. Below is the transcript of a portion of one of his shows that focused on employee benefits. Evaluate Wilson's reponses to the callers' questions, and identify the errors.

Caller 1	"Wilson, tell me about Xyloclick!"
Wilson	"The company is a fraud! It has a defined contribution plan for its employees and does not list the pension assets and liabilities on its books! Sell, sell, sell!"
Caller 2	"Wilson, tell me about Fling Media!"
Wilson	"You have to love this company. They are very conservative. They even accrue a liability for health insurance coverage relating to future retirees. Nobody does that! This company's real earnings are much higher than they are letting on. Buy, buy, buy!"
Caller 3	"Wilson, tell me about Big Foot Shoe!"
Wilson	"Well, it's true that peoples' feet are growing larger, so maybe this a good play. But, beware because the company is not accruing costs related to employee sick leave. They offer some lame excuse about not meeting all four criteria of an applicable accounting rule. Wrong, you only need to meet one of the criteria! Sell, sell, sell!"
Caller 4	"Wilson, tell me about Optic Sky!"
Wilson	"Buy! The company offers employees a defined benefit pension plan. The pension trust is loaded with loot, yet the company continues to show a pension liability on its books. It's a hidden asset."

Involved Problems

Following are selected transactions or events of Amazon Company relating to its first month of operation.

1-May	Amazon borrowed $100,000 via a note payable bearing interest at 1% per month. This note and all accrued interest is due at the end of July.
10-May	Purchased $25,000 of inventory, terms 2/10, n/30. The purchase was initially recorded at the net amount. The obligation was not paid during May.
17-May	The company adopted an employee health insurance plan. The total estimated cost is $100 per day. None of this cost was funded during May.
20-May	Sold goods for $80,000 cash. Amazon offers a warranty on the goods, and anticipates that total warranty cost will be 2% of sales.
25-May	Amazon was involved in an accident that resulted in damage to another person's property. Amazon expects to be held responsible for an estimated $10,000 in damages.

31-May   At month end, it was estimated that employees are owed for $13,000 in accrued wages. In addition, $400 was spent on warranty service work.

(a)   Prepare any initial journal entries necessary to record the preceding transactions or events.

(b)   Prepare month-end adjusting journal entries that are deemed appropriate related to the preceding transactions or events.

(c)   Prepare the current liability section of the company's balance sheet as of the end of the month. The only obligations are those related to the preceding transactions or events.

I-12.02   *Various notes payable transactions*

Following are selected borrowing transactions by Campus Housing Corporation.

1-Jun   Campus purchased new furniture in exchange for a $500,000 promissory note. The note was due in 6 months and bears interest at 8% per annum.

1-Jul   Borrowed cash of $90,000, giving a $100,000 one-year note. The interest is implicit in the difference between the cash borrowed and the note's $100,000 maturity value.

1-Oct   Campus was experiencing a temporary cash flow crunch. The company issued a $40,000 one-year note in settlement of an outstanding account payable. The note bears interest at 8% per annum. The agreement with the creditor was that Campus would repay the note as soon as possible, and the total interest would be allocated to each month based on the "rule of 78s."

31-Oct   Campus paid the note and accrued interest resulting from the October 1 transaction.

1-Nov   Borrowed $75,000 cash from a local bank by issuing a 2-year, 6% promissory note. The interest is to be calculated based on actual days, using a 365-day year assumption.

1-Dec   Campus paid the note and accrued interest resulting from the June 1 transaction.

(a)   Prepare journal entries necessary to record the above transactions.

(b)   Prepare year-end adjusting journal entries pertinent to the above borrowing transactions.

I-12.03   *Various issues relating to contingencies*

Camo Max manufactures camouflage apparel for paintball enthusiasts. In the normal course of business, the company encounters various situations giving rise to contingencies. Evaluate the following situations and prepare an explanation of the appropriate accounting considerations for each.

The company is subject to several lawsuits by plaintiffs. These claims assert that the camouflage is so effective that opposing paintballers come into too close range, and are therefore hurt by high-velocity, close-up shots. The company's attorney views the likelihood of any adverse judgment as highly remote. Further, the company generally has seen increased sales because of publicity associated with these claims.

The company manufactures a face shield that has been prone to crack. As a result, several serious injuries have been reported. The company is generally willing to settle each documented claim for $20,000. Currently, it is estimated that 45 such claims will be submitted and settled.

The company has issued a full product recall of the defective face shields and expects to spend $700,000 on issuing replacement shields. The new shields will not be distributed until the next fiscal year.

The company has been notified by a competitor that one of Camo Max's camouflage designs violates a copyright held by the competitor. The competitor is asking for a $250,000 paid-up license to the use the design. Camo Max disagrees, but believes that it is reasonably possible the competitor will file suit and win on a copyright infringement action.

Subsequent to year end (but before preparing financial statements), an employee was seriously injured by a fabric cutting machine. The company has agreed to a large financial settlement with the employee. This payment will eliminate any hope of profitability during the next several years.

| *Payroll records and entries* | *I-12.04* |

SFCC Corporation has 8 employees. Information about the October payroll follows:

SPREADSHEET TOOL:

Data sort routines

Name	Hours Worked	Pay Rate	Federal Income Tax Withheld
Breschi, K	95	$12 per hour	$200
Carballo, P	n/a	$3,000 per month	$850
Dangelo, J	180	$14 per hour	$625
Gaines, T	n/a	$4,500 per month	$1,100
Goseco, M	n/a	$10,100 per month	$3,575
Skolnick, J	180	$12 per hour	$480
Williams, R	172	$9 per hour	$140
Wong, O	195	$16 per hour	$800

Additional information is as follows:

SFCC is in a state without an income tax. Employees' federal income tax withholdings depend on various factors, and the amounts are as indicated in the above table.

No employees worked overtime, with the exception of Oscar Wong, who worked 15 hours of overtime. Overtime is paid at 150% of the normal hourly rate.

Assume that gross pay is subject to social security taxes at a 6.5% rate, on an annual base of $150,000. Assume that Medicare/Medicaid taxes are 1.5% of gross earnings. These taxes are matched by the employer. Only Marcia Goseco had earned more than $140,000 during the months leading up to October. Because of overtime and a bonus, she had earned $140,900 during that time period.

SFCC has 100% participation in a $10 per month employee charitable contribution program. These contributions are withheld from monthly pay.

SFCC pays for workers' compensation insurance at a 2% of gross pay rate. None of this cost is paid by the employee.

SFCC provides employees with a group health care plan; however, the cost is fully paid by employees. The rate is $250 per month, per employee.

SFCC's payroll is subject to federal (0.5%) and state (1.5%) unemployment taxes on each employee's gross pay, up to $8,000 per year. All employees had earned in excess of $8,000 in the months leading up to October, with the exception of Karen Breschi. Karen was first employed during the month of October.

SFCC contributes 5% of gross pay to an employee retirement program. Employees do not contribute to this plan.

(a)   Complete the payroll schedule on the website's accompanying blank worksheet.

(b)   Prepare journal entries for SFCC's payroll and the related payroll expenses.

I-12.05   *Team-based approach for retirement plans/other post-employment benefits*

Form a four-person team. Each team member should identify a public company and obtain its financial reports (available at www.sec.gov, or from the company website). If using the SEC website, look under the section for "search for company filings" and select the company's Form 10-K (annual report). Each member should locate the company disclosures relative to employee benefits and retirement plans. Make copies of the company's balance sheet and benefits/retirement plan related footnotes to share with your team mates.

Meet as a team and examine each company's data. Specifically, determine if each company has a defined contribution or defined benefit pension plan (or both). Also, which companies provide post-retirement benefits like health care coverage? What appears on the corporate balance sheet as an asset or liability related to such benefits? What is the magnitude of the costs and obligations related to the various plans and benefits? Are there any other interesting observations you can glean from the company disclosures? Do such costs and obligations bear on global competitiveness, and what are the potential implications? Summarize your conclusions on the worksheet template.

Chapter 13:
Long-Term Obligations

Goals:

Long-term notes and present value concepts.

The nature of bonds and related terminology.

Accounting for bonds payable, whether issued at par, a premium
    or discount.

Effective-interest amortization methods.

Bonds issued between interest dates, bond retirements, and fair
    value measurements.

Analysis, commitments, and leases.

Long-Term Notes

Prior chapters illustrate notes payable of short duration. However, borrowers may desire a longer term for a loan. It would be common to find two-, three-, five-year, and even longer term notes. These notes may evidence a "term loan," where "interest only" is paid during the period of borrowing and the balance of the note is due at maturity. To illustrate, assume that a $10,000, five-year, 8% term note, is issued on October 1, 20X3 :

10-01-X3	Cash	10,000	
	Note Payable		10,000
	To record note payable at 8% per annum; maturity date on 9-30-X8		

Interest on the note must be accrued each December 31, with payment following on September 30.

12-31-XX	Interest Expense	200	
	Interest Payable		200
	To record year-end interest accrual for 3 months ($10,000 X 8% X 3/12)		
09-30-XX	Interest Expense	600	
	Interest Payable	200	
	Cash		800
	To record the September interest payment ($10,000 X 8% = $800, of which $200 was previously accrued at the end of the prior year)		

The following entry is needed at maturity on September 30, 20X8:

09-30-X8	Interest Expense		600	
	Interest Payable		200	
	Note Payable		10,000	
	Cash			10,800
	To record final interest payment and balance of note at maturity			

OTHER TYPES OF NOTES

With the term note illustration, it is easy to calculate interest of $800 per year, and observe the $10,000 balance due at maturity. Other loans may require level payments over their terms, so that the interest and principal are fully paid by the end of the loan. This type of arrangement is commonly used for real estate financing. The payment of the note is usually secured by the property, allowing the lender to take possession for nonpayment. Real estate notes thus secured are called "mortgage notes." How are payments calculated? The first step is to learn about future value and present value calculations.

FUTURE VALUE

Let's start by thinking about how invested money can grow with interest. What will be the **future value** of an investment? If $1 is invested for one year, at 10% interest per year, it will grow to $1.10. This is calculated by multiplying the $1 by 10% ($1 X 10% = $0.10) and adding this $0.10 to the original dollar.

And, if the resulting $1.10 is invested for another year at 10%, it will grow to $1.21. That is, $1.10 X 10% = $0.11, which is added to the $1.10 value from the end of the first year. This process will continue year after year. The annual interest each year is larger than the year before because of "compounding."

Compounding simply means that the investment is growing with accumulated interest and earning interest on previously accrued interest. The contrast to **compound interest** is **simple interest.** Simple interest does not provide for compounding, such that $1 invested for two years at 10% would only grow to $1.20.

The preceding observations lead to this compound interest calculation:

$$(1+i)^n$$

Where "i" is the interest rate per period and "n" is the number of periods

This calculation reveals how much an investment of $1 will grow to after "n" periods. If $1 was invested for 5 years at 6%, then it would grow to about $1.34 [$(1.06)^5 = 1.33823$]. Of course, if $1,000 was invested for 5 years at 6%, it would grow to $1,338.23; this is determined by multiplying the derived factor times the amount invested at the beginning of the 5-year period. This calculation is aptly termed the "future value of a lump sum amount."

Future value amounts can always be calculated using the preceding formulation. However, spreadsheet software and business calculators frequently include built-in routines to return appropriate values. Another useful tool is a future value table (see principlesofaccounting.com supplements). These tables include values corresponding to various rates and periods. Use a table, spreadsheet, or business calculator to verify the 1.33823 factor for a 5-period, 6% investment. Likewise, determine that $5,000, invested for 10 years, at 4%, will grow to $7,401.20 ($5,000 X 1.48024).

Present value is the opposite of future value, as it reveals how much a dollar to be received in the future is worth today. The math is simply the reciprocal of future value calculations:

$$\frac{1}{(1+i)^n}$$

Where "i" is the interest rate per period and "n" is the number of periods

For example, $1,000 to be received in 5 years, when the interest rate is 7%, is presently worth $712.99 [$1,000 X (1/(1.07)^5)]. Stated differently, if $712.99 is invested today at 7%, it will grow to $1,000 in 5 years. Present value amounts are also determinable from spreadsheets, calculators, or tables. Verify that the present value of $50,000 to be received in 8 years at 8% is $27,013.50 ($50,000 X .54027).

Streams of level payments (i.e., the same amount each period) occurring on regular intervals are termed **annuities**. For example, if one invests $1 *at the beginning* of each year at 5% per annum, after 5 years it would accumulate to $5.80. This can be painstakingly calculated by summing the future value amount associated with each individual payment, as shown in the following calculations.

Investment Period	Future Value Factor	Payment	Value of Payment at End of 5th Year
Year 1 (amount will be invested 5 years)	1.27628	$1	$1.27628
Year 2 (amount will be invested 4 years)	1.21551	$1	1.21551
Year 3 (amount will be invested 3 years)	1.15763	$1	1.15763
Year 4 (amount will be invested 2 years)	1.10250	$1	1.10250
Year 5 (amount will be invested 1 year)	1.05000	$1	1.05000
			$5.80192

But, it is much easier to use spreadsheets, calculators, or annuity future value tables. The annuity table is simply the summation of individual factors. Verify the "5.80" factor from the 5% row, 5-year column of a table. These calculations are useful in financial planning. For example, one may wish to have a target amount accumulated by a certain age, such as with a retirement account. These factors help calculate the amount that must be set aside each period to reach the goal.

Conversely, one may be interested in the present value of an annuity which reveals the current worth of a level stream of payments to be received *at the end* of each period. Use a table, calculator, or spreadsheet to find the present value of $1,000 to be received at the end of each year for 5 years, if the interest rate is 8% per year. The 5-year column, 8% row of the appropriate table shows a factor of 3.99271, indicating that the present value of the annuity is $3,992.71.

How does one compute the payment on a typical loan that involves level periodic payments, with the final payment satisfying the remaining balance due? The answer to this question is found in the present value of annuity calculations. Remember that an annuity involves a stream of level payments, just like many loans. The payments on a loan are a series of level payments that cover both the principal and interest. The present value of those payments is the amount borrowed, in essence "discounting" out the interest component. This concept may still be a bit abstract, but can be further clarified mathematically with some equations:

Present Value of Annuity = Payments X Annuity Present Value Factor

A loan that is paid off with a series of equal payments is also an annuity, therefore:

Loan Amount = Payments X Annuity Present Value Factor

Thus, to determine the annual payment to satisfy a $100,000, 5-year loan at 6% per annum:

$100,000 = Payment X 4.21236 (from table)

$$\text{Payment} = \frac{\$100,000}{4.21236} = \$23,739.64$$

The five payments of $23,739.64 will exactly pay off the $100,000 loan plus all interest at a 6% annual rate. Simply stated, the payments on a loan are just the loan amount divided by the appropriate present value factor. To fully prove this point, look at the following typical loan amortization table. This table shows how each payment is applied to first satisfy the accumulated interest for the period, and then reduce the principal. Note that the final payment will extinguish any remaining principal.

Yr	Beginning of Year Loan Balance	Interest on Beginning Balance	Amount of Payment	Principal Reduction (payment minus interest)	End of Year Loan Balance
1	$100,000.00	$6,000.00 ($100,000.00 X 6%)	$23,739.64	$17,739.64 ($23,739.64 - $6,000.00)	$82,260.36 ($100,000.00 - $17,739.64)
2	$82,260.36	$4,935.62 ($82,260.36 X 6%)	$23,739.64	$18,804.02 ($23,739.64 - $4,935.62)	$63,456.34 ($82,260.36 - $18,804.02)
3	$63,456.34	$3,807.38 ($63,456.34 X 6%)	$23,739.64	$19,932.26 ($23,739.64 - $3,807.38)	$43,524.08 ($63,456.34 - $19,932.26)
4	$43,524.08	$2,611.44 ($43,524.08 X 6%)	$23,739.64	$21,128.20 ($23,739.64 - $2,611.44)	$22,395.89 ($43,524.38 - $21,128.20)
5	$22,395.89	$1,343.75 ($22,395.89 X 6%)	$23,739.64	$22,395.89 ($23,739.64 - $1,343.75)	$0 ($22,395.89 - $22,395.89)

The journal entries associated with the preceding loan would flow as follows:

01-01-X1	Cash	100,000.00	
	Note Payable		100,000.00
	To record note payable		
12-31-X1	Interest Expense	6,000.00	
	Note Payable	17,739.64	
	Cash		23,739.64
	To record note payment		
12-31-X2	Interest Expense	4,935.62	
	Note Payable	18,804.02	
	Cash		23,739.64
	To record note payment		
12-31-X3	Interest Expense	3,807.38	
	Note Payable	19,932.26	
	Cash		23,739.64
	To record note payment		
12-31-X4	Interest Expense	2,611.44	
	Note Payable	21,128.20	
	Cash		23,739.64
	To record note payment		
12-31-X5	Interest Expense	1,343.75	
	Note Payable	22,395.89	
	Cash		23,739.64
	To record note payment		

A FEW FINAL COMMENTS ON FUTURE AND PRESENT VALUE

Note that some scenarios may involve payments at the beginning of each period, while other scenarios might require end-of-period payments. Later chapters of this book include additional future and present value calculations for alternatively timed payment streams (e.g., present value of an annuity with payments at the beginning of each period).

Also note that payments may occur on other than an annual basis. For example, a $10,000, 8% per annum loan may involve quarterly payments over two years. The quarterly payment would be $1,365.10 ($10,000/7.32548). The 7.32548 present value factor is reflective of 8 periods (4 quarters per year for 2 years) and 2% interest per period (8% per annum divided by 4 quarters per year). This type of modification applies to annuities and lump-sum amounts. For example, the present value of $1 invested for 5 years at 10% compounded semiannually can be determined by referring to the 5% row, 10-period factor.

As previously noted, spreadsheet software normally includes functions to help with fundamental present value, future value, and payment calculations. Following is a screen shot of one such routine:

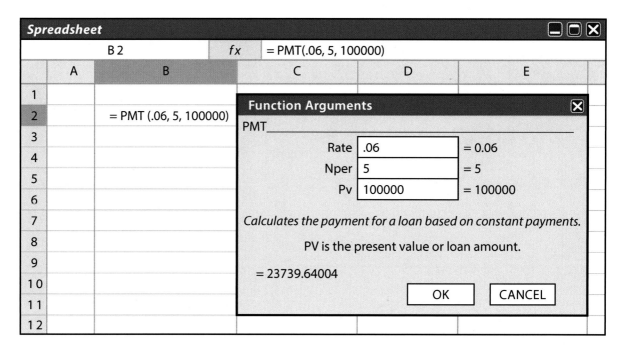

Bonds Payable

Bonds payable result when a borrower splits a large loan into many small units. Each of these units (or bonds) is essentially a note payable. Investors will buy these bonds, effectively making a loan to the issuing company. Bonds were introduced, from an investor's perspective, in Chapter 9.

The terms of a bond issue are specified in a bond indenture. In addition to making representations about the interest payments and life of the bond, the indenture may also address questions such as:

- Are the bonds **secured** by specific assets pledged as collateral to insure payment? If not, the bonds are said to be **debenture** bonds, meaning they do not have specific collateral but are only as good as the general faith and credit of the issuer.

- What is the preference in liquidation in the event of failure? Agreements may provide that some bonds are paid before others.

- To whom and when is interest paid? In the past, some bonds were **coupon bonds**, and those bonds literally had detachable interest coupons that could be stripped off and cashed in on specific dates. One reason for coupon bonds was to ease the record keeping burden on bond issuers. Companies merely issued coupons that were turned in for redemption.

  However, in recent times, most bonds are registered to an owner. Computerized information systems now facilitate tracking bond owners, and interest payments are commonly transmitted electronically to the registered owner. **Registered bonds** are in contrast to *bearer bonds*, where the holder of the physical bond instrument is deemed to be the owner (bearer bonds are rare in today's economy).

- Must the company maintain a required sinking fund? A **sinking fund bond** may sound bad, but it is actually not. In the context of bonds, a sinking fund is a required account into which monies are periodically transferred to insure that funds will be available at maturity to satisfy the bond obligation.

- Some companies will issue **serial bonds**. Rather than the entire issue maturing at once, portions of the serial issue will mature on select dates spread over time.

- Can the bond be converted into stock? **Convertible bonds** enable the holder to exchange the bond for a predefined number of shares of corporate stock. The holder may plan to be paid the interest plus face amount of the bond, but if the company's stock explodes upward in value, the holder may benefit by trading the bonds for appreciated stock.

Why would a company issue convertibles? First, investors may prefer these securities and are usually willing to accept lower interest rates than must be paid on bonds that are not convertible. Another factor is that the company may contemplate its stock going up; by initially borrowing money and later exchanging the debt for stock, the company may actually get more money for its stock than it would have had it issued the stock on the earlier date.

- Is the company able to call the debt? **Callable bonds** provide a company with the option of buying back the debt at a prearranged price before its scheduled maturity. If interest rates go down, the company may not want to be saddled with the higher cost obligations and can escape the obligation by calling the debt.

Sometimes, bonds cannot be called. For example, suppose a company is in financial distress and issues high interest rate debt (known as **junk bonds**) to investors who are willing to take a chance to bail out the company. If the company is able to manage a turn-around, the investors who took the risk and bought the bonds don't want to have their "high yield" stripped away with an early payoff before scheduled maturity.

- Bonds that cannot be paid off earlier are sometimes called **nonredeemable**. Be careful not to confuse nonredeemable with nonrefundable. **Nonrefundable bonds** can be paid off early, so long as the payoff money is generated from business operations rather than an alternative borrowing arrangement. Some specialized securities may be legally structured as equity instruments, but nonetheless possess mandatory redemption features. These attributes make the securities more like long-term debt, and the accounting should mirror this economic substance.

Note that convertible bonds will almost always be callable, enabling the company to force a bond holder to either cash out or convert. The company will reserve this call privilege because they will want to stop paying interest (by forcing the holder out of the debt) once the stock has gone up enough to know that a conversion is inevitable.

Bonds are potentially complex financial instruments. Who enforces all of the requirements for a company's bond issue? Within the bond indenture agreement should be a specified bond trustee. This trustee may be an investment company, law firm, or other independent party. The trustee is to monitor compliance with the terms of the agreement and has a fiduciary duty to intervene to protect the investor group if the company runs afoul of its covenants.

Accounting for Bonds Payable

A bond payable is just a promise to pay a series of payments over time (the interest component) and a fixed amount at maturity (the face amount). Thus, it is a blend of an annuity (the interest) and lump sum payment (the face). To determine the amount an investor will pay for a bond, therefore, requires present value computations to determine the current worth of the future payments. Assume that Schultz Company issues 5-year, 8% bonds. Bonds frequently have a $1,000 face value and pay interest every six months. Using these assumptions, consider the following three alternative scenarios:

PAR SCENARIO	MARKET RATE OF INTEREST IS 8%

If 8% is the market rate of interest for companies like Schultz (i.e., companies having the same perceived integrity and risk) at the time when Schultz issues its 8% bonds, then Schultz's bonds should sell at face value (also known as "par" or "100"). That is to say, investors will pay $1,000 for a bond and get back $40 every six months ($80 per year, or 8% of $1,000). At maturity they will also get their $1,000 investment back. Thus, the return on the investment will equate to 8%.

PREMIUM SCENARIO	MARKET RATE OF INTEREST IS 6%

If the market rate is only 6%, then the Schultz bonds are attractive because of their higher stated 8% interest rate. This higher rate will induce investors to pay a premium for the Schultz bonds. But, how much more will they pay? The answer to this question is that they will bid up the price to the point that the *effective yield* (in contrast to the stated rate of interest) drops to only equal the going market rate of 6%. Thus, investors will pay more than $1,000 to gain access to the $40 interest payments every six months and the $1,000 payment at maturity. The exact amount they will pay is determined by discounting (i.e., calculating the present value) the stream of payments at the market rate of interest. This calculation is demonstrated in the following table.

DISCOUNT SCENARIO	MARKET RATE OF INTEREST IS 10%

If the market rate is 10% when the 8% Schultz bonds are issued, then no one would want the 8% bonds unless they can be bought at a discount. How much discount would it take to get one to buy the bonds? The discount would have to be large enough so that the *effective yield* on the initial investment would be pushed up to 10%. That is to say, the price for the bonds would be low enough so that the $40 semiannual payment and the $1,000 at maturity would yield the 10% market rate of return. The exact amount is again determined by calculating the present value of the stream of payments at the market rate of interest.

The following table shows calculations of the price of the bond under different scenarios:

CASH FLOW FACTS 8% STATED RATE		PAR SCENARIO MARKET RATE OF 8%		PREMIUM SCENARIO MARKET RATE OF 6%		DISCOUNT SCENARIO MARKET RATE OF 10%	
Payment	Amount	Present Value Factors at 4%, 10 Periods	Present Value (amount X factor)	Present Value Factors at 3%, 10 Periods	Present Value (amount X factor)	Present Value Factors at 5%, 10 Periods	Present Value (amount X factor)
Periodic Interest	$40.00	8.11090	$324.44	8.53020	$341.21	7.72173	$308.87
Maturity Value	$1,000.00	0.67556	$675.56	0.74409	$744.09	0.61391	$613.91
			$1,000.00		$1,085.30		$922.78

To further explain, the interest amount on the $1,000, 8% bond is $40 every six months. Because the bonds have a 5-year life, there are 10 interest payments (or periods). The periodic interest is an annuity with a 10-period duration, while the maturity value is a lump-sum payment at the end of the tenth period. The 8% market rate of interest equates to a semiannual rate of 4%, the 6% market rate scenario equates to a 3% semiannual rate, and the 10% rate is 5% per semiannual period.

The present value factors are taken from the present value tables (annuity and lump-sum, respectively). Take time to verify the factors by reference to the appropriate tables, spreadsheet, or calculator routine. The present value factors are multiplied by the payment amounts, and the sum of the present value of the components would equal the price of the bond under each of the three scenarios.

Note that the 8% market rate assumption produced a bond priced at $1,000, the 6% assumption produced a bond priced at $1,085.30 (which includes an $85.30 premium), and the 10% assumption produced a bond priced at $922.78 (which includes a $77.22 discount).

These calculations are not only correct theoretically, but are very accurate financial tools. However, one point is noteworthy. Bond pricing is frequently to the nearest 1/32nd. That is, a bond might trade at 103.08. One could easily misinterpret this price as $1,030.80. But, it actually means 103 and 8/32. In dollars, this would amount to $1,032.50 ($1,000 X 103.25). Having learned the financial mechanics of bonds, it is now time to examine the correct accounting.

If Schultz issued 100 of its 5-year, 8% bonds at par, the following entries would be required :

BONDS ISSUED AT PAR

01-01-X1	Cash	100,000	
	Bonds Payable		100,000
	To record issuance of 100, 8%, 5-year bonds at par (100 X $1,000 each)		
periodically	Interest Expense	4,000	
	Cash		4,000
	To record interest payment (this entry occurs on every interest payment date at 6 month intervals -- $100,000 X 8% X 6/12)		
12-31-X5	Bonds Payable	100,000	
	Cash		100,000
	To record payment of face value at maturity		

BONDS ISSUED AT A PREMIUM

One simple way to understand bonds issued at a premium is to view the accounting relative to counting money! If Schultz issues 100 of the 8%, 5-year bonds when the market rate of interest is only 6%, then the cash received is $108,530 (see the previous calculations). Schultz will have to repay a total of $140,000 ($4,000 every 6 months for 5 years, plus $100,000 at maturity).

Thus, Schultz will repay $31,470 more than was borrowed ($140,000 - $108,530). This $31,470 must be expensed over the life of the bond; uniformly spreading the $31,470 over 10 six-month periods produces periodic *interest expense* of $3,147 (not to be confused with the actual periodic *cash payment* of $4,000).

Another way to illustrate this problem is to note that total borrowing cost is reduced by the $8,530 premium, since less is to be repaid at maturity than was borrowed up front. Therefore, the $4,000 periodic *interest payment* is reduced by $853 of premium amortization each period ($8,530 premium amortized on a straight-line basis over the 10 periods), also producing the periodic *interest expense* of $3,147 ($4,000 - $853).

This topic is inherently confusing, and the journal entries are actually clarifying. Notice that the premium on bonds payable is carried in a separate account (unlike accounting for investments in bonds covered in a prior chapter, where the premium was simply included with the Investment in Bonds account).

01-01-X1	Cash		108,530	
	Premium on Bonds Payable			8,530
	Bonds Payable			100,000
	To record issue of 8%, 5-year bonds at premium			
periodically	Interest Expense		3,147	
	Premium on Bonds Payable		853	
	Cash			4,000
	To record interest payment (this entry occurs on every interest payment date at 6 month intervals) and amortization of premium			
12-31-X5	Bonds Payable		100,000	
	Cash			100,000
	To record payment of face value at maturity			

Study the following illustration, and observe that the Premium on Bonds Payable is established at $8,530, then reduced by $853 every interest date, bringing the final balance to zero at maturity.

Period Ending	Bonds Payable	Unamortized Premium	Net Book Value (Bonds Payable plus Unamortized Premium)	Interest Expense (Cash Paid less Premium Amortization)
	$100,000	$8,530	$108,530	
06-30-X1	100,000	7,677	107,677	$3,147
12-31-X1	100,000	6,824	106,824	3,147
06-30-X2	100,000	5,971	105,971	3,147
12-31-X2	100,000	5,118	105,118	3,147
06-30-X3	100,000	4,265	104,265	3,147
12-31-X3	100,000	3,412	103,412	3,147
06-30-X4	100,000	2,559	102,559	3,147
12-31-X4	100,000	1,706	101,706	3,147
06-30-X5	100,000	853	100,853	3,147
12-31-X5	100,000	0	100,000	3,147

On any given financial statement date, Bonds Payable is reported on the balance sheet as a liability, along with the unamortized Premium balance (known as an "adjunct" account). To illustrate, the balance sheet disclosures would appear as follows on December 31, 20X3 and 20X4:

Long-term Liabilities (20X3)

Bonds payable	$100,000	
Plus: Unamortized premium on bonds payable	3,412	$103,412

Long-term Liabilities (20X4)

Bonds payable	$100,000	
Plus: Unamortized premium on bonds payable	1,706	$101,706

The income statement for all of 20X3 would include $6,294 of interest expense ($3,147 X 2). This method of accounting for bonds is known as the straight-line amortization method, as interest expense is recognized uniformly over the life of the bond. Although simple, it does have one conceptual shortcoming. Notice that interest expense is the same each year, even though the net book value of the bond (bond plus remaining premium) is declining each year due to amortization.

As a result, interest expense each year is not exactly equal to the effective rate of interest (6%) that was implicit in the pricing of the bonds. For 20X1, interest expense can be seen to be roughly 5.8% of the bond liability ($6,294 expense divided by beginning of year liability of $108,530). For 20X4, interest expense is roughly 6.1% ($6,294 expense divided by beginning of year liability of $103,412).

Accountants have devised a more precise approach to account for bond issues called the effective-interest method. Be aware that the more theoretically correct effective-interest method is actually the required method, except in those cases where the straight-line results do not differ materially. Effective-interest techniques are introduced in a following section of this chapter.

If Schultz issues 100 of the 8%, 5-year bonds for $92,278 (when the market rate of interest is 10%), Schultz will still have to repay a total of $140,000 ($4,000 every 6 months for 5 years, plus $100,000 at maturity). Thus, Schultz will repay $47,722 ($140,000 - $92,278) more than was borrowed. Spreading the $47,722 over 10 six-month periods produces periodic *interest expense* of $4,772.20 (not to be confused with the periodic *cash payment* of $4,000).

BONDS ISSUED AT A DISCOUNT

Another way to consider this problem is to note that the total borrowing cost is increased by the $7,722 discount, since more is to be repaid at maturity than was borrowed initially. Therefore, the $4,000 periodic *interest payment* is increased by $772.20 of discount amortization each period ($7,722 discount amortized on a straight-line basis over the 10 periods), producing periodic *interest expense* that totals $4,772.20.

Like bond premiums, discounts are also carried in a separate account. The following entry is needed to record the initial bond issuance:

01-01-X1	Cash	92,278	
	Discount on Bonds Payable	7,722	
	Bonds Payable		100,000
	To record issue of 8%, 5-year bonds at discount		

The following entries reflect periodic interest and repayment at maturity:

periodically	Interest Expense	4,772	
	Discount on Bonds Payable		772
	Cash		4,000
	To record interest payment (this entry occurs on every interest payment date at 6 month intervals) and amortization of discount		
12-31-X5	Bonds Payable	100,000	
	Cash		100,000
	To record payment of face value at maturity		

Carefully study this illustration, and observe that the Discount on Bonds Payable is established at $7,722, then reduced by $772.20 on every interest date, bringing the final balance to zero at maturity. On any given financial statement date, Bonds Payable is reported on the balance sheet as a liability, along with the unamortized Discount that is subtracted (known as a "contra" account). The illustration below shows the balance sheet disclosure as of June 30, 20X3. Note that the unamortized discount on this date is determined by calculations revealed in the table that follows:

Long-term Liabilities

Bonds payable	$100,000	
Less: Unamortized discount on bonds payable	(3,861)	$ 96,139

Period Ending	Bonds Payable	Unamortized Discount	Net Book Value (Bonds Payable less Unamortized Discount)	Interest Expense (Cash Paid plus Discount Amortization)
	$100,000.00	$7,722.00	$92,278.00	
06-30-X1	100,000.00	6,949.80	93,050.20	$4,772.20
12-31-X1	100,000.00	6,177.60	93,822.40	4,772.20
06-30-X2	100,000.00	5,405.40	94,594.60	4,772.20
12-31-X2	100,000.00	4,633.20	95,366.80	4,772.20
06-30-X3	100,000.00	3,861.00	96,139.00	4,772.20
12-31-X3	100,000.00	3,088.80	96,911.20	4,772.20
06-30-X4	100,000.00	2,316.60	97,683.40	4,772.20
12-31-X4	100,000.00	1,544.40	98,455.60	4,772.20
06-30-X5	100,000.00	772.20	99,227.80	4,772.20
12-31-X5	100,000.00	0	100,000.00	4,772.20

Each yearly income statement would include $9,544.40 of interest expense ($4,772.20 X 2). The straight-line approach suffers from the same limitations discussed earlier, and is acceptable only if the results are not materially different from those resulting with the effective-interest technique.

Effective-Interest Amortization Methods

The theoretically preferable approach to recording amortization is the **effective-interest method**. Interest expense is a constant *percentage* of the bond's carrying value, rather than an equal dollar amount each year. The theoretical merit rests on the fact that the interest calculation aligns with the basis on which the bond was priced.

Interest expense is calculated as the effective-interest rate times the bond's carrying value for each period. The amount of amortization is the difference between the cash paid for interest and the calculated amount of bond interest expense.

Recall that when Schultz issued its bonds to yield 6%, it received $108,530. Thus, effective interest for the first six months is $108,530 X 6% X 6/12 = $3,255.90. Of this amount, $4,000 is paid in cash and $744.10 ($4,000 - $3,255.90) is premium amortization. The premium amortization reduces the net book value of the debt to $107,785.90 ($108,530 - $744.10). This new balance would then be used to calculate the effective interest for the next period. This process would be repeated each period, as shown in the following table:

PREMIUM EXAMPLE

Period Ending	Beginning of Period Net Book Value of Bonds Payable	Interest Expense (Net Book Value X 6% X 6/12)	Amount of Payment	Premium Amortization (payment minus expense)	End of Period Net Book Value (beginning balance less amortization)
06-30-X1	$108,530.00	$3,255.90	$4,000.00	$744.10	$107,785.90
12-31-X1	107,785.90	3,233.58	4,000.00	766.42	107,019.48
06-30-X2	107,019.48	3,210.58	4,000.00	789.42	106,230.06
12-31-X2	106,230.06	3,186.90	4,000.00	813.10	105,416.96
06-30-X3	105,416.96	3,162.51	4,000.00	837.49	104,579.47
12-31-X3	104,579.47	3,137.38	4,000.00	862.62	103,716.86
06-30-X4	103,716.86	3,111.51	4,000.00	888.49	102,828.36
12-31-X4	102,828.36	3,084.85	4,000.00	915.15	101,913.21
06-30-X5	101,913.21	3,057.40	4,000.00	942.60	100,970.61
12-31-X5	100,970.61	3,029.39	4,000.00	970.61	100,000.00

The initial journal entry to record the issuance of the bonds, and the final journal entry to record repayment at maturity would be identical to those demonstrated for the straight-line method. However, each journal entry to record the periodic interest expense recognition would vary and can be determined by reference to the preceding amortization table.

The following entry would record interest on June 30, 20X3:

06-30-X3	Interest Expense	3,162.51	
	Premium on Bonds Payable	837.49	
	Cash		4,000.00
	To record interest payment and amortization		

The following balance sheet disclosure would be appropriate as of June 30, 20X3:

Long-term Liabilities

Bonds payable	$100,000	
Plus: Unamortized premium on bonds payable	4,579	$104,579

DISCOUNT EXAMPLE

Recall that when Schultz issued its bonds to yield 10%, it received only $92,278. Thus, effective interest for the first six months is $92,278 X 10% X 6/12 = $4,613.90. Of this amount, $4,000 is paid in cash, and $613.90 is discount amortization. The discount amortization increases the net book value of the debt to $92,891.90 ($92,278.00 + $613.90). This new balance would then be used to calculate the effective interest for the next period. This process would repeat each period as shown:

Period Ending	Beginning of Period Net Book Value of Bonds Payable	Interest Expense (Net Book Value X 10% X 6/12)	Amount of Payment	Discount Amortization (expense minus payment)	End of Period Net Book Value (beginning balance plus amortization)
06-30-X1	$92,278.00	$4,613.90	$4,000.00	$613.90	$92,891.90
12-31-X1	92,891.90	4,644.60	4,000.00	644.60	93,536.50
06-30-X2	93,536.50	4,676.82	4,000.00	676.82	94,213.32
12-31-X2	94,213.32	4,710.67	4,000.00	710.67	94,923.99
06-30-X3	94,923.99	4,746.20	4,000.00	746.20	95,670.19
12-31-X3	95,670.19	4,783.51	4,000.00	783.51	96,453.70
06-30-X4	96,453.70	4,822.68	4,000.00	822.68	97,276.38
12-31-X4	97,276.38	4,863.82	4,000.00	863.82	98,140.20
06-30-X5	98,140.20	4,907.01	4,000.00	907.01	99,047.21
12-31-X5	99,047.21	4,952.79	4,000.00	952.79	100,000.00

Each journal entry to record the periodic interest expense recognition would vary, and can be determined by reference to the preceding amortization table. For instance, the following entry would record interest on June 30, 20X3, and result in the balance sheet disclosure below:

06-30-X3	Interest Expense	4,746.20	
	Discount on Bonds Payable		746.20
	Cash		4,000.00
	To record interest payment and amortization		

Long-term Liabilities

Bonds payable	$100,000	
Less: Unamortized discount on bonds payable	(4,330)	$ 95,670

Bonds Issued Between Interest Dates, Bond Retirements, and Fair Value

Bonds issued between interest dates are best understood in the context of a specific example. Suppose Thompson Corporation proposed to issue $100,000 of 12% bonds, dated April 1, 20X1. However, despite the April 1 date, the actual issuance was slightly delayed, and the bonds were not sold until June 1. Nevertheless, the covenant pertaining to the bonds specifies that the first 6-month interest payment date will occur on September 30 in the amount of $6,000 ($100,000 X 12% X 6/12). In effect, interest for April and May has already accrued at the time the bonds are actually issued ($100,000 X 12% X 2/12 = $2,000). To be fair, Thompson will collect $2,000 from the purchasers of the bonds at the time of issue, and then return it within the $6,000 payment on September 30. This effectively causes the net difference of $4,000 to represent interest expense for June, July, August, and September ($100,000 X 12% X 4/12). The resulting journal entries are:

06-01-X1	Cash	102,000	
	Interest Payable		2,000
	Bonds Payable		100,000
	To record issuance of 100, 12% bonds		
09-30-X1	Interest Expense	4,000	
	Interest Payable	2,000	
	Cash		6,000
	To record interest payment (includes return of accrued interest from June 1)		

Notice that interest was paid in full through September 30. Therefore, the December 31 year-end entry must reflect the accrual of interest for October through December:

YEAR-END INTEREST ACCRUALS

12-31-X1	Interest Expense	3,000	
	Interest Payable		3,000
	To record accrued interest at year end for three months ($100,000 X 12% X 3/12)		

When the next interest payment date arrives on March 31, the actual interest payment will cover the previously accrued interest, and additional amounts pertaining to January, February, and March:

03-31-X2	Interest Expense	3,000	
	Interest Payable	3,000	
	Cash		6,000
	To record interest payment (includes accrued interest payable from prior year)		

If these bonds had been issued at other than par, end-of-period entries would also include adjustments of interest expense for the amortization of premiums or discounts relating to elapsed periods.

BONDS RETIRED BEFORE SCHEDULED MATURITY

Early retirements of debt may occur because a company has generated sufficient cash reserves from operations, and the company wants to stop paying interest on outstanding debt. Or, interest rates may have changed, and the company wants to take advantage of more favorable borrowing opportunities by "refinancing."

Whether the debt is being retired or refinanced in some other way, accounting rules dictate that the extinguished obligation be removed from the books. The difference between the old debt's net carrying value and the amounts used for the payoff should be recognized as a gain or loss.

For instance, assume that Cabano Corporation is retiring $200,000 face value of its 6% bonds payable on June 30, 20X5. The last semiannual interest payment occurred on April 30. The unamortized discount on the bonds at April 30, 20X5, was $6,000, and there was a 5-year remaining life on the bonds as of that date. Further, Cabano is paying $210,000, plus accrued interest to date ($2,000), to retire the bonds; this "early call" price was stipulated in the original bond covenant. The first step to account for this bond retirement is to bring the accounting for interest up to date:

06-30-X5	Interest Expense	2,200	
	Discount on Bonds Payable		200
	Interest Payable		2,000
	To record interest accrual and amortization of discount ($200,000 X 6% X 2/12 months = $2,000; $6,000 discount X 2/60 months = $200)		

Then, the actual bond retirement can be recorded, with the difference between the up-to-date carrying value and the funds utilized being recorded as a loss (debit) or gain (credit). Notice that Cabano's loss relates to the fact that it took more cash to pay off the debt than was the debt's carrying value of $194,200 ($200,000 minus $5,800).

06-30-X5	Bonds Payable	200,000	
	Interest Payable	2,000	
	Loss on Bond Retirement	15,800	
	Discount on Bonds Payable		5,800
	Cash		212,000
	To record retirement of debt [loss = $210,000 - ($200,000 - $5,800) = $15,800]		

THE FAIR VALUE OPTION

Be aware that bonds can change in value. Remember that the value of a bond is a function of the bond's stated rate of interest in relation to the going market rate of interest. If market interest rates rise, look for a market value decline (reflecting a lower present value based on the higher discount rate) and vice versa. Companies are permitted, but not required, to recognize changes in value of such liabilities. Entities that opt for this approach are to report unrealized gains and losses in earnings at each reporting date, and the balance sheet will be revised to reflect the fair value of the obligation.

Specific rules dictate the process and judgment for determining fair value. If a company's debt is traded in a public market, the valuation would be based on its observable price ("Level 1"). If the debt does not have a clearly determinable market, pricing would be tied to similar securities ("Level 2"). Management may develop their own pricing models in the rare case where the value is not otherwise observable ("Level 3").

Careful analysis is essential to judge an entity's financial health. One form of analysis is ratio analysis where certain key metrics are evaluated against one another. The "debt to total assets" ratio shows the percentage of total capitalization that is provided by the creditors of a business:

$$\textbf{Debt to Total Assets Ratio} = \frac{\textbf{Total Debt}}{\textbf{Total Assets}}$$

A related ratio is "debt to equity" that compares total debt to total equity:

$$\textbf{Debt to Equity Ratio} = \frac{\textbf{Total Debt}}{\textbf{Total Equity}}$$

The debt to asset and debt to equity ratios are carefully monitored by investors, creditors, and analysts. The ratios are often seen as signs of financial strength when "small," or signs of vulnerability when "large." Of course, small and large are relative terms. Some industries, like the utilities, are inherently dependent on debt financing but may, nevertheless, be very healthy. On the other hand, some high-tech companies may have little or no debt but be seen as vulnerable due to their intangible assets with potentially fleeting value. In short, one must be careful to correctly interpret a company's debt-related ratios. One must also be careful to recognize the signals and trends that may be revealed by careful monitoring of these ratios.

Another ratio, the "times interest earned ratio," demonstrates how many times the income of a company is capable of covering its unavoidable interest obligation.

$$\textbf{Times Interest Earned Ratio} = \frac{\textbf{Income Before Income Taxes and Interest}}{\textbf{Interest Charges}}$$

If this number is relatively small, it may signal that the company is on the verge of not generating sufficient operating results to cover its mandatory interest obligation. While ratio analysis is an important part of evaluating a company's financial health, one should be careful to not place undue reliance on any single evaluative measure.

CONTRACTS

A company may enter into a variety of long-term agreements. For example, a company may agree to buy a certain quantity of supplies from another company, agree to make periodic payments under a lease, or agree to deliver products at fixed prices in the future. There is effectively no limit or boundary on the nature of these **commitments** and agreements. Oftentimes, such situations do not result in a presently recorded obligation, but may give rise to an obligation in the future.

This introduces a myriad of accounting issues, and a few generalizations are in order. First, footnote disclosures are generally required for the aggregate amount of committed payments that must be made in the future (with a year-by-year breakdown). Second, changes in the value of such commitments may require loss recognition when a company finds itself locked into a future transaction that will have negative economic effects. These observations should make it clear that an evaluation of a company should not be limited to just the numbers on the balance sheet.

FINANCING LEASES

Chapter 10 introduced the idea of a "financing lease." Such transactions enable the lessee to acquire needed productive assets, not by outright purchase, but by leasing. The economic substance of financing leases, in sharp contrast to their legal form, is such that the lessee effectively acquires an asset right. Further, the accompanying obligation for lease payments is akin to a note payable. That is, the lessee is under contract to make a stream of payments over time. Accounting rules attempt to track economic substance ahead of legal form. When an asset is acquired under a financing lease, the initial recording is to establish both the asset and related obligation on the lessee's balance sheet.

Assume that equipment with a five-year life is leased on January 1, 20X1, and the lease agreement provides for five end-of-year lease payments of $23,739.64 each. At the time the lease was initiated, the lessee's incremental borrowing rate (the interest rate the lessee would have incurred on similar debt financing) is assumed to be 6%. The accountant would discount the stream of payments using the 6% interest rate and find that the present value of the fixed noncancelable lease payments is $100,000. Therefore, the following entry would be necessary to record the lease:

01-01-X1	Equipment	100,000	
	Obligation Under Financing Lease		100,000
	To record financing lease at present value of fixed noncancelable lease payments ($23,739.64 X PV Factor of 4.21236)		

After the initial recording, the accounting for the asset and obligation take separate paths. Essentially, the leased asset is accounted for like any other owned asset of the company. The asset is typically depreciated over the lease term (or useful life, depending on a variety of conditions). The depreciation method might be straight-line or an accelerated approach. The Obligation Under Financing Lease liability is accounted for like a note payable. In the lease example, the amounts correspond to those illustrated for the mortgage note introduced earlier in the chapter. The first lease payment would be accounted for as follows:

12-31-X1	Interest Expense	6,000.00	
	Obligation Under Financing Lease	17,739.64	
	Cash		23,739.64
	To record first lease payment (interest portion = $100,000 X 6%)		

Notice that this entry results in recording interest expense, not rent. This strategy would be applied for each successive payment, until the final payment extinguishes the Obligation Under Financing Lease account. The accounting outcome is virtually identical to that associated with the mortgage note illustrated earlier in the chapter.

Chapter 13 Quiz

Q13-1.   As a general rule, which type of note payable involves interest-only payments, with the full principal being due at maturity?

level pay note   or   term loan

Q13-2.   At the time a bond is issued, the Bonds Payable account is established for the face amount of the bond.

true   or   false

Q13-3.   If a bond is issued at a premium, what relation will interest expense bear to the amount of cash paid for interest each period over the life of the bond?

greater than   or   less than

Q13-4.   When bonds are issued between interest payment dates, the first interest payment will involve cash flow for:

a full period's interest   or   a partial period's interest

Q13-5.   It is a safe bet that all contractual commitments involving future payments are reported on the balance sheet as a liability.

true   or   false

Q13-6.   _____ is the amount to which an outlay will grow by the end of a designated time period, while _____ is the inverse or reciprocal technique.

Q13-7.   The provisions of a bond issue are normally stipulated in an accompanying document called a _____.

Q13-8.   A fund that is set aside to provide for the eventual repayment of bonds at maturity is known as a _____.

Q13-9.   The interest rate printed on the face of a bond certificate is called the _____, whereas the actual interest rate is the _____.

Q13-10. When bonds are sold at more than face value, the difference between the issue price and the face value is commonly referred to as a _____.

Q13-11. Premium amortization causes interest expense to _____.

Multiple Choice

Q13-12. The present value factor at 8% for one period is 0.92593, for two periods is 0.85734, for three periods is 0.79383, for four periods is 0.73503, and for five periods is 0.68058. Given these factors, what amount should be deposited in a bank today to grow to $100 three years from now?

a. $100/0.79383

c. ($100/0.92593 + $100/0.85734 + $100/0.79383)

b. $100/(0.92593/3)

d. $100 X 0.79383

Q13-13. Assume that Kamchatny Vladimir borrowed $100,000 on January 1 of Year 1, at 5% interest per annum. On December 31, of Year 1, an $8,000 payment is made. On December 31, of year 2, another $8,000 payment is made. Using normal assumptions about interest and principal reduction, how much is the unpaid balance of Vladimir's loan after the second payment?

a. $100,000

c. $93,850

b. $94,000

d. $84,000

Q13-14. On June 1, Surge Corporation issued $100,000 of 9%, 5-year bonds. The bonds are dated June 1, 20X1. The bonds were issued at 96, and pay interest on December 1 and June 1. The entry to record issuance of the bonds is:

a. Cash	100,000		c. Cash	104,000	
Bonds Payable		100,000	Bond Int. Payable		4,000
			Bonds Payable		100,000

b. Cash	96,000		d. Cash	96,000	
Disc. on Bonds Payable	4,000		Bond Int. Expense	4,000	
Bonds Payable		100,000	Bonds Payable		100,000

Q13-15. Jeske Company issued $1,000,000 of 8% bonds at a time when the market rate of interest was 10%. If the bonds were issued at a $50,000 discount and interest was paid annually, how much was interest expense for the first full year of the bond issue (utilize the effective-interest amortization technique)?

a. $76,000

c. $95,000

b. $80,000

d. $100,000

Q13-16. When interest payment dates on a bond are June 1 and December 1, and the bond is sold on July 1, the amount of cash received at issuance will be:

a. Decreased by accrued interest from July 1 to December 1.

c. Increased by accrued interest from July 1 to December 1.

b. Decreased by accrued interest from June 1 to July 1.

d. Increased by accrued interest from June 1 to July 1.

Chapter 13 Problems

Basic Problems

On April 1, 20X4, Rojas purchased land by giving $100,000 in cash and executing a $400,000 note payable to the former owner. The note bears interest at 10% per annum, with interest being payable annually on March 31 of each year. Rojas is also required to make a $100,000 payment toward the note's principal on every March 31.

(a) Prepare the appropriate journal entry to record the land purchase on April 1, 20X4.

(b) Prepare the appropriate journal entry to record the year-end interest accrual on December 31, 20X4.

(c) Prepare the appropriate journal entry to record the payment of interest and principal on March 31, 20X5.

(d) Prepare the appropriate journal entry to record the year-end interest accrual on December 31, 20X5.

(e) Prepare the appropriate journal entry to record the payment of interest on March 31, 20X6.

Review the discussion on future value from the textbook, and complete the following requirements (you will find it helpful to access the future value tables within the online version of the textbook).

(a) Prepare basic calculations showing how much a lump sum of $10,000 invested at 7% per year will become after 6 years. For this requirement, do not refer to the future value table.

(b) Verify your answer to part (a) by utilizing the appropriate future value factor from the applicable table.

(c) Construct a table of basic calculations showing how much $10,000 invested every year (as of the beginning of each year) at 7% per year will become after 6 years. For this requirement, you may refer to the future value table for $1 (but do not utilize the annuity table).

(d) Verify your answer to part (c) by utilizing the annuity future value factor from the applicable table.

SPREADSHEET TOOL:

Formulas

Review the discussion on present value from the textbook, and complete the following requirements (you will find it helpful to access the present value tables within the online version of the textbook).

(a) Prepare basic calculations showing the current value of a $25,000 sum to be received in 4 years. You may assume that 6% is the appropriate discount rate. For this requirement, do not refer to the present value table.

(b) Verify your answer to part (a) by utilizing the appropriate present value factor from the applicable table.

(c) Construct a table of basic calculations showing how much an annuity of $25,000 received at the end of each year for four years is worth today. Assume a 6% discount rate. For this requirement, you may refer to the present value table for $1 (but, do not utilize the annuity table).

(d) Verify your answer to part (c) by utilizing the annuity present value factor from the applicable table.

B-13.04   *Calculating note payments and preparing entries*

On January 1, 20X5, Juan Silvia borrowed $500,000 to purchase a new office building. The loan is to be re-paid in 2 equal annual payments, beginning December 31, 20X5. The annual interest rate on the loan is 9%.

(a) Calculate the annual payment on the loan.

(b) Prepare the appropriate journal entries to record the loan and subsequent payments at the end of 20X5 and 20X6.

(c) If the loan was to be repaid in 24 equal monthly payments (0.75% interest rate per month), how much would the monthly payment equal?

B-13.05   *Terminology relating to bonds*

The contractual conditions of specific bond issues vary. Therefore, it becomes important to understand exactly what is meant by the terminology used to describe a bond agreement. Every sentence in the following narrative contains a misstatement. Mark up and correct the narrative. The blank worksheet found on the website can be used to facilitate your answering this question.

> The specific terms of a bond issue are specified in a bond debenture. Secured bonds are backed up only by the general faith and credit of the issuer. Computerization has resulted in the virtual elimination of registered bonds. Serial bonds must be matched with funds set aside in a fund to provide for the eventual retirement of the issue. Callable bonds can be exchanged for common stock of the issuer. Low-yield bonds of distressed firms are frequently called junk bonds. Bonds will sell at a premium when the effective rate is above the stated rate.

B-13.06   *Bonds at par*

Ace Brick company issued $100,000 of 5-year bonds. The bonds were issued at par on January 1, 20X1, and bear interest at a rate of 8% per annum, payable semiannually.

(a) Prepare the journal entry to record the bond issue on January, 20X1.

(b) Prepare the journal entry that Ace would record on each interest date.

(c) Prepare the journal entry that Ace would record at maturity of the bonds.

(d) How much cash flowed "in" and "out" on this bond issue, and how does the difference compare to total interest expense that was recognized?

Bonds at a premium, straight-line amortization   *B-13.07*

Horton Micro Chip Company issued $100,000 of face amount of 6-year bonds on January 1, 20X1. The bonds were issed at 103, and bear interest at a stated rate of 8% per annum, payable semiannually. The premium is amortized by the straight-line method.

(a) Prepare the journal entry to record the initial issue on January, 20X1.

(b) Prepare the journal entry that Horton would record on each interest date.

(c) Prepare the journal entry that Horton would record at maturity of the bonds.

(d) How much cash flowed "in" and "out" on this bond issue, and how does the difference compare to total interest expense that was recognized?

Bonds at a discount, straight-line amortization   *B-13.08*

Erik Food Supply Company issued $100,000 of face amount of 4-year bonds on January 1, 20X1. The bonds were issued at 98, and bear interest at a stated rate of 8% per annum, payable semiannually. The discount is amortized by the straight-line method.

(a) Prepare the journal entry to record the initial issuance on January, 20X1.

(b) Prepare the journal entry that Erik would record on each interest date.

(c) Prepare the journal entry that Erik would record at maturity of the bonds.

(d) How much cash flowed "in" and "out" on this bond issue, and how does the difference compare to total interest expense that was recognized?

Bonds at a premium, effective-interest amortization   *B-13.09*

Standard Atlantic Shipping issued $5,000,000, face amount, of 7% bonds on January 1, 20X3. The bonds are 5-year bonds, and Interest is payable every 6 months. At the time of issue, the market rate of interest was only 6%, so the bonds were issued at a premium.

(a) Prepare calculations showing that issue price was approximately $5,213,235.

(b) Use the effective-interest method of amortization, and prepare the journal entries that Standard Atlantic Shipping would record on January 1, 20X3, June 30, 20X3, and December 31, 20X3.

(c) Show how the bonds would appear on Standard Atlantic Shipping's December 31, 20X3 balance sheet.

Bonds at a discount, effective-interest amortization

Standard Pacific Shipping issued $5,000,000, face amount, of 5% bonds on January 1, 20X3. The bonds are 5-year bonds, and Interest is payable every 6 months. At the time of issue, the market rate of interest was 6%, so the bonds were issued at a discount.

(a)   Prepare calculations showing that issue price was approximately $4,786,725.

(b)   Use the effective-interest method of amortization, and prepare the journal entries that Standard Pacific Shipping would record on January 1, 20X3, June 30, 20X3, and December 31, 20X3.

(c)   Show how the bonds would appear on Standard Pacific Shipping's December 31, 20X3 balance sheet.

Bonds issued between interest dates

My Chase is devoted to tracking the performance of amateur athletes. The company issued $1,000,000 face amount of 9% bonds. The bonds were dated January 1, 20X4, and pay interest on June 30 and December 31 of each year. The initial bond offering was delayed until March 1, 20X4, and the issue price was $100 plus accrued interest.

(a)   Prepare the journal entry to record the bond issue on March 1, 20X4.

(b)   Prepare the journal entry that My Chase would record on June 30, 20X4.

(c)   Prepare the journal entry that My Chase would record on December 31, 20X4.

Basic bond retirement

Clear Water Coffee issued $100,000 of 7% bonds on January 1, 20X1. The bonds were issued at par and pay interest on June 30 and December 31 of each year. By December 31, 20X5, the market rate of interest had increased, and Clear Water was able to reacquire and retire the bonds for $97,500, plus accrued interest.

Prepare the journal entry to record the interest payment and bond retirement on December 31, 20X5.

Debt analysis

Jacob Joseph has identified five different companies in which he is interested in investing, based upon their products and prospects. However, Jacob is concerned about a general economic downturn and desires to invest in companies with the lowest debt exposure. Following is a list of the data for the five potential investments. Jacob has compiled the data and has ranked the companies based upon total debt. He has requested your help in evaluating the risk profiles for each company.

To complete your evaluation, you need to know that each company faces an income tax rate that is equivalent to 30% of income before taxes (which also means that net income is 70% of income before taxes). In addition, assume that each company incurs an average interest cost that is 8% of total debt.

	Total Assets	Total Liabilities	Net Income
A	$10,000,000	$ 1,000,000	$ 200,000
B	20,000,000	3,000,000	1,000,000
C	6,000,000	4,000,000	250,000
D	15,000,000	6,000,000	1,600,000
E	30,000,000	22,000,000	4,000,000

(a) Calculate the debt to total asset ratio, and reorder the list from least risky to most risky, based upon that ratio.

(b) Calculate the debt to equity ratio, and reorder the list from least risky to most risky, based upon that ratio.

(c) Calculate the times interest earned ratio, and reorder the list from least risky to most risky, based upon that ratio.

(d) Do the ratios suggest that risk is a function of total debt, or other factors? Do all the ratios produce the same signals?

Commitments and leases   B-13.14

Mike Davis Company entered into two lease agreements. One lease was for office space and the other was for office equipment.

The office space lease is <u>not</u> a financing lease. It is an operating lease because the risks and rewards of owning the property remain with the lessor (owner of the property). The lease agreement is for 1 year and provides for monthly payments of $2,500. These rent payments are charged to rent expense as incurred. No liability is recorded for the lease contract.

The office equipment lease is a financing lease. This lease is for 5 years. Payments at the end of each month are $2,500, and their present value at the inception of the lease is $112,388. The interest rate implicit in the lease is 1% per month.

(a) Prepare the journal entry needed to record a payment under the office space lease.

(b) Prepare the initial journal entry to record the office equipment lease.

(c) Prepare the journal entries necessary to record the first and second payments under the office equipment lease.

(d) Assuming straight-line depreciation over 60 months, prepare the journal entry to record monthly depreciation of the office equipment.

(e) How would the financial reporting differ for the office space versus the office equipment?

Involved Problems

Each of the following scenarios is independent. Utilize the appropriate future value or present value table, and calculate the requested amount. Then, if available, utilize the related function in an electronic spreadsheet (or financial calculator) to verify your calculation.

SPREADSHEET TOOL:

Future value/ Present value functions

(a) How much will a lump sum of $10,000, invested at 7% per annum, grow to in 20 years?

(b) How much will be in account after 2 years, if $50 is placed into the account at the beginning of each month? Assume the account's interest rate is 6%, with monthly compounding.

(c) How much should be set aside today, so that it will grow to $30,000 in 15 years? The discount rate is 9%.

(d) What is the present worth of an income stream that includes annual end-of-period payments of $100,000 for 20 years? Assume the appropriate discount rate is 8% per year.

Rodriquez Oil and Gas borrowed $1,000,000 from a local bank to obtain funds needed for the construction of a new drilling rig. This "construction" loan was represented by a 2-year, 7%, promissory note, dated April 1, 20X3. Interest (only) is payable on March 31, 20X4, and again at maturity. The $1,000,000 principal is due on March 31, 20X5. Rodriguez repaid the promissory note on March 31, 20X5, as agreed.

On April 1, 20X5, Rodriguez secured permanent equipment financing via a $1,200,000, 5-year loan. This loan was at 6% per annum, and requires level quarterly payments so that the loan will be completely repaid at its maturity.

(a) Prepare journal entries for the $1,000,000 loan to record the loan's issuance (April 1, 20X3); accrued interest at December 31, 20X3; the interest payment on March 31, 20X4; accrued interest at December 31, 20X4; and the final payment at maturity (March 31, 20X5).

(b) Calculate the required quarterly payment for the 5-year loan.

(c) Prepare journal entries to record the 5-year loan, and its first two quarterly payments.

(d) Optional: Use an electronic spreadsheet to prepare a 20-quarter amortization schedule, showing how the loan will be fully amortized by its maturity.

On January 1, 20X2, Paisley Corporation issued $2,000,000 face amount of 6% bonds. These bonds are dated January 1, and mature in 6 years, with semiannual interest payments. The market rate of interest at the time of issue was 5%, and the bonds priced at $2,102,578. Paisley uses the effective-interest method of amortization.

(a) Prepare a 6-year amortization table for Paisley's bonds.

(b) Prepare 20X2's entries for these bonds; specifically, the initial bond issuance, the June 30 interest payment, and the December 31 interest payment.

(c) Demonstrate the appropriate balance sheet presentation for the bonds, as of December 31, 20X4.

Bonds issued at a discount; effective interest　　　　　　　　　　　　　　　　　　*I-13.04*

On January 1, 20X3, Daisy Corporation issued $5,000,000 face amount of 6% bonds. These bonds are dated January 1, and mature in 5 years, with semiannual interest payments. The market rate of interest at the time of issue was 7%, and the bonds priced at $4,792,085. Daisy uses the effective-interest method of amortization.

(a) Prepare a 5-year amortization table for Daisy's bonds.

(b) Prepare 20X3's entries for these bonds; specifically, the initial bond issuance, the June 30 interest payment, and the December 31 interest payment.

(c) Demonstrate the appropriate balance sheet presentation for the bonds, as of December 31, 20X5.

Team-based approach to bond pricing　　　　　　　　　　　　　　　　　　　　　*I-13.05*

You will need a pair of dice for this problem! Form a four-person team. Each team member is assumed to be the CFO for a company that is considering issuing bonds. Each team member will roll the dice twice and record the results (e.g., 7, 9). The first value will be the "stated rate of interest" for that team member's proposed bond issue. The value of the second roll will be the "effective rate."

Each team member should explain to the remainder of the team if they would expect their company's bonds to be issued at par, a premium, or a discount (and why!).

Following the general explanation, assume the bonds are $100,000 of 5-year bonds, paying interest semiannually. Each team member should perform calculations showing the actual premium or discount, then compare results. How do the premiums and discounts compare to the expected outcomes? Are they a function of the "spread" between the stated rate and effective rate?

Bond pricing, effective-interest amortization, and retirement　　　　　　　　　　　*I-13.06*

Cold Creek Confections issued $1,000,000 of 6% bonds on January 1, 20X5. The bonds were issued at 86.15 (note that bonds are frequently priced in increments of 1/32, so this nomenclature is taken to mean 86 and 15/32 of par, or $864,688). The issue price resulted in an effective yield of 8%, and Cold Creek amortizes bond discounts by the effective interest method. The bonds pay interest on June 30 and December 31 of each year, and had a life of 10 years. By December 31, 20X6, the market rate of interest had declined to 5%. At that time, Cold Creek reacquired and retired the bonds for $1,065,270.

(a) Determine the carrying value of the bonds on December 31, 20X6 (immediately after recording the interest payment due on that date).

(b) Prepare the journal entry to record the interest payment and bond retirement on December 31, 20X6.

(c) Prepare calculations showing that the bonds would be fairly priced at $1,065,270 on December 31, 20X6.

Chapter 14:
Corporate Equity Accounting

Goals:

Characteristics of the corporate form of organization.
Common and preferred stock.
Treasury stock.
Stock splits and stock dividends.
The statement of stockholders' equity.

The Corporate Form of Organization

A corporation is a legal entity having existence separate and distinct from its owners (i.e., stockholders). Corporations are artificial beings existing only in contemplation of law. A corporation is typically created when one or more individuals file "articles of incorporation" with a Secretary of State in a particular jurisdiction. The articles of incorporation generally specify a number of important features about the purpose of the entity and how governance will be structured.

After reviewing the articles of incorporation, the Secretary of State will issue a charter (or certificate of incorporation) authorizing the corporate entity. The persons who initiated the filing (the "incorporators") will then collect the shareholders' initial investment in exchange for the "stock" of the corporation (the **stock** is the financial instrument evidencing a person's ownership interest). Once the initial stock is issued, a shareholders' meeting will be convened to adopt bylaws and elect a board of directors. These directors appoint the corporate officers who are responsible for commencing the operations of the business. In a small start-up venture, the initial incorporators may become the shareholders, then elect themselves to the board, and finally appoint themselves to become the officers. This leads one to wonder why go to all the trouble of incorporating?

ADVANTAGES

The reasons for incorporating can vary, but there are certain unique advantages to this form of organization that have led to its popularity. One advantage of the corporate form of organization is that it permits otherwise unaffiliated persons to join together in *mutual ownership* of a business entity. This objective can be accomplished in other ways (like a partnership), but the corporate form of organization is arguably one of the better vehicles. Large amounts of venture capital can be drawn together from many individuals and concentrated into one entity under shared ownership. The stock of the corporation provides a clear and unambiguous point of reference to identify who owns the business and in what proportion. Further, the democratic process associated with shareholder voting rights (typically one vote per share of stock) permits shareholder "say so" in selecting the board of directors. In addition to electing the board, shareholders may vote on other matters such as selection of an independent auditor, stock option plans, and corporate mergers. The voting "ballot" is usually referred to as a "proxy."

Corporate stock has the benefit of *transferability of ownership*. It is easily transferable from one person to another. Transferability provides liquidity as it enables stockholders to quickly enter or exit an ownership position in a corporate entity. As a corporation grows, it may bring in additional shareholders by issuing more stock. The entity may become sufficiently large that its shares become "listed" on a stock exchange.

An "IPO" is the **initial public offering** of the stock of a corporation. Rules require that such IPOs be accompanied by regulatory registrations and filings, and that potential shareholders be furnished with a **prospectus** detailing corporate information. *Publicly traded* corporate entities are subject to a number of continuing regulatory registration and reporting requirements to ensure full and fair disclosure.

Another benefit of a corporation is *perpetual existence*. A corporate entity is typically of unlimited duration enabling it to effectively outlive its shareholders. Changes in stock ownership do not cause operations to cease. What would cause a corporation to cease to exist? At some point, a corporation may be acquired by another and merged in with the successor. Or, a corporation may fail and cease operations. Finally, some businesses may find that liquidating operating assets and distributing residual monies to the creditors and shareholders is a preferable strategy to continued operation.

Not to be overlooked in considering why a corporation is desirable is the feature of *limited liability* for stockholders, who normally understand that their investment can be lost if the business fails. However, stockholders are not liable for debts and losses of the company beyond the amount of their investment. There are exceptions to this rule. In some cases, shareholders may be called upon to sign a separate guarantee for corporate debt. And, shareholders in closely held companies can inadvertently be drawn into having to satisfy corporate debts when they commingle their personal finances with those of the company or fail to satisfy the necessary legal procedures to maintain a valid corporate existence. A Limited Liability Corporation (LLC) is a unique business structure allowed by state statute which may be treated as either a corporation, partnership, or individual for tax purposes and which may protect its owners (members) from some debts or actions.

DIS-ADVANTAGES

Corporations are not without certain disadvantages. Most corporations are taxable entities, and their income is subject to taxation. This "income tax" is problematic as it oftentimes produces double taxation. This effect occurs when shareholders receive cash dividends that they must include in their own calculation of taxable income. Thus, a dollar earned at the corporate level is reduced by corporate income taxes; to the extent the remaining after-tax profit is distributed to shareholders as dividends, it is again subject to taxes at the shareholder level. So, a large portion of the profits of a dividend-paying corporation are apt to be shared with governmental entities.

Governments are aware that this double-taxation outcome can limit corporate investment and be potentially damaging to an economy. Various measures of relief are sometimes available, depending on the prevailing political climate (including "dividends received deductions" for dividends paid between affiliated companies, lower shareholder tax rates on dividends, and S-Corporation provisions that permit closely held corporations to attribute their income to the shareholders thereby avoiding one level of tax). Some countries adopt "tax holidays" that permit newer companies to be exempt from income taxes, or utilize different approaches to taxing the value additive components of production by an entity.

Another burden on the corporate form of organization is *costly regulation*. In the U.S., larger (usually public) companies are under scrutiny of federal (The Securities and Exchange Commission (SEC) and other public oversight groups) and state regulatory bodies. History shows that the absence or failure of these regulators will quickly foster an environment where rogue business persons will launch all manner of stock fraud schemes. These frauds can quickly corrupt public confidence without which investors become unwilling to join together to invest in new ideas and products.

It seems almost unavoidable that governmental regulation must be a part of the corporate scene. However, the cost of compliance with such regulation is high. Public companies must prepare and file quarterly and annual reports with the SEC, along with a myriad of other documents. Many of these documents must be certified or subjected to independent audit. Further, companies are required to have strong internal controls and even ethical training.

Common and Preferred Stock

Companies may issue different types of stock. For example, some companies have multiple classes of common stock. A "family business" that has grown very large and become a public company may be accompanied by the creation of Class A stock (held by the family members) and Class B stock (held by the public), where only the Class A stock can vote. This enables raising needed capital but preserves the ability to control and direct the company. While **common stock** is the most typical, another way to gain access to capital is by issuing **preferred stock**. The customary features of common and preferred stock differ, providing some advantages and disadvantages for each. The following tables reveal general features that can be modified on a company by company basis.

TYPICAL COMMON STOCK FEATURES

Dividends

Receives a portion of dividends that are declared and issued to common shareholders.

Preemptive right

An option to buy a proportional part of any additional shares that may be issued by the company. This **preemptive right** is intended to allow a shareholder to avoid ownership dilution by being assured an opportunity to acquire a fair part of any corporate stock expansion. (Numerous companies have done away with this provision.)

Voting

The right to vote on certain general governance matters like election of the board of directors, employee stock award plans, mergers, and similar corporate matters.

Proceeds from liquidation

Receives proceeds of liquidation after creditors and other priority claims are settled.

Periodic financial reports

The right to periodic financial reports about corporate performance.

POSSIBLE PREFERRED STOCK FEATURES

Preferred position for dividends

Paid a dividend prior to any distribution to common stockholders, and the dividend is more or less expected each period. The amount of the dividend is usually stated as a percentage of the preferred stock's "par value." Furthermore, preferred stock is frequently **cumulative**; if the annual dividend requirement cannot be satisfied, it will become a **dividend in arrears**, and all dividends in arrears must be paid before any dividends can be paid to common shareholders (in contrast to "noncumulative" where a missed dividend is not required to be made up in the future).

The absence of voting rights

Usually lacking in voting rights.

Position in liquidation

In the event of a corporate liquidation, to be "paid-off" before common shareholders. Of course, creditors must first be satisfied before any funds will flow to either the preferred or common stockholders.

Callable

Can be forced to cash out in exchange for a preagreed "call price" that is oftentimes set at a certain percentage of "par value" (e.g., **callable** at 105, would mean the company can buy back the preferred stock at 105% of its par value). A call provision can effectively limit the upside value of an investment in preferred stock.

Convertible

May be exchanged for common stock at a preagreed ratio (e.g., 3 shares of common for 1 share of preferred). A **convertible** preferred stock can effectively provide significant upside potential if the related common stock increases value.

Fixed maturity date

Intent to be bought back by the company ("mandatory redeemable") on a certain future date.

A comparative review of the preceding tables reveals a broad range of potential attributes. Every company has different financing and tax considerations and will tailor its package of features to match those issues. For instance, a company can issue preferred that is much like debt (cumulative, mandatory redeemable), because a fixed periodic payment must occur each period with a fixed amount due at maturity. On the other hand, some preferred will behave more like common stock (noncallable, noncumulative, convertible).

WHAT IS PAR? In the preceding discussion, there were several references to **par value.** Many states require that stock have a designated par value (or in some cases "stated value"). Thus, par value is said to represent the "legal capital" of the firm. In theory, original purchasers of stock are contingently liable to the company for the difference between the issue price and par value if the stock is issued at less than par. However, as a practical matter, par values on *common stock* are set well below the issue price, negating any practical effect of this latent provision.

It is not unusual to see *common stock* carry a par value of $1 per share or even $.01 per share. In some respects, then, par value is merely a formality. But, it does impact the accounting records, because separate accounts must be maintained for "par" and **paid-in capital in excess of par**. Assume that Godkneckt Corporation issues 100,000 shares of $1 par value stock for $10 per share. The entry to record this stock issuance would be:

05-01-XX	Cash		1,000,000	
	Common Stock			100,000
	Paid in Capital in Excess of Par			900,000
	To record issuance of 100,000 shares of $1 par value common stock at $10 per share			

Occasionally, a corporation may issue no-par stock, which is recorded by debiting Cash and crediting Common Stock for the issue price. A separate Paid-in Capital in Excess of Par account is not needed.

Sometimes, stock may be issued for land or other tangible assets, in which case the debit in the preceding entry would be to the specific asset account (e.g., Land instead of Cash). When stock is issued for noncash assets, the amount of the entry would be based upon the fair value of the asset (or the fair value of the stock if it can be more clearly determined).

Begin by assuming that a company has only common shares outstanding. There is no mandatory dividend requirement, and the dividends are a matter of discretion for the board of directors to consider. To pay a dividend the company must have sufficient cash and a positive balance in retained earnings (companies with a "deficit" (negative) Retained Earnings account would not pay a dividend unless it is part of a corporate liquidation action). Many companies pride themselves in having a long-standing history of regular and increasing dividends, a feature that many investors find appealing. Other companies view their objective as one of continual growth via reinvestment of all earnings; their investors seem content relying on the notion that their investment value will gradually increase due to this earnings reinvestment activity. Whatever the case, a company has no obligation to pay a dividend, and there is no "liability" for dividends until such time as they are actually declared. A "declaration" is a formal action by the board of directors to indicate that a dividend will be paid at some stipulated future date. On the date of declaration, the following entry is needed on the corporate accounts:

07-01-XX	Dividends	50,000	
	Dividends Payable		50,000
	To record declaration of dividends on common stock (assumed $0.50 per share on 100,000 shares outstanding); to be paid on September 1		

In observing the preceding entry, it is imperative to note that the declaration on July 1 establishes a liability to the shareholders that is legally enforceable. Therefore, a liability is recorded on the books at the time of declaration. Recall (from earlier chapters) that the Dividends account will directly reduce retained earnings (it is not an expense in calculating income; it is a distribution of income)! When the previously declared dividends are paid, the appropriate entry would require a debit to Dividends Payable and a credit to Cash.

Some shareholders may sell their stock between the date of declaration and the date of payment. Who is to get the dividend? The former shareholder or the new shareholder? To resolve this question, the board will also set a "date of record;" the dividend will be paid to whomever the owner of record is on the date of record. In the preceding illustration, the date of record might have been set as August 1, for example. To further confuse matters, there may be a slight lag of just a few days between the time a share exchange occurs and the company records are updated. As a result, the date of record is usually slightly preceded by an **ex-dividend** date.

The practical effect of the ex-dividend date is simple: if a shareholder on the date of declaration continues to hold the stock at least through the ex-dividend date, that shareholder will get the dividend. But, if the shareholder sells the stock before the ex-dividend date, the new shareholder can expect the dividend. In the illustrated time line, if one were to own stock on the date of declaration, that person must hold the stock at least until the "green period" to be entitled to receive payment.

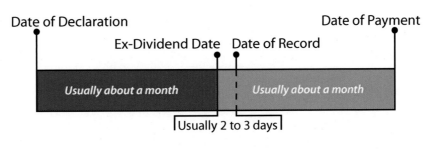

Recall that preferred dividends are expected to be paid before common dividends, and those dividends are usually a fixed amount (e.g., a percentage of the preferred's par value). In addition, recall that cumulative preferred requires that unpaid dividends become "dividends in arrears." Dividends in arrears must also be paid before any distributions to common can occur. The following illustration will provide the answer to questions about how these concepts are to be implemented.

To develop the illustration, begin by looking at the equity section of Embassy Corporation's balance sheet. Note that this section of the balance sheet is quite extensive. A corporation's stockholders' equity (or related footnotes) should include rather detailed descriptions of the type of stock outstanding and its basic features. This will include mention of the number of shares *authorized* (permitted to be issued), *issued* (actually issued), and *outstanding* (issued minus any shares reacquired by the company). In addition, be aware of certain related terminology: **legal capital** is the total par value ($20,400,000 for Embassy), and **total paid-in capital** is the legal capital plus amounts paid in excess of par values ($56,400,000 for Embassy).

Stockholders' Equity

Capital stock:

Preferred stock, $100 par value, 8% cumulative, 500,000 shares authorized, 200,000 shares issued and outstanding	$20,000,000		
Common stock, $1 par value, 2,000,000 shares authorized, 400,000 shares issued and outstanding	400,000	$20,400,000	
Additional paid-in capital			
Paid-in capital in excess of par - preferred stock	$ 1,000,000		
Paid-in capital in excess of par - common stock	35,000,000	36,000,000	
Total paid-in capital			$56,400,000
Retained earnings			6,600,000
Total stockholders' equity			$63,000,000

Note that the par value for each class of stock is the number of shares issued multiplied by the par value per share (e.g., 200,000 shares X $100 per share = $20,000,000). The preferred stock description makes it clear that the $100 par stock is 8% cumulative. This means that each share will receive $8 per year in dividends, and any "missed" dividends become dividends in arrears.

If the notes to the financial statements appropriately indicate that Embassy has not managed to pay its dividends for the preceding two years, and Embassy desired to pay $5,000,000 of total dividends during the current year, how much would be available to the common shareholders?

The answer is only $200,000 (or $0.50 per share for the 400,000 common shares). The reason is that the preferred stock is to receive annual dividends of $1,600,000 ($8 per share X 200,000 preferred shares), and three years must be paid consisting of the two years in arrears and the current year requirement ($1,600,000 X 3 years = $4,800,000 to preferred, leaving only $200,000 for common).

Treasury Stock

Treasury stock is the term that is used to describe shares of a company's own stock that it has reacquired. A company may buy back its own stock for many reasons. A frequently cited reason is a belief by the officers and directors that the market value of the stock is unrealistically low. As such, the decision to buy back stock is seen as a way to support the stock price and utilize corporate funds to maximize the value for shareholders who choose not to sell back stock to the company.

Other times, a company may buy back public shares as part of a reorganization that contemplates the company "going private" or delisting from some particular stock exchange. Further, a company might buy back shares and in turn issue them to employees pursuant to an employee stock award plan.

Whatever the reason for a treasury stock transaction, the company is to account for the shares as a purely equity transaction, and "gains and losses" are ordinarily not reported in income. Procedurally, there are several ways to record the "debits" and "credits" associated with treasury stock, and the specifics can vary globally. The "cost method" is generally acceptable. Under this approach, acquisitions of treasury stock are accounted for by debiting Treasury Stock and crediting Cash for the cost of the shares reacquired:

04-01-X1	Treasury Stock	1,000,000	
	Cash		1,000,000
	To record acquisition of 40,000 treasury shares at $25 per share		

The effect of treasury stock is very simple: cash goes down and so does total equity by the same amount. This result occurs no matter what the original issue price was for the stock. Accounting rules do not recognize gains or losses when a company *issues its own stock*, nor do they recognize gains and losses when a company *reacquires its own stock*. This may seem odd, because it is certainly different than the way one thinks about stock investments. But remember, this is not a stock investment from the company's perspective. It is instead an expansion or contraction of its own equity.

Treasury Stock is a contra equity item. It is not reported as an asset; rather, it is subtracted from stockholders' equity. The presence of treasury shares will cause a difference between the number of shares issued and the number of shares outstanding. Following is Embassy Corporation's equity section, modified (see highlights) to reflect the treasury stock transaction portrayed by the entry.

Stockholders' Equity

Capital stock:

Preferred stock, $100 par value, 8% cumulative, 500,000

  shares authorized, 200,000 shares issued and outstanding $20,000,000

Common stock, $1 par value, 2,000,000 shares authorized,

  400,000 shares issued and 360,000 shares outstanding   400,000 $20,400,000

Additional paid-in capital

  Paid-in capital in excess of par - preferred stock $ 1,000,000

  Paid-in capital in excess of par - common stock   35,000,000 36,000,000

  Total paid-in capital $56,400,000

Retained earnings   6,600,000

    $63,000,000

Less: Treasury stock, 40,000 shares at cost   (1,000,000)

Total stockholders' equity $62,000,000

If treasury shares are reissued, Cash is debited for the amount received and Treasury Stock is credited for the cost of the shares. Any difference may be debited or credited to Paid-in Capital in Excess of Par.

Stock Splits and Stock Dividends

Stock splits are events that increase the number of shares outstanding and reduce the par or stated value per share. For example, a 2-for-1 stock split would double the number of shares outstanding and halve the par value per share. Existing shareholders would see their shareholdings double in quantity, but there would be no change in the proportional ownership represented by the shares (i.e., a shareholder owning 1,000 shares out of 100,000 would then own 2,000 shares out of 200,000).

Why would a company bother with a stock split? The answer is not in the financial statement impact, but in the financial markets. Since the same company is now represented by more shares, one would expect the market value per share to suffer a corresponding decline. For example, a stock that is subject to a 3-1 split should see its shares initially cut in third. But, holders of the stock will not be disappointed by this share price drop since they will each be receiving proportionately more shares; it is very important to understand that existing shareholders are getting the newly issued shares for no additional investment outlay. The benefit to the shareholders comes about, in theory, because the split creates more attractive opportunities for other future investors to ultimately buy into the larger pool of lower priced shares.

Rapidly growing companies often have share splits to keep the per share price from reaching stratospheric levels that could deter some investors. In the final analysis, understand that a stock split is mostly cosmetic as it does not change the underlying economics of the firm.

Importantly, the *total* par value of shares outstanding is not affected by a stock split (i.e., the number of shares times par value per share does not change). Therefore, no journal entry is needed to account for a stock split. A memorandum notation in the accounting records indicates the decreased par value and increased number of shares. If the *initial* equity illustration for Embassy Corporation was modified to reflect a four-for-one stock split of the common stock, the revised presentation would appear as follows (the only changes are underlined):

Stockholders' Equity

Capital stock:

Preferred stock, $100 par value, 8% cumulative, 500,000

    shares authorized, 200,000 shares issued and outstanding $20,000,000

Common stock, $0.25 par value, 2,000,000 shares authorized,

    1,600,000 shares issued and outstanding   400,000 $20,400,000

Additional paid-in capital

    Paid-in capital in excess of par - preferred stock $ 1,000,000

    Paid-in capital in excess of par - common stock   35,000,000   36,000,000

    Total paid-in capital $56,400,000

Retained earnings   6,600,000

Total stockholders' equity $63,000,000

By reviewing the changes, one can see that the par has been reduced from $1.00 to $0.25 per share, and the number of issued shares has quadrupled from 400,000 shares to 1,600,000 (be sure to note that $1.00 X 400,000 = $0.25 X 1,600,000 = $400,000). None of the account balances have changes.

Splits can come in odd proportions: 3 for 2, 5 for 4, 1,000 for 1, and so forth depending on the scenario. A reverse split (1 for 5, etc.) is also possible and will initially be accompanied by a reduction in the number of issued shares along with a proportionate increase in share price.

In contrast to cash dividends discussed earlier in this chapter, **stock dividends** involve the issuance of additional shares of stock to existing shareholders on a proportional basis. Stock dividends are very similar to stock splits. For example, a shareholder who owns 100 shares of stock will own 125 shares after a 25% stock dividend (essentially the same result as a 5 for 4 stock split). Importantly, all shareholders would have 25% more shares, so the percentage of the total outstanding stock owned by a specific shareholder is not increased.

Although shareholders will perceive very little difference between a stock dividend and stock split, the accounting for stock dividends is unique. Stock dividends require journal entries. Stock dividends are recorded by moving amounts from retained earnings to paid-in capital. The amount to move depends on the size of the distribution. A *small stock dividend* (generally less than 20-25% of the existing shares outstanding) is accounted for at market price on the date of declaration. A *large stock dividend* (generally over the 20-25% range) is accounted for at par value.

To illustrate, assume that Childers Corporation had 1,000,000 shares of $1 par value stock outstanding. The market price per share is $20 on the date that a stock dividend is declared and issued:

Small Stock Dividend: Assume Childers Issues a 10% Stock Dividend

XX-XX-XX	Retained Earnings	2,000,000	
	Common Stock		100,000
	Paid in Capital in Excess of Par		1,900,000
	To record issuance of a 10% stock dividend (1,000,000 shares X 10% X $20 per share price)		

Large Stock Dividend: Assume Childers Issues a 40% Stock Dividend

XX-XX-XX	Retained Earnings	400,000	
	Common Stock		400,000
	To record issuance of a 40% stock dividend (1,000,000 shares X 40% X $1 per share par)		

It may seem odd that rules require different treatments for stock splits, small stock dividends, and large stock dividends. There are conceptual underpinnings for these differences, but it is primarily related to bookkeeping. The total par value needs to correspond to the number of shares outstanding. Each transaction rearranges existing equity, but does not change the amount of total equity.

Statement of Stockholders' Equity

Remember that a company must present an income statement, balance sheet, statement of retained earnings, and statement of cash flows. However, it is also necessary to present additional information about changes in other equity accounts. This may be done by notes to the financial statements or other separate schedules.

However, most companies will find it preferable to simply combine the required statement of retained earnings and information about changes in other equity accounts into a single **statement of stockholders' equity**. Following is an example of such a statement.

PEPPER CORPORATION
Statement of Stockholders' Equity
For the Year Ending December 31, 20X9

	Common Stock, $1 Par	Paid-in Capital in Excess of Par	Retained Earnings	Treasury Stock	Total Stockholders' Equity
Balance on January 1	$20,000,000	$25,000,000	$11,000,000	$(5,000,000)	$51,000,000
Issued shares for cash	3,000,000	12,000,000			15,000,000
Purchase of treasury stock				(2,000,000)	(2,000,000)
Net income			4,000,000		4,000,000
Cash dividends			(1,500,000)		(1,500,000)
Stock dividends	1,150,000	4,600,000	(5,750,000)		
Balance on December 31	$24,150,000	$41,600,000	$ 7,750,000	$(7,000,000)	$66,500,000

Note that the company had several equity transactions during the year, and the retained earnings column corresponds to a statement of retained earnings. Companies may expand this presentation to include comparative data for multiple years. Under international reporting guidelines, the preceding statement is sometimes replaced by a statement of recognized income and expense that includes additional adjustments for allowed asset revaluations ("surpluses"). This format is usually supplemented by additional explanatory notes about changes in other equity accounts.

Chapter 14 Quiz

Q14-1.   Which of the following types of stock is accounted for similar to par-value stock?

no-par   or   stated-value

Q14-2.   For a cash dividend, stockholders' equity would be reduced on the:

date of declaration   or   date of payment

Q14-3.   If a corporation has dividends in arrears on preferred stock for two years ($5,000 per year), and declares $20,000 of dividends during the current (third) year, how much will be paid to the common shareholders?

$5,000   or $10,000

Q14-4.   A small stock dividend (one that is less than 20-25%) should be accounted for based on:

par value   or   fair value

Q14-5.   In lieu of the Statement of Retained Earnings, many companies will prepare an expanded Statement of Stockholders' Equity.

true   or   false

Q14-6.   A corporation is created by obtaining a _____ from one of the states.

Q14-7.   The _____ allows existing shareholders the opportunity to maintain their respective interests in a corporate entity by acquiring additional shares on a pro rata basis.

Q14-8.   The significance of par value is that it represents _____ per share of stock.

Q14-9.   The _____ is the date that corporate records are reviewed to determine who will receive a previously declared dividend.

Q14-10.   For a preferred stock to have dividends in arrears, it must be _____.

Q14-11.   A _____ involves increasing the number of shares outstanding and reducing the stock's par or stated value per share.

Multiple Choice

Q14-12. Of the following characteristics, which is not generally regarded as a right of common shareholders?

a. Preemptive right

c. Preference in liquidation

b. Voting rights

d. Transferability of shares

Q14-13. If 1,000 shares of $10 par-value common stock are issued in exchange for land with a fair market value of $25,000, the land and common stock (along with any additional paid-in capital) should be recorded at:

a. $0

c. $10,000

b. $1,000

d. $25,000

Q14-14. Jackson Corporation has 500,000 shares of common stock outstanding. On April 10, the board of directors declared a $0.60 per share cash dividend, to be paid to stockholders of record on April 25. The dividend was distributed on June 6. The proper journal entry to record on June 6 is:

a. Dividends Expense   300,000
        Cash   300,000

c. Retained Earnings   300,000
        Cash   300,000

b. Dividends Payable   300,000
        Cash   300,000

d. Dividends Payable   300,000
        Retained Earnings   300,000

Q14-15. Magic Corporation paid $100,000 in dividends. The corporation had 10,000 shares of common stock outstanding and 5,000 shares of $100 par value 5% preferred stock. The preferred stock was two years in arrears prior to the current year. How much was paid to the common stockholders?

a. $0

c. $50,000

b. $25,000

d. $75,000

Q14-16. Which of the following statements about treasury stock is false?

a. Gains are not recorded on treasury stock transactions, but losses are.

c. Treasury stock is reported as a deduction from stockholders' equity.

b. Acquiring treasury stock causes stockholders' equity to decrease.

d. The excess of the sales price of treasury stock over its cost should be credited to Paid-in Capital from Treasury Stock.

Chapter 14 Problems

Basic Problems

Following is a list describing various features of the corporate form of organization. Match each feature with an appropriate descriptive term, and note whether this feature is an advantage or disadvantage of the corporate entity.

	Term	Advantage/Disadvantage
The ability of a company to raise capital by issuing shares to the public	Publicly Traded	Advantage
The ability of an existing shareholder to sell shares without corporate approval		
The ability of the government to tax corporate earnings and dividends		
Periodic regulatory filings		
The ability of different individuals to pool resources		
The inability of creditors to pursue individual shareholders		
The life of the entity can exceed the life of the shareholders		

Terms:

Limited Liability

Double Taxation

Perpetual Existence

Transferability of Ownership

Mutual Ownership

Cost of Regulation

Publicly Traded

Evaluate the following list, and decide if each described attribute more likely relates to a common stock or preferred stock issue.

	Common	Preferred
The stock is described as 6%, cumulative		✓
The stock includes voting rights		
The stock is last in line in the event of liquidation		
The stock is convertible		
The stock ordinarily pays a fixed dividend		
The stock may be subject to significant appreciation		
The stock has a "call price"		
The stock has a mandatory redemption date		

B-14.03 *Recording stock issues*

Prepare journal entries to record each of the following independent stock issue situations.

(a) Sherri Hui Corporation issued 100,000 shares of $1 par value common stock. The issue price was $30 per share.

(b) Ariana Corporation issued 50,000 shares of no par common stock for $10 per share.

(c) Laser Golf issued 40,000 shares of $100 par value preferred stock. The issue price was $102 per share.

(d) Charleston Industries issued 5,000 shares of $5 par value common stock for land with a fair value of $75,000.

B-14.04 *Dividend calculations and journal entries*

Krull Corporation presented the following selected information. The company has a calendar year end.

Before considering the effects of dividends, if any, Krull's net income for 20X7 was $2,500,000.

Before considering the effects of dividends, if any, Krull's net income for 20X8 was $3,000,000.

Krull declared $750,000 of dividends on November 15, 20X7. The date of record was January 15, 20X8. The dividends were paid on February 1, 20X8.

Stockholders' equity, at January 1, 20X7, was $5,000,000. No transactions impacted stockholders' equity throughout 20X7 and 20X8, other than the impact of earnings and dividends on retained earnings.

(a) Prepare journal entries, if needed, to reflect the dividend declaration, the date of record, and the date of payment.

(b) How much was net income for 20X7 and 20X8?

(c) How much was total equity at the end of 20X7 and 20X8?

(d) Is total "working capital" reduced on the date of declaration, date of record, and/or date of payment?

Equity concepts and preferred dividends	*B-14.05*

Wiggins Corporation has 10,000,000 shares of $1 par value common stock outstanding. This stock was originally issued at $7 per share. The company also has 1,000,000 shares of $50, 4%, cumulative preferred stock outstanding. The preferred stock was originally issued at par. During 20X5, the company experienced a significant business interruption and was unable to pay any dividends. Prior to 20X5, the preferred shareholders had always received the expected dividend. During 20X6, the company returned to profitability, and paid $7,000,000 in dividends.

(a) How much is the company's legal capital, additional paid-in capital, and total paid-in capital?

(b) What accounting/disclosure is needed relating to the dividends in arrears on the preferred stock as of the end of 20X5 (i.e., should a liability be established)?

(c) How would the 20X6 dividends be divided between common and preferred stock?

Treasury stock	*B-14.06*

Kenya Corporation had an equity structure that consisted of $1 par value common stock, $3,500,000; paid-in capital in excess of par, $17,500,000; and retained earnings, $22,700,000.

Transaction A — Believing that its share price was depressed due to general market conditions, Kenya's board of directors authorized the reacquisition of 250,000 shares of common stock. These treasury shares were purchased at $10 per share.

Transaction B — Subsequent to Transaction A, the stock price increased to $17 per share, and half of the treasury shares were sold in the open market.

Transaction C — Subsequent to Transaction B, Kenya experienced business difficulties that necessitated it selling the remaining treasury shares to raise additional cash. The shares were sold for $6 per share.

(a) Assuming that all 3,500,000 shares of Kenya were issued at the same time and at the same price per share, what was the original issue price? How does this compare to the price paid in Transaction A, and is it rational for a company to pay more to buy back shares than it originally received upon the initial issuance?

(b) Prepare an appropriate journal entry to record Transaction A. Kenya records treasury shares at cost.

(c) Prepare an appropriate journal entry for Transaction B.

(d) Prepare an appropriate journal entry for Transaction C.

(e) Is there any income statement impact from these transactions? What is the impact on total stockholders' equity from each of the three transactions?

B-14.07   *Stock dividends and splits*

SPREADSHEET TOOL:

Holding a cell reference constant

Magic Blade's stock has risen rapidly to $50 per share. The increase is due to excitement about its new knife that uses a light beam to slice fruits and vegetables. This process enhances the final appearance and quality of salads and fruit trays.

The board of directors is considering strategies to divide the corporate ownership into more shares of stock, and bring about some reduction in the price per share. They are considering a stock split, small stock dividend, or large stock dividend. The board is unsure of the accounting effects of such transactions, and has requested information about how stockholders' equity would be impacted.

Prior to the contemplated stock transaction, equity consisted of:

Stockholders' Equity

Common stock, $2 par value, 2,000,000 shares authorized,	
500,000 shares issued and outstanding	$1,000,000
Paid-in capital in excess of par	2,000,000
Retained earnings	6,000,000
Total stockholders' equity	$9,000,000

(a) Assuming the board were to declare a 2 for 1 split, how would the revised stockholders' equity appear?

(b) Assuming the board were to declare a 15% stock dividend, how would the revised stockholders' equity appear?

(c) Assuming the board were to declare a 50% stock dividend, how would the revised stockholders' equity appear?

(d) Prepare journal entries that would be needed (if necessary) to record the proposed transactions from part (a), (b), and (c).

B-14.08   *The statement of stockholders' equity*

Pasquali Corporation was incorporated on January 1, 20X4. The following equity-related transactions occurred during 20X4. Evaluate these activities and prepare a statement of stockholders' equity for the year ending December 31, 20X4.

Issued 4,000,000 shares of $1 par value common stock at $3 per share.

Declared and issued a 5% stock dividend (200,000 shares) at a time when the market value of the stock was $6 per share.

Reacquired 15,000 treasury shares at $5 per share.

Declared and paid cash dividends of $100,000.

Reported net income for the full year of $1,500,000.

Involved Problems

Equity structure and impact *I-14.01*

Summary information for Branford Corporation's balance sheet follows:

BRANFORD CORPORATION Balance Sheet August 15, 20X4		
Assets		
Cash		$ 125,000
Accounts receivable		250,000
Inventory		750,000
Property, plant, & equipment (net)		860,000
Total assets		$1,985,000
Liabilities		
Accounts payable	$125,000	
Accrued liabilities	260,000	
Notes payable	290,000	
Total liabilities		$ 675,000
Stockholders' equity		
Common stock, $5 par	$700,000	
Paid-in capital in excess of par	300,000	
Retained earnings	310,000	
Total stockholders' equity		1,310,000
Total liabilities and equity		$1,985,000

Branford's business is growing rapidly, and the company needs to expand its manufacturing facilities. This expansion will require the company to obtain an additional $1,000,000 in cash. The company is exploring five alternatives to obtain the necessary capital:

DEBT OPTION:

> Branford is able to borrow, on a 5-year note, the full amount needed. The interest rate on this note would be 7%, and the note would require monthly payments.

COMMON STOCK OPTION:

> Branford has identified an investor who is willing to pay $1,000,000 for 40,000 newly issued common shares. Common shares have been paying a dividend of $0.50 per share. Branford anticipates that this dividend rate will be maintained.

NONCUMULATIVE PREFERRED STOCK OPTION:

> Branford has identified a hedge fund that will pay $1,000,000 for 8% noncumulative preferred stock to be issued at par.

CUMULATIVE PREFERRED STOCK OPTION:

> Branford has identified an insurance company that will pay $1,000,000 for 6% cumulative preferred stock to be issued at par.

CONVERTIBLE PREFERRED STOCK OPTION:

> Branford has identified a retirement fund that will pay $1,000,000 for 4% cumulative preferred stock to be issued at par. The preferred stock must be convertible into 25,000 shares of common stock at the option of the retirement fund.

(a) Prepare the revised balance sheets that would result under each of the five alternative financing scenarios.

(b) Which of the alternative financing scenarios involve fixed committed payments to investors, and which involve discretionary payments?

(c) Which one of the alternative financing scenarios presents the least risk to existing shareholders? Which one of the scenarios involves the most ownership dilution for existing shareholders?

(d) Which scenario is most risky, and does it require any ownership dilution for existing shareholders?

(e) What is the price per share that is implicit in the common stock alternative? What price per share must the common stock reach before convertible preferred shares might logically be converted? Why might the preferred share alternatives involve different yields?

(f) Evaluate the balance sheets prepared in part (a). Which appear similar? Given that certain balance sheets appear similar, yet the fundamental economic positions vary, what is to be learned about carefully examining financial statements and notes?

I-14.02 *Dividend considerations and strategies*

Buchanan Air Corporation's board of directors is elected by a vote of the common stockholders. As such, the board believes that it owes a fiduciary duty to maximize the returns for common shareholders. The board is evaluating a proposal to raise an additional $10,000,000 in capital by issuing preferred stock. The company's underwriter for the preferred stock offering has determined that the preferred stock will carry a 3% rate if the preferred shares are offered as cumulative shares and a 4% rate if noncumulative.

The board plans to pay out annual dividends equal to net income for each of the next four years. The anticipated income is $300,000 in 20X1, $0 in 20X2, $900,000 in 20X3, and $1,800,000 in 20X4.

Prepare a table showing how much in dividends would be paid to common shareholders if the preferred stock is issued as cumulative versus noncumulative. To maximize the anticipated return to common over the next 4 years, should the board conclude to issue the preferred stock as cumulative or noncumulative? If the anticipated income pattern were different, could a different conclusion be reached?

Impact of various stock transactions   *I-14.03*

Evaluate the following types of transactions, and identify the impact (increase (▲), decrease (▼), or no change (**N/C**)) on total equity, common or preferred stock, additional paid-in capital, treasury stock, and retained earnings. The first transaction type is done as an example.

	Total Equity	*Common Stock/ Preferred Stock*	*Additional Paid-in Capital*	*Treasury Stock*	*Retained Earnings*
Issue common stock at par	▲	▲	N/C	N/C	N/C
Issue common stock at > par					
Issue preferred stock at par					
Issue preferred stock at > par					
Buy treasury stock (cost method)					
Resell treasury stock > cost (cost method)					
Resell treasury stock < cost (cost method)					
Declare cash dividend					
Pay previously declared cash dividend					
Declare and issue large stock dividend					
Declare and issue small stock dividend (fair value > par)					
Declare and issue stock split					

Dry Dock Container Corporation began operations in early 20X5, when it issued 200,000 shares of $3 par value common stock for $10 per share. The following additional equity-related transactions occurred during 20X5.

Transaction A:

Issued 50,000 shares of $100 par value, 6%, cumulative preferred at $102 per share.

Transaction B:

Reacquired 10,000 common shares for treasury at $12 per share.

Transaction C:

Declared the full cash dividend on the preferred and $0.10 per share on the outstanding common shares.

Transaction D:

Paid the previously declared dividends.

Transaction E:

Sold 10,000 treasury shares at $15 per share.

Transaction F:

Declared and issued a 2% common stock dividend. The dividend occurred subsequent to the above described treasury stock transactions. The market value of the stock was $13 per share.

Transaction G:

Reacquired 20,000 common shares for treasury at $11 per share.

Transaction H:

Closed the annual net income of $800,000 from Income Summary to Retained Earnings.

(a) Prepare journal entries for the above described transactions.

(b) Prepare the 20X5 statement of stockholders' equity reflecting the above described transactions.

(c) Prepare the stockholders' equity section of Dry Dock's balance sheet at December 31, 20X5.

Panther Partners is an investment management company and was recently faxed the stockholders' equity statement for a company in which an investment was contemplated. The fax machine malfunctioned and certain information was not legible. The following is the smudged fax:

PALOMA CORPORATION
Statement of Stockholders' Equity
For the Year Ending December 31, 20X7

	Preferred Stock, $$Ж Par	Common Stock, $2 Par	Paid-in Capital in Excess of Par - PS	Paid-in Capital in Excess of Par - CS	Retained Earnings	Treasury Stock	Total Stockholders' Equity
Balance on January 1	▮▮▮▮	$600,000		$400,000	$550,000		$1,550,000
Issuance of common		200,000		▮▮▮▮			700,000
Issuance of preferred	500,000		$5,000				▮▮▮▮
Purchase treasury stock						▮▮▮▮	▮▮▮▮
Net income					275,000		▮▮▮▮
Preferred cash dividends					▮▮▮▮		▮▮▮▮
Common cash dividends					(25,000)		▮▮▮▮
Stock dividend	-	▮▮▮▮	-	60,000	(90,000)	-	▮▮▮▮
Balance on December 31	$500,000	▮▮▮▮	▮▮▮▮	$960,000	$690,000	$(160,000)	▮▮▮▮

Examine the smudged statement of stockholders' equity, and determine the correct reply to each of the following questions:

If 10,000 preferred shares were issued, what was the per share par value and issue price?

Assuming the preferred dividend reflected a full-year amount at the normal yield, what is the percentage rate associated with preferred stock?

What price per share was received for the newly issued common shares?

How much was the aggregate price paid for the treasury stock purchase?

How many common shares were issued as of December 31?

What was the market price per share on the date of the stock dividend?

Team-based approach to comparison of equity issues　　　　　　　　　　　　　　　　*I-14.06*

Form a team of 4 to 6 members. Each team member should go to the website of the Securities and Exchange Commission (www.sec.gov). Follow the links that allow you find the latest filings by corporate issuers of securities (filings and forms - company filings - latest filings) and enter "form type" as "S-1". This will retrieve all of the recent S-1's which are filed pursuant to corporate issuances of securities. Each team member should select a unique example of a company that is issuing an equity security (common stock, preferred stock, or some other option or warrant for such securities).

Examine the S-1 filing and answer the following questions. Then, meet as a group and compare results. Were any unique features identified for your company?

What is the name of the business, and what is their product or service?

What is the history of the business? Is it a new company, or does it have an established operating history?

What type of security is being offered for sale?

What are the primary features of the offering, such as number of shares, par value, and so forth?

How will the money that is being raised be used? Will it all flow to the company for use, or is some of it earmarked for existing shareholders who are "selling" their stock?

Chapter 15:
Financial Reporting and Concepts

Goals:

Special reporting situations.
Earnings per share and other key indicators.
The objectives and qualities of accounting information.
The development of generally accepted accounting principles.
Key assumptions of financial accounting and reporting.
Issues in accounting for global commerce.

principlesofaccounting.com

The accounting profession uses an "all inclusive" approach to measuring income. Virtually all transactions, other than shareholder related transactions like issuing stock and paying dividends, are eventually channeled through the income statement. However, there are certain situations where the accounting rules have evolved in sophistication to provide special disclosures. The reason for the added disclosure is to make it easier for users of financial statements to sort out the effects that are related to ongoing operations versus those that are somehow unique. The following discussion will highlight the correct handling of special situations.

CORRECTIONS OF ERRORS

Errors consist of mathematical mistakes, incorrect reporting, omissions, oversights, and other things that were simply handled wrong in a previous accounting period. Once an error is discovered, it must be corrected.

The temptation is to simply force the books into balance by making a compensating error in the current period. For example, assume that a company failed to depreciate an asset in 20X4, and this fact is discovered in 20X5. Why not just catch up by "double depreciating" the asset in 20X5, and then everything will be fine, right? Wrong! While it is true that accumulated depreciation in the balance sheet would be back on track at the end of 20X5, income for 20X4 and 20X5 would now both be wrong. It is not technically correct to handle errors this way.

Instead, U.S. generally accepted accounting principles dictate that error corrections (if material) must be handled by **prior period adjustment**. This means that the financial statements of prior periods must be subjected to a **restatement** to make them correct. In essence, the financial statements of prior periods are redone to reflect the correct amounts. Global GAAP follows a similar approach but provides an exception for adjustments that are impractical to determine.

The following 20X5 entry reveals the method of adjusting the general ledger for failure to record depreciation of $50,000 in 20X4. The debit to Retained Earnings reflects the expense that would have been recorded and closed to Retained Earnings in the prior year, while the credit to Accumulated Depreciation provides a catch-up adjustment to reflect the account's correct balance.

XX-XX-X5	Retained Earnings	50,000	
	Accumulated Depreciation		50,000
	To record correction of error for previously omitted 20X4 depreciation expense		

Importantly, if comparative financial statements (i.e., side-by-side financial statements, for two or more years) are presented for 20X4 and 20X5, depreciation would be reported at the correct amounts in each years' statements (along with a note indicating that the prior years' data have been revised for an error correction). If an error related to prior periods for which comparative data are not presented, then the statement of retained earnings would be amended as follows:

GOOF UP CORPORATION **Statement of Retained Earnings** **For the Year Ending December 31, 20X5**	
Retained earnings - January 1, 20X5 - as previously reported	$500,000
Less: Effect of correction of depreciation error from 20X4	(50,000)
Corrected beginning retained earnings	$450,000
Plus: Net income	125,000
	$575,000
Less: Dividends	(25,000)
Retained earnings - December 31, 20X5	$550,000

DIS-CONTINUED OPERATIONS

A company may decide to exit a unit of operation by sale to some other company, or by outright abandonment. For example, a computer maker may sell its personal computer manufacturing unit to a more efficient competitor and instead focus on its server and service business. Or, a chemical company may decide to close a unit that has been producing a specialty product that has become an environmental liability.

When an entity plans to dispose of a component, it will invoke the unique reporting rules related to **discontinued operations**. To trigger these rules requires that the disposal represent a strategic shift with major impact on operations and financial resources. This would typically entail discontinuance of a major segment, unit, subsidiary, or group of assets that are clearly distinguishable operationally and for reporting purposes.

Following is an illustrative income statement for Bail Out Corporation. Bail Out distributes farming implements and sporting goods. During 20X7, Bail Out sold its sporting equipment business and began to focus only on farm implements.

In examining this illustration, be aware that revenues and expenses only relate to the continuing farming equipment operations. *All* amounts relating to operations of the sporting equipment business, along with the loss on the sale of assets used in that business, are removed from the upper portion of the income statement and placed in a separate category below income from continuing operations. If material, a company may separate the operating gain/loss from the gain/loss on the actual disposal of assets within this section.

BAIL OUT CORPORATION
Income Statement
For the Year Ending December 31, 20X7

Sales		$5,500,000
Cost of goods sold		3,300,000
Gross profit		$2,200,000
Operating expenses		
Salaries	$635,000	
Rent	135,000	
Other operating expenses	300,000	1,070,000
Income from continuing operations before income taxes		$1,130,000
Income taxes		400,000
Income from continuing operations		$ 730,000
Discontinued operations		
Loss from operation of sports equip. unit, including loss on disposal	$600,000	
Less: Income tax benefit from loss on disposal of business unit	130,000	
Loss on discontinued operations		470,000
Net income		$ 260,000

In addition to the shown modification on the face of the income statement, a company may also be required to provide extensive supplemental disclosures. These disclosures identify the disposal unit's specific income statement impacts such as revenues, cost of sales, and so forth. Additional information may be provided explaining the discontinuation and detail impacts on assets, liabilities, and cash flows.

If a company disposes of a facility or some other set of assets that is not judged to be a major strategic shift, then discontinued operations reporting is *not* invoked. Suppose Sail Out sold its facility in Georgia, but continued to distribute the same products at other locations. This would not constitute a discontinued operation because the company will continue to operate in the same line of business. The income statement might include a separate line item for the gain or loss on the sale of the location, but it would not constitute a discontinued operation:

SAIL OUT CORPORATION
Income Statement
For the Year Ending December 31, 20X7

Sales		$5,900,000
Cost of goods sold		3,900,000
Gross profit		$2,000,000
Operating expenses		
Salaries	$635,000	
Rent	135,000	
Other operating expenses	300,000	
Loss on sale of Georgia location	400,000	1,470,000
Income from continuing operations before income taxes		$ 530,000
Income taxes		270,000
Net income		$ 260,000

Look again at Bail Out and note that income taxes were "split" between continuing operations and discontinued operations. This method of showing tax effects for discontinued operations is mandatory and is called **intraperiod tax allocation**. Intraperiod tax allocation is applicable to other items reported below continuing operations (and some prior period and selected equity adjustments), but only one income tax number is attributed to income from continuing operations.

COMPRE-
HENSIVE
INCOME

The Long-Term Investments chapter introduced *other comprehensive income*. OCI arose from changes in the fair value of investments classified as "available for sale." OCI can also result from certain pension plan accounting adjustments and translation of the financial statements of foreign subsidiaries.

OCI does not enter into the determination of net income or retained earnings, but it does enter into the determination of a broader concept of income. When OCI is present, it may be presented as a separate component in a statement of comprehensive income. Alternatively, a company may present a reconciliation of net income to total comprehensive income.

In the following illustration take note that **net income** or **earnings** is income from continuing operations plus/minus discontinued operations. **Comprehensive income** is *net income* plus *other comprehensive income*. OCI is closed to the Accumulated Other Comprehensive Income account that is presented within stockholders' equity (similar to, but separate from, retained earnings). Additional reconciliations are sometimes necessary to more fully explain the detailed nature of specific changes in Accumulated OCI.

RECAP CORPORATION Statement of Comprehensive Income For the Year Ending December 31, 20X7		
Sales		$6,500,000
Cost of goods sold		4,000,000
Gross profit		$2,500,000
Operating expenses		
Salaries	$ 750,000	
Rent	250,000	
Other operating expenses	300,000	1,300,000
Income from continuing operations before income taxes		$1,200,000
Income taxes		500,000
Income from continuing operations		$ 700,000
Discontinued operations		
Profit on operations of food processing unit, including gain on disposal	$1,700,000	
Less: Income tax on disposal of business unit	450,000	
Gain on discontinued operations		1,250,000
Net income/earnings		$1,950,000
Other comprehensive income adjustments from certain investments		100,000
Comprehensive income		$2,050,000

A company may adopt an alternative accounting principle. Such **accounting changes** relate to changes from one acceptable method to another. For instance, a company may conclude that it wishes to adopt FIFO instead of average cost. Such changes should only occur for good cause (not just to improve income), and flip-flopping is not permitted. When a change is made, the company must make a **retrospective**

adjustment. This means that the financial statements of prior accounting periods should be reworked as if the new principle had always been used.

Disclosures that must accompany a change in accounting principle are extensive. Notes must indicate why the newly adopted method is preferable. In addition, a substantial presentation is required showing amounts that were previously presented versus the newly derived numbers, with a clear delineation of all changes. And, the cumulative effect of the change that relates to all years *prior to the earliest financial data presented* must be disclosed.

Do not confuse a change in accounting method with a change in accounting estimate. Changes in estimate are handled prospectively. This type of change was illustrated in the Property, Plant, and Equipment chapter. If a change in principle cannot be separated from a change in estimate, the adjustment would be handled as a change in estimate. Similar treatment is required for any change in depreciation method.

Investors may discuss a company's "earnings before interest and taxes" (**EBIT**) and "earnings before interest, taxes, depreciation, and amortization" (**EBITDA**). These numbers can be calculated from information available in the statements. Some argue that EBIT (pronounced with a long "E" sound and "bit") and EBITDA (pronounced with a long "E" sound and "bit" and "dah") are important and relevant to decision making, because they reveal the core performance before considering financing costs and taxes (and noncash charges like depreciation and amortization).

These numbers are sometimes used in evaluating the intrinsic value of a firm, in that they reveal how much the business is producing in earnings without regard to how the business is financed and taxed. These numbers should be used with great care, as they can provide an overly simplistic view of business performance.

Earnings Per Share and Other Indicators

How is one to meaningfully compare the net income of a large corporation that has millions of shares outstanding to smaller companies that may have less than even one million shares? The larger company is probably expected to produce a greater amount of income. But, the smaller company might be doing better per unit of ownership. To adjust for differences in size, public companies must supplement their income reports with a number that represents earnings on a per common share basis.

Earnings per share, or EPS, is a widely followed performance measure. Corporate communications and news stories will typically focus on EPS, but care should be taken in drawing any definitive conclusions. Nonrecurring transactions and events can positively or negatively impact income. Companies that present an income statement that segregates income from continuing operations from other components of income must also subdivide per share data (e.g., EPS from continuing operations, discontinued operations, etc.).

BASIC EPS   **Basic EPS** may be thought of as a fraction with income in the numerator and the number of common shares in the denominator. Expanding this thought, consider that income is for a period of time (e.g., a quarter or year), and during that period of time, the number of shares might have changed because of share issuances or treasury stock transactions. Therefore, a *more correct* characterization is income divided by the weighted-average number of common shares outstanding.

Further, consider that some companies have both common and preferred shares. Dividends on common and preferred stock are not expenses and do not reduce income. However, preferred dividends do lay claim to a portion of the corporate income stream. Therefore, one more modification is needed to *correctly* portray the basic EPS fraction:

$$\text{Basic EPS} = \frac{\text{Income Available to Common}}{\text{Weighted-Average Number of Common Shares Outstanding}}$$

The basic EPS calculation entails a reduction of income by the amount of preferred dividends for the period. To illustrate, assume that Kooyul Corporation began 20X4 with 1,000,000 shares of common stock outstanding. On April 1, 20X4, Kooyul issued 200,000 additional shares of common stock, and 120,000 shares of common stock were reacquired on November 1. Kooyul reported net income of $2,760,000 for the year ending December 31, 20X4. Kooyul also had 50,000 shares of preferred stock on which $500,000 in dividends were rightfully declared and paid during 20X4. Kooyul paid $270,000 in dividends to common shareholders. Therefore, Kooyul's basic EPS is $2 per share ($2,260,000/1,130,000), as discussed in the following paragraph.

Income available to Kooyul's common shareholders is $2,260,000. This amount is calculated as the net income ($2,760,000) minus the preferred dividends ($500,000). Dividends on common stock do not impact the EPS calculation. Weighted-average common shares outstanding during 20X4 are 1,130,000. The following table illustrates this calculation:

Time Interval	Portion of Year	Shares Outstanding During Time Interval	Calculation	Weighted-Average Impact
Jan. 1 - March 31	3 months	1,000,000	3/12 X 1,000,000 =	250,000
April 1 - Oct. 31	7 months	1,200,000 (1,000,000 + 200,000)	7/12 X 1,200,000 =	700,000
Nov. 1 - Dec. 31	2 months	1,080,000 (1,200,000 - 120,000)	2/12 X 1,080,000 =	180,000
				1,130,000

DILUTED EPS   Some companies must report an *additional* **diluted EPS** number. The diluted EPS is applicable to companies that have **complex capital structures**. Examples include companies that have issued stock options and warrants that entitle their holders to buy additional shares of common stock from the company, and convertible bonds and preferred stocks that are exchangeable for common shares. These financial instruments represent the possibility that more shares of common stock will be issued and are potentially "dilutive" to existing common shareholders.

Companies with **dilutive securities** take the potential effect of dilution into consideration in calculating diluted EPS. These calculations require a series of assumptions about dilutive securities being converted into common stock.

The hypothetical calculations are imaginative; even providing guidelines about how *assumed* money generated from *assumed* exercises of options and warrants is *assumed* to be "reinvested." Diluted EPS provides existing shareholders a measure of how the company's income is potentially to be shared with other interests.

Financial analysts often incorporate reported EPS information into the calculation of the **price/earnings ratio** (P/E). This is simply the stock price per share divided by the annual EPS:

$$\text{Price Earnings Ratio} = \frac{\text{Market Price Per Share}}{\text{Earnings Per Share}}$$

For example, a stock selling at $15 per share with $1 of EPS would have a P/E of 15. Other companies may have a P/E of 5 or 25. Wouldn't investors always be drawn to companies that have the lowest ratios since they may represent the best earnings generation per dollar of required investment? Perhaps not, as the "E" in P/E is past earnings. New companies may have a bright future, even if current earnings are not great. Other companies may have great current earnings, but no room to grow.

Another ratio is the "PEG" ratio that relates P/E to the earnings "growth" rate, with growth expressed as a whole number. For example, a company with a P/E of 20 that is experiencing average annual increases in income of 20% would have a PEG of 1 (20 divided by 20). If the same company instead had annual earnings increases of 10%, then the PEG would be 2 (20 divided by 10). Lower PEG numbers sometimes help identify more attractive investments.

Another per share amount that analysts frequently calculate is the **book value per share**. This refers to the amount of reported stockholders' equity for each share of common stock. Book value is not the same thing as market value or fair value. Book value is based on reported amounts within the balance sheet.

Many items included in the balance sheet are based on historical costs which can be well below fair value. On the other hand, do not automatically conclude that a company is worth more than its book value, as some balance sheets include significant intangibles that cannot be easily converted to value.

For a corporation that has only common stock outstanding, the calculation of book value per share is simple. Total stockholders' equity is divided by common shares outstanding at the end of the accounting period.

To illustrate, assume that Fuller Corporation has the following stockholders' equity, which results in a $24 book value per share ($12,000,000/500,000 shares):

Stockholders' Equity	
Common stock, $1 par value, 2,000,000 shares authorized, 500,000 shares issued and outstanding	$ 500,000
Paid-in capital in excess of par - common stock	10,000,000
Retained earnings	1,500,000
Total stockholders' equity	$12,000,000

A company with preferred stock must allocate total equity between the common and preferred shares. The amount of equity attributable to preferred shares is generally considered to be the call price (i.e., redemption or liquidation price) plus any dividends that are due. The remaining amount of "common" equity (total equity minus equity attributable to preferred stock) is divided by the number of common shares to calculate book value per common share:

$$\text{Book Value Per Share} = \frac{\text{"Common" Equity}}{\text{Common Shares Outstanding}}$$

Assume that Muller Corporation has the following stockholders' equity:

Stockholders' Equity

Capital stock:			
Preferred stock, $100 par value, callable at 110, 6%, cumulative, 300,000 shares authorized, 100,000 shares issued and outstanding	$10,000,000		
Common stock, $1 par value, 1,000,000 shares authorized, 600,000 shares issued and outstanding		600,000	$10,600,000
Additional paid-in capital			
Paid-in capital in excess of par - preferred stock	$ 700,000		
Paid-in capital in excess of par - common stock	20,000,000	20,700,000	
Total paid-in capital			$31,300,000
Retained earnings			4,900,000
Total stockholders' equity			$36,200,000

Mike Kreinhop is a financial analyst for an investment fund, and is evaluating the merits of Muller Corporation. Pursuant to this task, he has diligently combed through the notes to the financial statements and found that the preferred dividends were *not paid in the current or prior year*. He notes that the annual dividend is $600,000 (6% X $10,000,000) and the preferred stock is cumulative in nature. Although Muller has sufficient retained earnings to support a dividend, it is presently cash constrained due to reinvestment of all free cash flow in a new building and expansion of inventory. Kreinhop correctly prepared the following book value per share calculation:

Total Equity		$36,200,000
Less: Amount of equity attributable to preferred		
Call price ($10,000,000 X 110%)	$11,000,000	
Dividends claim (2 years @ $600,000 per year)	1,200,000	(12,200,000)
Residual equity for common shares		$24,000,000
Number of common shares		÷600,000
Book value per common share		$40 per share

Many companies do not pay dividends. One explanation is that the company is not making any money. Hopefully, the better explanation is that the company needs the cash it is generating from operations to reinvest in expanding a successful concept. On the other hand, some profitable and mature businesses can easily manage their growth and still have plenty of cash left to pay a reasonable dividend to shareholders. In evaluating the dividends of a company, analysts calculate the **dividend rate** (also known as yield).

The dividend rate is the annual dividend divided by the stock price:

$$\textbf{Dividend Rate} = \frac{\textbf{Annual Cash Dividend}}{\textbf{Market Price Per Share}}$$

If Pustejovsky Company pays dividends of $1 per share each year, and its stock is selling at $20 per share, it is yielding 5% ($1/$20). Analysts may be interested in evaluating whether a company is capable of sustaining its dividends and will compare the dividends to the earnings:

$$\textbf{Dividend Payout Ratio} = \frac{\textbf{Annual Cash Dividend}}{\textbf{Earnings Per Share}}$$

If Pustejovsky earned $3 per share, its payout ratio is .333 ($1/$3). On the other hand, if the earnings were only $0.50, giving rise to a **dividend payout ratio** of 2 ($1/$0.50), one would begin to question the "safety" of the dividend.

Some financial statement analysts will compare income to assets, in an attempt to assess how effectively assets are being utilized to generate profits. The specific income measure that is used in the **return on assets** ratio varies with the analyst, but one calculation is:

$$\textbf{Return on Assets Ratio} = \frac{\textbf{(Net Income + Interest Expense)}}{\textbf{Average Assets}}$$

These calculations of "ROA" attempt to focus on income (excluding financing costs) in relation to assets. The point is to demonstrate how much operating income is generated by the deployed assets of the business. This can prove useful in comparing profitability and efficiency for companies in similar industries.

The **return on equity ratio** evaluates income for the common shareholder in relation to the amount of invested common shareholder equity:

$$\textbf{Return on Equity Ratio} = \frac{\textbf{(Net Income - Preferred Dividends)}}{\textbf{Average Common Equity}}$$

"ROE" enables comparison of the effectiveness of capital utilization among firms. What it does not do is evaluate risk. Sometimes, firms with the best ROE also took the greatest gambles. For example, a high ROE firm may rely heavily on debt to finance the business, thereby exposing the business to greater risk of failure when things don't work out. Analysts may compare ROE to the rate of interest on borrowed funds. This can help them assess how effective the firm is in utilizing borrowed funds ("leverage").

Objectives and Qualities of Accounting Information

Of what value is accounting? Why is so much time and money spent on the development of accounting information? To fairly answer these questions, one must think broadly. Investors and creditors have limited resources and seek to place those resources where they will generate the best returns. Accounting information is the nexus of this capital allocation decision process. Without good information, misallocation of capital would occur and result in inefficient production and shortages.

Most organizations devote a fair amount of time and effort to considering their goals and objectives. The accounting profession is no different. Foremost among the objectives of accounting and reporting is to provide useful information for investors, creditors, analysts, governments, and others.

Accounting information is general purpose and should be designed to serve the information needs of all types of interested parties. To be useful, information should be helpful in assessing an entity's economic resources, claims against resources, and what causes changes in resources and claims. Such assessments are generally benefited by accrual accounting, coupled with consideration of cash flows. Care must be taken to differentiate between resource changes resulting from economic performance and other factors (e.g., earnings vs. issuing additional shares of stock). The following qualities help to make accounting useful.

Fundamental Qualities	
Relevancy	Information should be timely and bear on the decision-making process by possessing predictive or confirmatory (feedback) value.
Faithful Representation	Information must be truthful; complete, neutral, and free from error.

Enhancing Qualities	
Comparability	Even though different companies may use different accounting methods, there is still sufficient basis for valid comparison.
Consistency	Deviations in measured outcomes from period to period should be the result of deviations in underlying performance (not accounting quirks).
Verifiability	Different knowledgeable and independent observers reach similar conclusions.
Timeliness	Available in sufficient time to be capable of influence.
Understandability	Clear and concise to those with reasonable business knowledge.

Be aware of the growing complaint that accounting has become too complex. Many persons within and outside the profession protest the ever growing number of rules and their level of detail. The debate is generally couched under the heading "principles versus rules." Advocates of a **principles-based** approach argue that general concepts should guide the judgment of individual accountants. Others argue that the world is quite complex, and accounting must necessarily be **rules-based**. They believe that reliance on individual judgment may lead to wide disparities in reports that could render meaningful comparisons impossible.

Generally accepted accounting principles, or **GAAP**, encompass the rules, practices, and procedures that define the proper execution of accounting. It is important to note that this definition is quite broad, taking in more than just the specific rules issued by standard setters. It encompasses the long-standing methodologies and assumptions that have become ingrained within the profession through years of thought and development. Collectively, GAAP form the foundation of accounting by providing comprehensive guidance and a framework for addressing most accounting issues.

THE FASB, IASB, AND SEC

The Financial Accounting Standards Board (FASB) has been the primary U.S. accounting rule maker since the early 1970s. The FASB maintains an excellent website at FASB.org. There one can find information on all **Accounting Standard Updates** (ASU), as well as numerous helpful videos and news releases related to developments in financial reporting. The FASB is a large organization with the board being supported by a large staff and special groups. These groups include the Emerging Issues Task Force (EITF) and Private Company Council (PCC). The latter is charged with simplifying accounting rules generally applicable to companies without large groups of "public" shareholders.

Prior to the FASB's creation, rules were set by the **Accounting Principles Board** (APB). The APB was created in 1959 by the **American Institute of Certified Public Accountants** (AICPA). The AICPA is a large association of professional accountants who seek to advance the practice of accounting. Before 1959, the duty of standard development fell on the shoulders of an AICPA committee known as the Committee on Accounting Procedure (CAP).

The many rulings of the FASB and its predecessors are updated and codified in an online database called the **Accounting Standards Codification**. This collection provides a research tool that is deemed to be the primary authoritative source and reference guide on accounting standards.

The International Accounting Standards Board (IASB) is the global counterpart to the FASB. The standards of the IASB are oftentimes referred to as IFRS (**International Financial Reporting Standards**). The FASB and IASB are working harmoniously to converge toward a single set of accounting standards. This project is receiving considerable interest from financial institutions, investors, and governmental units around the world. Convergence of accounting standards is seen as an important tool in the facilitation and coordination of international commerce and the global economy.

In a 1930s-era effort to bring credibility to capital markets, the U.S. Congress created the **Securities and Exchange Commission** (SEC). The SEC was charged with the administration of laws that regulate the reporting practices of companies with publicly traded stock. Today, U.S. public companies must register and report to the SEC on a continuing basis. Although the SEC has ultimate authority to set accounting rules, it has elected to operate under a tradition of cooperation and largely defers to the private sector for most specific accounting rules.

THE AUDIT FUNCTION

To provide a measure of integrity, financial reports of public companies are required to be audited by independent CPAs. Auditors evaluate the systems and data that lead to the reported financial statements. The auditor will usually issue an opinion letter on the fairness of the reports. This letter is rather brief and to the point and includes a paragraph similar to the following:

In our opinion, the financial statements present fairly, in all material respects, the financial position of the Company as of [at] December 31, 20X3 and 20X2, and the results of its operations and its cash flows for each of the three years in the period ended December 31, 20X3, in conformity with U.S. generally accepted accounting principles.

Note that the auditor is expressing an opinion about the conformity of the financial statements with generally accepted accounting principles. Thus, conformity with GAAP is the key to obtaining the desired audit opinion. Being alert to the detection of potential fraud is important, but it is not the primary mission of a financial statement audit.

The U.S. Congress created the **Sarbanes-Oxley Act** of 2002 (SOX). It imposed stringent financial statement certification requirements on corporate officers, raised the fiduciary duty of corporate boards, imposed systematic ethics awareness, and placed a greater burden on auditors.

In addition, Section 404 of the Act requires public companies to implement a robust system of internal control; an independent auditor must issue a separate report on the effectiveness of this control system. The Act also created the **Public Company Accounting Oversight Board** (PCAOB). The PCAOB is a private-sector, non-profit corporation, charged with overseeing the auditors of public companies.

Key Assumptions

Many associate accounting with math in terms of absolute precision. However, accounting is actually more like art and social science and depends on certain fundamental assumptions.

ENTITY   Accounting information should be presented for specific and distinct reporting units. In other words, the **entity assumption** requires that separate transactions of owners and others not be commingled with the reporting of economic activity for a particular business. On one hand, an individual may prepare separate financial statements for a business he or she owns even if it is not a separate legal entity. On the other hand, consolidated financial statements may be prepared for a group of entities that are economically commingled but are technically separate legal units.

GOING-CONCERN   In the absence of contrary evidence, accountants base measurement and reporting on the **going-concern assumption**. This means that accountants are not constantly assessing the liquidation value of a company in determining what to report, unless of course liquidation looks like a possibility. This allows for allocation of long-term costs and revenues based on a presumption that the business will continue to operate into the future. Accountants are typically conservative (when in doubt, select the lower asset/revenue measurement choice and the higher liability/expense measurement choice) but not to the point of introducing bias based on an unfounded fear for the future.

If conditions or events raise substantial doubt about the ability to continue to operate as a going concern, and management does not have a viable plan to alleviate those concerns, disclosure is required. This disclosure must accompany the financial statements and include details about the conditions and events giving rise to the doubts, the potential impact on entity obligations, and plans to attempt to mitigate the problem.

PERIODICITY   Accountants assume they can divide time into specific measurement intervals (i.e., months, quarters, years). This periodicity assumption is necessitated by the regular and continuing information needs of financial statement users. More precision could be achieved if accountants had the luxury of waiting many years to report final results, but users need timely information. For instance, a health club may sell lifetime memberships for a flat fee, not really knowing how long its customers will utilize the club. But, the club cannot wait years and years for their customers to die before reporting any financial results. Instead, methods are employed to attribute portions of revenue to each reporting period. This is justified by the periodicity assumption.

MONETARY UNIT

The **monetary unit assumption** means that accounting measures transactions and events in units of money. This assumption overcomes the problems that would arise by mixing measures in the financial statements (e.g., imagine the confusion of combining acres of land with cash). The monetary unit assumption is core and essential to the double-entry, self-balancing accounting model.

STABLE CURRENCY

Inflation can wreak havoc on the usefulness of financial data. For example, suppose a power plant that was constructed in 1970 is still in operation. Accounting reports may show a profit by matching currently generated revenues with depreciation of old ("cheap") construction costs.

A different picture might appear if one reconsidered the "value" of the power plant that is being "used up" in generating the current revenue stream. Inflation can distort performance measurement. Inflation also has the potential to limit the usefulness of the balance sheet by reporting amounts at costs that differ greatly from current value.

Accountants have struggled with this issue for many years, and even experimented with supplemental reporting requirements. However, accounting generally operates under the **stable currency assumption**, going along as though costs and revenues incurred in different time periods need not be adjusted for changes in the value of the monetary unit over time.

Issues in Global Commerce

Understand that international trade no longer simply means importing and exporting. Companies have added subsidiaries in many countries, formed cooperative alliances, listed shares on multiple stock exchanges around the globe, engaged in global cross-border debt financing, and set up service centers that utilize technology to provide seamless customer support around the world.

Companies engaging in global business face some specific reporting challenges. Two of those challenges are (1) how to consolidate global subsidiaries and (2) how to account for global transactions denominated in alternative currencies.

GLOBAL SUBS

When a parent corporation has a subsidiary outside of its home country, the financial statements of that subsidiary may be prepared in the "local" currency of the country in which it operates. But, the parent's financials are prepared in the "reporting" currency of the country in which it is domiciled. Thus, to consolidate the parent and sub first requires converting the sub's financial information into the reporting currency. Facts and circumstances will dictate whether the conversion process occurs by a process known as the functional currency **translation** approach or an alternative approach known as **remeasurement**.

Translation: Used when the subsidiary is somewhat autonomous

The subsidiary is self-supporting by virtue of generating and reinvesting cash flows in its own operations; the parent is primarily an investor. This approach converts the assets and liabilities to the reporting currency based upon prevailing exchange rates at the balance sheet date. A "plug" translation adjustment may be needed to maintain a "balanced" translated set of financials, and that plug is an item of "other comprehensive income" (not operating income).

Remeasurement: Used when translation is not appropriate

This approach converts assets and liabilities at a variety of exchange rates, depending on the type of asset or liability and the date of its origination. Again, a "plug" may be needed to balance, but this plug will produce a positive (credit) or negative (debit) effect on operating income.

GLOBAL TRADING

Many firms buy goods from foreign suppliers and/or sell goods to foreign customers. The terms of the transaction will stipulate how payment is to occur and the currency for making settlement. If the currency is "foreign," then some additional thought must be given to the bookkeeping. Suppose Bentley's Bike Shop purchases bicycles from GiroCycle of Switzerland. On July 1, 20X6, Bentley purchased bicycles, agreeing to pay 20,000 Swiss francs within 60 days. Bentley is in Cleveland, Ohio, and the U.S. dollar is its primary currency. On July 1, Bentley will record the purchase by debiting Inventory and crediting Accounts Payable. But, what amount should be debited and credited? If 20,000 were used, the accounts would cease to be logical. The total Inventory balance would be illogical since it would include this item, and all other transactions in other currencies. Total Accounts Payable would become unintelligible as well. Therefore, Bentley needs to measure the transaction in dollars. On July 1, assume that the current exchange rate (i.e., the "spot rate") is 0.90 U.S. dollars to acquire 1 Swiss franc. The correct entry would be:

07-01-X6	Inventory	18,000	
	Accounts Payable		18,000
	Purchased bicycles, agreeing to pay 20,000 Swiss francs in 60 days (spot rate is $0.90: 20,000 X $0.90 = $18,000)		

By the August 29 settlement date, assume that the dollar has weakened and the spot rate is $0.95. Bentley will have to pay $19,000 (20,000 X $0.95) to buy the 20,000 francs needed to settle the obligation. The following entry shows that the difference between the initially recorded payable ($18,000) and the cash settlement amount ($19,000) is to be recorded as a foreign currency transaction loss:

08-29-X6	Accounts Payable	18,000	
	Currency Exchange Loss	1,000	
	Cash		19,000
	Paid foreign currency payable and recorded exchange loss (20,000 Swiss francs X $0.95 = $19,000)		

If the exchange rate had gone the other way, a foreign currency transaction gain (credit) would have been needed to balance the payable and required cash disbursement.

It is important to know that foreign currency payables and receivables that exist at the close of an accounting period must also be adjusted to reflect the spot rate on the balance sheet date. Suppose Vigeland Corporation sold goods to a customer in England, agreeing to accept payment of 100,000 British pounds in 90 days. On the date of sale, December 1, 20X1, the spot rate for the pound was $1.75. Vigeland prepared financial statements at its year end on December 31, 20X1, at which time the spot rate for the pound was $1.90. The foreign currency receivable was collected on February 28, 20X2, and Vigeland immediately converted the 100,000 pounds to dollars at the then current exchange rate of $1.70. The following illustrates Vigeland's sale, year-end adjustment, and subsequent collection:

12-01-X1	Accounts Receivable	175,000	
	Sales		175,000
	Sold goods to a customer in England, agreeing to accept 100,000 British pounds (100,000 pounds X $1.75 spot rate = $175,000)		
12-31-X1	Accounts Receivable	15,000	
	Currency Exchange Gain		15,000
	Year-end adjustment to increase accounts receivable to the spot rate (100,000 pounds X $1.90 spot rate = $190,000; $190,000 - $175,000 = $15,000 gain)		
02-28-X2	Cash	170,000	
	Currency Exchange Loss	20,000	
	Accounts Receivable		190,000
	Collected 100,000 pounds and converted them to dollars (100,000 x $1.70 spot rate). Recorded loss for decline in value of receivable since year end ($190,000 vs. $170,000)		

Some companies may wish to avoid foreign currency exchange risks like those just illustrated. The simplest way is to convince a trading partner to make or take payment in the home currency. In the alternative, various financial agreements can be structured with banks or others to hedge this risk.

Chapter 15 Quiz

Goals Achievement

Q15-1. Continuing operations, discontinued operations, and prior period adjustments should all be reported net of their related tax effect.

true or false

Q15-2. Changing from one generally accepted accounting method to another one should be accounted for via:

retrospective adjustment or restatement

Q15-3. When two classes of stock are outstanding, the book value per share computation involves dividing total stockholders' equity by the sum of the number of common and preferred shares outstanding.

true or false

Q15-4. A presumption that a business will continue to operate for an indefinite period of time unless there is substantial evidence to the contrary is the:

going-concern assumption or periodicity assumption

Q15-5. If a foreign currency account payable is established in the accounts at $0.50 per unit, and the exchange rate subsequently changes to $0.60 per unit, then which of the following will result?

exchange gain or exchange loss

Fill in the Blanks

Q15-6. Correction of an error that occurred in the computation of the net income of a previous period is accomplished by the use of a _____.

Q15-7. _____ earnings per share is calculated by ignoring the dilutive effect of convertible securities.

Q15-8. Information is deemed to be _____ if it influences the actions of a decision maker.

Q15-9. _____ are the assumptions, concepts, and procedures that collectively serve as the underlying foundation of accounting.

Q15-10. The _____ assumption holds that an entity's life can be divided into discrete time periods.

Q15-11. Foreign currency payables and receivables will result in exchange gains and losses if exchange rates _____.

Q15-12. Which of the following is correct?

a. Net income is included in total comprehensive income.

b. Discontinued operations is an example of an item that is classified as other comprehensive income.

c. Intraperiod tax allocation means that all tax is attributed to income from continuing operations.

d. If a company has discontinued operations, net income excludes the effects thereof.

Q15-13. Sparks Corporation had 15,000 shares of common stock outstanding on January 1, and issued an additional 5,000 shares on June 1. There was no preferred stock outstanding. The corporation reports net income of $200,000. How much is basic earnings per share (to the nearest cent) for the calendar year?

a. $10.00

b. $11.16

c. $11.43

d. $13.33

Q15-14. If a corporation has total stockholders' equity of $1,000,000, 100,000 shares of common stock outstanding, and 1,000 shares of $100 par value preferred stock outstanding, how much is book value per common share? Assume that the preferred stock is callable at $110 and dividends of $4,000 on preferred stock are due.

a. $8.86

b. $9.00

c. $9.96

d. $10.00

Q15-15. Which of the following is a stated objective of financial reporting?

a. To provide information useful in assessing resources, claims against those resources, and changes therein.

b. To provide information useful in preparing tax returns and other governmental reports.

c. To provide information about the current cost of an enterprise's assets.

d. To ensure that all companies use the same financial accounting principles.

Q15-16. Darland Corporation (U.S.) purchased goods on account for 1,000 Swiss francs. On the date of purchase, the spot rate for the Swiss franc was $0.70. By the time the corporation settled its obligation, the spot rate had fallen to $0.65 per Swiss franc. How much was the foreign currency exchange gain or loss?

a. $0

b. $50 gain

c. $50 loss

d. $83 gain

Chapter 15 Problems

Basic Problems

Roll Call manufactures a unique keychain with a built-in radio frequency identification chip. This device is issued to students at State University, and a host computer tracks student attendance at each class by automatically monitoring the whereabouts of the keychains.

Roll Call's ending inventory at December 31, 20X3 was $1,670,000. However, this value was transposed and entered into the accounting system at $1,760,000. As a result, ending inventory was overstated and cost of goods sold was understated by $90,000. This error was discovered in March of 20X4, when the CFO was preparing a presentation for potential investors.

The 20X3 books have long-since been closed, and financial reports were already released. The CFO proposed to correct the error by debiting Cost of Goods Sold and crediting Inventory for $90,000. Net income for 20X3 was $900,000, and 20X4 should be at about the same level.

(a) What is the appropriate journal entry to correct the error? You may assume the firm uses a periodic inventory system, and the balance of the Inventory account is shown as $1,760,000.

(b) In the CFO presentation to potential investors, how much should be reported as 20X3 net income? How much should be reported as inventory on hand at December 31, 20X3?

(c) Is the amount of the error material? If you are an accountant for Roll Call and instructed by the CFO to record the erroneous entry, what should you do?

Work safety regulations require that the side walls of ditches and trenches be supported by various devices to protect workers from collapse. Trench Coat manufactures and sells a spray on concrete product that supports the walls of recently excavated trenches.

Several years back, the company formed a separate business unit that provides spray on surface linings for swimming pools. That business unit has failed to meet management's goals. At the beginning of 20X8, Trench Coat sold the swimming pool business, resulting in a $250,000 pretax gain.

The trench coating product continues to be very successful. During 20X8, product sales were $7,000,000, at a gross margin of 35%. Selling expenses totaled $800,000 and administrative expenses totaled $1,200,000. Trench Coat is subject to a 40% income tax rate.

(a) Prepare the 20X8 income statement assuming that management views the disposal of the swimming pool business as a strategic shift.

(b) Prepare the 20X8 income statement assuming that the disposal of the swimming pool business is not a strategic shift.

Melanie Mielke Construction Corporation is considering the appropriate accounting for two unrelated events during the year. The first event related to the effects of a labor strike that resulted in a work stoppage on a major construction project. $2,000,000 of building material that was left exposed to weather conditions during the strike was lost. The second event was a $3,000,000 unrealized gain on available-for-sale securities that continue to be held as an investment.

Melanie Mielke's annual sales were $9,000,000, at a gross margin of 15%. Selling expenses totaled $300,000, and administrative expenses totaled $800,000. Mielke is subject to a 30% income tax rate.

Prepare the 20XX income statement for Melanie Mielke Construction Corporation.

At the beginning of 20X2, Devin Company changed its method of accounting for certain operating expenses. The change in methods shifted from one acceptable method to another acceptable method. Devin Company's accounting department was not sure how to report the effect of the change, and has prepared the following alternative comparative income statements.

The first option includes a cumulative effect catch-up adjustment for the change.

The second option results in changing the amount of operating expenses previously reported for 20X1. The company faces a 35% tax rate.

Which of the two income statements should be used? What was the dollar impact of the change in method, before and after tax. Did the change impact any years prior to 20X1?

DEVIN COMPANY Income Statement For the Years Ending December 31, 20X1 and 20X2		
	20X2	20X1
Sales	$6,500,000	$5,000,000
Cost of goods sold	3,000,000	2,700,000
Gross profit	$3,500,000	$2,300,000
Operating expenses	2,100,000	1,650,000
Income from continuing operations before income tax	$1,400,000	$ 650,000
Income tax on income from continuing operations	490,000	227,500
Income from continuing operations	$ 910,000	$ 422,500
Cumulative effect of change in method, net of tax	190,000	-
Net income	$1,100,000	$ 422,500

DEVIN COMPANY
Income Statement
For the Years Ending December 31, 20X1 and 20X2

	20X2	20X1
Sales	$6,500,000	$5,000,000
Cost of goods sold	3,000,000	2,700,000
Gross profit	$3,500,000	$2,300,000
Operating expenses	2,100,000	1,357,692
Income from continuing operations before income taxes	$1,400,000	$ 942,308
Income tax on income from continuing operations	490,000	329,808
Net income	$ 910,000	$ 612,500

B-15.05   *Concepts including OCI/ROA/EBIT/EBITDA/etc.*

Three of the following statements are patently false. Find the three false statements. The other statements are true, and may include additional insights beyond those mentioned in the textbook.

"Earnings" is synonymous with "income from continuing operations plus or minus the effects of any discontinued operations."

Changes in accounting estimates must be reported by retrospective adjustment.

EBIT and EBITDA are accounting values that are required to be reported on the face of the income statement.

Other comprehensive income can be reported on the face of a statement of comprehensive income or in a separate reconciliation.

When there is reported change in value for available for sale securities, "comprehensive income" becomes synonymous with "net income."

Book value per share is an amount related to shares of common stock.

B-15.06   *Earnings per share*

Trinity Railway began 20X5 with 900,000 shares of common stock outstanding. On March 1, 20X5, Trinity Railway issued 300,000 additional shares of common stock. 50,000 shares of common stock were reacquired on October 1. Trinity Railway reported net income of $2,275,000 for the year ending December 31, 20X5. Trinity Railway paid $250,000 in common dividends during 20X5.

(a) Calculate the weighted-average common shares outstanding for 20X5.

(b) Calculate basic earnings per share for 20X5.

(c) If Trinity Railway also had preferred stock outstanding, and declared and paid $227,500 in dividends on these shares during 20X5, calculate the revised amount for basic earnings per share.

(d) Explain the concept of diluted EPS. What types of additional securities would Trinity Railway likely need to issue before it would be become necessary to calculate a diluted EPS amount?

P/E, PEG, Dividend rates B-15.07

Calculate the price earnings ratio, PEG ratio, dividend rate, and dividend payout ratio for each of the following companies. Will each ratio consistently rank the companies from "best" to "worst" performer?

SPREADSHEET
TOOL:

Data sort

	Earnings Per Share	Dividends Per Share	Market Price Per Share	Average Annual Increase in Earnings
Andrews Corporation	$2.50	$0.00	$25.00	5%
Borger Corporation	$1.00	$1.00	$18.00	10%
Calvert Corporation	$5.00	$2.50	$20.00	5%
Dorchester Corporation	$1.25	$0.00	$10.00	25%
Easton Corporation	$2.50	$0.75	$50.00	30%
Flores Corporation	$2.00	$0.10	$25.00	20%
Gerber Corporation	$0.10	$0.00	$ 5.00	10%
Houston Corporation	$0.50	$0.25	$20.00	3%

Book value per share B-15.08

Brazil Corporation has a simple capital structure, and its equity section follows:

Stockholders' Equity	
Common stock, $0.50 par value, 800,000 shares authorized, 300,000 shares issued and outstanding	$ 150,000
Paid-in capital in excess of par - common stock	750,000
Retained earnings	2,400,000
Total stockholders' equity	$3,300,000

Chile Corporation has a complex capital structure, and its equity section follows:

Stockholders' Equity

Capital stock:			
Preferred stock, $50 par value, callable at 103, 5%, cumulative, 100,000 shares authorized, 60,000 shares issued and outstanding	$3,000,000		
Common stock, $1 par value, 500,000 shares authorized, 200,000 shares issued and outstanding	200,000	$3,200,000	
Additional paid-in capital			
Paid-in capital in excess of par - preferred stock	$ 60,000		
Paid-in capital in excess of par - common stock	800,000	860,000	
Total paid-in capital			$ 4,060,000
Retained earnings			6,910,000
Total stockholders' equity			$10,970,000

With the exception of the current year's preferred dividend which is now due, Chile has paid all dividends on the preferred stock.

Determine the issue price of each company's common and preferred stock. Determine the book value per common share for each company.

B-15.09   *Return on assets and return on equity*

Calculate the return on assets and return on equity for the following companies. What appears to be the average interest rate faced by the companies? As a broad generalization, which companies appear to be effectively utilizing debt to improve financial performance?

	Net Income	Interest Expense*	Preferred Dividends	Average Assets	Average Equity
Alejando Corp.	$120,000	$10,000	$0	$1,100,000	$1,000,000
Ling Corp.	$100,000	$80,000	$20,000	$1,900,000	$1,100,000
Beaufort Corp.	$700,000	$200,000	$15,000	$4,000,000	$2,000,000
Robinson Corp.	$300,000	$200,000	$100,000	$6,000,000	$4,000,000

* Note: Many analysts use the "after tax" cost of interest (i.e., $1 of interest only costs $0.75 if a company faces a 25% tax rate) in calculating the return on assets. The idea is to determine how much higher income would be without the interest impact. For purposes of this problem you may simply use the interest expense shown.

Match the following accounting qualities to the appropriate explanations that follow:

Relevancy

Faithful representation

Comparability

Consistency

Verifiability

Timeliness

Understandability

(a) Deviations in measured outcomes from period to period should be the result of deviations in underlying performance (not accounting quirks).

(b) Clear and concise to those with reasonable business knowledge.

(c) Available in sufficient time to be capable of influence.

(d) Even though different companies may use different accounting methods, there is still sufficient basis for valid comparison.

(e) Information must be truthful; complete, neutral, and free from error.

(f) Information should be timely and bear on the decision-making process by possessing predictive or confirmatory (feedback) value.

(g) Different knowledgeable and independent observers reach similar conclusions.

Provide the correct name of the organization that is being referenced by the following descriptions.

This organization is viewed as centric to the coordination of global harmonization of accounting standards.

This organization passed "Section 404" requiring public companies to implement a robust system of internal control.

This organization is the primary private-sector accounting rule-making body in the U.S.

This organization is no longer in existence, but once issued "opinions" on acceptable accounting practices.

This organization is a professional association of accountants who are seeking to advance the practice of accounting.

This organization was created many years ago, and it is charged with administration of laws that regulate the reporting practices of companies whose stock is publicly traded.

This organization is charged with overseeing the auditors of public companies.

Match the following accounting assumptions to the appropriate explanations that follow:

Entity assumption

Going-concern assumption

Periodicity assumption

Monetary unit assumption

Stable currency assumption

(a)   Overcomes mixing alternative measurements into the financial statements.

(b)   A continuous business process can be segmented into discrete intervals.

(c)   Provides for an orderly allocation of costs and revenues over extended time periods.

(d)   Justification for consolidating the accounts of separate legal entities.

(e)   Because of this, changing currency values due to inflation effects are disregarded.

Match the following terms and concepts to the appropriate explanations that follow:

International Accounting Standards Board

Translation

Remeasurement

Convergence

Reporting currency

Local currency

(a)   The currency of the country in which a subsidiary operates.

(b)   The anticipated direction of global GAAP development.

(c)   The world-wide equivalent of the FASB.

(d)   The currency of the country in which financial statements are prepared for owners.

(e)   Conversion process that uses a variety of exchange rates for assets.

(f)   The "plug" adjustment is an item of "other comprehensive income."

Universal Instruments is based in the U.S. and prepares its financial statements in dollars. The company uses a perpetual inventory system. On December 5, 20X5, Universal had two separate purchase transactions from suppliers in Europe.

The first transaction was for $100,000. Terms of sale provide for settlement in dollars. The account was paid in full on January 11, 20X6.

The second transaction was for 100,000€. Terms of sale provide for settlement in euros. The account was paid in full on January 11, 20X6.

The exchange rate of dollars for euros fluctuated as follows:

December 5, 20X5:	$1.47 per euro
December 31, 20X5:	$1.46 per euro
January 11, 20X6:	$1.49 per euro

Prepare journal entries showing the inventory purchase, year-end adjustment (if necessary), and final settlement for each of these two transactions.

Global Technology is based in the U.S. and prepares its financial statements in dollars. On December 5, 20X5, Global had two sales transactions with customers in Europe.

The first transaction was for $100,000. Terms of sale provide for settlement in dollars. Payment in full was received on January 11, 20X6.

The second transaction was for 100,000€. Terms of sale provide for settlement in euros. Payment in full was received on January 11, 20X6.

The exchange rate of dollars for euros fluctuated as follows:

December 5, 20X5:	$1.47 per euro
December 31, 20X5:	$1.46 per euro
January 11, 20X6:	$1.49 per euro

Prepare journal entries showing the sale (you may ignore cost of sales), year-end adjustment (if necessary), and final settlement for each of these two transactions.

Involved Problems

Stearns Corporation was a diversified company with two separate lines of business - chemicals and financial services. At the beginning of 20X7, a strategic shift resulted in Stearns selling its financial services unit, resulting in a $3,000,000 pretax gain. The following additional transactions and events pertain to 20X7:

The chemical unit sold a paint factory at pretax loss of $500,000. This asset sale did not represent a strategic shift for Stearns.

General information for 20X7 is as follows: Sales, $7,500,000; Cost of Goods Sold, $3,200,000; Selling Expenses, $1,000,000; and General & Administrative Expenses, $1,500,000. The company's income tax rate is 30%.

Stearns changed its method of accounting for inventory at the beginning of 20X7. The cost of goods sold of $3,200,000 is based on the new method. Cumulatively, prior years' income would have been $2,400,000 higher (net of tax effects) had the new method been in use all along.

The company discovered an error in a prior year's report. The error resulted in a $420,000 overstatement of 20X5 net income.

(a)   Prepare the 20X7 income statement for Stearns Corporation.

(b)   Retained earnings at January 1, 20X7, was $5,500,000 before giving consideration to the correction of error or accounting change described above. What is the balance of the revised beginning retained earnings?

(c)   If the company had $400,000 of other comprehensive income (net of any tax effects) related to holding gains on available for sale securities, how much is total "comprehensive income?"

Case Corporation has common and preferred stock outstanding at December 31, as follows:

3,400,000 shares of $1 par value common stock. The company started the year with 3,000,000 shares, issued 600,000 shares on July 1, and reacquired 200,000 shares on October 1.

100,000 shares of $100 par value, 5% preferred. These shares have been outstanding all year, and the $500,000 dividend was declared and paid during the year.

The company's net income for the full year was $2,600,000.

(a)   Compute the company's basic earnings per share.

(b) Additionally, assume the preferred stock is convertible into 1,000,000 shares of common stock. Compute the company's diluted earnings per share. For this calculation, the numerator will be net income, as you will assume that the preferred dividend was not paid ("if" the preferred was converted to common, the preferred dividend would not have been paid). The denominator will be the weighted-average common shares plus the number of shares that would be issued on conversion (i.e., 1,000,000).

Ratios and valuations   *I-15.03*

Roscovis Corporation's December 31, 20X6, equity section follows:

Stockholders' Equity

Capital stock:			
Preferred stock, $100 par value, callable at 105, 4%, cumulative, 200,000 shares authorized, 50,000 shares issued and outstanding	$5,000,000		
Common stock, $2 par value, 1,000,000 shares authorized, 400,000 shares issued and outstanding	800,000	$5,800,000	
Additional paid-in capital			
Paid-in capital in excess of par - preferred stock	$ 50,000		
Paid-in capital in excess of par - common stock	4,000,000	4,050,000	
Total paid-in capital			$ 9,850,000
Retained earnings			7,400,000
Total stockholders' equity			$17,250,000

Roscovis Corporation has annually paid all preferred dividends. There were no changes in paid-in capital during all of 20X6. The beginning retained earnings was $5,400,000. The ending balance of retained earnings is the result of $3,000,000 in net income and $1,000,000 in total dividends.

Determine the maximum price you would pay for a share of common stock in Roscovis if you have the following investment constraints:

Maximum Price/Earnings Ratio	15 X
Maximum Multiple of Book Value	3 X
Minimum Dividend Yield	3%

This problem requires you to team with one other person. One of you will assume the role of accountant for Company A (based in Miami), and the other for Company B (based in London). You should each prepare your company's journal entries for the following purchase and sale transactions. On the sale transactions, you may disregard recording of any cost of goods sold. Compare your results and consider why Company A's foreign currency transaction gain or loss is not offset on Company B's books (and vice versa).

Sale of inventory by Company A to Company B:

> This transaction was for $5,000, on account. The date of sale was March 1, and settlement occurred on April 1.

Sale of inventory by Company A to Company B:

> This transaction was for £2,500, on account. The date of sale was April 1, and settlement occurred on May 1.

Purchase of inventory by Company A from Company B:

> This transaction was for $7,000, on account. The date of purchase was May 1, and settlement occurred on June 1.

Purchase of inventory by Company A from Company B:

> This transaction was for £3,500, on account. The date of purchase was June 1, and settlement occurred on July 1.

The exchange rate of dollars ($) for pounds (£) fluctuated as follows:

March 1:	$2.00 per pound
April 1:	$2.10 per pound
May 1:	$2.05 per pound
June 1:	$1.95 per pound
July 1:	$2.00 per pound

Chapter 16:

Financial Analysis and the Statement of Cash Flows

Goals:

Tools for financial statement analysis.
Evaluating cash flow and the statement of cash flows.
The direct approach to preparing a statement of cash flows.
The indirect approach to presenting operating activities.
Using a worksheet to prepare a statement of cash flows.

principlesofaccounting.com

Anyone wishing to study this textbook can learn valuable insights about accounting. Does the mere fact that this book exists mean that everyone knows about accounting? Obviously not. By analogy, the same can be said about financial information. Many companies spend substantial amounts of money preparing and presenting financial statements that are readily available (the reports for U.S. public companies can be found at www.sec.gov). Does this mean that everyone has in-depth knowledge about these companies? Again, no. Some degree of study is required to benefit from the information.

It is important to know that CPAs and the SEC provide safeguards to protect the *integrity of reported information*, but this is entirely different than suggesting that reporting companies are necessarily good investments. For example, a company could report that its revenue stream is in decline, expenses are on the rise, and significant debt is coming due without a viable plan for making the payments. The financial statements may fully report this predicament. But, if financial statement users choose to ignore that report, only they are to blame.

Investors must be very thorough in examining the financial statements of companies in which they are considering making an investment. Sometimes, the evaluation of complex situations can be assisted by utilization of key metrics or ratios. For example, a doctor will consider a patient's health by taking measurements of blood pressure, heart rate, cholesterol level, and so forth. Likewise, consideration of a company's health can be measured with certain important ratios.

This book has introduced financial statement ratios and analysis techniques throughout many of the previous chapters. The following tables include a recapitulation of those ratios, including cross references back to chapters where the ratios were first introduced. If any of the ratios are unclear, it may prove helpful to refer back to the earlier chapters for more detail on the calculation and interpretation of the ratios. The right hand column of the tables include specific calculations for Emerson Corporation. Comprehensive financial statements for Emerson follow the tables. Be sure to verify each ratio calculation to the data included in those financial statements.

DETAILED
EXAMPLE

Liquidity Ratios	Formula	Ratios For Emerson
Current (Chapter 4: A measure of liquidity; the ability to meet near-term obligations)	$$\frac{\text{Current Assets}}{\text{Current Liabilities}}$$	$$\frac{\$1,730,000}{\$290,000} = 5.97$$
Quick (Chapter 4: A narrow measure of liquidity; the ability to meet near-term obligations)	$$\frac{\text{Cash + Short-term Investments + Accts. Rec.}}{\text{Current Liabilities}}$$	$$\frac{\$1,550,000}{\$290,000} = 5.34$$

Debt Service Ratios	Formula	Ratios For Emerson
Debt to Total Assets (Chapter 13: Percentage of assets financed by long-term and short-term debt)	$$\frac{\text{Total Debt}}{\text{Total Assets}}$$	$$\frac{\$1,190,000}{\$4,100,000} = 0.29$$
Debt to Total Equity (Chapter 13: Proportion of financing that is debt-related)	$$\frac{\text{Total Debt}}{\text{Total Equity}}$$	$$\frac{\$1,190,000}{\$2,910,000} = 0.41$$
Times Interest Earned (Chapter 13: Ability to meet interest obligations)	$$\frac{\text{Income Before Income Taxes and Interest}}{\text{Interest Charges}}$$	$$\frac{\$1,400,000}{\$100,000} = 14$$

Turnover Ratios	Formula	Ratios For Emerson
Accounts Receivable Turnover (Chapter 7: Frequency of collection cycle; to monitor credit policies)	$$\frac{\text{Net Credit Sales}}{\text{Average Net Accounts Receivable}}$$	$$\frac{\$3,250,000}{\$725,000} = 4.48$$
Inventory Turnover (Chapter 8: Frequency of inventory rotation; to monitor inventory management)	$$\frac{\text{Cost of Goods Sold}}{\text{Average Inventory}}$$	$$\frac{\$1,160,000}{\$200,000} = 5.8$$

Profitability Ratios	Formula	Ratios For Emerson	
Net Profit on Sales (Chapter 5: Profitabilty on sales; for comparison and trend analysis)	$\dfrac{\text{Net Income}}{\text{Net Sales}}$	$\dfrac{\$1,000,000}{\$3,250,000}$	= 31%
Gross Profit Margin (Chapter 5: Gross profit rate; for comparison and trend analysis)	$\dfrac{\text{Gross Profit}}{\text{Net Sales}}$	$\dfrac{\$2,090,000}{\$3,250,000}$	= 64%
Return on Assets (Chapter 15: Asset utilization in producing returns)	$\dfrac{\text{Net Income} + \text{Interest Expense}}{\text{Average Assets}}$	$\dfrac{\$1,100,000}{\$3,865,000}$	= 28%
Return on Equity (Chapter 15: Effectiveness of equity investment in producing returns)	$\dfrac{\text{Net Income} - \text{Preferred Dividends}}{\text{Average Common Equity}}$	$\dfrac{\$1,000,000}{\$2,095,000}$	= 48%

Other Indicators	Formula	Ratios For Emerson	
EPS (Chapter 15: Amount of earnings attributable to each share of common stock)	$\dfrac{\text{Income Available to Common}}{\text{Weighted-Average Number of Common Shares}}$	$\dfrac{\$1,000,000}{905,000}$	= $1.11
P/E (Chapter 15: The price of the stock in relation to earnings per share)	$\dfrac{\text{Market Price Per Share}}{\text{Earnings Per Share}}$	$\dfrac{\$10}{\$1.11}$	= 9
Dividend Rate/Yield (Chapter 15: Direct yield to investors through dividend payments)	$\dfrac{\text{Annual Cash Dividend}}{\text{Market Price Per Share}}$	$\dfrac{\$0.055}{\$10}$	= 0.55%
Dividend Payout Ratio (Chapter 15: Proportion of earnings distributed as dividends)	$\dfrac{\text{Annual Cash Dividend}}{\text{Earnings Per Share}}$	$\dfrac{\$0.055}{\$1.11}$	= 5.0%
Book Value (Chapter 15: The amount of stockholders' equity per common share outstanding)	$\dfrac{\text{"Common" Equity}}{\text{Common Shares Outstanding}}$	$\dfrac{\$2,610,000}{910,000}$	= $2.87

BALANCE
SHEET

EMERSON CORPORATION Comparative Balance Sheet December 31, 20X5 and 20X4		
Assets	**20X5**	**20X4**
Current assets		
Cash	$ 700,000	$ 170,000
Accounts receivable	850,000	600,000
Inventory	180,000	220,000
Total current assets	$1,730,000	$ 990,000
Property, plant, & equipment		
Land	$ 800,000	$1,400,000
Building	1,000,000	700,000
Equipment	1,050,000	900,000
	$2,850,000	$3,000,000
Less: Accumulated depreciation	(480,000)	(360,000)
Total property, plant, & equipment	$2,370,000	$2,640,000
Total assets	$4,100,000	$3,630,000
Liabilities		
Current liabilities		
Accounts payable	$ 270,000	$ 200,000
Wages payable	20,000	50,000
Total current liabilities	$ 290,000	$ 250,000
Long-term liabilities		
Long-term loan payable	900,000	1,800,000
Total liabilities	$1,190,000	$2,050,000
Stockholders' equity		
Preferred stock	$ 300,000	$ -
Common stock ($1 par)	910,000	900,000
Paid-in capital in excess of par	370,000	300,000
Retained earnings	1,330,000	380,000
Total stockholders' equity	$2,910,000	$1,580,000
Total liabilities and equity	$4,100,000	$3,630,000

ADDITIONAL FACTS FOR EMERSON

No dividends were due or paid on the $300,000 of preferred stock which was issued in exchange for a building in late 20X5. Average common equity is assumed to be $2,095,000 ((($2,910,000 - $300,000) + $1,580,000)/2). Assume most other balance sheet items change uniformly throughout the year (e.g., average receivables = ($600,000 + $850,000)/2 = $725,000, etc.). The year-end market value of the common stock was $10 per share, and the cash dividend was paid on shares outstanding at the end of the year ($50,000/910,000 shares = $0.055 per share).

It appears that Emerson is doing fairly well. Its liquidity suggests no problem in meeting obligations, the debt is manageable, receivables and inventory appear to be turning well, and profits are good.

EMERSON CORPORATION
Statement of Retained Earnings
For the Year Ending December 31, 20X5

Beginning retained earnings, Jan. 1	$ 380,000
Net income	1,000,000
	$1,380,000
Less: Dividends on common	50,000
Ending retained earnings, Dec. 31	$1,330,000

EMERSON CORPORATION
Income Statement
For the Year Ending December 31, 20X5

Revenues		$3,250,000
Cost of goods sold		1,160,000
Gross profit		$2,090,000
Operating expenses		
Wages	$450,000	
Interest	100,000	
Depreciation	120,000	
Other operating expenses	270,000	(940,000)
Gain on sale of land		150,000
Income before income taxes		$1,300,000
Income taxes		300,000
Net income		$1,000,000

Analysts often reproduce financial statement data in percentage terms. For example, Emerson's cash is 17% of total assets ($700,000/$4,100,000). These data provide investors and managers with a keen sense of subtle shifts that can foretell changes in the business environment. This approach is sometimes called "common size" financial statements, as applied to the balance sheet data below:

Assets	20X5	20X4
Cash	17%	5%
Accounts receivable	21%	16%
Inventory	4%	6%
Property, plant, & equipment	58%	73%
Total assets	100%	100%
Liabilities		
Total current liabilities	7%	7%
Long-term loan payable	22%	50%
Total stockholders' equity	71%	43%
Total liabilities and equity	100%	100%

Cash Flow and the Statement of Cash Flows

Accounting is based upon accrual concepts that report revenues as earned and expenses as incurred, rather than when received and paid. Accrual information is perhaps the best indicator of business success or failure. However, one cannot ignore the importance of cash flows.

For example, a rapidly growing successful business can be profitable and still experience cash flow difficulties in trying to keep up with the need for expanded facilities and inventory. On the other hand, a business may appear profitable, but may be experiencing delays in collecting receivables, and this can impose liquidity constraints. Or, a business may be paying dividends, but only because cash is produced from the disposal of core assets. Sophisticated analysis will often reveal such issues.

Rather than depending upon financial statement users to do their own detailed cash flow analysis, the accounting profession has seen fit to require another financial statement that clearly highlights the cash flows of a business entity. This required financial statement is named the **Statement of Cash Flows**.

One objective of financial reporting is to provide *information that is helpful in assessing the amounts, timing, and uncertainty of an organization's cash inflows and outflows.* As a result, the statement of cash flows provides three broad categories that reveal information about operating activities, investing activities, and financing activities. In addition, businesses are required to reveal significant noncash investing/financing transactions.

OPERATING, INVESTING, AND FINANCING ACTIVITIES

Cash inflows from **operating activities** consist of receipts from customers for providing goods and services, and cash received from interest and dividend income (as well as the proceeds from the sale of "trading securities"). Cash outflows consist of payments for inventory, trading securities, employee salaries and wages, taxes, interest, and other normal business expenses. To generalize, cash from operating activities is generally linked to those transactions and events that enter into the determination of income. However, another way to view "operating" cash flows is to include anything that is not an "investing" or "financing" cash flow.

Cash inflows from **investing activities** result from items such as the sale of longer-term stock and bond investments, disposal of long-term productive assets, and receipt of principal repayments on loans made to others. Cash outflows from investing activities include payments made to acquire plant assets or long-term investments in other firms, loans to others, and similar items.

Cash inflows from **financing activities** include proceeds from a company's issuance of its own stock or bonds, borrowings under loans, and so forth. Cash outflows for financing activities include repayments of amounts borrowed, acquisitions of treasury stock, and dividend distributions.

There are potential distinctions between U.S. GAAP and international accounting standards. IFRS permits interest received (paid) to be disclosed in the investing (financing) section of a cash flow statement. The global viewpoint also provides more flexibility in the classification of dividends received (and paid). Additionally, international standards encourage disclosures of cash flows that are necessary to maintain operating capacity, versus cash flows attributable to increasing capacity.

NONCASH INVESTING AND FINANCING ACTIVITIES

Some investing and financing activities occur without generating or consuming cash. For example, a company may exchange common stock for land or acquire a building in exchange for a note payable. While these transactions do not entail a direct inflow or outflow of cash, they do pertain to significant investing and/or financing events. Under U.S. GAAP, the statement of cash flows includes a separate section reporting these noncash items. Thus, the statement of cash flows is actually enhanced to reveal the totality of investing and financing activities, whether or not cash is actually involved. The international approach is to present such information in the notes to the financial statements.

Direct Approach to the Statement of Cash Flows

Spend just a few moments reviewing the preceding balance sheet, statement of retained earnings, and income statement for Emerson Corporation. Then, examine the following statement of cash flows. Everything within this cash flow statement is derived from the data and additional comments presented for Emerson. The tan bar on the left is not part of the statement; it is to facilitate the "line by line" explanation that follows.

	EMERSON CORPORATION Statement of Cash Flows (Direct Approach) For the Year Ending December 31, 20X5		
	Cash flows from operating activities:		
O1	Cash received from customers		$ 3,000,000
	Less cash paid for:		
O2	Merchandise inventory	$1,050,000	
O3	Wages	480,000	
O4	Interest	100,000	
O5	Other operating expenses	270,000	
O6	Income taxes	300,000	(2,200,000)
	Net cash provided by operating activities		$ 800,000
	Cash flows from investing activities:		
I1	Sale of land	$ 750,000	
I2	Purchase of equipment	(150,000)	
	Net cash provided by investing activities		600,000
	Cash flows from financing activities:		
F1	Proceeds from issuing stock	$ 80,000	
F2	Dividends on common	(50,000)	
F3	Repayment of long-term loans	(900,000)	
	Net cash used in financing activities		(870,000)
C1	**Net increase in cash**		$ 530,000
C2	**Cash balance at January 1, 20X5**		170,000
C3	**Cash balance at December 31, 20X5**		$ 700,000
	Noncash investing/financing activities:		
N1	Issued preferred stock for building		$ 300,000

Notice that Line 01 appears as follows:

OPERATING ACTIVITIES

Line 01	Cash received from customers	$ 3,000,000

Emerson's customers paid $3,000,000 in cash. Emerson's information system could be sufficiently robust that a "database query" could produce this number. On the other hand, one can infer this amount by reference to sales and receivables data found on the income statement and balance sheet:

Cash Received From Customers
=
Total Sales Minus the Increase in Net Receivables
(or, plus a decrease in net receivables)
=
$3,250,000 - ($850,000 - $600,000)
=
$3,000,000

Accounts receivable increased by $250,000 during the year ($850,000 - $600,000). This means that of the total sales of $3,250,000, a net $250,000 went uncollected. Thus, cash received from customers was $3,000,000. If net receivables had decreased, cash collected would have exceeded sales.

Line 02	Merchandise inventory	$1,050,000

Emerson paid $1,050,000 of cash for inventory. Bear in mind that cost of goods sold is the dollar amount of inventory sold. But, the amount of inventory actually purchased will be less than this amount if inventory on the balance sheet decreased. This would mean that some of the cost of goods sold came from existing stock on hand rather than having all been purchased during the year. On the other hand, purchases would be greater than cost of goods sold if inventory increased.

Inventory Purchased
=
Cost of Goods Sold Minus the Decrease in Inventory
(or, plus an increase in inventory)
=
$1,160,000 - ($220,000 - $180,000)
=
$1,120,000

Inventory purchased is only the starting point for determining cash paid for inventory. Inventory purchased must be adjusted for the portion that was purchased on credit. Notice that Emerson's accounts payable increased by $70,000 ($270,000 - $200,000). This means that cash paid for inventory purchases was $70,000 less than total inventory purchased:

Cash Paid for Inventory
=
Inventory Purchased Minus the Increase in Accounts Payable
(or, plus a decrease in accounts payable)
=
$1,120,000 - ($270,000 - $200,000)
=
$1,050,000

Line O3	Wages	480,000

Emerson paid $480,000 of cash for wages during the year. Emerson's payroll records would indicate the amount of cash paid for wages, but this number can also be determined by reference to wages expense in the income statement and wages payable on the balance sheet:

Cash Paid for Wages
=
**Wages Expense Plus the Decrease in Wages Payable
(or, minus an increase in wages payable)**
=
$450,000 + ($50,000 - $20,000)
=
$480,000

Emerson not only paid out enough cash to cover wages expense, but an additional $30,000 as reflected by the overall decrease in wages payable. If wages payable had increased, the cash paid would have been less than wages expense.

Line O4	Interest	100,000
Line O5	Other operating expenses	270,000
Line O6	Income taxes	300,000

Emerson's cash payments for these items equaled the amount of expense in the income statement. Had there been related balance sheet accounts (e.g., interest payable, taxes payable, etc.), then the expense amounts would need to be adjusted in a manner similar to that illustrated for wages.

Overall, operations generated net positive cash flows of $800,000. Notice that two items within the income statement were not listed in the operating activities section of the cash flow statement:

- Depreciation is not an operating cash flow item. It is a <u>noncash</u> expense. Remember that depreciation is recorded via a debit to Depreciation Expense and a credit to Accumulated Depreciation. No cash is impacted by this entry (the "investing" cash outflow occurred when the asset was purchased), and

- The gain on sale of land in the income statement does not appear in the operating cash flows section. While the land sale may have produced cash, the entire proceeds will be listed in the investing activities section; it is a "nonoperating" item.

INVESTING ACTIVITIES

The next major section of the cash flow statement is the cash flows from investing activities. This section can include both inflows and outflows related to investment-related transactions. Emerson Corporation had one example of each; a cash inflow from sale of land, and a cash outflow for the purchase of equipment. The sale of land requires some thoughtful analysis. Notice that the statement of cash flows for Emerson reports the following line item:

Line I1	Sale of land	$ 750,000

This line item reports that $750,000 of cash was received from the sale of land during the year. In actuality, it would be possible to look up this transaction in the company's journal. The journal entry would appear as follows:

XX-XX-X5	Cash	750,000	
	Gain		150,000
	Land		600,000
	Sold land costing $600,000 for $750,000		

But, it is not necessary to refer to the journal. Notice that land on the balance sheet decreased by $600,000 ($1,400,000 - $800,000), and that the income statement included a $150,000 gain. Applying a little "forensic" accounting allows one to deduce that $600,000 in land was sold for $750,000, to produce the $150,000 gain.

Line I2	Purchase of equipment	(150,000)

Emerson purchased equipment for $150,000 during the year. Notice that equipment on the balance sheet increased by $150,000 ($1,050,000 - $900,000). One could confirm that this was a cash purchase by reference to the journal; such is assumed in this case.

FINANCING **ACTIVITIES**	Line F1	Proceeds from issuing stock	$ 80,000

This line reveals that $80,000 was received from issuing common stock. This cash inflow is suggested by the $10,000 increase in common stock ($910,000 - $900,000) and $70,000 increase in additional paid-in capital ($370,000 - $300,000).

Line F2	Dividends on common	(50,000)

The statement of retained earnings reveals that Emerson declared $50,000 in dividends. Since there is no dividend payable on the balance sheet, one can assume that all of the dividends were paid.

Line F3	Repayment of long-term loans	(900,000)

The balance sheet reveals a $900,000 decrease in long-term debt ($1,800,000 - $900,000). This represented a significant use of cash.

Line C1	**Net increase in cash**	$ 530,000	*CASH FLOW*
Line C2	**Cash balance at January 1, 20X5**	170,000	*RECAP*
Line C3	**Cash balance at December 31, 20X5**	$ 700,000	

Emerson had a $530,000 increase in cash during the year ($800,000 from positive operating cash flow, $600,000 from positive investing cash flow, and $870,000 from negative financing cash flow). This change in cash is confirmed by reference to the beginning and ending cash balances.

Line N1	Issued preferred stock for building	$ 300,000	*NONCASH INVESTING/ FINANCING ACTIVITIES*

The noncash investing and financing section reports that preferred stock was issued for a building.

RECON- CILIATION

The statement of cash flows just presented is known as the **direct approach**. It is so named because the cash items entering into the determination of operating cash flow are specifically identified. In many respects, this presentation of operating cash flows resembles a cash basis income statement.

An acceptable alternative is the "indirect" approach. Before moving on to the indirect approach, be aware that companies using the direct approach must supplement the cash flow statement with a reconciliation of income to cash from operations. This reconciliation may be found in notes accompanying the financial statements:

Net income		$1,000,000
Add (deduct) noncash effects on operating income		
Depreciation expense	$ 120,000	
Gain on sale of land	(150,000)	
Increase in accounts receivable	(250,000)	
Decrease in inventory	40,000	
Increase in accounts payable	70,000	
Decrease in wages payable	(30,000)	(200,000)
Net cash provided by operating activities		$ 800,000

Notice that this reconciliation starts with the net income, and adjusts to the $800,000 net cash from operations. Some explanation may prove helpful:

- Depreciation is added back to net income, because it reduced income but did not consume any cash.

- Gain on sale of land is subtracted, because it increased income, but is not related to operations (remember, it is an investing item and the "gain" is not the sales price).

- Increase in accounts receivable is subtracted, because it represents uncollected sales included in income.

- Decrease in inventory is added, because it represents cost of sales from existing inventory (not a new cash purchase).

- Increase in accounts payable is added, because it represents expenses not paid.

- Decrease in wages payable is subtracted, because it represents a cash payment for something expensed in an earlier period.

This can become rather confusing. Most can probably see why depreciation is added back. But, the gain may be fuzzy. It must be subtracted because one is trying to remove it from the operating number; it increased net income, but it is viewed as something other than operating, and that is why it is backed out. Conversely, a loss on such a transaction would be added. Remember, the full proceeds of an asset sale are reported within investing activities, regardless of whether the sale produced a gain or loss.

The following drawing is useful in simplifying consideration of how changes in current assets and current liabilities result in reconciliations of net income to operating cash flows. Begin by thinking about a reconciling item that is fairly easy to grasp. Emerson's accounts receivable increased on the balance sheet, but the amount of the increase was subtracted in the reconciliation (again, this increase reflects sales not yet collected in cash, and thus the subtracting effect). In the drawing below, consider that accounts receivable is a current asset, and it increased. This condition relates to the upper left quadrant; hence the increase is shown as "subtracted."

RECONCILIATION ADJUSTMENTS RELATED TO:

	Current Assets	Current Liabilities
Account Increased	subtracted	added
Account Decreased	added	subtracted

With the drawing it mind, it becomes a simple matter that all increasing current assets result in subtractions in the reconciliation. This relationship is inverse for current liabilities, as shown in the upper right quadrant of the drawing. Similarly, these relationships are inverse for account decreases as shown in the bottom half of the drawing. With the drawing in mind, it becomes a simple matter to examine changes in specific current accounts to determine whether they are generally added or subtracted in the reconciliation of net income to cash flows from operating activities. Using the Emerson example:

	Current Assets	Current Liabilities
Account Increased	subtracted increase in Accounts Receivable	added increase in Accounts Payable
Account Decreased	added decrease in Inventory	subtracted decrease in Wages Payable

Indirect Approach to Presenting Operating Activities

Although accounting standards encourage the direct approach, most companies actually present an indirect statement of cash flows. The **indirect approach** is so named because the "reconciliation" replaces the direct presentation of the operating cash flows. Except for the shaded areas, this statement is identical to the direct approach. The first shaded area reflects the substitution of the operating cash flow calculations. The second shaded area reflects that the indirect approach must be supplemented with information about cash paid for interest and taxes.

EMERSON CORPORATION
Statement of Cash Flows (Indirect Approach)
For the Year Ending December 31, 20X5

Cash flows from operating activities:		
Net income		$1,000,000
Add (deduct) noncash effects on operating income		
Depreciation expense	$ 120,000	
Gain on sale of land	(150,000)	
Increase in accounts receivable	(250,000)	
Decrease in inventory	40,000	
Increase in accounts payable	70,000	
Decrease in wages payable	(30,000)	(200,000)
Net cash provided by operating activities		$ 800,000
Cash flows from investing activities:		
Sale of land	$ 750,000	
Purchase of equipment	(150,000)	
Net cash provided by investing activities		600,000
Cash flows from financing activities:		
Proceeds from issuing stock	$ 80,000	
Dividends on common	(50,000)	
Repayment of long-term loans	(900,000)	
Net cash provided by financing activities		(870,000)
Net increase in cash		$530,000
Cash balance at January 1, 20X5		170,000
Cash balance at December 31, 20X5		$ 700,000
Noncash investing/financing activities:		
Issued preferred stock for building		$ 300,000
Supplemental information:		
Cash paid for interest		$ 100,000
Cash paid for income taxes		300,000

Using a Worksheet to Prepare a Statement of Cash Flows

Given enough time and careful thought, one can generally prepare a statement of cash flows by putting together a rough shell that approximates the statements illustrated throughout this chapter, and then filling in all of the bits and pieces that can be found. Ultimately, the correct solution is reached when the change in cash is fully explained. This is like working a puzzle without reference to a supporting picture. But, complex tasks are simplified by taking a more organized approach. To that end, consider the value of a worksheet for preparing the statement of cash flows.

The worksheet examines the change in each balance sheet account and relates it to any cash flow statement impacts. Once each line in the balance sheet is contemplated, the ingredients of the cash flow statement will be found! A sample worksheet for Emerson is presented on the following page.

In this worksheet, the upper portion is the balance sheet information, and the lower portion is the cash flow statement information. The change in each balance sheet row is evaluated and keyed to a change(s) in the cash flow statement. When one has explained the change in each balance sheet line, the accumulated offsets (in the lower portion) reflect the information necessary to prepare a statement of cash flows.

Specific explanations for each keyed item in the worksheet are found in the following table. The cash flow statement explanations are color coded such that blue is the final balancing step, red is cash outflow, black is cash inflow, and green is special.

	Upper/Balance Sheet	Lower/Cash Flow Statement
(a)	debit (increase) cash	credit to balance - the remaining effect as net positive cash flow
(b)	debit (increase) accounts receivable	credit reflecting negative cash effect via receivables increase
(c)	credit (decrease) inventory	debit reflecting positive cash effect via inventory reduction
(d)	credit (decrease) land	credit gain and debit sale of land reflecting source of cash
(e)	debit building (increase)/ credit preferred stock (increase)	debit and credit reflecting noncash investing/financing
(f)	debit (increase) equipment	credit reflecting use of cash to purchase equipment
(g)	credit (increase) accum. depreciation	debit reflecting noncash adjustment of income
(h)	credit (increase) accounts payable	debit reflecting positive cash effect via increased payables
(i)	debit (decrease) wages payable	credit reflecting negative cash effect via payables reduction
(j)	debit (decrease) loan payable	credit reflecting use of cash via loan repayment
(k)	credit (increase) stock and paid-in capital	debit reflecting source of cash via stock issue
(l)	debit (decrease) retained earnings	credit reflecting use of cash for dividends
(m)	credit (increase) retained earnings	debit reflecting source of cash via income

EMERSON CORPORATION
Cash Flow Statement Worksheet
For the Year Ending Dec. 31, 20X5

	20X4		Debit		Credit	20X5
Debits						
Cash	$ 170,000	(a)	$ 530,000			$ 700,000
Accounts receivable	600,000	(b)	250,000			850,000
Inventory	220,000			(c)	$ 40,000	180,000
Land	1,400,000			(d)	600,000	800,000
Building	700,000	(e)	300,000			1,000,000
Equipment	900,000	(f)	150,000			1,050,000
	$3,990,000					$4,580,000
Credits						
Accumulated depreciation	$ 360,000			(g)	120,000	$ 480,000
Accounts payable	200,000			(h)	70,000	270,000
Wages payable	50,000	(i)	30,000			20,000
Long-term loan payable	1,800,000	(j)	900,000			900,000
Preferred stock	-			(e)	300,000	300,000
Common stock ($1 par)	900,000			(k)	10,000	910,000
Paid-in capital in excess of par	300,000			(k)	70,000	370,000
Retained earnings	380,000	(l)	50,000	(m)	1,000,000	1,330,000
	$3,990,000					$4,580,000
Cash flows from operating activities:						
Net income		(m)	1,000,000			
Depreciation expense		(g)	120,000			
Gain on sale of land				(d)	150,000	
Increase in accounts receivable				(b)	250,000	
Decrease in inventory		(c)	40,000			
Increase in accounts payable		(h)	70,000			
Decrease in wages payable				(i)	30,000	
Cash flows from investing activities:						
Sale of land		(d)	750,000			
Purchase of equipment				(f)	150,000	
Cash flows from financing activities:						
Proceeds from issuing stock		(k)	80,000			
Dividends on common				(l)	50,000	
Repayment of long-term loan				(j)	900,000	
Noncash investing/financing activities:						
Issue preferred stock for building		(e)	300,000	(e)	300,000	
Increase in cash				(a)	530,000	
			$4,570,000		$4,570,000	

Chapter 16 Quiz

Goals Achievement

Q16-1. Which type of ratio is useful for measuring the ability of a business to meet current debts as they come due?

liquidity ratio   or   profitability ratio

Q16-2. The numerator for the return on assets ratio includes net income plus:

preferred dividends   or   interest expense

Q16-3. Which activities relate primarily to the production and sale of goods and services and enter into the determination of income?

operating activities   or   financing activities

Q16-4. Cash received from customers can be calculated by starting with accrual basis sales and adding:

decreases in accounts receivable   or   increases in accounts receivable

Q16-5. Both the direct and indirect methods are acceptable for external financial reporting.

true   or   false

Fill in the Blanks

Q16-6. _____ measure the ability of a business to meet current debts and obligations as they come due.

Q16-7. Insight into the amount of protection that is afforded the long-term creditors is provided by a ratio called _____.

Q16-8. _____ activities are those that involve investment of an entity's resources.

Q16-9. Under both the direct and indirect approaches to preparing a statement of cash flows, a separate schedule of _____ investing/financing transactions should be presented.

Q16-10. Under the _____ method, operating cash flows are calculated by starting with accrual basis net income, then adding and subtracting amounts to convert to the cash basis.

Q16-11. The payment of dividends and receipt of proceeds from bond issues are examples of _____ activities.

Q16-12. Financial statement ratio analysis may be undertaken to study liquidity, turnover, profitability, and other indicators. To which does the current ratio most relate?

a. Liquidity

c. Profitability

b. Turnover

d. Other indicator

Q16-13. Selected information for 20X1 for the Bernstein Company is as follows:

Cost of goods sold	$6,000,000
Average inventory	$2,000,000
Net sales	$8,000,000
Average receivables	$3,000,000
Net income	$1,000,000

Assuming a 360-day business year, what was the inventory turnover ratio for Bernstein?

a. 3

c. 5

b. 4

d. 6

Q16-14. Which of the following activities would generally be regarded as a financing activity in preparing a statement of cash flows?

a. Dividend distribution

c. Loans made by the entity to other businesses

b. Proceeds from the sale of stocks of other firms

d. Employees' salaries and wages paid

Q16-15. As a generalization, the adjustment of accrual basis income to cash provided by operating activities requires which of the following to be added?

a. Increases in current assets related to operating activities

c. Decreases in current liabilities related to operating activities

b. Increases in current liabilities related to operating activities

d. Both (a) and (c) are correct.

Q16-16. In preparing a work sheet for the statement of cash flows, the lower portion corresponds to a statement of cash flows prepared using the indirect method. Items in the debit column of this lower portion most closely correspond to items which:

a. Explain increases in cash.

c. Relate to financing activities.

b. Explain decreases in cash.

d. Relate to investing activities.

Chapter 16 Problems

Basic Problems

Liquidity analysis

Fairfield Corporation owns three separate subsidiaries. The Board of Directors is developing a strategy to withdraw $1,000,000 in cash from one of the subsidiaries to finance the acquisition of a fourth business.

Prepare the current and quick ratio for each subsidiary, and rank order the subsidiaries based on their ability to pay a dividend to the parent company without jeopardizing liquidity.

	Sub A	Sub B	Sub C
Cash	$1,000,000	$3,000,000	$ 5,000,000
Trading securities	3,000,000	2,000,000	1,000,000
Accounts receivable	6,000,000	5,000,000	14,000,000
Inventory	4,000,000	8,000,000	7,000,000
Prepaid rent	2,000,000	2,000,000	3,000,000
Accounts payable	5,000,000	2,000,000	8,000,000
Interest payable	1,000,000	1,000,000	6,000,000
Note payable (due in 6 months)	4,000,000	1,500,000	4,000,000
Unearned revenues	3,000,000	500,000	2,000,000

Debt service ratios

Billy Covington is a loan analyst for DotBanc. DotBanc accepts online business loan applications. The data are stored in a spreadsheet ("data set"). Billy imports this data into an analysis spreadsheet and calculates the debt to total assets ratio, debt to stockholders' equity ratio, and times interest earned ratio.

SPREADSHEET TOOL:

Importing data

The calculated ratios are used to screen applicants for further evaluation. To qualify, a company must have a debt to total assets ratio of less than 0.5, debt to total equity of less than 1.0, and a times interest earned ratio of at least 5.

In calculating the ratios, DotBanc makes certain assumptions as follows:

Total equity is the sum of paid-in capital and retained earnings.

Total assets equal total equity plus total liabilities.

Total interest cost is 7% of total liabilities.

Use the accompanying data set to calculate the indicated ratios. Identify companies that meet the preliminary screening.

DATA SET

Applicant	Total Liabilities	Paid-in Capital	Retained Earnings	Net Income for Past Year	Taxes for Past Year
Berkley	5,000,000	2,000,000	2,000,000	1,000,000	250,000
Costnor	2,500,000	1,000,000	500,000	400,000	100,000
Dalia	3,000,000	400,000	5,200,000	500,000	110,000
Fergusen	500,000	700,000	3,500,000	800,000	90,000
Hernandez	2,000,000	200,000	700,000	600,000	75,000
Indio	1,600,000	1,200,000	8,000,000	250,000	50,000
Jordanson	4,400,000	5,000,000	(400,000)	(60,000)	-
Kervin	3,000,000	1,500,000	1,800,000	10,000	1,000
Lensmire	600,000	500,000	500,000	250,000	60,000

Analysis of receivables and inventory turnover	B-16.03

Stanley Corporation has no material problem with uncollectible accounts or obsolete inventory. All sales and purchases are on account. The company provided the following information for the year ending 20X7:

Total sales	$2,600,000
Beginning accounts receivable	700,000
Total purchases of inventory	1,800,000
Beginning inventory	50,000
Collections on accounts receivable	2,400,000
Payments on accounts payable	1,850,000
Cost of goods sold	1,775,000

(a) Calculate the "accounts receivable turnover ratio."

(b) Calculate the "inventory turnover ratio."

(c) If Stanley's competitors have a receivables turnover ratio of "6" and an inventory turnover ratio of "4," would you initially conclude that Stanley is better or worse than its competitors in managing receivables and inventory?

Liz Marett is the chief financial officer for Fulton Construction. She delivered the following comments in a recent conference call with analysts that follow the company:

"20X5 was another excellent year. Net income was a record setting $10,000,000. We maintained our overall net profit on sales at the historic 10% level. This occurred despite an increase in raw material costs that lowered our gross margin to 60%. We are proud that we continue to maintain a healthy balance sheet that is free of any liablities.

All of our financing continues to be provided by our common and preferred shareholders. Our beginning of year equity of $75,000,000 was sufficient to fund our capital needs, and no additional shares were issued this year. Our "5% preferred shareholders" have again received their full $2,000,000 in dividends for the year. The remaining earnings have been reinvested in the company."

(a)   Use profitability ratios to determine Fulton's sales, cost of goods sold, gross profit, and net income.

(b)   Calculate Fulton's return on assets and return on equity. Which is higher, and why?

Jean Neftin was chatting with friends about stock investment ideas. One of his friends suggested that he consider Cabela Corporation. The friend noted that Cabela was coming out with a new product line that could be really hot.

Cabela's stock sells for $21 per share, and has a P/E of 15. The dividend yield is 3%. The company has had 10,000,000 shares outstanding for all of the past year, and the stock price is two times book value per share.

(a)   Calculate Cabela's earnings per share, net income, dividend per share, and total stockholders' equity.

(b)   In addition to the preceding facts, assume that Cabela's also has $10,000,000 of 6% preferred stock outstanding all year. Dividends are current. The preferred stock was issued at par, but has a 110 call price. Recalculate net income and book value per common share based on this revised set of facts.

Examine the listed business activities and decide if each is to be classified as a:

Cash flow from operating activity

Cash flow from investing activity

Cash flow from financing activity

Non-cash investing/financing activity

(a) Issue common stock for land

(b) Issue common stock for cash

(c) Pay interest on loan

(d) Sell goods for cash

(e) Pay employee salaries

(f) Pay dividends to common shareholders

(g) Receive dividend on an investment

(h) Obtain proceeds of long-term loan

(i) Acquire treasury shares

(j) Purchase land for cash

(k) Buy inventory for resale

Direct calculation of operating cash flows   *B-16.07*

Gainesville Corporation's income statement revealed sales of $700,000; gross profit of $300,000; selling and administrative costs of $140,000; and income taxes of $45,000. The selling and administrative expenses included $10,000 for depreciation. The company's operating activities generated positive cash flow of $129,000. Use the "direct" approach to demonstrate how this amount was calculated. The following additional information is available:

	Beginning-of-Period Balance	End-of-Period Balance
Account receivable	$70,000	$82,000
Inventory	50,000	41,000
Accounts payable	37,000	44,000

Indirect calculation of operating cash flows   *B-16.08*

Gainesville Corporation's income statement revealed sales of $700,000; gross profit of $300,000; selling and administrative costs of $140,000; and income taxes of $45,000. The selling and administrative expenses included $10,000 for depreciation. The company's operating activities generated positive cash flow of $129,000. Use the "indirect" approach to demonstrate how this amount was calculated. The following additional information is available:

	Beginning-of-Period Balance	End-of-Period Balance
Account receivable	$70,000	$82,000
Inventory	50,000	41,000
Accounts payable	37,000	44,000

Following is an incorrectly prepared statement of cash flows for Herman Corporation. Review and correct this presentation, using a direct approach.

HERMAN CORPORATION
Statement of Cash Flows
For the Year Ending December 31, 20X2

Cash balance at January 1, 20X2:		$ 175,000
Cash receipts during 20X2:		
Sale of building	$ 800,000	
Dividend received on investments	10,000	
Cash received from customers	2,350,000	
Proceeds from issuing stock	1,400,000	4,560,000
Cash payments during 20X2:		
Purchase of inventory	$ 760,000	
Interest on loans	56,000	
Income taxes	124,000	
Repayment of long-term note payable	2,000,000	
Purchase of equipment	435,000	
Selling and administrative expenses	696,000	
Dividends on common	175,000	(4,246,000)
Cash balance at December 31, 20X2		$ 489,000
Noncash investing/financing activities:		
Bought land by issuing promissory note payable		$ 450,000

The accountant for Rimmerex Corporation used a spreadsheet to prepare information needed to prepare the statement of cash flows for the year ending December 31, 20X5. However, the data were accidentally sorted alphabetically into the following listing of items. To compound the problem, the "add" and "subtract" notations for each line item were also deleted.

Review the information, and prepare a correct presentation, using the indirect approach. The beginning cash balance was $63,800, and the ending cash balance was $415,000.

Bought building by issuing common stock	$850,000
Decrease in accounts payable	34,000
Decrease in accounts receivable	21,000

continued...

Depreciation expense	68,000
Dividends on common	50,000
Gain on sale of land	20,000
Increase in income taxes payable	7,000
Increase in inventory	27,800
Increase in prepaid insurance	3,000
Net income	215,000
Purchase of equipment	75,000
Repayment of long-term note payable	180,000
Sale of land	430,000

Knowledge of cash flow statement components   *B-16.11*

Review the following technical comments about the presentation methodology for the statement of cash flows. Identify if the comment pertains to the "direct" or "indirect" approach, or "both."

The operating cash flows section typically begins with net income.

Separate disclosure is provided for noncash investing/financing activities.

Requires supplemental disclosure reconciling net income to operating cash flows.

Conceptually, the preferred approach.

Includes three separate sections - operating, investing, and financing.

Requires supplemental disclosure of cash paid for interest and cash paid for taxes.

A loss on the sale of a plant asset would be added back in operating cash flows.

Company cash flow evaluation   *B-16.12*

Waguespack Corporation and Hedrick Corporation had identical cash positions at the beginning and end of 20X9. Each company also reported a net income of $150,000 for 20X9. Evaluate their cash flow statements that follow.

Which company is displaying elements of cash flow stress? What factors cause you to reach this conclusion? What is the importance of evaluating a company's cash flow statement?

WAGUESPACK CORPORATION
Statement of Cash Flows
For the Year Ending December 31, 20X9

Cash flows from operating activities:

Net income		$150,000
Add (deduct) noncash effects on operating income		
Depreciation expense	$ 20,000	
Gain on sale of equipment	(185,200)	
Increase in accounts receivable	(45,000)	
Decrease in inventory	37,500	
Increase in accounts payable	11,400	
Decrease in income taxes payable	(3,000)	(164,300)
Net cash provided by operating activities		$ (14,300)
Cash flows from investing activities:		
Sale of equipment		204,900
Cash flows from financing activities:		
Proceeds from long-term borrowing		20,000
Net increase in cash		$210,600
Cash balance at January 1, 20X9		66,000
Cash balance at December 31, 20X9		$276,600

HEDRICK CORPORATION
Statement of Cash Flows
For the Year Ending December 31, 20X9

Cash flows from operating activities:

Net income		$150,000
Add (deduct) noncash effects on operating income		
Depreciation expense	$160,000	
Decrease in accounts receivable	43,700	
Increase in inventory	(87,500)	
Decrease in accounts payable	(8,100)	
Decrease in income taxes payable	(8,600)	99,500
Net cash provided by operating activities		$249,500
Cash flows from investing activities:		
Purchase of equipment		(20,400)
Cash flows from financing activities:		
Repayment of long-term borrowing		(18,500)
Net increase in cash		$210,600
Cash balance at January 1, 20X9		66,000
Cash balance at December 31, 20X9		$276,600

Ozark Corporation reported net income of $100,000 for 20X5. The income statement revealed sales of $1,000,000; gross profit of $520,000; selling and administrative costs of $340,000; interest expense of $20,000; and income taxes of $60,000.

The selling and administrative expenses included $25,000 for depreciation.

No equipment was sold during the year. Equipment purchases were made with cash.

Prepaid insurance included in the balance sheet related to administrative costs.

All accounts payable included in the balance sheet relate to inventory purchases.

The change in retained earnings is attributable to net income and dividends.

The increase in common stock and additional paid-in capital is due to issuing additional shares for cash.

Using the direct approach, prepare a statement of cash flows (excluding the supplemental reconciliation of net income to operating cash flow) for Ozark for the year ending December 31, 20X5.

Comparative balance sheets for Ozark follow.

OZARK CORPORATION Balance Sheet December 31, 20X5 and 20X4		
Assets	**20X5**	**20X4**
Cash	$ 458,700	$ 471,450
Accounts receivable	199,250	171,500
Inventories	248,600	278,800
Prepaid insurance	13,000	11,000
Land	250,000	250,000
Building and equipment	1,500,000	1,300,000
Less: Accumulated depreciation	(205,000)	(180,000)
Total assets	$2,464,550	$2,302,750
Liabilities		
Accounts payable	$ 85,700	$ 93,400
Interest payable	10,500	15,000
Income taxes payable	22,000	8,000
Stockholders' equity		
Common stock	710,000	700,000
Paid-in capital in excess of par	990,000	900,000
Retained earnings	646,350	586,350
Total liabilities and equity	$2,464,550	$2,302,750

Ozark Corporation reported net income of $100,000 for 20X5. The income statement revealed sales of $1,000,000; gross profit of $520,000; selling and administrative costs of $340,000; interest expense of $20,000; and income taxes of $60,000.

The selling and administrative expenses included $25,000 for depreciation.

No equipment was sold during the year. Equipment purchases were made with cash.

Prepaid insurance included in the balance sheet related to administrative costs.

All accounts payable included in the balance sheet relate to inventory purchases.

The change in retained earnings is attributable to net income and dividends.

The increase in common stock and additional paid-in capital is due to issuing additional shares for cash.

Using the indirect approach, prepare a statement of cash flows for Ozark for the year ending December 31, 20X5.

Comparative balance sheets for Ozark follow.

OZARK CORPORATION Balance Sheet December 31, 20X5 and 20X4		
Assets	**20X5**	**20X4**
Cash	$ 458,700	$ 471,450
Accounts receivable	199,250	171,500
Inventories	248,600	278,800
Prepaid insurance	13,000	11,000
Land	250,000	250,000
Building and equipment	1,500,000	1,300,000
Less: Accumulated depreciation	(205,000)	(180,000)
Total assets	$2,464,550	$2,302,750
Liabilities		
Accounts payable	$ 85,700	$ 93,400
Interest payable	10,500	15,000
Income taxes payable	22,000	8,000
Stockholders' equity		
Common stock	710,000	700,000
Paid-in capital in excess of par	990,000	900,000
Retained earnings	646,350	586,350
Total liabilities and equity	$2,464,550	$2,302,750

Involved Problems

Weaver Corporation's stock is selling for $16 per share. Weaver provided the following financial statements. Use these statements to prepare comprehensive ratio analysis tables similar to those illustrated in the chapter.

WEAVER CORPORATION **Comparative Balance Sheet** **December 31, 20X3 and 20X2**		
Assets	**20X3**	**20X2**
Current assets		
Cash	$ 500,000	$ 370,000
Accounts receivable	350,000	290,000
Inventories	90,000	110,000
Total current assets	$ 940,000	$ 770,000
Property, plant, & equipment		
Land	$ 200,000	$200,000
Building	650,000	650,000
Equipment	950,000	900,000
	$1,800,000	$1,750,000
Less: Accumulated depreciation	(365,000)	(325,000)
Total property, plant, & equipment	$1,435,000	$1,425,000
Total assets	$2,375,000	$2,195,000
Liabilities		
Current liabilities		
Accounts payable	$ 160,000	$ 200,000
Interest payable	40,000	30,000
Total current liabilities	$ 200,000	$ 230,000
Long-term liabilities		
Long-term note payable	800,000	700,000
Total liabilities	$1,000,000	$ 930,000
Stockholders' equity		
Common stock ($0.50 par)	$ 100,000	$ 100,000
Paid-in capital in excess of par	655,000	655,000
Retained earnings	620,000	510,000
Total stockholders' equity	$1,375,000	$1,265,000
Total liabilities and equity	$2,375,000	$2,195,000

WEAVER CORPORATION
Statement of Retained Earnings
For the Year Ending December 31, 20X3

Beginning retained earnings, Jan. 1	$510,000
Plus: Net income	160,000
	$670,000
Less: Dividends	50,000
Ending retained earnings, Dec. 31	$620,000

WEAVER CORPORATION
Income Statement
For the Year Ending December 31, 20X3

Revenues		$1,685,000
Cost of goods sold		980,000
Gross profit		$ 705,000
Operating expenses		
Salaries	$245,000	
Interest	65,000	
Depreciation	40,000	
Other operating expenses	155,000	505,000
Income before income taxes		$ 200,000
Less: Income taxes		40,000
Net income		$ 160,000

I-16.02   *Preparation of statement of cash flows (direct)*

Travis Engineering presented the following comparative balance sheet:

TRAVIS ENGINEERING
Balance Sheet
December 31, 20X3 and 20X2

Assets	20X3	20X2
Cash	$ 672,200	$ 145,300
Accounts receivable	219,600	175,600
Inventories	234,500	316,900
Land	1,300,000	300,000
Building and equipment	900,000	856,000
Less: Accumulated depreciation	(501,800)	(435,000)
Total assets	$2,824,500	$1,358,800

continued...

Liabilities

Accounts payable	$ 111,100	$ 93,400
Utilities payable	2,500	4,000
Interest payable	5,000	-
Long-term note payable	1,000,000	-
Stockholders' equity		
Common stock , $1 par	300,000	250,000
Paid-in capital in excess of par	560,000	450,000
Retained earnings	845,900	561,400
Total liabilities and equity	$2,824,500	$1,358,800

Additional information about transactions and events occurring in 20X3 is as follows:

Dividends of $105,700 were declared and paid.

Accounts payable and accounts receivable relate solely to purchases and sales of inventory.

The increase in land resulted from the purchase of land via issuance of the long-term note payable. No buildings were purchased or sold. Equipment was purchased.

In January of 20X3, equipment with an original cost of $75,000 was sold for $50,000.

The increase in paid-in capital all resulted from issuing additional shares for cash.

The income statement for the year ending 20X3 follows:

TRAVIS ENGINEERING
Income Statement
For the Year Ending December 31, 20X3

Sales		$2,856,000
Cost of goods sold		1,576,300
Gross profit		$1,279,700
Operating expenses and other		
Salaries	$433,500	
Utilities	64,200	
Interest	60,000	
Depreciation	76,800	
Loss on sale of equipment	15,000	649,500
Income before income taxes		$ 630,200
Income taxes		240,000
Net income		$ 390,200

Prepare Travis Engineering's statement of cash flows for the year ending 20X3. Use the direct approach, and prepare the supplemental reconciliation of net income to operating cash flows.

Fred Slezak presented the following comparative balance sheet:

COMPARATIVE BALANCE SHEET December 31, 20X5 and 20X4		
Assets	**20X5**	**20X4**
Current assets		
Cash	$ 664,000	$ 9,000
Accounts receivable	375,000	345,000
Inventories	150,000	160,000
Prepaid expenses	35,000	25,000
Total current assets	$1,224,000	$ 539,000
Property, plant, & equipment		
Land	$ 300,000	$ 400,000
Building	700,000	700,000
Equipment	530,000	450,000
	$1,530,000	$1,550,000
Less: Accumulated depreciation	(300,000)	(270,000)
Total property, plant, & equipment	$1,230,000	$1,280,000
Total assets	$2,454,000	$1,819,000
Liabilities		
Current liabilities		
Accounts payable	$ 112,000	$ 119,000
Interest payable	2,000	-
Total current liabilities	$ 114,000	$ 119,000
Long-term liabilities		
Long-term note payable	80,000	-
Total liabilities	$ 194,000	$ 119,000
Stockholders' equity		
Common stock ($1 par)	$ 700,000	$ 600,000
Paid-in capital in excess of par	800,000	400,000
Retained earnings	760,000	700,000
Total stockholders' equity	$2,260,000	$1,700,000
Total liabilities and equity	$2,454,000	$1,819,000

Additional information about transactions and events occurring in 20X5 follows:

Dividends of $55,000 were declared and paid.

Accounts payable and accounts receivable relate solely to purchases and sales of inventory. Prepaid items related only to advertising expenses.

The decrease in land resulted from the sale of a parcel at a $45,000 loss. No land was purchased during the year. Equipment was purchased during the year in exchange for a promissory note payable. No equipment was sold.

The increase in paid-in capital resulted from issuing additional shares for cash.

The income statement for the year ending December 31, 20X5, included the following key amounts:

Sales	$2,000,000
Cost of goods sold	1,200,000
Salaries expense	400,000
Advertising expense	150,000
Depreciation expense	30,000
Utilities expense	15,000
Interest expense	5,000
Loss on sale of land	45,000
Income tax expense	40,000
Net income	115,000

Prepare Fred Slezak's statement of cash flows for the year ending 20X5. Use the indirect approach, and include required supplemental information about cash paid for interest and taxes.

Worksheet for a statement of cash flows	*I-16.04*

Live Oak presented a similar comparative balance sheet and income statement as in problem I-16.03.

Additional information about transactions and events occurring in 20X5 follows:

Dividends of $55,000 were declared and paid.

Accounts payable and accounts receivable relate solely to purchases and sales of inventory. Prepaid items related only to advertising expenses.

The decrease in land resulted from the sale of a parcel at a $45,000 loss. No land was purchased during the year. Equipment was purchased during the year in exchange for a promissory note payable. No equipment was sold.

The increase in paid-in capital resulted from issuing additional shares for cash.

Prepare a cash flow statement worksheet similar to the one illustrated in the text. Use the worksheet to prepare the statement of cash flows under the indirect approach. Be sure to include supplemental information about noncash investing/financing activities, and information about cash paid for interest and taxes.

I-16.05   *Team-based approach to evaluation of cash flows*

Each student should obtain the statement of cash flows from the annual report of a favorite company. Annual reports are usually downloadable from the website of a public company, or are otherwise available from the website of the Securities and Exchange Commission (www.sec.gov). An annual report filed on the SEC website is referenced as a form 10-K.

Each student should examine their statement of cash flows and determine:

Did the company use the direct or indirect approach?

Was the company's operating cash flow positive or negative?

Is the company involved in financial services (bank, insurance, investments)?

In class, physically separate classmates into two groups on either side of the room - those whose company used the direct approach versus those whose company used the indirect approach. What is the relative proportion, and how does this compare to the "preference" expressed by the FASB for a direct presentation?

Remaining in the groups formed above, by show of hands, identify students who picked a company with positive versus negative operating cash flows. Is there any seeming correlation between the direct and indirect methods and positive versus negative operating flows?

By show of hands, identify students who picked a company in the financial sector. Is there any seeming correlation between the direct and indirect methods and the financial services sector?

Appendix

(Chapter Quiz Solutions)

Chapter 1 Quiz

Q1-1.	Financial Accounting	Q1-9.	objective, verifiable
Q1-2.	assets	Q1-10.	income statement, statement of retained earnings, balance sheet, statement of cash flows
Q1-3.	decrease	Q1-11.	Net income
Q1-4.	remain the same	Q1-12.	c
Q1-5.	balance sheet	Q1-13.	d
Q1-6.	Managerial	Q1-14.	d
Q1-7.	Financial Accounting Standards Board (FASB)	Q1-15.	b
Q1-8.	assets, liabilities, owners' equity	Q1-16.	b

Chapter 2 Quiz

Q2-1.	debit	Q2-9.	equal total credits
Q2-2.	incorrect	Q2-10.	trial balance
Q2-3.	posting	Q2-11.	chart of accounts
Q2-4.	correct	Q2-12.	c
Q2-5.	running balance form	Q2-13.	b
Q2-6.	accounts	Q2-14.	a
Q2-7.	debit	Q2-15.	d
Q2-8.	accounting equation	Q2-16.	d

Chapter 3 Quiz

Q3-1.	periodicity assumption	Q3-9.	Unearned, accrued
Q3-2.	matching principle	Q3-10.	adjusted trial balance
Q3-3.	Interest Payable	Q3-11.	income statement
Q3-4.	income statement approach	Q3-12.	c
Q3-5.	accrual basis	Q3-13.	b
Q3-6.	periodicity assumption	Q3-14.	b
Q3-7.	rendered, sold, delivered	Q3-15.	b
Q3-8.	Prepaid expenses	Q3-16.	b

Chapter 4 Quiz

Q4-1.	net loss		Q4-9.	reversing entry
Q4-2.	balance sheet accounts		Q4-10.	liquidity
Q4-3.	right		Q4-11.	current liabilities, current assets
Q4-4.	long-term investments		Q4-12.	a
Q4-5.	3		Q4-13.	b
Q4-6.	worksheet		Q4-14.	a
Q4-7.	income statement, retained earnings, balance sheet		Q4-15.	a
Q4-8.	Income Summary		Q4-16.	a

Chapter 5 Quiz

Q5-1.	contra-revenue accounts		Q5-9.	multi-step
Q5-2.	net method		Q5-10.	control environment
Q5-3.	true		Q5-11.	prenumbered
Q5-4.	perpetual inventory system		Q5-12.	a
Q5-5.	single-step approach		Q5-13.	b
Q5-6.	credit memorandum		Q5-14.	b
Q5-7.	cash discount		Q5-15.	c
Q5-8.	debit, payment		Q5-16.	d

Chapter 6 Quiz

Q6-1.	true		Q6-9.	current asset
Q6-2.	false		Q6-10.	market
Q6-3.	true		Q6-11.	income
Q6-4.	correct		Q6-12.	a
Q6-5.	false		Q6-13.	a
Q6-6.	Cash, postdated checks		Q6-14.	c
Q6-7.	cash budget		Q6-15.	a
Q6-8.	bank statement		Q6-16.	a

Chapter 7 Quiz

Q7-1.	nontrade receivables		Q7-9.	maker
Q7-2.	at the time of sale		Q7-10.	Interest, principal, rate, time
Q7-3.	balance sheet		Q7-11.	principal, interest
Q7-4.	net credit sales		Q7-12.	a
Q7-5.	transferred to accounts receivable		Q7-13.	c
Q7-6.	Trade		Q7-14.	c
Q7-7.	net realizable value		Q7-15.	a
Q7-8.	matching		Q7-16.	b

Chapter 8 Quiz

Q8-1.	wrong		Q8-9.	Cost of Goods Sold, Inventory, Purchases
Q8-2.	less than		Q8-10.	gross profit
Q8-3.	sales price less selling costs		Q8-11.	overstated
Q8-4.	false		Q8-12.	a
Q8-5.	right		Q8-13.	b
Q8-6.	consignor		Q8-14.	a
Q8-7.	specific identification		Q8-15.	a
Q8-8.	Consistency		Q8-16.	c

Chapter 9 Quiz

Q9-1.	debt	Q9-9.	equity
Q9-2.	all inclusive	Q9-10.	subsidiaries
Q9-3.	true	Q9-11.	intercompany
Q9-4.	dividends are paid	Q9-12.	a
Q9-5.	Investment in Subsidiary	Q9-13.	b
Q9-6.	amortized cost	Q9-14.	b
Q9-7.	all inclusive	Q9-15.	b
Q9-8.	discount	Q9-16.	c

Chapter 10 Quiz

Q10-1.	included in an asset's cost	Q10-9.	declining balance
Q10-2.	allocation	Q10-10.	modified accelerated cost recovery system
Q10-3.	stated in output	Q10-11.	lessee, lessor
Q10-4.	true	Q10-12.	b
Q10-5.	operating lease	Q10-13.	a
Q10-6.	lump-sum	Q10-14.	c
Q10-7.	physical deterioration, obsolescence, inadequacy	Q10-15.	c
Q10-8.	depreciable base, book value	Q10-16.	b

Chapter 11 Quiz

Q11-1.	betterments	Q11-9.	Depletion
Q11-2.	true	Q11-10.	intangible assets
Q11-3.	gains	Q11-11.	Goodwill
Q11-4.	income	Q11-12.	c
Q11-5.	false	Q11-13.	d
Q11-6.	Betterments	Q11-14.	b
Q11-7.	loss	Q11-15.	c
Q11-8.	gain, loss	Q11-16.	c

Chapter 12 Quiz

Q12-1.	true	Q12-9.	Federal Insurance Contributions Act
Q12-2.	true	Q12-10.	unemployment tax
Q12-3.	estimated	Q12-11.	pension fund
Q12-4.	gross earnings	Q12-12.	c
Q12-5.	liability	Q12-13.	a
Q12-6.	third party	Q12-14.	d
Q12-7.	discount amortization	Q12-15.	c
Q12-8.	probable, reasonably estimable	Q12-16.	c

Chapter 13 Quiz

Q13-1.	term loan	Q13-9.	contract interest rate, effective interest rate
Q13-2.	true	Q13-10.	premium
Q13-3.	less than	Q13-11.	decrease
Q13-4.	a full period's interest	Q13-12.	d
Q13-5.	false	Q13-13.	c
Q13-6.	Future value, present value	Q13-14.	b
Q13-7.	bond indenture	Q13-15.	c
Q13-8.	bond sinking fund	Q13-16.	d

Chapter 14 Quiz

Q14-1.	stated-value		Q14-9.	date of record
Q14-2.	date of declaration		Q14-10.	cumulative
Q14-3.	$5,000		Q14-11.	stock split
Q14-4.	fair value		Q14-12.	c
Q14-5.	true		Q14-13.	d
Q14-6.	charter		Q14-14.	b
Q14-7.	preemptive right		Q14-15.	b
Q14-8.	legal capital		Q14-16.	a

Chapter 15 Quiz

Q15-1.	true		Q15-9.	Generally accepted accounting principles
Q15-2.	retrospective adjustment		Q15-10.	periodicity
Q15-3.	false		Q15-11.	change (fluctuate)
Q15-4.	going-concern assumption		Q15-12.	a
Q15-5.	exchange loss		Q15-13.	b
Q15-6.	prior period adjustment		Q15-14.	a
Q15-7.	Basic		Q15-15.	a
Q15-8.	relevant		Q15-16.	b

Chapter 16 Quiz

Q16-1.	liquidity ratio		Q16-9.	noncash
Q16-2.	interest expense		Q16-10.	indirect
Q16-3.	operating activities		Q16-11.	financing
Q16-4.	decreases in accounts receivable		Q16-12.	a
Q16-5.	true		Q16-13.	a
Q16-6.	Liquidity ratios		Q16-14.	a
Q16-7.	debt to total assets (and times interest earned)		Q16-15.	b
Q16-8.	Investing		Q16-16.	a

Glossary

A

accelerated depreciation methods. Several alternative depreciation approaches that result in relatively more depreciation in early years of use, and smaller amounts during later years *(p. 271)*.

account. A record that is kept for each asset, liability, equity, revenue, expense, and dividend component of an entity *(p. 25)*.

accounting. A set of concepts and techniques that are used to measure and report financial information about an economic unit *(p. 1)*.

accounting changes. Changes from one acceptable method of accounting to another acceptable method; like straight-line depreciation to a declining balance approach *(p. 377)*.

accounting cycle. The procedures needed to process transactions through an accounting system; including journalization, posting, adjusting, and preparing financial statements *(p. 96)*.

accounting equation. A financial relationship at the heart of the accounting model: Assets = Liabilities + Owners' Equity *(p. 4)*.

Accounting Principles Board. The private sector group charged with developing accounting standards from 1959 to 1973; primary authoritative pronouncements were known as "opinions" *(p. 383)*.

Accounting Standards Codification. Research tool deemed to be the primary authoritative source and reference guide on accounting standards. *(p. 383)*.

accounts payable. Amounts due to suppliers relating to the purchase of goods and services on credit *(p. 302)*.

accounts receivable. Amounts due from customers from credits sales of products or services; "trade receivables" *(p. 179)*.

accrual. Expenses and revenues that gradually accumulate throughout an accounting period *(p. 66)*.

accrual basis. The accounting process whereby revenues are measured and recorded as earned, while expenses are recorded as incurred *(p. 58)*.

accrued expenses. Unpaid expenses that have already been incurred *(p. 66)*.

accrued revenues. Revenues that have been earned and recorded, but are not as yet collected *(p. 66)*.

adjusted trial balance. A trial balance prepared after adjusting entries have been prepared and posted to the ledger *(p. 68)*.

adjusting process. To analyze account balances and update them at the end of an accounting period to reflect the correct measure of revenues and expenses *(p. 60)*.

aging of accounts receivable. Analysis used to estimate the uncollectible accounts; involves stratification of receivables based upon age *(p. 182)*.

AICPA. American Institute of CPAs; an organization whose members are CPAs interested in advancing the accounting profession *(p. 383)*.

all inclusive approach. A concept of income by which virtually all nonequity-based transactions and events are captured and reported in the income statement; the preferred approach for income theory *(p. 235)*.

allowance method for uncollectibles. A method that estimates uncollectibles as a portion of total receivables and establishes an offsetting contra allowance account *(p. 182)*.

amortization. The process used to allocate the cost of an intangible asset to the accounting periods benefited *(p. 291)*.

amortized cost method. The approach mandated for held-to-maturity securities; investments are reported at their cost with any premium or discount amortized over the life of the investment *(p. 238)*.

annuities. Streams of level (i.e., the same amount each period) payments occurring on regular intervals *(p. 325)*.

assets. The economic resources owned by an entity; entailing probable future benefits to the entity *(p. 4)*.

auditing. The examination of transactions and systems that underlie an organization's financial statements with the goal or reporting thereon *(p. 3)*.

available-for-sale securities. Investments that are neither "held-to-maturity" or "trading;" a default category that is accounted for at fair value with changes in value recognized in other comprehensive income *(p. 235)*.

B

balance sheet. A financial statement that presents a firm's assets, liabilities, and owners' equity at a particular point in time *(p. 4)*.

bank reconciliation. A control procedure to establish and verify the correct cash balance via identification of errors, irregularities, and adjustments *(p. 159)*.

bank statement. The document received from a bank which summarizes deposits and other credits, and checks and other debits to a bank account *(p. 159)*.

basic EPS. The simplest earnings per share number; earnings available to common shares divided by weighted average shares, without factoring in potential dilution *(p. 378)*.

betterment. Expenditures that improve or increase the service potential of an asset even beyond its original new condition; such costs may be capitalized by increasing the asset's cost *(p. 285)*.

bonds payable. An obligation divided into transferable units requiring the issuer to make periodic interest payments and an eventual repayment of the face amount *(p. 328)*.

book value. Cost minus accumulated depreciation; the net amount at which an asset is reported on the balance sheet *(p. 65)*.

book value per share. Common stockholders' equity divided by common shares outstanding, to indicate stockholders' equity per share *(p. 379)*.

boot. Term used to describe additional monetary consideration that may accompany an exchange transaction *(p. 288)*.

C

callable bond. A bond that provides the issuer an option to reacquire the bonds before scheduled maturity at a preset price *(p. 329)*.

callable preferred. Preferred stock that can be repurchased by issuer for a preset price *(p. 354)*.

capital expenditures. Ordinary and necessary costs incurred to place an item of property, plant, or equipment in its condition for intended use; such amounts are included in the asset account *(p. 264)*.

capital stock. A non-specific reference to the ownership interests of shareholders in a corporation *(p. 101)*.

cash. Items acceptable to a bank for deposit and free from restrictions for satisfying current debts; includes coins, currency, bank deposits, etc. *(p. 157)*.

cash basis. An accounting approach where revenue is recorded when cash is received (no matter when "earned"), and expenses are recognized when paid (no matter when "incurred") *(p. 69)*.

cash budget. A major component of a cash planning system that depicts cash inflows and outflows for a stated period of time *(p. 158)*.

cash discount. A reduction in invoice price offered to customers to encourage prompt payment of invoices *(p. 123)*.

cash equivalents. Short-term interest-earning financial instruments that are deemed to be highly secure and will convert back into cash within 90 days *(p. 157)*.

certified public accountant (CPA). An individual who is licensed by a state to practice public accounting *(p. 3)*.

change in accounting estimate. A revision of assumptions used in a related accounting calculation (e.g., change in estimated useful life of an asset); handled prospectively by revising current and future periods *(p. 273)*.

chart of accounts. A listing of the accounts of an entity, along with any identification coding *(p. 34)*.

closing process. The process by which temporary accounts are "zeroed" out and the effects transferred to retained earnings *(p. 96)*.

commercial substance. The quality of an exchange transaction such that it changes the future cash flow potential of the entity *(p. 287)*.

commitments. Promises to engage in some future action; not necessarily creating a recordable accounting liability but potentially necessitating enhanced disclosure *(p. 339)*.

common stock. The residual equity interest in a corporation; last in liquidation but usually receiving the full benefits of any corporate growth *(p. 353)*.

comparability. An enhancing quality of accounting such that even though different companies may use different accounting methods, there is still sufficient basis for valid comparison *(p. 382)*.

compensated absences. Term to describe paid time off; vacations, sick leave, etc. *(p. 311)*.

compensating balance. An amount that must be left on deposit and cannot be withdrawn *(p. 157)*.

complex capital structure. Companies with options, warrants, or convertible bonds and stocks that may result in the issuance of additional shares *(p. 378)*.

compound interest. Interest calculations that provide for periodic inclusion of accumulated interest into the base on which interest is calculated; "interest on the interest" *(p. 324)*.

comprehensive income. Net income plus items of other comprehensive income (e.g., market value adjustments of available for sale securities) *(p. 376)*.

conservatism. A general principle of accounting measurement; when in doubt, understate assets and income and overstate liabilities *(p. 214)*.

consignment. To place inventory in the custody of another party without requiring them to purchase it, as a sales agent *(p. 204)*.

consistency. An enhancing quality of accounting such that deviations in outcomes from period to period should be the result of deviations in underlying performance (not accounting quirks) *(p. 382)*.

consolidation. To prepare financial reports for a parent and subsidiary company as a single economic unit *(p. 247)*.

contingent liabilities. Events that may or may not give rise to an actual liability because the outcome is uncertain; examples include lawsuits, environmental damage issues, and so forth *(p. 306)*.

contra asset. An account that is subtracted from a related account -- contra accounts have opposite debit/credit rules *(p. 64)*.

control account. The total of all subcomponent account records for an account; e.g., the sum of all individual accounts receivable *(p. 35)*.

convertible bond. A bond that may be converted by the holder into stock of the issuing company *(p. 329)*.

convertible preferred. Preferred stock that can be exchanged for common stock at some preagreed ratio *(p. 354)*.

corporation. A form of business organization where ownership is represented by divisible units called shares of stock *(p. 4)*.

cost flow assumption. An assumption about how costs are assigned to inventory in the accounting records *(p. 206)*.

cost of goods sold. The total cost attributed to units of inventory actually sold during a period *(p. 132)*.

coupon bond. A bond that has detachable coupons that are exchanged for interest payments; historically popular but falling into disuse *(p. 328)*.

credit. The nature of an action to an account to indicate an increase (liabilities, equity, and revenue) or decrease (assets, expenses, and dividends); usually right-justified in an entry *(p. 26)*.

credit memorandum. A seller-prepared document evidencing an approved return of merchandise for credit against an account *(p. 122)*.

cumulative preferred. Preferred stock that is entitled to a periodic dividend, and those dividends must be paid (eventually) before any monies can be distributed to common stockholders *(p. 353)*.

current assets. Assets that will be converted into cash or consumed within one year or the operating cycle, whichever is longer *(p. 101)*.

current liabilities. Obligations that will be liquidated within one year or the operating cycle, whichever is onger *(p. 101)*.

current operating approach. A concept of income where income is limited to transactions related to central ongoing operations; not an acceptable approach for income theory *(p. 235)*.

current ratio. A measure of liquidity, calculated by dividing current assets by current liabilities *(p. 103)*.

D

debenture bond. A bond that lacks specific collateral; payment is only assured by the general faith and creditworthiness of the issuer *(p. 328)*.

debit. The nature of an action to an account to indicate an increase (assets, expenses, and dividends) or decrease (liabilities, equity, and revenue); usually left-justified in an entry *(p. 26)*.

debit card. Transactions are equivalent to an electronically generated check that results in an almost immediate withdrawal of funds *(p. 163)*.

debit memorandum. A purchaser-prepared document evidencing a return of merchandise to a seller *(p. 126)*.

declining balance depreciation method. An accelerated depreciation method by which a constant rate (that is a multiple of the straight-line rate) is multiplied by each period's beginning (constantly declining) book value *(p. 272)*.

defined benefit plan. A type of pension plan where the benefits are a function of years of service, pay, and age; the ultimate employer cost is not known in advance *(p. 312)*.

defined contribution plan. A type of pension plan where the benefits are based on amounts in trust for the benefit of the employee; employer contributions are usually a fixed percentage of pay *(p. 312)*.

depletion. The process used to allocate the cost of a natural resource asset to the accounting periods benefited *(p. 289)*.

deposits in transit. Receipts entered on company records but not yet posted by the bank *(p. 159)*.

depreciable base. Cost minus salvage value; the amount of cost that will be allocated to the service life *(p. 268)*.

depreciation. The process used to allocate the cost of a long-lived property to the accounting periods benefited *(p. 64)*.

derivatives. Investments accounted for a fair value that generally derive their value from some other item; examples include commodity futures, options, and so forth *(p. 168)*.

diluted EPS. An earnings per share number; adjusted to reflect the potential effect of dilutive securities *(p. 378)*.

dilutive securities. Options, warrants, convertible bonds, convertible stocks, and other items that have the potential to increase the number of shares outstanding *(p. 379)*.

direct approach. The preferred method for preparing the statement of cash flows; operating cash flows are presented according to their direct source (e.g., cash received from customers) *(p. 411)*.

direct write-off method. A simple, non-GAAP, method that expenses uncollectible accounts only as they are determined to be uncollectible and are written off *(p. 180)*.

discontinued operations. The special income statement reporting of the impact of disposing or abandoning of a component of a business *(p. 374)*.

discount on bonds. The difference between face value and issue price of a bond, where the issue price is less; causes the effective yield to be higher than that stated *(p. 241)*.

dishonoring a note. To fail to pay a note at maturity *(p. 187)*.

dividend payout ratio. Dividend per share divided by earnings per share *(p. 381)*.

dividend rate. Dividend per share divided by stock price; also called dividend yield *(p. 381)*.

dividends. Amounts paid from profits of a corporation to shareholders as a return on their investment in the stock of the entity *(p. 4)*.

dividends in arrears. An omitted dividend on cumulative preferred stock that must eventually be paid before any monies can be distributed to common stockholders *(p. 353)*.

double-declining balance depreciation. An accelerated depreciation method by which a constant rate (that is 200% of the straight-line rate) is multiplied by each period's beginning (constantly declining) book value *(p. 271)*.

E

earnings. A concept that relates to income from continuing operations plus/minus discontinued operations *(p. 376)*.

Earnings per share. EPS; generally understood as the amount of income for each share of stock, but is actually better refined as basic and diluted EPS (see those definitions) *(p. 377)*.

EBIT. An analyst's calculation to reflect "earnings before interest and taxes" *(p. 377)*.

EBITDA. An analyst's calculation to reflect "earnings before interest, taxes, depreciation, and amortization" *(p. 377)*.

effective-interest amortization. A theoretically preferable method for amortizing premiums and discounts on bonds; interest expense is a constant percentage of the bonds ever-changing carrying value *(p. 335)*.

employee. A person who works for a specific business and whose activities are directed by that business *(p. 308)*.

entity assumption. Accounting information should be presented for circumscribed distinct economic units *(p. 384)*.

equity method. Method to account for stock investment when significant influence is present; changes in equity of the investee are recognized by the investor on a pro rata basis *(p. 243)*.

exchange transaction. Trading one asset for another; to be booked at fair value if the transaction has commercial substance *(p. 287)*.

ex-dividend. The event (date) when a transfer of stock ownership between shareholders will occur without the right for the purchaser to receive any previously declared dividends *(p. 355)*.

expenses. The costs incurred in producing revenues *(p. 5)*.

F

F.O.B. destination. Free on Board destination; meaning the transfer of ownership of inventory will occur when the goods reach their destination and the seller will incur the freight charges *(p. 130)*.

F.O.B. shipping point. Free on Board shipping point; meaning the transfer of ownership of inventory will occur when the goods are shipped and the purchaser will incur the freight charges *(p. 130)*.

fair value accounting. Sometimes called "mark-to-market;" to record an investment at its fair value and recognize changes in value as they occur *(p. 166)*.

faithful representation. A fundamental quality of accounting such that information must be truthful; complete, neutral, and free from error *(p. 382)*.

FICA. Federal Insurance Contributions Act (also known as social security and Medicare); establishes a tax that employers must withhold and match for government-based retiree benefit *(p. 309)*.

financial accounting. An area of accounting that deals with external reporting to parties outside the firm; usually based on standardized rules an procedures *(p. 2)*.

Financial Accounting Standards Board (FASB). An organization charged with producing standards for financial reporting in the USA *(p. 2)*.

financial statements. Core financial reports that are prepared to represent the financial position and results of operations of a company *(p. 9)*.

financing activities. A cash flow category; including receipts from stock issues, bonds, notes and loans, -- and payments for loan repayment, acquisitions of treasury stock, and dividend distributions *(p. 406)*.

financing lease. A lease that effectively transfers the risks and rewards of ownership to the lessee *(p. 340)*.

first-in, first-out. FIFO; An inventory cost flow assumption based on the notion that the earliest costs are to be assigned to units sold *(p. 206)*.

fiscal year. A one-year accounting period that does not correspond to a calendar year *(p. 58)*.

Form 1099. A form required to be issued to an independent contractor reporting amounts paid; to assist with tax compliance issues (this form used to report other payments like interest, etc.) *(p. 308)*.

full disclosure principle. All relevant facts that would influence investors' and creditors' judgments about the company are disclosed in the financial statements or related notes *(p. 103)*.

FUTA. Federal Unemployment Tax levied on employer to provide funds for unemployed workers; rate is dependent on existence of SUTA and employer history of layoffs, etc. *(p. 310)*.

future value. The amount to which an interest-earning amount is expected to grow over a stipulated time period at a given interest rate *(p. 324)*.

G

GAAP. Generally accepted accounting principles -- encompass the rules, practices, and procedures that define the proper execution of accounting *(p. 383)*.

general ledger. A record of the accounts comprising financial statements, and their respective balances *(p. 31)*.

going-concern assumption. In the absence of evidence to the contrary, accountants assume that a business will continue to operate well into the future *(p. 384)*.

goods available for sale. A calculated amount corresponding to the beginning inventory plus net purchases; represents the total pool of inventory available during a period from which sales can occur *(p. 133)*.

goods in transit. Goods in the process of being transported to the buyer; ownership is based on freight terms *(p. 203)*.

goodwill. The excess of the purchase price of an acquired company over the fair value of the identifiable net assets acquired *(p. 246)*.

gross method. A method of recording purchases of inventory at invoice price *(p. 127)*.

gross pay. Also known as gross earnings; this it is the total amount earned by an employee before any deductions *(p. 308)*.

gross profit. A calculated amount corresponding to net sales minus cost of goods sold *(p. 121)*.

gross profit method. A technique that purports to estimate inventory and cost of goods sold by applying historic percentage relationships to observable sales information *(p. 215)*.

H

held-to-maturity investments. Investments purchased with intent to hold to maturity; usually investment in debt; accounted for by amortized cost method *(p. 238)*.

historical cost principle. The concept that many transactions and events are to be measured and reported at acquisition cost *(p. 3)*.

I

impairment. When the carrying amount of an asset is not recoverable from its future cash flow *(p. 289)*.

income statement. A financial statement that summarizes the revenues, expenses, and results of operations for a specified period of time *(p. 9)*.

income summary. A non-financial statement account used only to facilitate the closing process by summarizing and zeroing-out the revenue and expense accounts *(p. 96)*.

income taxes. Taxes that are based on the amount income; for employees such amounts must be withheld by employers and remitted to the government *(p. 308)*.

independent contractor. One who performs a designated task or service for a company, and the company has the right to control or direct only the result of the work done *(p. 308)*.

indirect approach. An alternative method for preparing the statement of cash flows; operating cash flows are presented as a reconciliation of income to cash from operating activities *(p. 413)*.

initial public offering. The first time stock in a corporation is offered to the investing public; registration and other requirements must be met; proceeds may flow to the corporation or private shareholders *(p. 352)*.

intangible asset. (Chapter 4) Lack physical existence, and include items like purchased patents and copyrights *(p. 101)*.

intangible asset. (Chapter 11) Long-term asset that lacks physical existence; contract rights, copyrights, patents, trademarks, etc. *(p. 290).*

interest. The charge imposed on the borrower of funds for the use of money *(p. 186).*

internal auditor. A person within an organization who reviews and monitors the controls, procedures, and information of the organization *(p. 3).*

International Accounting Standards Board (IASB). An organization charged with producing accounting standards with global acceptance *(p. 2).*

International Financial Reporting Standards (IFRS). The specific accounting rules developed by the International Accounting Standards Board *(p. 383).*

intraperiod tax allocation. Separately reported items like discontinued operations, prior period adjustments, and other comprehensive income, are to reported net of their specifically related tax effects *(p. 376).*

inventory. Goods held for resale to others *(p. 125).*

investee. The company in which another has an investment *(p. 243).*

investing activities. A cash flow category; including receipts from disposal of investments and long-term assets -- and payments to acquire long-term assets and investments *(p. 406).*

invoice price. List price less any trade discounts *(p. 123).*

issue price. The amount a company receives in exchange for the initial issue of debt or other financial instrument *(p. 238).*

J

journal. A chronological listing of the transactions and events of an organization, in debit/credit format *(p. 29).*

journalizing. The process of recording transactions and events into the journal *(p. 29).*

junk bond. A bond that is issued by a company of low credit worthiness, and entails substantial risk of nonpayment; generally offers a high interest rate to compensate for the high risk *(p. 329).*

L

land improvements. Includes the cost of parking lots, sidewalks, landscaping, irrigation systems, and similar expenditures that are incurred to better land *(p. 264).*

last-in, first-out method. LIFO; An inventory cost flow assumption based on the notion that the most recent costs are to be assigned to units sold *(p. 206).*

lease/lessee and lessor. Periodic payment from the user (lessee) of an asset to an owner (lessor) of the asset *(p. 274).*

legal capital. Usually the par value of the stock of a corporation *(p. 356).*

liabilities. Amounts owed by an entity to others *(p. 4).*

liquidity. The ability of a firm to meet its near-term obligations as they come due *(p. 103).*

list price. An established price determined by reference to a catalog or general price list; before any discounts *(p. 123)*.

long-term investments. Investments made for long-term holding purposes; including land for speculation, securities of other companies, etc. *(p. 101)*.

long-term liabilities. Any obligation that is not current, and include bank loans, mortgage notes, and the like *(p. 101)*.

lower of cost or net realizable value. To report inventory at the lower of its cost or net realizable value *(p. 214)*.

lump-sum purchase. A single price paid for a package of assets; the purchase price must be allocated to each of the components *(p. 264)*.

M

maker. The party creating the note and agreeing to make payment *(p. 186)*.

managerial accounting. An area of accounting concerned with reporting results to managers and others who are internal to an organization *(p. 2)*.

matching principle. To associate expenses with revenues, and record them in simultaneous accounting periods *(p. 60)*.

materiality. A matter of accounting judgment; when amounts involved are slight, expediency may dictate waiving the technically correct alternative in lieu of a simpler approach *(p. 265)*.

maturity date. The date on which a note and related interest are due to be paid *(p. 186)*.

maturity value. The amount due at maturity of a note; includes principal and interest *(p. 186)*.

Modified Accelerated Cost Recovery. A "depreciation" approach common to the tax code; generally permits more rapid "recovery" of asset cost than GAAP approaches; MACRS - pronounced "makers" *(p. 273)*.

modified cash basis. Like the cash basis, except that certain large expenditures for durable assets may be recorded as assets initially *(p. 69)*.

moving-average method. Under the perpetual inventory system; to recompute running average cost with each purchase transaction *(p. 213)*.

multiple-step income statement. A complex income statement with sections that segregate cost of goods sold calculations and other components of income and expense; enables enhanced evaluations of data *(p. 136)*.

N

natural business year. Applicable to certain businesses that have a seasonal business pattern, and an attempt is made to establish an accounting fiscal year to match *(p. 58)*.

natural resources. Oil and gas reserves, mineral deposits, thermal energy sources, and standing timber are just a few examples of such assets that a firm may own *(p. 289)*.

net income. (Chapter 1) The excess of revenues over expenses for a designated period of time *(p. 9)*.

net income. (Chapter 15)Income from continuing operations plus/minus discontinued operations, but before items of "other comprehensive income" *(p. 376)*.

net loss. The excess of expenses over revenues for a designated period of time *(p. 9)*.

net method. A method of recording purchases of inventory at invoice price less available cash discounts *(p. 128)*.

net pay. Also known as net earnings; this is the gross pay less all applicable deductions ("take home pay") *(p. 308)*.

net realizable value (inventories). Estimated selling price in the normal course of business, less reasonably predictable costs of completion, disposal, and transportation *(p. 214)*.

net realizable value (receivables). The amount of cash expected to be collected on outstanding accounts receivable; accounts receivable minus the allowance for uncollectibles *(p. 182)*.

nominal accounts. Accounts that will be reset to a zero balance with each new accounting period; revenue, expense, and dividend accounts (also called "temporary" accounts) *(p. 96)*.

nonredeemable bond. A bond that cannot be paid off before scheduled maturity *(p. 329)*.

nonrefundable bond. A bond that cannot be paid off with the proceeds of a new debt issue *(p. 329)*.

nontrade receivables. Amounts due from transactions and events not directly related to sales of products or services *(p. 179)*.

notes payable. Formal short-term borrowings usually evidenced by a specific written promise to pay *(p. 302)*.

notes receivable. A written promise from a client or customer to pay a definite amount of money on a specific future date *(p. 186)*.

NSF check. Nonsufficient funds check; a customer check returned for lack of funds (a "hot check") *(p. 159)*.

O

operating activities. A cash flow category; generally related to transactions that enter into the determination of income -- items that are not investing or financing *(p. 406)*.

operating cycle. The period of time it takes to convert cash back into cash (i.e., purchase inventory, sell the inventory on account, and collect the receivable) *(p. 101)*.

operating expenses. General expense category for selling and administrative costs *(p. 121)*.

operating lease. A lease of less than one year where the lessee makes periodic payments for periodic use of an asset, but does not assume the ultimate risks and rewards of owning the asset *(p. 274)*.

other assets. The category of a classified balance sheet for reporting assets that are not logically attached to one of the other specific sections *(p. 101)*.

other comprehensive income. An account for changes in value of available for sale securities; not part of net income but is included in the broader concept of total comprehensive income *(p. 235)*.

outstanding checks. Checks entered on company records but not yet cleared by the bank *(p. 159)*.

owner investments. Resources provided to an organization by a person in exchange for a position of ownership in the organization *(p. 4)*.

owners' equity. The residual of assets minus liabilities, representing the collective interest or position of the entity's owners *(p. 4)*.

P

paid-in capital in excess of par. The amount by which a stock's issue price exceeds its par value; also referred to as "additional paid-in capital" *(p. 354)*.

par value on bonds. The face or contract amount of a bond; the amount to be repaid at maturity along with any interest *(p. 238)*.

partnership. A non-corporation representing an association of two or more persons organized to carry out a business plan for a profit motive *(p. 4)*.

payee. The party to whom a note is made payable *(p. 186)*.

PCAOB. Public Company Accounting Oversight Board -- a private-sector, non-profit corporation, charged with overseeing the auditors of public companies *(p. 384)*.

pension plan. A general term to describe some form of arrangement for continuing payments to retirees *(p. 312)*.

periodic inventory system. An inventory system that utilizes a Purchases account and does not update inventory with each sale; inventory is updated by physical count at the end of accounting periods *(p. 125)*.

periodicity assumption. An accounting assumption that purports to divide a continuous business process into measurement intervals, such as months, quarters, and years *(p. 58)*.

perpetual inventory system. A "real-time" inventory system that updates inventory records with each purchase and sale *(p. 125)*.

petty cash. A fund established for making small payments that are impractical to pay by check; also known as imprest cash fund *(p. 164)*.

physical inventory. The process of counting inventory actually on hand *(p. 215)*.

post-closing trial balance. Reveals the balance of accounts after the closing process, and consists of balance sheet accounts only *(p. 98)*.

posting. The process of transferring journal entry effects into the respective general ledger accounts *(p. 31)*.

preemptive right. A right that may or may not be provided to shareholders enabling them with a first right of refusal to buy any additional shares offered by a corporation *(p. 353)*.

preferred stock. A class of stock that generally benefits from a stipulated periodic dividend and priority in liquidation; but, usually lacking in upside participation in corporate growth *(p. 353)*.

premium on bonds. The difference between face value and issue price of a bond, where the issue price is more; causes the effective yield to be lower than that stated *(p. 239)*.

prepaid expenses. Goods or services purchased in advance of their consumption *(p. 61)*.

present value. The calculated value today of an amount to be received in the future, based upon an assumed interest rate (the reciprocal of future value) *(p. 325)*.

price earnings ratio. The per share market value of a stock divided by its earnings per share *(p. 379)*.

principal. The basic stated amount of a note on which interest is usually calculated; generally relating to the amount borrowed *(p. 186)*.

principles-based. The idea that accounting standards should articulate broad-based principles rather than specific and detailed rules *(p. 382)*.

prior period adjustment. To correct errors from prior years; prior financial statements are retroactively changed to make them correct *(p. 373)*.

proof of cash. A detailed bank reconciliation that verifies not only beginning and end balances, but also validates deposits and withdrawals during the month *(p. 164)*.

property, plant, and equipment. Assets with long lives that will be used in an entity's production processes; land, buildings, and equipment *(p. 101)*.

prospectus. The documentation describing financial and business aspects of an initial public offering *(p. 352)*.

public accounting. Accounting activities provided by a person to the general public, typically relating to audit, tax and similar services *(p. 3)*.

purchase discounts. A cash discount available on purchases of merchandise on account; encourages prompt payment *(p. 126)*.

Q

quick ratio. An extreme measure of liquidity, calculated by dividing quick assets (cash, short-term investments, and accounts receivable) by current liabilities *(p. 104)*.

R

real accounts. Asset, liability, and equity accounts; balances are carried forward from the end of one period into the beginning of the next period *(p. 96)*.

registered bond. A bond for which ownership records are maintained, and interest is paid to the registered owner *(p. 328)*.

relevancy. A fundamental quality of accounting such that information should be timely and bear on the decision-making process by possessing predictive or confirmatory (feedback) value *(p. 382)*.

remeasurement. Uses a variety of exchange rates to convert assets and liabilities of a foreign affiliate to the reporting currency; adjustment may impact operating income *(p. 385)*.

replacement. A restoration of an asset, at least partially, to its original condition; such costs may be capitalized by reducing accumulated depreciation *(p. 285)*.

residual value. Amount expected be realized at the end of an asset's service life; "salvage value" *(p. 268)*.

restatement. The financial statements of prior periods are redone to reflect the correct amounts *(p. 373)*.

retail inventory method. An inventory costing technique used by retailers that extrapolates inventory values by applying cost-to-retail percentages to known sales and purchase transactions *(p. 216)*.

retained earnings. The excess of a corporation's income over its dividends *(p. 4)*.

return on assets ratio. A ratio comparing income (net income plus interest) to the average total assets *(p. 381)*.

return on equity ratio. A ratio comparing income (net income minus preferred dividends) to the average total equity *(p. 381)*.

revenue. Inflows and other benefits received in exchange for the providing of goods and services *(p. 5)*.

revenue expenditure. Not a capital expenditure; to be expensed as incurred *(p. 285)*.

revenue recognition. The point at which revenue is recognized in the accounting records; ordinarily the point of sale *(p. 59)*.

reversing entry. Optional accounting procedure which may prove useful in simplifying record keeping; a journal entry to "undo" an adjusting entry *(p. 98)*.

rules-based. The idea that accounting standards must be very specific to provide adequate guidance and drive consistency in reporting *(p. 382)*.

S

sales discounts. A cash discount offered to customers to encourage prompt payment of invoices *(p. 123)*.

Sarbanes-Oxley. "SOX" -- Legislation that imposes stringent controls over reporting and auditing; created the Public Accounting Oversight Board *(p. 384)*.

secured bond. A bond that provides specific assets as collateral to help assure the payment stream *(p. 328)*.

Securities and Exchange Commission. "SEC" -- regulatory body with which public companies must file and report *(p. 383)*.

serial bond. A bond issue that has multiple repayment dates, rather than the entire issue maturing at one fixed maturity date *(p. 329)*.

service life. The period of time that a depreciable asset will be in use by an entity; the time interval over which the asset will be depreciated *(p. 266)*.

significant influence. The ability to sway management and decision making of another entity, but generally not enough to assert absolute control *(p. 243)*.

simple interest. Interest calculations that do not provide for periodic inclusion of accumulated interest into the base on which interest is calculated *(p. 324)*.

single-step income statement. A simple income statement with a section for all revenues and another for all expenses; there is no direct association between specific revenue and expense components *(p. 136)*.

sinking fund bond. A bond issue that requires periodic setting aside of monies into a separate fund to provide for eventual repayment of the debt at maturity *(p. 328)*.

sole proprietorship. A non-corporation business owned by a sole individual *(p. 4)*.

source document. A document evidencing a transaction or event and potentially providing for the initiation of a journal entry *(p. 27)*.

specific identification method. Inventory costing method where the actual cost of each unit of merchandise is tracked and used for accounting purposes *(p. 210)*.

stable currency assumption. An accounting assumption that presumes the currency is not impacted over time by inflation *(p. 385)*.

statement of cash flows. A financial statement that summarizes the cash flows relating to operating, investing, financing, and noncash investing/financing activities of an entity *(p. 406)*.

statement of retained earnings. A financial statement that discloses changes in retained earnings during a designated period of time; those changes usually attributable to income and dividends *(p. 10)*.

statement of stockholders' equity. A financial statement that is often presented in lieu of a statement of retained earnings and other disclosures about equity accounts *(p. 360)*.

stock. Transferable units of ownership in a corporation *(p. 351)*.

stock dividend. A noncash corporate activity to provide shareholders with additional shares in proportion to existing ownership; makes for more shares outstanding, but does not change total equity *(p. 359)*.

stock split. A corporate action to increase the number of shares and reduce the par per share by a stipulated ratio (e.g., 2 for 1) *(p. 358)*.

straight-line amortization. A method for amortizing premiums and discounts on bonds; the premium or discount is spread uniformly over the life of the bond as an adjustment of interest *(p. 240)*.

straight-line depreciation. A simple depreciation method by which the depreciable base is spread uniformly over the service life *(p. 269)*.

subsidiary account. A subcomponent account record providing individual balance details; e.g., the record for one customer out of a group of customers comprising all accounts receivable *(p. 35)*.

SUTA. State Unemployment Tax levied on employer to provide funds for unemployed workers; rate is adjusted for employer history of layoffs, etc. *(p. 310)*.

T

T-account. An abstract representation of an account, with the left side of the "T" representing debits and the right side credits *(p. 37)*.

temporary accounts. Accounts that will be reset to a zero balance with each new accounting period; revenue, expense, and dividend accounts (also called "nominal" accounts) *(p. 96)*.

timeliness. An enhancing quality of accounting such that information is available in sufficient time to be capable of influence *(p. 382)*.

total paid-in capital. The sum of legal capital plus paid-in capital in excess of par *(p. 356)*.

trade discount. A reduction from list price that is not entered in the accounting records; customarily offered in "setting" the invoice amount *(p. 123)*.

trade receivables. Amounts due from customers from credits sales of products or services *(p. 179)*.

trading securities. Investments acquired with the intent of generating profits by reselling the investment in the very near future; classified as current assets *(p. 235)*.

translation. Uses prevailing exchange rates to convert assets and liabilities of a foreign affiliate to the reporting currency; adjustment may impact other comprehensive income *(p. 385)*.

treasury stock. Shares of a company's own stock that it has reacquired *(p. 356)*.

trial balance. A listing of account balances from the ledger, used to test the equality of debits and credits *(p. 33)*.

U

understandability. An enhancing quality of accounting such that information is clear and concise to those with reasonable business knowledge *(p. 382)*.

unearned revenue. Revenue that has been collected in advance of providing goods and services to "earn it;" reported as a liability until earned *(p. 65)*.

units of output depreciation. A depreciation approach where the depreciable base is allocated to the expected total units of output; mileage, hours, etc. *(p. 270)*.

V

verifiability. An enhancing quality of accounting such that different knowledgeable and independent observers reach similar conclusions *(p. 382)*.

W

W-2. An annual statement provided to employees stating the amount of earnings and withholdings; assists employee in preparing their own tax returns *(p. 311)*.

W-4. A form filled out by an employee stating the amount of exemptions to which they are entitled for tax purposes; such exemptions bear on the amount of income tax withholdings *(p. 309)*.

warranty liability. A liability that is recorded for the future costs of claims that are anticipated because of product warranty agreements *(p. 307)*.

weighted-average inventory method. Under the periodic inventory system; inventory cost is based on the average cost of units purchased giving consideration to the quantities purchased at different prices *(p. 209)*.

workers compensation insurance. Insurance paid by the employer to cover work related injuries sustained by employees *(p. 310)*.

working capital. The difference between current assets and current liabilities *(p. 103)*.

Index

Made in the USA
Columbia, SC
10 April 2021